PLATO'S THOUGHT

G. M. A. GRUBE

with new introduction,
bibliographic essay,
and bibliography by
DONALD J. ZEYL

TO THE "DILLETANT"
FROM GARRETH '94

HACKETT PUBLISHING COMPANY, INC.

Copublished in the United Kingdom by
The Athlone Press

For further information, please address
Hackett Publishing Company, Inc.
P.O. Box 44937, Indianapolis, Indiana 46244-0937

Library of Congress Cataloging in Publication Data

Grube, G. M. A.
  Plato's Thought.

  Reprint of the 1935 ed. published by
Methuen, London
  Bibliography: p.
  Includes index.
  1. Plato I. Title
  B395.G67   1980   184   80-14588
  ISBN 0-915144-79-4
  ISBN 0-915144-80-8 (pbk.)

TO

R. CARY GILSON

τροφεῖα

CONTENTS

Before his death in 1982 at age 83, G.M.A. GRUBE devoted an extraordinarily productive life to the service of scholarship. Appointed full professor of classics at the University of Toronto in 1928, he headed the classics department of the university's Trinity College from 1931 until his retirement in 1970. His translations of Aristotle and of Plato are renowned for their lucidity and their sensitivity to nuances of argument and the interplay of philosophical ideas. In addition, Grube wrote several original works, including *The Greek and Roman Critics,* recipient in 1968 of the American Philological Association's award for outstanding contribution to classical scholarship; *Plato's Thought*; and *The Drama of Euripides.*

Grube was also very active in Canadian politics. A leading member of the provincial Cooperative Commonwealth Federation (forerunner of the New Democratic Party), he was president of the provincial party in the 1940s. He served on the Toronto Board of Education and ran unsuccessfully for Parliament a number of times.

PREFACE

NOT only classical students but other friends, sometimes specialists in other subjects, frequently ask me where they can find a reliable exposition of this or that aspect of Platonic philosophy. To answer this question is not easy for it implies a different method of approach from that generally adopted except in specialist books that treat only of a small part of Plato's thought. Even of these there are remarkably few available in English. Those who interpret Plato, whether superficially or in detail, usually take the reader through the dialogues one by one and deal with several or all subjects more or less simultaneously. It is, of course, true that we can only get into close and intimate contact with Plato's genius by reading and re-reading his dialogues as far as possible in chronological order and by making a painstaking study of each of them. As a guide to this approach A. E. Taylor's *Plato, The Man and His Work* cannot be too highly recommended, nor am I so foolhardy as to compete with a scholar to whose published works I am, and have been for many years, most deeply indebted. But even those who have the leisure and enthusiasm necessary to read Plato as he should be read know well that even for them another method is at times necessary, that it is essential to pause now and again to collect together the scattered pronouncements of the great philosopher on each of a number of subjects and to follow the development of his thought in regard to them.

The two methods, the study of individual works and of the philosophy subject by subject, are not mutually exclusive; they supplement one another. The approach

adopted in this book is all the more essential in that
Plato himself never wrote any important dialogue on
a single topic, except perhaps the *Symposium*, in that
he always appears to be following the argument whither-
soever it may lead, and because his way of imaginative presentation and the glorious naturalness of the
conversations he professes merely to report do not make
it easy even for those familiar with his writings to
keep all the golden threads of thought simultaneously
before their dazzled eyes. When one is consulted about
the ethical doctrines of Aristotle it is easy to refer the
inquirer to the *Ethics*, when about art, to the *Poetics*,
where he will at least get a clear idea of the fundamental Aristotelian position on these subjects. In the
case of Plato it is always necessary to refer to several
dialogues, and one should in most cases refer to all his
works.

Plato's mind was synthetic rather than analytic. He
never treats subjects separately. That is why commentators find it impossible to explain his ethics for
example without at the same time explaining the rest
of his philosophy. If however we deal with the cog-
nate subjects, though separately, within the compass
of the same book, the difficulty is considerably lessened.
It is essential also to select one's subjects in a manner
which Plato himself would have understood. Exposition is made much harder by forcing upon pre-Aris-
totelian philosophers the formal framework of modern
thought. Metaphysics, Ethics and Psychology would
have seemed to Plato a meaningless classification and
he would certainly have protested against its application to himself. Each of these terms he would have
thought to include all the others. But he would have
understood what was meant by the theory of Ideas
(the core of his metaphysics), by the problem of pleasure
(the root of all ethics) and the nature of the soul (the
basis of all psychology). The difference is, I think,

important, for it means that, as subjects of discussion, the last three would have appeared to him capable of separate treatment.

In each of the eight chapters of this book the reader will find an account, as complete and as concise as I can make it, of what Plato said on the subject discussed and an explanation of what he meant when he said it. The different subjects are, of course, intimately connected and, taken together, will give an adequate understanding of Plato's view of life as a whole and of his philosophy of man. The order I have adopted, or something very like it, follows from that philosophy itself. The Ideas stand first because the whole edifice is built upon this fundamental hypothesis, but the reader unfamiliar with Plato should perhaps be warned that the exposition is here inevitably harder to follow than elsewhere. Then Pleasure, as the first problem that faces man as soon as he begins to reflect upon good and evil. From this we go on to discuss Eros, the emotional drive, and the Soul generally, as those forces within the individual that make for the good life. The question naturally arises how far those forces direct the world at large ; hence the Gods. To know how man can be led to the good life requires a study of Art and Education. Finally we shall see the Platonic philosopher in his relation to the state at large, the Statesman.

Inevitably, the atmosphere of each dialogue is for the most part lost where relevance to the subject discussed is the first consideration, and this must be so if clarity, which is my chief aim, is to be attained. Further, no adequate description of the historical, literary and mental background against which the dialogues must ultimately be read and understood can be attempted. Fortunately, since the publication of G. C. Field's *Plato and His Contemporaries*, such an attempt would be superfluous.

I have deliberately refrained from going beyond Plato, from trying to improve upon him by filling in gaps which he himself has left unfilled. True, I have not shirked interpretation of what he did say or hesitated to tackle notoriously difficult but extremely important passages which are not infrequently glossed over in any but special treatises ; and where my interpretation differs from that generally accepted I have tried to justify my views in a brief appendix more definitely addressed to specialists. On the other hand I have, I hope, scrupulously avoided putting in what Plato should have said (in my opinion) where in fact he said nothing. For example, the relation of the different kinds of gods and souls to each other in the *Timaeus* is treated at some length, but not the relation of the mathematical realities to the other Ideas. The former question is one of interpretation of the Platonic text; the latter is not raised there, but in Aristotle.

Aristotle's criticism of Plato, especially of the theory of Ideas, is a special subject and a thorny one which does not come within the scope of this book. The reliability of Aristotle's evidence is questionable ; even the existence of the ' unwritten doctrines ' of Plato to which he refers has been called in question by no less a person than Constantin Ritter. In any case, a sound knowledge of Plato's own writings is obviously an essential prerequisite to any such study. My only aim is to help the reader to that knowledge. Having omitted tempting references to Aristotle, I have also omitted all reference to modern thought and philosophy. Many parallels are obvious ; they will occur to a reader probably more familiar with modern thought than I. On the other hand, if I may trust my own experience, parallels are frequently more confusing than helpful and the attempt to explain Plato by means of modern philosophic terminology is, except in the most expert

hands, disastrous. In a book of this kind I thought
it better to sin by omission than to expose the reader
to the dreadful confusion that inevitably follows an
unsuccessful attempt.

There remain two notorious hurdles which any one
who writes on Plato must inevitably clear : the chronology of the dialogues and the Socratic question.

Before we can speak of development in Plato's thought
it is obviously necessary to know the order in which
the dialogues were written. But that is just what we
do not know. Commentators who relied entirely upon
their own ideas of development have in the past come to
the most remarkably varied conclusions. Fortunately,
about the middle of last century Lewis Campbell
discovered a more objective method, since perfected
by German scholars. It is the method of stylometry :
as it is indisputable that the *Laws* (with the *Epinomis*,
if genuine) is Plato's last work, a study of its
style and a comparison of it with that of other
dialogues allow definite conclusions as to their relative
order if special attention is paid to the frequency of
certain expressions and particles which any writer uses
all but unconsciously. Some turns of phrase that occur
in the early works gradually disappear and vice versa.
The leading exponent of this method is Constantin
Ritter and the results of his own and other people's
researches are given in his *Platon*.[1] His main conclusions are generally admitted and, as we intend to study
the content of the dialogues exclusively, it is prudent
to start from a chronological order arrived at by a
completely different method. I accept Ritter's conclusions then *in so far as they are based on stylometry*.
This means that I follow his division of Plato's works
into three main groups, written at different periods of
his life.

[1] I, 232–73.

The earliest group includes all the smaller, so-called Socratic, dialogues and six longer : the *Gorgias*, the *Protagoras*, the *Euthydemus*, the *Cratylus*, the *Phaedo* and the *Symposium*. To the second or middle period belong the *Republic*, the *Phaedrus*, the *Parmenides* and the *Theaetetus*. To the third and last group the *Sophist*, the *Politicus*, the *Philebus*, the *Timaeus*, the *Critias* and the *Laws*. But when we come to further detail, to the order of the dialogues within a particular group, Ritter himself admits that stylometry cannot help much and his own conclusions are due to much more subjective arguments. For example, he places the *Hippias Minor* and the *Protagoras* very early in the first group because he believes that Plato could not have published such an unflattering picture of Socrates after the latter's death. It will appear from my discussion of those dialogues that the picture is not inconsistent with others, and in any case it is very doubtful whether Plato wrote anything at all before 399 B.C. With such arguments I feel entirely at liberty to disagree. With the *Hippias Minor*, which is an apparent *reductio ad absurdum* of the equation 'virtue is knowledge', in its simplest form, I find it more convenient to deal after other dialogues in which this equation is explained. It could have been written at any time within the first period.

But even so, the only changes of any import which I would make in Ritter's detailed order [1] are that I would definitely place the *Protagoras* after the *Gorgias* and the *Symposium* after the *Phaedo* ; I would also

[1] op. cit., 273. First period : *Hippias Minor, Laches, Protagoras, Charmides (Hippias Major), Euthyphro, Apology, Crito, Gorgias, Meno, Euthydemus, Cratylus, Menexenus, Lysis, Symposium, Phaedo*.
Second period : *Republic, Phaedrus, Theaetetus, Parmenides*.
Third period : *Sophist, Politicus, Timaeus, Critias, Philebus, Laws (Epinomis)*.
In *The Essence*, p. 27, he gives this order, but divided into six groups, as due to a combination of stylistic and other considerations. Reference to his larger work will show that stylometry only takes him as far as I have stated.

prefer, but this is not essential, to put the *Theaetetus* after the *Parmenides* and the *Timaeus* after the *Philebus*. On all these points except the first Ritter confesses himself in doubt. Certainty of detail is clearly impossible to attain and as regards the lesser dialogues we may legitimately be guided by convenience in exposition as long as consistency is maintained.

Let me add that if, always within the framework of the three groups, I were to be definitely proved wrong in any particular case, it would not greatly matter. It is quite certain, as a matter of ascertainable fact, that pleasure is discussed in a far more subtle and advanced manner in the *Protagoras* than in the *Gorgias*. Yet the *Protagoras* might have been written first and the difference be due to the different situation, the different angle from which the problem is discussed, the different audience or even the mood of the artist, the last factor being quite unaccountable. For Plato was a dramatist as well as a philosopher, and even as a philosopher he never reduced his thought to a system developed in an orderly manner. So with the *Symposium* and the *Phaedo*. A different chronological order would mean that the very different moods therein depicted had possessed Plato in the reverse order. I consider this unlikely, but it is possible.

The Socratic question is the problem of how far Plato's picture of Socrates is historical. As is well known it does not tally with that given in Xenophon, and the latter used to be regarded as the more trustworthy historian. But of late years John Burnet and A. E. Taylor have championed the view that the Socrates of the Platonic dialogues is in all essentials the Socrates of history and that the doctrines put in his mouth were actually held by him. The view that is now finding general acceptance is that Burnet and Taylor have proved that Socrates must have been very much the kind of *man* we find him to be in Plato, but that it is unlikely that he held all the *doctrines* there attributed to him, especially the theory of Ideas in its developed form. I will deal with this point when discussing the Ideas (pp. 4 ff.) though it will not be necessary for me to refute the general position of Burnet and Taylor. This has been convincingly done by others. I may perhaps add that even Plato might well have found it difficult to draw the line accurately between himself and Socrates. I feel sure he must often have thought that he was merely expounding and amplifying his master's views when the latter, if alive, would not have recognized them as his own. They were Platonic views in any case and in what follows the name Socrates must be understood to refer to the Platonic Socrates unless the historical Socrates is specifically indicated.

As this book is addressed to all who are interested in Plato, whether in translation or in the original, no Greek word has been used anywhere in the text without immediate translation or explanation. In the Appendix, which is more specifically addressed to specialists and where the actual interpretation of the Greek words is the question at issue, this could not be done.

I have referred the reader in the footnotes to passages in other works on Plato where, and only where, these directly contribute something to the question in hand or where I was conscious of a specific debt. A complete list of the books referred to in this way will be found at the end. If author and page only are given in the note, the reference is to the first work of that author on the list. The greater debt which all students of Plato owe to the many who have come before them cannot be thus specifically indicated, and is but the greater for that. In common with others of my generation I owe most to the works of Burnet, Taylor, Shorey,

Dies, Ritter and Wilamowitz.   Wilamowitz' *Platon* is to
me the most inspiring work on the subject.

My thanks are due to many colleagues, students and
friends who have helped me over a period of years with
helpful suggestions and criticism, especially so to Mr.
L. H. G. Greenwood of Emmanuel College, Cambridge ;
and to Professor Gilbert Norwood who very kindly read
through the book in proof.   In very large measure am I
also indebted to the great teacher to whom this book is
dedicated.   His were the words that first opened for
me the golden gates.

G. M. A. GRUBE

TRINITY COLLEGE,
   TORONTO
MARCH 1935

NOTE

Professor Cornford's *Plato's Theory of Knowledge*
appeared after this book was already in proof, and
I was therefore unable to refer the reader to it as a
most illuminating analysis and interpretation of the
Theaetetus and the *Sophist*, when discussing those dialogues.   I am encouraged to find in such an eminent
authority confirmation of certain views expressed below,
especially those on pp. 36–43 and in Appendix II.

G. M. A. G.

INTRODUCTION

It is a pleasure to welcome a new edition of Professor Grube's *Plato's Thought*. This book has proved its usefulness to several generations of students and scholars, and its recent unavailability has been an inconvenience to those who have looked to it for a basic, reliable exposition of the central themes of Plato's philosophy. The new edition is all the more welcome in that no general book on Plato has appeared, since the first publication of this book, which accomplishes as well the goals of this book. Stated in the author's words, these are to give "an account, as complete and concise as I can make it, of what Plato said on the subject discussed, and an explanation of what he meant by it." The need for such an account has not diminished over the years, and may even be said to have increased. For although the volume of studies of Plato's thought continues to grow unabated, almost all recent work is highly technical or specialized, and ill-suits the needs of students who encounter Plato for the first time.

It is unusual that a book on Plato written nearly half a century ago should continue to be as serviceable as this book is. Anyone even casually acquainted with the recent history of Platonic scholarship is aware of the truly revolutionary metamorphosis of method that the study of the Platonic dialogues has undergone. I shall say more of this development later; here I want to point out and explain why it has not rendered *Plato's Thought* out of date, as it has many other contemporary, and indeed subsequent, studies of Plato. The chief reason for this immunity is the fact that Grube's account of Plato's philosophy does not ally Plato with philosophical positions and interests which were prevalent in the earlier part of the century, but find little allegiance today. In Grube's book Plato is interpreted against the background of his own culture and the intellectual climate of this own time, rather than in the context of philosophical concerns which were alien to Plato

and have come to be alien to us. I am not faulting in principle
the attempts to connect Plato with current philosophical questions; this indeed should be done, anew by each generation,
and is of great value in understanding both Plato and modern
thought, provided that it is done with due caution. But such
studies simply do not survive the shifts in philosophical focus
which occur from time to time.

The continuing timeliness of *Plato's Thought* should not be
taken to imply that Grube's interpretations have been unanimously accepted by Plato scholars over the years. There
neither is nor has been, and indeed there need not be, scholarly unanimity on such matters. But the book has enjoyed the admiration of scholars to this day, and deservedly, for Grube's interpretations are always balanced and sane, his skill in getting
the right sense of Plato's Greek superb (as is well demonstrated
by the translations of Plato which he has produced in recent
years), and his perception of the drift of a Platonic argument
very sound. The positions taken by Grube do in the main
represent a wide consensus, and they are always well thought
out, clearly stated and ably defended. It should be frankly
acknowledged that the issues and controversies which
dominate current Platonic scholarship are, in the nature of the
case, not reflected in this book. This is why a survey of the
more recent scholarship has been provided, with a new
bibliography, at the end of the book. But in order to understand and appreciate the significance of those issues, a basic
familiarity with the contours of Plato's philosophy is essential.
Plato's Thought is an excellent first book on Plato, and it is
hoped that for most of its readers it will not be the last. And it
can answer to no higher calling than to stimulate them to a
closer study of the dialogues themselves.

What, then, is the "revolutionary metamorphosis of
method" which has changed the shape of Platonic scholarship?
We can best understand it by referring it, in Aristotelian
fashion, to its causes. These are largely the developments in
philosophy which have taken place predominantly in the
English-speaking world since the turn of the century, usually
referred to as "analytical philosophy". One of these developments, the advance in the field of formal logic, made
available to philosophers an important tool which better

equipped them for two tasks: (1) to examine the meaning, in the sense of the logical structure, of linguistic expressions, and (2) to assess more accurately the logical relations among propositions. Thus, first, by casting sentences and phrases, including those in the writings of philosophers, into symbolic form, scholars became aware of hitherto unnoticed ambiguities and other logical troubles in the writings of past philosophers, prompting a reexamination and reassessment of their theories. Second, a more accurate way of assessing the logical relations among propositions diverted interest in attending to the content of this or that doctrine advanced by a given philosopher, to attending to the argument upon which the doctrine was based. This approach has led to a greater appreciation of the stature of the philosophers of the past as thinkers, rather than as propounders of doctrines.

These new ways of approach have proved immensely fruitful in their application to the Platonic texts, and both are well illustrated in the literature on what is by now undoubtedly the most famous (or notorious) argument in the dialogues, the "Third Man" argument at *Parmenides* 132a1–b2. A glance at the literature (surveyed in the Bibliographical Essay at the end of the book) shows at once that the major questions in the assessment of that argument are concerned with the logical relations among, and the logical structure of, its premises. Is the argument valid as it stands? If not, what further premises are required to make it valid? What is the logical status of the argument once such premises have been supplied? And what is the logical structure of those new premises, particularly the "self-predication" premise? This premise, in the context of the *Parmenides* argument, states that the Form, the Large, is itself large. But how are we to construe that? If the infinite regress is to eventuate, the premise needs to be understood as assigning to the Form, the Large, the property of being large in the same way as that property is assigned to large particulars. This gives rise to a crucial question: could Plato have believed this, or believed himself committed to such a view? A glance back to dialogues such as the *Phaedo* and the *Republic,* and indeed as far back as the *Protagoras,* shows Plato using or requiring the use of such "self-predicative" expressions as: the Beautiful is beautiful, the Equal is equal, and so forth. But what is the logical structure of these expressions in those contexts? Is it the same as that evidently required for a "Third Man" regress? If so, Plato is exposing a fatal logical flaw in his theory of Forms; if not, then some other construction of these expressions must be suggested and defended, in such a way that a cardinal feature of the theory of Forms, its paradeigmatism (see the Bibliographical Essay), is nevertheless preserved.

Another, if related, development within analytical philosophy which deserves attention for its influence on Platonic studies has been the rise of linguistic and conceptual analysis. Professor Gilbert Ryle (1900–1976), whose own work in the classification and clarification of concepts has been widely influential, led the way to a new appreciation of certain passages in the later dialogues. This development also promoted a vigorous interest in Plato's philosophy of language, his theories of meaning and truth, and led to a new interest in problems broached by Plato in the *Cratylus*, the *Theaetetus* and the *Sophist*. An aspect of Plato's thought which had hitherto received only passing attention now came into its own.

Both the issues raised by a study of the "Third Man" argument and the attention given to Plato's philosophy of language, and to the later dialogues in general, are representative of a larger issue which has dominated recent work on Plato. This is the question of the development of Plato's philosophy. An earlier generation of scholars, represented preeminently by Paul Shorey, whose work predated the importation of analytical methods in Platonic scholarship, insisted on the "unity of Plato's thought", i.e., on the view that all of the Platonic dialogues, from the earliest to the last, present successively the components of a single system of doctrines which from the beginning was already complete in all its essentials. It is wrong, according to these scholars, to read the dialogues as the record of a development in Plato's views, and disastrous to take some of the later ones as recanting, in whole or in part, views expressed in the earlier ones. Scholars of this persuasion maintain, for example, that the epistemology of the *Theaetetus* reaffirms, rather than revises, the epistemology of the *Meno* and that of the *Phaedo* and the *Republic*. Any difference can be accounted for in terms of a difference in point of view or approach. This "unitarian" position has suffered greatly at the hands of scholars whose approach to the texts has been vigorously analytical, and it is now hard to see how such a view could have been so insistently maintained. It is now generally agreed that Plato's philosophy does develop through the course of the dialogues, though the nature and extent of this process are still subjects of debate. Is the development one in which later views extend but do not recant earlier ones, or did Plato modify his views to the point of abandoning in later dialogues positions which he had held earlier? Supporters for either alternative are not lacking. In either case, a new picture of Plato has emerged, one which represents him as facing new problems with which his earlier views did not equip him to deal, and expanding or revising those views to deal with them. No doubt his colleagues and students in the Academy stimulated this process. Still, in his courage to "follow the argument wherever it may lead", even if it led into paths beyond territory previously staked out, and uncongenial to that territory, Plato has shown himself to be in the best sense a disciple of his master Socrates—that is, in adopting Socrates' practice of rethinking things out for himself—and Plato deserves (and indeed has won) the admiration of his modern students and colleagues.

The University of Rhode Island   Donald J. Zeyl
Kingston, R.I.

I

THE THEORY OF IDEAS

THE theory of 'ideas' is the belief in eternal, unchanging, universal absolutes, independent of the world of phenomena ; in, for example, absolute beauty, absolute justice, absolute goodness, from which whatever we call beautiful, just or good derives any reality it may have. Its meaning and scope— for there are Ideas of much more than ethical concepts—will become clear as we proceed, but a warning is necessary at the outset : it is well known, but cannot be too often repeated, that the word Idea in this connexion is a very misleading transliteration, and in no way a translation, of the Greek word ἰδέα which, with its synonym εἶδος, Plato frequently applies to these supreme realities. The nearest translation is ' form ' or ' appearance ', that is, the ' look ' of a person or thing. We shall see how the meaning of the word probably developed. Suffice it for the moment to say that ' theory of forms ' is much nea.er the Greek, though the expression ' theory of ideas ' is so firmly established that it is all but impossible, and perhaps undesirable, to avoid it altogether. But it must be quite clear that we are not speaking of ideas in any sense which the word can carry in ordinary English.[1]

The Milesian school of philosophy, some two centuries before Plato, had sought to reduce the baffling variety of the physical world to one underlying substance. To the question : what is the world made of ? Thales had answered water, Anaximenes air, while Anaximander had said that all things were made out of one material substratum which he called the indefinite or infinite (τὸ ἄπειρον). By following up this conception to its logical conclusion Parmenides came to assert

---

[1] In the sequel, to avoid misunderstanding, the words Idea and Form are printed with a capital when they refer to Platonic εἴδη.

the existence of the One, eternal and immovable, and to deny
the reality of all change and therefore of all sensibles. He
thus proved that the Milesian hypothesis was insufficient : if
the only Real is one ultimate homogeneous substance, there
is nothing to account for any movement, change or plurality.
Being the only thing that exists it must remain ever and always
the same, it cannot become anything else, and nothing else can
exist. Heraclitus, on the other hand, insisted on the change-
ability of things ; he said that everything was in a state of flux
(the famous πάντα χωρεῖ, 'everything flows'), though he
insisted also on a Logos, a balance or proportion, in these
changes, and attached some kind of superior reality to fire.
Empedocles, to solve the riddle set by Parmenides, postulated
four permanent elements—fire, air, water and earth—and two
principles of motion, attraction and repulsion, or Love and
Hate as he poetically called them. Anaxagoras, whose philosophy was probably obscure even to his contemporaries, seems
to have insisted on the permanence of qualities and posited
Nous or mind as the origin of motion and the guiding principle
of the universe. The Pythagorean school continued to develop
well into the fourth century and we have not enough evidence
to decide when the various theories associated with their name
originated. The general trend of their philosophy, however,
was to insist that the essential reality of things was to be found
not in the material components but in their Logos, that is,
in the mathematical ratios and proportions of the different
mixtures, so that they said that things were numbers or like
numbers. And, leaving out of account the magic and mysti-
cism which led them to attach all kinds of symbolic meanings
to particular numbers, we may give them credit for having
built on the solid fact that all physics, if not all science, has a
mathematical basis.

With all these conflicting theories before them, the Sophists
of the fifth century helped to turn men's minds from philosophical speculation to practical life. They taught many
different things, these travelling teachers who have been well
called 'itinerant university extension professors without a
university base ',[1] and it is a grave mistake to lump them all
together as if they belonged to one school of thought or had

[1] Shorey, p. 13.

any one method of teaching. They tried to supply the need for a general education, as this need grew with the growth of democracy, by laying special emphasis on public speaking and the management of household or state. But one thing, if we may judge from Plato's account of the greatest of them (and we have little else from which to judge), they had in common : a disbelief in the possibility of knowledge about ultimate realities or of absolute standards. ' Man is the measure of all things ' Protagoras had said, and this Plato at any rate interpreted to mean that what I perceive or feel is true for me, what you feel or perceive is true for you, and there is no other criterion of knowledge. The *Theaetetus* shows that it follows from this that knowledge and sensation are identical, so that real knowledge is impossible and there can be neither science nor philosophy. Gorgias is reported to have said that there was nothing to know, if there were we could not know it, if we did we could not communicate our knowledge to any one.[1] This denial of universally valid standards led minor sophists to regard law and morality as mere conventions and Plato represents them as not hesitating to preach a doctrine of pure selfishness. Thus scepticism was flourishing in the second half of the fifth century, when Socrates was active in Athens. It probably also faced Plato at the beginning of the fourth, for the disturbed decade that preceded Socrates' death is not likely to have steadied men's minds, and a general attitude to life like that fostered by the Sophists is wont to last for a considerable time.

It is in opposition to this hopeless scepticism, the influence of which upon moral, social and political life he saw far more clearly than the Sophists themselves, that Plato insisted upon the possibility of knowledge and upon the existence of absolute values. To do this he had to establish the existence of an objective, universally valid reality, and this he found in his Forms or Ideas. How far Socrates led him to this there is no certain means of knowing, though there is no possible doubt that they both travelled along the same road, and that the pupil went on from where the master left off.

Aristotle has told us [2] that Plato accepted the Socratic

---

[1] See Diels, Protagoras Fragm. 1 ; Gorgias fragm. 3.

[2] *Metaphysics* A, 987 *a* 30 : ' From youth on Plato had first been a disciple of Cratylus and his Heraclitean opinions : that all sensibles are ever in a

method of definition with the addition that, for a definition
to be universally valid, he felt it must be the definition of a
constant reality, independent of any particular specimen of
the thing defined. A definition of man is not that of any
particular man, but of Man, which is a reality quite independent of you or me, and which continues to exist even if we both
die this instant. This reality is the ' eidos,' the Platonic Form,
of man. The statement of Aristotle as to the origin of the
theory of Ideas need not necessarily be true, for he probably
knew little about Socrates which he did not learn in the
Academy, where he arrived as a youth of seventeen thirty
years after Socrates' death. But it is all the more remarkable
that he did draw this distinction between Socrates and Plato,
since we find Socrates in the Platonic dialogues expounding
the theory of Forms fully developed.

Apart from the Socratic method of definition, it is probable
that Plato drew his inspiration also from the Eleatic school of
Parmenides, whose conception of the One must have led him
directly to the notion of abstract reality ; certainly nothing
could be further removed from the world as we know it than
this One. The Pythagoreans also quite clearly had a great
influence on Plato, as probably on Socrates, and from them
Plato derived the more mathematical aspects of his theory.
There is, however, no need to derive the Platonic Forms directly
from either school.[1] Nor must Plato's debt to Anaxagoras'
conception of Mind as the ruling principle be forgotten.

state of flux, and that there is no knowledge concerning them. These
theories he held later also. While Socrates was preoccupied with Ethics
and not at all with nature as a whole, yet in the former he sought for the
universal and was the first to reflect upon definitions. Plato, who had
accepted the theories of Cratylus, was thus led to believe that the Socratic
search was concerned with other than sensible things. For it was impossible for a universal definition to be that of a particular sensible, since
sensibles are for ever changing. It thus came about that he called this
kind of reality Forms ($\varepsilon\iota\delta\eta$) and maintained that sensibles exist side by side
with them, and are named after them.'

For a discussion of this passage see the introduction and notes in Ross's
edition. The reader will find there a very convincing refutation of the
view that the theory of Ideas as we know it from the *Phaedo*, &c., belonged
to the historical Socrates. See also Appendix I below, and Field, pp.
202–13.

[1] Natorp (p. 228) seems to exaggerate the Eleatic, A. E. Taylor the
Pythagorean influence (*Varia Socratica* and *Commentary* passim). For an
excellent account of the origin of the theory see Wilamowitz, I, 346 ff.

It may help us to realize more clearly what problems the theory of Ideas was intended to solve if we consider very briefly the various arguments by which it seems to have been supported. We do not find any complete presentation of these either in Plato or in Aristotle. Plato never professed to give a systematic account of his philosophy, while Aristotle wrote for those who were fully conversant with the philosophy of the Academy, so that he merely refers to these arguments by headings of which we find the explanations only in a comparatively late commentator.[1] Nevertheless, they probably derive from a lost work of Aristotle which, if extant, would give us just what we want. Aristotle refers to five different arguments which he calls : the argument from the sciences, that of the one over the many, the knowledge of things that are no more, the argument from relation, that implying the fallacy of the ' third man '.[2]

The first was established in three ways : (i) if every science fulfils its function by having some one thing as its object, there must be such a single thing which is the object of that science, it must be unchanging and eternal, an eternal model beyond the particular sensible things, for these cannot be objects of knowledge in any proper sense. The particular things or incidents in the physical world happen according to this model. This model is the Idea. (ii) The objects of science exist. But science is concerned with something beyond the particulars which are infinite in number and indeterminate, while science is of the determined. There are therefore certain things beyond the particulars, and these are the Ideas. (iii) Medicine is not the study of my health or yours, but of health as such. So the objects of geometry are not this or that equal or commensurate object, but equality and commensurability. These must exist and are Ideas. These three ways of stating the case all come to this : knowledge and science exist, they must have objects, therefore those objects exist ; they cannot be the particular things we know since these are in a perpetual state of change whereas the objects of science must be constant ; there must therefore be eternal and immutable realities, which we

---

[1] Alexander, c A.D. 220. These arguments are fully analysed in Robin, pp. 15–26. The account in the text is a brief summary of Robin's analysis.
[2] See on p. 34.

call the Ideas.   The best illustration is that of the mathematical sciences : no line we draw is a perfect line, or indeed a line at all since it has two dimensions ; no square that we draw is a perfect square.   But we study the properties of the perfect line and the perfect square.   The objects of mathematics therefore exist, though not in the physical world.

The second argument is as follows : Though every man in the mass of men is a man, and every animal an animal, yet in no case is the particular subject equivalent to its general predicate since this predicate is of wider application than the subject. There is therefore some external existent apart from the particulars, and it is equally applicable to all the individuals concerned.   That which is the unity of this multiplicity, eternal and apart from them, we call the Idea.

The third argument is : When we think ' man ' or ' horse ' our thought has an object which remains unaffected by the destruction of any particular man or horse, or any number of them.   Something therefore exists apart from the particulars, and this something is the Idea.

The fourth argument is : Things are designated by the same name or have the same predicate in one of three ways : (i) there may be merely a likeness in the name ; (ii) they may be similar in nature, e.g. Plato and Socrates are both men ; (iii) one may be a copy of the other, e.g. a picture of a man may be called a man.   Now when we draw two lines they are never truly equal ; they are not equality itself but an imitation of it.   The model of things is the Idea.   This argument is obviously cast in Aristotelian terminology.   Platonists were probably content to say that particular equals were obviously a mere copy or imitation of equality (we shall find this said in the *Phaedo*) and that there must therefore be eternal models.

The fifth argument restates the second in a slightly different way : When things are called by the same name, yet are not identical with this name in its widest application, they have this name only because they are all in the same relation to a universal reality, e.g. several men are called men because they are all in the same relation to the universal, Man.

Such were the most important arguments that seem to have been used in the Academy.

When we turn to the Platonic dialogues themselves we are at once struck by the fact that this theory of Forms which bulks so large in the commentaries on Plato actually occupies a relatively small space in the works themselves. If a graph were drawn of the appearance of the theory it would stay at zero for several of the earliest works, rise doubtfully in some of the so-called Socratic dialogues, leap up to maximum with the *Phaedo* and the *Symposium,* stay at that level in the central books of the *Republic,* the *Phaedrus* and the *Parmenides,* and then settle down to a level where the existence of some transcendental realities is definitely taken for granted but no full explanation of the extent of that belief is given, in spite of several outstanding questions clamouring for solution. In this last period the *Timaeus* is to some extent an exception.

Though the Ideas do not appear in the earliest works, some scholars maintain, as if they regard the theory as Socratic they must, that it was fully formed in Plato's mind from the first ; others try to determine the exact point at which Plato himself discovered them. However that may be, we will be satisfied to trace the development of the theory as we find it, *as Plato's hearers and readers found it.* For, whatever theories Plato may have held privately, there is in the earliest dialogues nothing whatever which Socrates' audience (or even we, with the *Republic* before us) could reasonably interpret as implying any belief in transcendental Forms. Equally clearly there comes a time when the Forms must be understood as transcendental realities and then their nature is carefully explained.

A good example of the early approach is the *Charmides.* It is a charming little work in which Socrates, together with the beautiful young Charmides and his uncle Critias, searches for a definition of sophrosyne, self-control or moderation. They fail to find one that will satisfy but the ground is, as usual, considerably cleared. Sophrosyne is equated with knowledge of self, but the exact meaning of this could not at this stage be described satisfactorily, for it presents many difficulties.[1] Not a word, not a hint about Ideas. The same absence of compromising expressions [2] will be found also in such more

[1] See on pp. 218–9.
[2] Such expressions as ' ὁποῖόν τινά σε ποιεῖ ἡ σωφροσύνη παροῦσα καὶ ποία τις οὖσα, ' what sort of a man self-control will make you when you have it and what it is ' have no special significance (*Charm.* 160 D).

substantial works as the *Gorgias* and the *Protagoras*. In the *Laches* we do find such phrases as αὐτὸ τὸ ἀνδρεῖον , 'courage itself', but neither Socrates nor his audience see in this anything more than a reference to that common quality inherent in all courageous actions, the common quality which they are trying to define. In some dialogues, however, the thing to be defined is described and considered more definitely 'in itself'. To this group belong the *Lysis*, the *Euthyphro*, the *Hippias Major* and the first *Alcibiades*. The genuineness of the last two has been doubted, probably without good reason.[1] The first two, however, are undoubtedly genuine and seem to give clear evidence of a slowly developing vocabulary. In the *Lysis*, which seeks to define love or affection (φιλία) and is in its small way a forerunner of the *Symposium*, we find such pregnant expressions as 'that which is the ultimate object of love, because of which we call dear all things that are dear to us'; the other beloved things are but 'images of that which is in truth the object of love'.[2] The same is true of the *Euthyphro*, though here we do find expressions which to us seem to imply the theory of Ideas and which *we* find difficult to interpret in any other way. Socrates says (5*d*) :

'But tell me now, by Heaven, what you just now professed to know so well. What is the pious and what is the impious as regards murder and other things? Is the righteous not similar in every action and the impious on the other hand the opposite of the righteous in every case, and like to itself? Do not all impious things have one Form (appearance?) owing to their impiety?'[3]

And again (6*d*) :

'My friend, you did not teach me properly when I asked you before what the righteous might be. You told me that what you were doing was righteous, to prosecute your father for murder.

---

[1] For a full discussion of the First *Alcibiades*, see P. Friedländer, *Der Grosse Alkibiades*. For the *Hippias Major*, see Miss D. Tarrant's edition and my articles in *Classical Quarterly*, 1926, and *Classical Philology*, 1929, where see references.

[2] *Lysis*, 219*d* : ἐκεῖνο ὅ ἐστιν πρῶτον φίλον, οὗ ἕνεκα καὶ τὰ ἄλλα φαμὲν πάντα φίλα . . . ὥσπερ εἴδωλα ἄττα ὄντα . . . ὃ ὡς ἀληθῶς ἐστι φίλον . . . τό γε τῷ ὄντι φίλον.

[3] ἢ οὐ ταὐτόν ἐστιν ἐν πάσῃ πράξει τὸ ὅσιον αὐτὸ αὑτῷ, καὶ τὸ ἀνόσιον αὖ τοῦ μὲν ὁσίου πάντος ἐναντίον, αὐτὸ δὲ αὑτῷ ὅμοιον καὶ ἔχον μίαν τινὰ ἰδέαν . . .

—And I was right, Socrates.

—Possibly. You would agree, however, that many other things are righteous?

—So they are.

—Remember then that I did not bid you teach me one or two out of many righteous things, but that Form itself which gives the quality of righteousness to things. For you agreed that it is through one Form (appearance?) that impious things are impious, righteous things righteous. Do you not remember?

—I do.

—Tell me then, what is the nature of this Form, so that by looking at it and using it as a pattern I may call righteous any action of yours or another's that is so, and say of whatever is not righteous that it is not.'

Yet in spite of his unhesitating assent no one has yet suggested that Euthyphro understood the theory of Ideas, or indeed had any suspicion that any such realities were being referred to. It follows that all these expressions, whatever hidden meaning, if any, they may hold for Socrates, are taken by the other speaker as describing no more than the common characteristics of particular things to which the same predicate is applied, these common qualities being considered *not as transcendentally existing but as immanent in the particulars*.[1] It follows, since Plato is no scribbler, that the words could at least be so understood.

It is in this transitional use of the words εἶδος and ἰδέα, where they naturally carry a meaning that will later become technical, that we have the best opportunity of finding an answer to the much-debated question of how, and from what primary meaning, the technical sense of these untranslatable words developed. Now the most common meaning of the word eidos, and one which occurs frequently in Plato, is that of physical stature or bodily appearance. The eidos of a man is ' what he looks like '. It is obvious that all righteous deeds, for example, or all beautiful things have something which looks alike, a common appearance to our observation, and that this is the thing which in each case Socrates is trying to define.

---

[1] So Wilamowitz (I, 208; II, 78–9) and Ritter (I, 570) avoid reading the theory of Ideas into this. The same is true of such phrases as ' you call good men good because of the presence of good things (ἀγαθῶν, a remarkable plural) and beautiful those in whom there is beauty ' in *Gorgias*, 497*e*, cp. 506*d*.

In fact he wants Euthyphro to tell him what all such actions 'look like', so that he can identify them as you would identify a man from a description of his appearance. It would seem that this is not an unnatural use of the word. Then, from asking what all righteous things 'look like' to asking 'what it is they look like', thus supposing the existence of something beyond them which they resemble, is but a step, and it is a step which Plato definitely took between the *Euthyphro* and the *Meno* on the one hand and the *Phaedo* on the other, for in the last-mentioned dialogue the separate existence of the eidos as an independent reality is explicit and explained at some length.[1]

Before leaving the early dialogues it may be well to examine one a little more closely. The *Meno* will serve this purpose excellently : it is not only a very good example of the Socratic method but it introduces some new conceptions which are intimately connected with the later development of the theory. The metaphysical vocabulary is on a par with the *Euthyphro* : mention is made of an eidos of virtue or excellence (ἀρετή) through which all virtues are what they are, and we are told that this Form is permanent and unchanging. Beyond this it does not go.[2] Meno has come to Athens from Larissa, a town in Thessaly, and hails Socrates with a question of which the directness, as well as the confident way he expects an immediate answer, are excellently in character. Meno has only recently been introduced to the great sophist Gorgias who, as we soon learn, has graced Larissa with his presence. He asks (70a) :

---

[1] For this development of the meaning of eidos see Natorp, p. 1 and Wilamowitz, I, 346. Taylor takes it rather as the equivalent of φύσις, nature ; see *Varia Socratica*, 179–267, for an exhaustive analysis of the uses of εἶδος and ἰδέα, in authors before Plato. Ritter, *Neue Uutersuchungen*, pp. 229–326, classifies all the uses of the words in Plato and concludes that the primary meaning was 'die Bedeutung der augenfälligen Áusserlichkeit' (p. 323).

[2] 72 c–e: ἕν γέ τι εἶδος ταὐτὸν ἅπασαι ἔχουσι δι᾽ οὗ εἰσὶν ἀρεταί, εἰς ὅ . . . ἀποβλέψαντα . . . There is an instructive parallel to this usage which seems to imply abstract existence without transcendentality in *Rep.*, V, 477c–d : 'of a δύναμις (power, potentiality, capacity) I see neither the colour nor the shape, nor any such quality as those of other things which I have in view when I say to myself that this is one thing, this another'. Cp. also what is said of memory in *Theaetetus* 163e. It is doubtful how far Plato clearly thought of such things as being Ideas.

' Can you tell me, Socrates, whether virtue can be taught ? Or is it the result not of teaching but of practice ? Or neither one nor the other, but it comes to men as a natural gift or in some other way ? '

Socrates, somewhat taken aback by the shattering naïvety of this question, replies in his usual ironic manner. Known hitherto for their wealth and horsemanship, the Larissans have evidently now acquired wisdom also. Here at Athens there is a dearth of wisdom, for, far from being able to answer Meno's question directly, we are in some doubt whether we know what virtue is. So at least it is with Socrates. Surprised, Meno wants to know whether that is the report that he must carry back home, that Socrates does not know what virtue is. It would seem so, replies the Athenian, but as Meno has been hearing the great Gorgias, perhaps *he* can tell us what virtue is. Indeed he can, and after this delightful introduction we settle down to the usual Socratic search for a definition, in this case of virtue or excellence, which constitutes the first part of the dialogue.

Meno makes the usual mistakes, which Socrates takes the opportunity to correct and explain. For Meno's first answer to the question : what is virtue ? is to give an enumeration and description of the virtue of a man, that of a woman, a child, ' and there are many others ' (71e). A whole swarm of them indeed, but Socrates points out that a mere enumeration is not a definition. If you are asked to define a bee and you merely exhibit to view all manner of bees, you are nowhere near answering the question. What we require is a description of the Form which all virtues have in common. Meno then suggests that it is the capacity for rule and management, but to this we must surely add the word δικαίως, justly or rightly. Well then, virtue is justice or righteousness (δικαιοσύνη). But there are others : courage, moderation, wisdom and so forth ; and we are back again to a mere enumeration. As an example of what he wants Socrates gives a definition of shape or figure (σχῆμα). There are many shapes, yet we can define the general term as ' that which ever accompanies colour ' or, as this is unsatisfactory unless colour has been previously defined, we can say shape is ' the limit of solids ' for the notion ' solid ' is well known to us. This digression (74b–76e) brings out the important point that a new concept must be defined in terms of others already known if the definition is to have any value. Returning to virtue, Meno now defines it as ' to take pleasure in fine things and to have the power to procure them ' (77*d*), but since all men desire what is good for them the first term of the definition may be ignored, and to the second we must surely again add the word ' justly '. This however leads us to include the term to be defined in the definition, for justice is a virtue, and it is the nature of this that we are trying to define.

In a short interlude Meno, after making the famous comparison of Socrates to a torpedo-fish who numbs his victims, expresses some doubt as to the possibility of knowledge and supports his doubt by the sophism that what you know you cannot learn since you know it already, while you cannot discover what you do not know because you will not recognize it when you see it. To refute this sophism, which delights the man from Larissa, Socrates introduces the theory that all knowledge is recollection (ἀνάμνησις). This is based, of course, on a belief in the immortality of the soul which, he tells us, he has heard expounded by priests and poets (81*c*) :

' The soul then is immortal and has come to life a number of times. It has seen what is here and in the underworld and everything, and there is nothing which it has not come to know. Small wonder it can call to mind what it has previously known about virtue and other things. In as much as the whole of nature is akin, and the soul has learned everything, there is nothing to prevent it, once it has recollected one thing—and this men call to learn—from rediscovering everything else, if the man is brave and does not tire of his investigation. For the whole of research and learning is only recollection.'

It should be noted that Recollection or Reminiscence is introduced in a mythical vein, to dispose of Meno's tiresome sophism which interrupted the argument. There is no mention of Ideas but only of ' what the soul has learned ', a very vague expression. Once the possibility of knowledge is thus vindicated we return to our quest for a definition of virtue or goodness. But Meno is an impatient sort of person and to please him Socrates consents to proceed by hypothesis : if goodness is knowledge it must be teachable. Let us see if we can find any teachers of it.

The rest of the dialogue is taken up by this unsuccessful quest, and in the course of it an important difference is established between knowledge and belief. The object of knowledge is not yet, and the Socratic search still ends in perplexity. But we are getting near, for what are those things which the mind or soul remembers? Socrates does not say. Perhaps he did not know. Perhaps Plato did not know, when he wrote the *Meno*. But the theory of Recollection points the way and the vocabulary by which the common characteristics of things are described is getting crystallized and is ready for a more technical usage.

To this usage the *Cratylus* comes even closer. The question to be solved there is whether the names of things are purely a matter of convention or whether there is a definite and natural relation between a thing and its name. Socrates takes this opportunity of gloriously ridiculing etymologists with a string of most outrageous derivations. In the course of conversation the saying of Protagoras that ' man is the measure of all things ' is somewhat summarily rejected by an affirmation of the existence of objective reality : ' things have a stable nature of their own ' which does not depend on our perception of them. And this is true not only of things but of actions. All our actions are in fact conditioned by circumstances in nature external to ourselves : we can cut only such things as are by nature liable to be cut, we can burn only such things as are by nature inflammable. In other words our actions, as well as our knowledge, are dependent upon objective realities, and can happen only in a manner objectively determined.[1]

A little later we find another illustration : a carpenter makes a weaver's shuttle ' with the natural function of a shuttle ' in mind or, more literally, ' looking at something of such a kind as will by nature close the web '.[2] If he breaks this shuttle,

---

[1] 386e : δῆλον δὴ ὅτι αὐτὰ αὑτῶν οὐσίαν ἔχοντά τινα βέβαιόν ἐστι τὰ πράγματα, οὐ πρὸς ἡμᾶς οὐδ᾽ ὑφ᾽ ἡμῶν ἑλκόμενα ἄνω καὶ κάτω τῷ ἡμετέρῳ φαντάσματι, ἀλλὰ καθ᾽ αὑτὰ πρὸς τὴν αὑτῶν οὐσίαν ἔχοντα ὥσπερ πέφυκεν . . . ἢ οὐ καὶ αὐταὶ ἕν τι εἶδος τῶν ὄντων εἰσὶν αἱ πράξεις ;
Note the use of εἶδος and καθ᾽ αὑτά of the physical world. For an excellent discussion of this passage see Diès, II, 477–9.
[2] πρὸς τοιοῦτόν τι (βλέπων) ὃ ἐπεφύκει κερκίζειν. This is definitely a stage further than *Gorgias*, 503e, where it is said that the good orator will

he makes another and, while doing this, he does not 'look at
the other which he broke' but 'at that eidos which he had in
view when he made the first' and this 'we might rightly call
that thing which is a shuttle in itself' (αὐτὸ δ ἔστι κερκίς).
This all shuttles have in common for 'they must all have the
eidos (form, appearance, look?) of a shuttle'. In the same
way the lawgiver who names things must look at 'that which
is a name in itself' and must give to each name the proper
eidos of name in whatever syllables is suitable.

These passages are of extreme importance in the development of Plato's technical vocabulary and the meaning it carries
at least to his hearers if not to himself. Indeed in the above
passages the vocabulary is laboured and the meaning obscure.
The carpenter makes a shuttle. This, like all other actions, is
conditioned by something in nature. He can only make the
instrument in a certain way, and this limitation is expressed
by saying that he can only make it with his mind's eye on the
essential properties of a shuttle. The eidos of a shuttle then
is the sum of its essential qualities as the carpenter 'sees' it.
It is what the shuttle looks like to his mind. For we should
note the constant use of the word to look (βλέπειν) in this
connexion ; it is very relevant to the meaning of eidos. In
this passage of the *Cratylus* we can almost see the change of
meaning taking place from 'what a thing looks like', its
appearance, to the pregnant meaning of eidos as 'that like
which the shuttle looks' and the transition is by way of a
metaphor, 'to look' from a physical becomes a mental act.
It may be fanciful to suppose that we are watching Plato's
own mind at work and the very birth of the transcendental
Forms, though if he had them all clear in his own mind it
seems strange that he should not express himself more clearly
to his audience. In any case it would seem that the Form
will not be so much a 'hypostatized concept' as it has been
called (a name that loses sight of the fact that we are never
dealing with concepts or ideas at all) as the hypostatized
appearance or look of a thing, its appearance given abstract
existence.

speak 'with the good in view, just as any other craftsman produces his
work so that it may have some Form for him'. ὅπως ἂν εἶδός τι αὐτῷ
σχῇ ὃ ἐργάζεται. The indefinite τι is especially interesting.

We may also note in passing that we are dealing here with the Form of a manufactured article, a point to which we shall have occasion to return, and that it is at least very doubtful whether this discussion leaves Socrates' audience with any notion that this Form 'which all shuttles have' and the 'appropriate Form which all names must have' are transcendental realities. Certainly they can have no clear notion of it and they may well be still thinking of these Forms as the uniformity of functions inherent in shuttles or names. And even when we find at the end of the dialogue (439c) that knowledge is only possible if 'something in itself beautiful exists', (τι εἶναι αὐτὸ καλόν) and so with good and everything else ; that the beautiful is ever the same and never leaves its Form (μηδὲν ἐξιστάμενον τῆς αὐτοῦ ἰδέας) ; that there is a Form of knowledge which does not change ; we are still somewhat confused. These things must be independent of their particular manifestations and are the same in them all, but their nature cannot be said to have been satisfactorily explained or even clearly expressed.

When we come to the *Phaedo* the case is very different. There is no longer any doubt that we are dealing with Forms which have an existence of their own quite apart from the particular phenomena of the world we know. Nor can the other speakers here remain in doubt that such is Socrates' meaning. The difference is so clear that it has been supposed that Socrates' hearers are here represented as familiar with the theory of Ideas from the beginning.[1] This seems very unlikely, were it only because the theory is introduced five times, a different and more difficult aspect of it being explained each time. These explanations we must follow carefully, for it is the only systematic explanation of the theory that we find in Plato. Not even that is complete.

In 65b Socrates is discussing the reliability of the senses, and Simmias agrees that they are unreliable. Socrates proceeds :

' How then does the mind (soul) grasp the truth ? For whenever it tries to examine something with the help of the senses, it is clearly deceived.

[1] For a discussion of this view, and my reasons for rejecting it, see Appendix I.

—True.

—Is it not in mathematical reasoning (λογίζεσθαι), if anywhere, that something real becomes clear to the soul?

—Yes.

—And mathematical reasoning is most successful when the mind is not troubled by hearing, sight, pleasure, pain or any of those things ; when it is alone as far as possible and without concern for the body ; when with the least possible contact or association with the body it reaches out towards reality.

—That is so.

—It is also then that the mind of the philosopher most ignores the body, flees from it and seeks solitude.

—It seems so.

—What about this, Simmias? Do we admit that the just exists as such, or not?

—We do, by Heaven.

—And again the beautiful as such, and the good?

—Of course.

—Have you ever seen any of those things with your eyes?

—Never, said he.

—Have you ever grasped them with any other bodily sense? I refer to all such things as size, health, strength and in short to all other existent things, what each of them is. Is what is most true of these apprehended through the body, or is the following the case : whoever of us prepares himself best and most exactly to perceive each thing in itself will come nearest to knowing each thing?

—Quite.

—And the purest knowledge will be that of the man who approaches each subject as far as possible with thought alone, who makes no use of his sight in his thinking, nor drags in any other perception along with his reason, but uses thought pure and by itself in an attempt to hunt down each thing pure and by itself, freeing himself as much as possible from eyes and ears and, in a word, from his body. For when the body participates, it does not allow the mind to acquire truth and wisdom. Is it not such a man, Simmias, who, if any one, will reach the truth.

—What you say is marvellously true, Socrates.'

The theory is here approached from the epistemological side : there exist certain things which we know and which we do not apprehend by means of the bodily senses, and these are the true. The problem of the *relation* between these absolutes and the particulars which we do perceive is not touched upon.

The second passage (72e ff.) is concerned with Reminiscence or Recollection which 'according to that argument you are wont to expound, Socrates' (we have seen it in the *Meno*) clearly implies the pre-existence of the soul. Socrates then proceeds (74a) :

'Whenever a man recollects anything through likeness, must he not also consider whether or not the thing he sees falls short in its likeness to that which it called to mind ?
—Necessarily so.
—Consider then whether this is the case : We say there is such a thing as equality (τι εἶναι ἴσον). I do not mean a stick equal to a stick or a stone to a stone or anything like that, but something else besides all these, the equal itself. Do we say that exists or not ?
—We do, by Heaven, certainly.
—Whence do we get this knowledge ? . . .'

And the discussion which follows points out that this equality does not exist in the world of sense perception (75a–b). We then conclude that we must have had the knowledge before we were born. We have here a much clearer explanation of the difference between things and Ideas. Things are *like* the Ideas and remind us of them. The mathematical examples are especially appropriate as Simmias and Kebes know something of Pythagoreanism. Indeed the particulars, we are told, are 'trying to be like' the Ideas and this important notion of imitation we find elaborated in many places both in Plato and in Aristotle.

The conversation then proceeds to discuss this knowledge which is recollection : it consists of examining the particulars in comparison with the universals, and of giving an account of things (δοῦναι λόγον), a phrase used in the *Meno* and one which will frequently recur. Then, in the course of one of the proofs of immortality, namely that the soul is simple (not compound) and therefore more likely to live on than other things, Socrates says (78d) :

'As for reality itself, of the existence of which we give an account by question and answer, the point is whether those things always remain the same and consistent with themselves, or vary at different times. Equality itself, Beauty itself, each thing that exists in itself, the real ; does that ever undergo any change ? or is whatever of those things exists, being of one kind with itself, ever existent in the same manner, and never at any time liable to any change ? —Necessarily, said Kebes, it is ever the same, Socrates. —What of the many beautiful things such as men, horses . . .'

The Ideas themselves are here described in a vocabulary most of which recurs again and again, but the words εἶδος and ἰδέα are not used yet. The contrast betwen the two worlds is then worked out (80*b*). On the one hand is the Ideal, 'that which is divine, deathless, intelligible, of one kind, indissoluble, always in the same way identical with itself' ; and opposed to this is the phenomenal world 'human, mortal, varied in kind, unintelligible, soluble, never in any way identical with itself'.

When next the theory of Ideas is mentioned Socrates is discussing knowledge. He gives a short history of his own mental development (96*a* ff.) and expresses his dissatisfaction with the purely 'scientific' account of causes. He desires mental and teleological reasons. It is, he tells us, as if one were to account for the fact that Socrates is sitting in prison by saying it is because 'my bones were lifted at the joints, and the sinews by straining and loosening forced my limbs to bend as they are bent ; and that this is the reason why I am sitting here'. Now such an account, he says, is clearly insufficient : it does not explain why he is in prison at all, nor the fact that he sat down by an act of will and as the result of a mental process. We must find a better account than that. He then continues (100*b*) :

'I am not introducing a new subject but those things about which I have continually been talking, both in the earlier part of our discussion and elsewhere. I am going to try to prove to you the kind of cause (εἶδος αἰτίας) with which I am concerned. And again I have recourse to those oft-mentioned things (πολυθρύλητα) and start from them : supposing there to be something beautiful in itself, and something good, and something great and the rest. And if you grant me those things and agree that they exist, I hope from them to deduce, and to show you, a reason why the soul is immortal.

—You may take it, said Kebes, that I certainly grant that, and proceed.

—Consider then whether you agree with me as to what follows from this. For it seems to me that if there is anything beautiful apart from beauty itself, it is beautiful for no other reason than because it partakes of that beauty. Do you agree that this is the reason ?

—I agree, he said.

—Now I do not know and cannot understand those other wise reasons. And if any one tells me why anything is beautiful, either because it has a blooming colour or shape or any such thing, I leave all that out, for I get confused by all those other reasons, but simply and ignorantly and perhaps foolishly I say to myself that nothing else makes things beautiful but the presence of that beauty we spoke of, or its company or however it is that it comes to be there. I am not dogmatic as to the manner of its presence but I insist that it is through beauty that all beautiful things are beautiful. For that seems to me the safest answer to make both to myself and to others, and if I hold on to this I do not think I shall stumble ; it is safe for me or any one else to answer that beautiful things become beautiful through beauty. Don't you think so ? '

This would seem at first sight to be a safe answer indeed, because completely tautological ; but in insisting that beauty in a particular object must be explained in relation to the Idea of beauty, does Socrates not obviously mean that it is no use analysing one example of it ? That we must first realize that beauty is common to many things and that we cannot give a satisfactory explanation of any particular thing without connecting it with the other things that belong to the same class ? Whereas if we have grasped the universal we shall be able to give an intelligible account also of the particular instances of it.

Socrates then discusses from this new angle the difference between properties and accidents in a far clearer manner than he could do in the *Euthyphro*. As he puts it here : The number three always participates in the Idea of oddness, for it is always an odd number ; so snow always participates in the Idea of cold, and can never admit the opposite Idea, heat, without ceasing to be snow. The Ideas which are always present by definition in a certain particular are its properties, those which are not always present in a particular are accidents. And it is at this stage, now that the meaning of the theory has been much clarified, that he first uses the words εἶδος, ἰδέα and μορφή in the sense of Ideas (103*e*). In the next few pages this usage is common.

From these elaborate explanations of the theory of Ideas in the *Phaedo* we have learnt : first, that there are realities such as the good, the equal, the beautiful, &c., which are absolutely true but cannot be perceived by the bodily senses. They can only be grasped by a process of reasoning akin to the mathematical, by the mind freed as far as possible from the errors of sense. In the second place that these are the realities which the mind saw before birth, as described in the *Meno*, and that we remember them because we are reminded of them by the objects of sense. This does not really contradict what was said before : Plato first emphasizes the necessity of abstract reasoning, then allows that this process is initiated by certain sense perceptions. Just as no material square is quite perfect, yet it starts us reasoning about the perfect square which is the object of mathematical reasoning, so no two sticks are perfectly equal, yet the sight of them makes us think of equality. In the third place these Ideas are unique, stable and eternal, and the contrast is clearly drawn between them and the world of sense. Too clearly, for the abyss thus created will have to be bridged later. Lastly, these eternal Ideas alone can lead us to a satisfactory theory of causation : no account of a particular thing is possible when it is considered in isolation, it must be brought into a class, the common characteristics it shares with other members of that class must first be understood ; and these common qualities, considered abstractly, are the Ideas. These Forms can also be variously present, as properties and accidents, in the particulars ; and contrary Forms cannot be participated in by the same particular.

The logical applications of the theory of Ideas, naturally enough, finds no place in the *Symposium*. But the supreme beauty which is there the ultimate aim of all desire is described in the same terms as were applied to the Ideas in the *Phaedo*, though the more technical words εἶδος and ἰδέα, and even μορφή (shape), are not here applied to it. At the end of the philosopher's journey of love (211a) :

' The beautiful will not appear to him as a face or hands or anything else in which body has a part, nor as some discourse (λόγος) or some science, nor as being contained in anything else, be it living creature, earth, sky or anything else, but by itself, of one kind and ever existing. All other beautiful things participate in this in some way, though they come to be and are destroyed while beauty itself never becomes more or less, nor is acted upon in any way.'

This Idea of beauty, for so it must be, reigns here supreme, as does the Good in the *Republic*. More so, for no other Ideas are mentioned. It is the supreme reality considered as object of love, the in-itself-beloved of the *Lysis*. That this supreme reality is thus the Beautiful in one dialogue, the Good in another, is not surprising. The two concepts were always closely allied in Plato's mind, and in this he was only expressing the ordinary Athenian point of view.

We may now turn to the *Republic*. The theory of Ideas does not make its appearance until the fifth book. In the first book Socrates tries to define justice in the usual early manner and there is nothing in the vocabulary to suggest that the *Phaedo* had ever been written. There is not even any ambiguous terminology such as we found in the *Cratylus* and the *Euthyphro*. Nor, with one exception, does anything of the kind occur in the next three books. It seems as if Plato was quite deliberately building up his city and the education of his guardians without introducing any metaphysics, only to return later to the whole question of the proper ruler and his duties from a more fundamental point of view. He takes his reader along a good way towards his goal, converting him by the way to belief in a great many things, without as yet disclosing the fundamental premises upon which these things are based. At most (and this is the exception mentioned above) is it said to be necessary in order to be truly cultured (μουσικός) to recognize ' the different Forms of moderation, courage, freedom and greatheartedness, their like and their contraries as they happen and are present everywhere, to perceive wherein they exist, themselves and their images, and to honour them in big things and small ' (402*c*). This is a typically ambiguous expression which, though quite vague, must by this time imply the Forms to Plato, but which certainly need not do so to those present.[1] There is not a single other

---

[1] It is *possible* that this passage was actually written before the *Phaedo*. See also note 3 on p. 235.

reference to the Ideas, expressed or implied, until the fifth book, where Socrates, repeatedly challenged to prove his city to be possible, finally replies that it is possible, but that nations will never find peace until philosophers are kings or kings become philosophers, a paradox which Glaucon fears will be ' laughed out of court '.[1]

Challenged to explain what a philosopher is, Socrates resorts to the theory of Forms, which he definitely expects Glaucon to know and to accept. For that it is here introduced as well known to Glaucon at least, is obvious from the way the technical term eidos is introduced at once. The beautiful and the ugly, he tells us, are two different things, each of them being one (476a) :

' And so about the just and the unjust, the good and the bad and all the Forms the same is true : each of them is one thing, but seems to be many because it everywhere appears in association with actions and bodies and with the other Forms.' [2]

From this point, the whole argument of this and the next two books centres upon the theory. The existence of the Forms is not established but taken for granted and the character of the philosopher or lover of wisdom is explained by means of them. Other men grasp at particular sights and sounds ; of the reality behind these they have no conception (476c) :

' As for the man who believes in beautiful things, but does not believe in beauty itself nor is able to follow if one lead him to the understanding of it—do you think his life is real or a dream ? Consider : is not to dream just this, whether a man be asleep or awake, to mistake the image for the reality ? '

And this is just what the ordinary man does. He confuses particular beautiful things, which are so only in as far as they

---

[1] See p. 272.
[2] This remarkable introduction takes for granted the relation between Forms and particulars, establishes the existence of negative Ideas (the bad), and even hints at association between the Forms themselves. It is however probable that ' association with one another ' (ἀλλήλων κοινωνία) refers only to the fact that several Ideas ' occupy ' the same particulars as explained in *Phaedo*, 104cd. For a discussion of this passage see Wilamowitz, I, 667 ; Shorey *Republic* note ad loc. and *Unity*, note 244 with references.

participate in beauty, with beauty itself. The philosopher has knowledge of reality, of the Forms ; the others can only have beliefs or opinions (δόξαι). There are then three stages : knowledge, belief and ignorance. The first is of the Forms ; the second of the physical world which, since no object in it retains its qualities but is for ever changing, cannot be an object of real knowledge at all, but both is and is not : while ignorance is not concerned with Being at all, since the things it affirms simply are not. That difference between knowledge and belief is the difference between the philosopher and other men.

Clearly it is the philosopher, whose mind apprehends goodness, who should rule the state. He alone has the pattern of the good in his soul and thus can use it as a painter does (500e) to try to realize eternal justice in the lives of men, to make the state approximate to the ethical realities of which he alone has understanding. He must have the highest kind of knowledge, which is knowledge of the good.

But what is the Good ? Some say it is pleasure, but they themselves must admit that some pleasures are bad. Others say it is knowledge, but knowledge must have an object, which can only be the good, the very term to be defined. Men will sometimes be satisfied with the appearance merely of beauty or justice, but when it comes to the good they want what is really so and are no longer satisfied with belief. Challenged to give his own definition, Socrates denies that he can do so off-hand, but he is willing to describe ' the offspring of the good ', and proceeds with his famous parallel between the sun and the Idea of good. The sun, he says, is the cause of light in the physical world, and light is necessary to sight which is the highest of our senses (508b) :

' It is the sun which I call the offspring of the good, made by the good in its own likeness to bear the same relation to sight and the objects seen in the physical world as the good itself, in the intelligible world, bears to mind and to what is known.

—How ? Explain more fully.

—You know that our eyes become dim and almost blind when we turn them upon objects of which the colours are no longer decked with the sunlight but with the gleam of night, as if sight were no longer present in us.

—Certainly.

—But when the sun shines we see distinctly and sight seems to inhabit those same eyes.

—Of course.

—Understand then the same to take place in the mind (soul). Whenever the mind is directed to something illumined by truth and reality, it knows this and understands it and thus appears gifted with intelligence. But when directed to what is mixed with darkness, what is subject to birth and destruction, the mind is dimmed, has only beliefs which change this way and that, and seems to have no intelligence.

—Yes, that seems true.

—That then which adds truth to the objects of knowledge and gives the knowing subject the power to know, consider this to be the Idea of good. As it is the cause of knowledge and of truth, so think of it also as being apprehended by knowledge. And although both knowledge and truth are beautiful, this other you will rightly consider more beautiful than they. As yonder light and sight are rightly called sun-like but should not be thought to be the sun, so here it is right to call both knowledge and truth good-like, but to identify either with the good is wrong, for goodness must be honoured even more than these.'

In the physical world then we have the sun from which derive light, sight and the eye that sees ; in the intelligible we have the good from which derive truth, knowledge and the mind that knows. It is to the good that the sun itself owes its existence. Furthermore, the sun is not only the cause of sight, its light makes existence possible on the physical plane ; so the good is not only the cause of knowledge, but causes the very existence of the knowable and, a fortiori of the physical which derives from the knowable.

Socrates proceeds at once to make his meaning clear by another image. Starting from the now familiar division of existence into two classes or forms (εἴδη), the visible and the intelligible, he bids Glaucon draw a line and divide it into two unequal parts, each part being then subdivided into two further sections, as follows, so that AD is to DC as CE is to EB as AC is to CB (509d).

The main division at C is between the world of sense and the world of Ideas. We must imagine the highest point in the ladder of truth and reality to be at B. A is the lowest point at which a thing can be said to exist at all. DC will then contain all the phenomena of the physical world, the things we apprehend with our bodily perceptions ' animals, plants and all manufactured objects ', whereas in the lowest section AD we place their images and shadows in water or mirrors, &c. (and possibly, though Plato does not say so, the products of the fine arts). The relation between the objects in DC and those in AD is one we easily understand : it is that between a model and a copy or imitation.

This relation Plato now uses to express also the relation between the objects of sense and the objects in the higher section CE. He makes his meaning clear by the example of mathematics : the objects studied in geometry are in truth perfect mathematical figures, but in his demonstrations the geometer draws material representations of the perfect square, &c., and uses these in his study of the perfect geo-metrical figures which can only be seen by the mind's eye. That is, he uses the sensible objects of DC as copies or images of those mathematical realities which have their being in the higher section CE. This section therefore contains the objects of such sciences as use concrete realities to represent them. Further, such sciences start from axioms and hypotheses which

they take for granted and which it is not their business to call
into question.

There is, however (we are told), a higher kind of science
which is purely abstract and uses no concrete illustrations or
images. The objects of these belong to the highest section EB.
It is the business of this science to test the truth of the hypotheses
and axioms of the lower sciences in terms of hypotheses of still
wider application and it will finally base the whole body of
knowledge upon one universal proposition which is then one
supreme truth. For as this final basis explains all the rest
and is consistent with the whole body of knowledge it can
no longer be called hypothetical. It is the first principle of
nature and existence. This is the Idea of good in the *Republic*,
which we must suppose to exist at B. EB will presumably contain the various truths which the philosopher discovers in the
course of his ascent from the hypotheses of mathematics to the
supreme truth. Once this is discovered he will descend again
through the whole realm of thought. The lower sciences will
now also become knowledge in the highest sense to him because
to him they are no longer based on the hypothetical. Plato
expresses this as follows (511*b*) :

' Understand then that by this other section of the intelligible
(EB) I mean that which reason (λόγος) grasps by means of dialectic.
It does not consider its hypotheses as first principles (ἀϱχαί) but as
hypotheses in the real sense of stepping stones or starting points so
that it may reach that which is beyond hypothesis and arrive at the
first principle of all that is. Having grasped this and keeping hold
of what follows from it, it makes its way down to a conclusion in this
manner without making use of anything visible at all but of Ideas,
and proceeding by way of Ideas to Ideas, its conclusions are Ideas.
—I understand, though not very well, for this is a great labour of
which you speak. You wish to establish that the kind of intelligible
reality viewed by the science of dialectic is more certain than that
viewed by the so called sciences (or crafts, τέχναι) which look upon
their hypotheses as first principles. While students are compelled
to study these by thought (διανοίᾳ) and not by the senses, yet because they do not go back and examine their premises, but work
from hypotheses, they do not appear to you to have any real understanding of their subject, though it can be so understood when
approached with a first principle. And I think you call the attitude
of mind of geometers and such men thought (διάνοια) but not

THE THEORY OF IDEAS

understanding (νοῦς), thought being midway between belief and understanding.
—You have grasped this admirably. Take it further that there are conditions of the mind (παθήματα ἐν τῇ ψυχῇ) corresponding to the four sections : understanding for the highest, thought for the second, belief (πίστις) for the third and imagination (εἰκασία) for the last. Place these in due order and consider that each of them gives as much certainty as there is truth in the corresponding section.'

It is interesting to dwell for a moment on the mental processes by which the different grades of reality are perceived. The main division at C is here, as elsewhere, between uncritical belief (δόξα) which is concerned with the phenomenal world and the critical function of the mind which leads to knowledge (νόησις). When we come to the subdivisions the lowest section contains the objects of εἰκασία which is usually translated as imagination, but it is rather the power of seeing images, for Plato is here thinking of it not so much as a creative faculty but rather as a completely uncritical perception which does not even attempt to relate one perception to another or to differentiate between an object and its reflection in a mirror. The phenomena themselves in DC are the objects of faith or belief (πίστις) which, though it does in a sense correlate its perceptions, does not submit them to critical analysis. Then knowledge is subdivided into διάνοια, the power of critical and logical analysis, of reasoning from given premises, and νοῦς, understanding, which enables one to go beyond the premises of particular sciences to the grasping of the absolute values behind all reality.[1]

As so often, Plato does not work out the scheme of the line in detail and scholars have differed as to what exactly each section of the line should include. Are works of art to be condemned to the lowest section? What, besides the objects of mathematics, should we place in CE? Are the natural sciences and such arts as strategy merely matters of belief? These and many similar questions Plato leaves unanswered.

---

[1] On the nature of this νοῦς see also pp. 253 ff. Any translation of these words must be arbitrary. I prefer to use ' understanding ' to mean the deeper and fuller knowledge, thus reversing Jowett's use of the word for the third section.

Having put vividly before us the different grades of reality
in broad outline, the main steps on the ladder of knowledge,
he goes on to do so again in the magnificent parable of the
cave. And it is better not to press his imagery further than
he does. It is not his way to schematize his philosophy and
it is not very wise to try to do it for him. Some of the
difficulties will recur. Meanwhile we should not forget that
the line is continuous, that it is *one* line, however subdivided,
and that it emphasizes the continuous nature of man's ascent
from ignorance to knowledge as well as the different stages
reached on the road.

The parable of the cave, which illustrates also the ascent
from the darkness of belief into the light of knowledge, is well
known. It does not really add anything new to the theory
of Ideas and there is no need to summarize it here (514 ff.).

The next passage which directly concerns us here, is that of
the Platonic number (546a ff.). When Socrates is proceeding
to give an analysis of the different types of state, the question
arises how, if the ideal republic were once established, any
degeneration could possibly set in. Socrates' answer is that all
human things are subject to change. He calls upon the Muses
to explain how dissensions first began. They are made to
speak ' grandiloquently and in jest ' to us as if we were children,
a sure indication that the following passage is mythical. They
explain how the guardians, who have but human reason tied
up with sense perception, will fail to understand the mathematical laws that govern the universe. In this connexion
Plato builds up both a human and a cosmic number, and in
doing so makes free use of Pythagorean number magic, for are
the Muses not speaking in jest ? [1]

He first builds the human number. Taking 3, 4 and 5, the
sides of the Pythagorean right-angled triangle from which they
derived all physical existence, he adds their cubes to one
another, thus getting 216. This number was supposed to
contain certain ' harmonies ' of which the following are the
most important : it is 210, the shortest period of gestation of
the human embryo reckoned in days, plus 6, which was the
' marriage-number ' because the product of the first even or

[1] The interpretation in the text is that of Adam in his edition of the
Republic.

female number 2 and the first male or odd number 3 (the unit was not considered to be a number but the source of all numbers) ; 210 is also 6 times 35 which is the sum of 6, 8, 9 and 12, the first whole numbers representing the ratios of the Greek musical scale. He then tries to establish a correspondence between man and the universe and to do this builds up the cosmic number : again we start from 3, 4, and 5, multiply them by one another (60) and raise this to the fourth power which gives 12,960,000. This can be written geometrically (as the Pythagoreans wrote their numbers) as a rectangle 4800 by 2700, or as a square with a side of 3600. Note the definite relation between the cosmic number and the human number 216. Not only are they both built up from 3, 4, 5, the first being $(3 \times 4 \times 5)^4$ and the second $(3^3 + 4^3 + 5^3)$, but one side of the rectangle is the longest period of human gestation in days multiplied by the Pythagorean magic number 10, while the other side is the sum of the shortest and longest periods (210 and 270) also multiplied by 10. On the other hand the square number 12,960,000 when divided by the number of days in the year (as was thought) 360, gives 36,000, which may stand for the number of years marking a period in the development of the universe. The cosmic number is also the square of the number of days in the year multiplied by the square of 10. Other harmonies can be found,[1] but we need not follow Plato's play with numbers any further.

It is quite obvious that all this need not be taken too seriously. But though Plato often speaks in jest he never speaks in vain, and it is a very grave mistake to ignore this passage in any interpretation of the doctrine of Ideas. For the Platonic number *is* the Idea of Good, or at any rate one aspect of the supreme Idea, mythically represented. Objectively considered the laws of the universe and the Ideas are mathematical. The conglomeration of elements which is a man, just as much as the movements of the stars, can be expressed in mathematical formulae. Time, space, sound are all mathematical from one point of view, and the purpose or supreme law of the universe can (or so Plato thought) be expressed in terms of numbers. Not of course that the number 12,960,000 does this, for it is only a myth. Plato is not in the least suggesting that this

[1] See Adam l.c.

number contains all the ratios, proportions, &c., in accordance with which the world is made, but he does definitely mean that the world is made in accordance with *some* mathematical formulae. And the sum total of these formulae or laws is surely one aspect of the supreme reality. And because it contains the most perfect ratios, proportions, &c., the best possible mathematical harmony between the manifold factors that make up the world, this reality is good, indeed the Good. In the same way the human number represents at least one aspect of the Idea of man, for it also would contain the essential properties of man expressed mathematically. We may well suppose that Plato meant to indicate that the essential human attributes were capable of mathematical formulation.

We have now seen the theory of Ideas come to its fullest expression in the *Republic*. As the common characteristics of all subjects to which the same predicate applies, the Idea is a logical entity, an aspect of it that recurs in the *Phaedrus* and will be more fully developed in the *Sophist*. It is here that the Idea naturally develops out of the Socratic definition. From this point of view there must be Forms corresponding to all general predicates ; so that at this stage it is not surprising to find a Form of evil in the fourth book ; there is also a Form of bed in the tenth. As metaphysical realities the Ideas belong to the highest and truest kind of real. The ' line ' at least implies some gradation among them, and that those of the widest application are the most fundamental, the highest place of all being claimed for the Idea of good. As the Ideas motivate order in chaos which is self-destructive, they are also beautiful ; and we saw the supreme Idea considered as beauty in the *Symposium*.[1]

In the *Phaedrus* the Forms first appear in the myth in praise of love where Socrates describes the nature of the soul and its journey through the heavens between incarnations. After emphasizing the essential kinship of the soul with the divine and the life of the gods as they journey along the outer rim of heaven, he says (247*c*) :

---

[1] Cp. Robin (*L'Amour*, 225) : ' Prise en elle-même, la Mesure, c'est absolument le Bon ; quand elle se manifeste à nous, c'est le Beau ; quand elle nous devient connaissable, c'est le Vrai.'

' But of the place beyond heaven no one of our poets has yet sung nor will ever sing in a manner worthy. It is as follows, for one must dare to speak the truth, especially when talking of the true : in that place truly existent reality dwells colourless, shapeless and intangible. As the object of true knowledge it is perceived only by that capacity for wisdom which is the pilot of the soul. The thought of the gods, nurtured by pure knowledge and wisdom, and that of every soul concerned to receive what is akin to it, seeing Being at last, rejoices, is nurtured by the contemplation of the true and is happy until it is brought back by the revolving circle to the same place. While thus going round it beholds justice itself, moderation itself and knowledge—not the knowledge that comes to be or that exists in another thing of those we call real, but that which is truly knowledge in that which truly is. And feasting on the contemplation of the other things that likewise truly are, diving back into the inner heaven, the soul goes homeward.'

Though the words εἶδος and ἰδέα are not used in this description, there is no possible doubt that these realities are the Forms. They are said to exist in a place above heaven, that is outside space and time.[1] As in the *Phaedo*, knowledge consists of the recollection of these Forms. Beauty is then mentioned as in a class by itself, not because it is different in nature from the other Ideas among which it shines but because the sense of sight is the clearest of our senses, so that we see more clearly the images and reflections of beauty in the world below than those of other Forms. That is why beauty is most clearly recollected on earth and most beloved.

In the rest of the dialogue, and once also in the myth, the Ideas appear as logical entities. No soul, we are told, that has not caught a glimpse of the Forms can be a human soul, for man must understand what is spoken ' according to a Form ' (249b). The meaning of this becomes clear in the sequel where the proper method of scientific discourse is said to be a right classification of things into classes each of which corresponds to an Idea in nature, a process which is compared to dissection along the joints (κατ' ἄρθρα). This logical method, here explained for the first time, consists then in dividing things into natural classes according to their common

---

[1] See p. 160 and cp. the expression ἐπέκεινα τῆς οὐσίας, beyond reality, in *Rep.*, 509b.

characteristics which correspond to the universal Forms.
Men who can do this are dialecticians, they unite scattered
things under one Idea (265*d*) by means of division and synthesis
(διαιρέσεις, συναγωγαί). The method is not explained at
length, but it should be noted that we have here all the essentials of the process of classification fully explained in the
Sophist and the *Politicus*.

A thorough criticism of the theory of Ideas appears in the
Parmenides, which must have appeared some years before the
dialogues of the third and last period of Plato's writings. The
first part of this remarkable dialogue is a discussion between
Parmenides and his disciple Zeno on the one hand, and
Socrates, here represented as a young man, on the other.
Zeno had exploited the apparent contradictions of the world
of sense to prove that those who believed the world to be
made of a plurality of elements were led to conclusions quite
as paradoxical as those of his master. To escape from this
dilemma Socrates brings up the theory of Forms. In the
course of the conversation he gives three kinds of examples
of Ideas : [1] Ideas of relation such as the big, the small, the
same and the different ; ethical Ideas such as the good and the
beautiful ; Ideas of concrete objects such as man. Parmenides
himself submits the theory to searching criticisms which may
be summarized as follows (130*c*–134*e*) :
First, are there Forms of such things as man, fire, water ?
Socrates is rather doubtful about them and when Parmenides
goes on to ask the same question about hair, mud and sealing-
wax it is too much for him. He fears he must deny that there
are Forms of these to avoid absurdity. But, says Parmenides,
Socrates must get over this fear of ridicule which is due to his
youth.
In the second place, how can the whole Form be present
in different objects of sense and yet remain one ? If it does
not retain its unity we have a plurality once more and the
original difficulty will only be transferred from the physical
to the intelligible world. Socrates suggests that the Forms
might be like day or night, which are each one and yet are
everywhere. Parmenides scoffs at this and retorts that you

[1] See Ritter, II, 79 ff.

might as well spread a big sail over a company and maintain that the sail as a whole is over the head of every person. The sail obviously has parts and is therefore a ' many '. Has the Form parts also ? Are we to suppose the Form of bigness, for example, to be split up into little bits, of which one exists in every big individual thing, so that one bit of bigness will be smaller than another bit ? This surely is absurd.

The third objection is that, if you postulate one Idea to account for the fact that all big things are big, you are still left with two classes of big things—the Idea and the particulars —and you still have to explain why both those classes of big things are big. You will then have to have a further Idea for both classes to participate in, and then in the same way a third Idea to account for the fact that the first and the second Idea have a common predicate, big, and so on *ad infinitum*.

Socrates now makes a very remarkable suggestion (132*b*) :

' Could not, Parmenides, each of these Forms be a concept (νόημα, i.e. idea in our sense) which cannot properly exist elsewhere than in minds (souls). For then each of them would be one and what you said just now would not apply to it.

To this Parmenides objects that thought must have an object, and this would be the Idea as originally brought forward. It is a reality and as such cannot be a thought, for then all things would be composed of thought and everything could think (since all things, Socrates had said, partake of the Forms).

Fourthly, another suggestion of Socrates is that the Ideas exist in nature as patterns or models, that things participate in them merely by being made like them. Parmenides answers as before : if, as Socrates asserts, particulars are like each other (have a common predicate) because they participate in a common Idea ; then, if particulars and this Idea are like each other also, they must both participate in a further Idea.

Fifthly : If the Ideas are not of our world (ἐν ἡμῖν), they are totally separate and there can be no connexion between the two. The Ideas cannot then be objects of knowledge. A particular slave has a particular master, but the Form slavery can only be related to the Form masterhood, not to any particular master, and is of no use to us. If any one has knowledge of it, a god has, but this knowledge of the Forms is beyond us human beings. We cannot know the god and the god cannot know us.

This thorough-going critique has always been a source of astonishment to students of Plato. Most of the main objections to the Ideas later brought forward by Aristotle are there. Is Plato criticizing himself? It has been suggested that he was rather criticizing the theory as *mis*understood by some of his own followers and it is true enough that he never regarded the Ideas as material entities and that it is upon this misconception that the second objection of Parmenides (how can the Form be present in many things and yet remain one?) is based. The same is true of the third and fourth objections which contend that a further Idea will be required to explain that the particulars and the first Idea are like one another and have the same predicate ; this is usually referred to as the argument of the ' third man ' because Aristotle again and again argues in this way that a second Idea of man or a ' third man ' will be required to explain the likeness between the Idea of man and particular men. In the form in which it is here attacked Plato certainly never held the theory, and we might be inclined to dismiss these objections as frivolous and irrelevant were it not that Aristotle is continually arguing in this way in all seriousness. That does not in itself make the arguments relevant, but it does point to the necessity of explaining clearly what is the nature of these Forms, a thing which Plato has not done. No doubt he would say it could not be done. But the difficulty remains.

Apart from these somewhat captious objections, however, others point to weaknesses which certainly belong to the theory of the *Phaedo* and the *Republic*. Are there Forms of man, fire, water, hair and sealing-wax ? and, we may add, of manufactured articles, of negative notions such as injustice ? We have not been told. Then the fifth objection of Parmenides raises the question of the relation between the Ideas and the phenomenal world, and no one will deny that this difficulty at least is very real and that no satisfactory answer has been given. Attempts have been made to bridge the gulf between the two worlds by means of Reminiscence in the *Meno*, the

Phaedo and the *Phaedrus* ; by intellect in the *Phaedo* and the *Republic* ; by Eros in the *Symposium* and the *Phaedrus* ; and all these are functions of the human soul. But a study of Plato's conception of the soul and of the gods in the later dialogues will show that he knew well enough that he had not solved the problem. And when he tells us that particulars participate in (μετέχειν) or imitate the Ideas, he is fully aware that those are only metaphors.

It seems therefore idle to deny that some at least of Parmenides' criticisms are pertinent enough against the theory of Forms as it is presented to us in the great dialogues we have been considering. Aristotle himself gives plenty of proof that one at least of the most able students in the Academy thought them all to be valid against the theory as he knew it. In view of all this it seems rather perverse to argue that there is no self-criticism in the *Parmenides* and it is surely a greater tribute to Plato to suppose that he put in the mouth of the old Eleatic all the arguments that had been advanced by others or that he could think of himself against the existence of his beloved Forms. And, though some are clearly unsound, it is not Plato's way to tell us what to think about them.

We shall deal only very briefly with the second, by far the longer, part of the *Parmenides*. Parmenides gives there an excellent display of his logical powers by taking eight hypotheses such as ' If One is ', ' If One is not ', ' If the many are ' (i.e. if reality is a plurality), and derives from these all kinds of contradictory conclusions.[1] This strange exhibition has been variously interpreted : some see in it little more than a *jeu d'esprit*, a headlong parody ; others, from the Neo-Platonists on, have sought, and of course found, all kinds of hidden meanings in every part. The truth probably lies somewhere between the two. A parody it certainly is and there is no need to suppose that Plato did not see through most of the fallacies ; but any sane analysis of this part of the dialogue shows a serious motive behind.[2] The fallacies and contradictions are mostly

[1] The reader will find an excellent summary of the eight arguments in Burnet, pp. 264–72.
[2] e.g. Marck, 81 ff., who somewhat corrects Natorp's extravagances (Natorp, 242 ff.). See also Taylor, 360 ff., who perhaps underestimates the serious purpose behind the ' play '.

due to two things : the confusion of the two uses of the verb
' to be ' (εἶναι) which, in Greek as in most languages, could
be used either as a copula or to mean ' exist ' ; and also the
way in which Parmenides isolates a single aspect of reality, e.g.
the One, and considers it in complete separation from anything else. We are tempted to infer that a Platonic Idea
considered in the same way will lead to much the same unsatisfactory conclusions. But did not Socrates remark in the
earlier part of the dialogue that while he was not disturbed by
the fact that contradictory predicates could be applied to the
same things in the physical world, he would be marvellously
surprised if any one could show how the Idea of likeness could
be said to be unlike in any way ? This marvellous surprise
Plato will give his readers in the *Sophist*. There too the
ambiguity of the verb to be will be clarified, so that the connexion between the two dialogues is obvious and generally
recognized.

This severe criticism would lead us to expect a restatement
of the theory of Ideas. As such we do not get it. Hence it
has sometimes been supposed that Plato abandoned, or at least
fundamentally altered,[1] his belief in the existence of Ideas ;
but it will soon appear that there is no evidence to indicate any
such change ; quite the contrary. Yet some of the questions
asked by Parmenides are never answered. We are nowhere
told whether there are Ideas of manufactured articles, for
example. On such points we must suppose that Plato was
not prepared to be dogmatic, at least in his writings. Perhaps
he thought it unnecessary. Having, as he obviously thought,
proved the existence of unchangeable absolutes, he probably
considered his main point established and he did not wish to
attempt a detailed schematization of the world of Ideas. At any
rate he has not done so.

The *Theaetetus* was probably written shortly after the *Parmenides*. It is a curious return to the earlier inconclusive
manner, for no satisfactory definition of knowledge is found.
The Ideas seem at times almost deliberately left aside, and I

[1] e.g. by Burnet, *Platonism*, pp. 46 ff., 119, and *passim*. Also in Jackson's
famous articles in *Journal of Philology*, vols. X, XI.

have no doubt that this is the case. When Theaetetus' suggestions that knowledge is perception, or that it is right belief, have been refuted, we expect at every moment the Ideas to appear and to solve the problem. They remain absent. The reason for this seems to be that the aim of the whole dialogue is to prove to the relativists, be they followers of Heraclitus or Protagoras, that on their premises knowledge is impossible. It is ever Plato's way to argue from his opponents' premises, not from his own. He disproves the equation of sense perception with knowledge, he proves that not even perception is reliable on the assumption of perpetual motion or of Protagoras' ' man is the measure of all things ', he proves that knowledge is to be found in the mind's converse with itself. Even so, however, a definition of knowledge that does not provide an object towards which the mind can be directed, a permanent reality for it to grasp firmly, is unsatisfactory. Theaetetus' last suggestion that ' knowledge is right belief, together with a power to give an account of things ' fails to satisfy because, if belief and knowledge have the same object or content, the difference must be that the latter is knowledge of that which was previously believed, and this is no definition of knowledge. Then, if, as is suggested, the elements of a thing are unknowable, a mere enumeration of those elements cannot be knowledge. Further, if the thing to be known is a whole which is more than the sum of its parts, we must suppose this to be a further unknowable besides the elements, and then the essence of a thing cannot be known.

Of course, Plato did not believe this to be the case, just because the Forms exist and are objects of knowledge, both the Form of the whole and the Forms of the elements. So that although the Forms are not mentioned, the *Theaetetus* might well be looked upon as an essay on the last words of Parmenides about the Forms : ' unless they exist, Socrates, all converse (διαλέγεσθαι) is impossible '.[1] And the existence of the Ideas, of ' things in themselves ' is always kept before us as the only alternative to the theory of flux. The denial of those ' things in themselves ' entails, as elsewhere, the denial of moral values also.[2]

The long digression which contrasts the rhetorician of the

[1] *Parm.*, 135*b*.   [2] 157*a–d*.

law-court with the philosopher, though it does not explicitly mention the Ideas, implies them at every turn. How else can we understand the search for 'justice itself' and for its nature as well as that of injustice, which occupies the thinker? (175c) Further (176e) :

'There are fixed patterns in reality, my friend, one of the divine and happiest, the other of the godless and most unhappy, but men do not see that this is so. Their simplicity and extreme ignorance hide from them the fact that unjust actions make them like the latter and unlike the first. And they pay the penalty by living a life similar to that pattern which they resemble.'

Lastly, it is by itself that the mind or soul perceives Being (as in the *Phaedo*), non-being, likeness, unlikeness, same, other, beauty, ugliness, good and evil, the nature of these things and their relationship to one another (185c ff.). This is the knowledge that cannot be perception. It follows that, although the words εἶδος and ἰδέα are not used and Plato is careful to keep his Ideas in the background, these realities are the Platonic Forms and none other.

The *Sophist* makes a more positive contribution to our problem. It contains a discussion of the logical method of classification ; the Eleatic stranger (the chief speaker here) gives six different illustrations of the method, each one an attempt to define a Sophist. Each division emphasizes a different aspect of the Sophist, and the difference in the results is enough to prove that the logical method of classification is not in itself enough to discover the essence of a thing, that it needs at least to be carefully controlled so that one's divisions will correspond to natural classes with common characteristics, that is, to Ideas.

In the course of this discussion Plato considers the two difficulties raised by the *Parmenides*, and one of them is dealt with for good and all. The positive meaning of negation, in its simplest form, relies on a proper understanding of the copulative meaning of the verb 'to be', that is, of the difference between the two statements : 'Socrates is not' and 'Socrates is not tall '. The first is a clear denial of Socrates' existence, the second an assertion that 'Socrates is not-tall' i.e. other-than-tall, and in this secondary sense is-not does express something about a subject or, as the Greeks put it, non-being is. Whether Plato himself had only now come to understand this we do not know (we do find the fallacy used to refute opponents in earlier dialogues), but we have here at any rate a time-honoured puzzle completely disposed of, and for the first time. One is tempted to suppose that he disposes at the same time of negative Ideas, such as injustice, which we have seen referred to now and again hitherto. It would, indeed, seem to follow (237*b* ff.), but he does not say so explicitly.

The second difficulty is the perennial one of the apparently complete divorce between the world of Ideas and the phenomenal world. This comes up in the course of an attempt to define the nature of being, the ultimate reality of Logic. Two schools of philosophy are opposed : on the one hand the materialists who will only admit as true what is material body which they can touch, on the other hand are the ' friends of the Ideas ' who, in opposition to the first (246*b*) :

' very discreetly from the invisible above defend themselves, and maintain that true reality consists of some kind of intelligible and immaterial Forms. They make short shrift in argument of the physical bodies which the others call truth, and call them a becoming in motion instead of reality.'

The materialists are easily dealt with : [1] they must admit the existence of soul and of that which, when present, makes the soul just, namely justice. They will then have to accept a definition of reality as ' that which has the power to act or be acted upon '.[2] The trouble with the friends of the

---

[1] The materialists are casually mentioned in *Theaet.*, 155*e*. There they are summarily dismissed, and Plato goes on to discuss the partisans of motion, the Heracliteans, with whom he links Protagoras. To these are later opposed ' the Parmenides' ' and ' Melissi ' who believe reality to be completely divorced from motion. When the Heraclitus-Protagoras point of view is disposed of, he refuses to discuss Parmenides' position (183*a*). In the *Sophist* there are two sets of opposing schools : the pluralists and the monists (including Parmenides) at 243*d* ff. ; then the materialists and the friends of the Ideas (probably including Parmenides again as a believer in one Idea) in the present passage. See p. 297.

[2] 247*e* : τὰ ὄντα ὡς ἐστιν οὐκ ἄλλο πλὴν δύναμις. Cp. *Theaet.*, 156*a*.

Ideas is, we are told, that they postulate a number of Forms which are completely inactive. How then do they explain the relation between these and the physical world? They will agree that these Ideas are known by the soul's intelligence. But surely, to be known is a form of activity (κίνησις), and the Ideas are at least capable of being known : they are in some manner subjected to an activity and are thus acted upon. And we cannot surely believe that this intelligible world or real being is entirely devoid of activity, life, soul, wisdom and intellect. Of that which is completely unmoved and inactive (in the sense defined) there cannot be knowledge (249c) : [1]

'The philosopher then, he who holds these things in honour (i.e. mind, intelligence, &c.) cannot possibly accept from those who assert the existence either of one or of many Ideas the theory that the whole of reality stands still. Nor must he listen at all to those who say that reality is ever in every kind of motion, but, like children in their wishes, he must insist on having it both ways ; what is immovable is also in motion, the whole and the real are both.'

How Plato thus brings soul and motion into the world of supreme reality is a question we shall discuss when speaking of Plato's gods.[2] Here our problem is not so much metaphysical as logical, namely that supreme Forms cannot be considered in absolute isolation from each other, a point that the mental acrobatics of the *Parmenides* made emphatically clear.

Scholars have been much exercised as to who 'the friends of the Ideas' could be who are here criticized. Apart from those who see here a reference to other philosophical schools, some have maintained the reference to be to Platonists who had misinterpreted their master's theories. No doubt intercourse with his fellow workers brought home to Plato the difficulties implied in the theory of Forms. It is true also, as we have seen, that he was always conscious of the necessity of bridging the gap between the Forms and the pheno-

[1] Cp. *Theaet.*, 153a, on the necessity of movement if there is to be any life.
[2] For a full discussion of the difficulties see also Appendix II ; and pp. 161–2.

mena. On the other hand it is quite clear that in no dialogue hitherto (with the possible exception of a hint in the *Republic* [1]) has there been any question of intercommunion or participation between the Forms themselves, or of the inclusion of mind and movement in the supra-sensual world. Even in the *Phaedrus* myth, where the gods are in heaven, the Forms are above and beyond heaven. All this drives us to conclude that the beliefs of the friends of the Ideas are, or at least include, the theory of Ideas as expressed by Socrates in the *Phaedo*, the *Republic* and the *Parmenides*. They may not have told the whole story and it is always possible that Plato made mental reservations regarding problems he intended to deal with later. But he can hardly claim to have been misunderstood, if he was criticized as the friends of the Forms are criticized here.

The stranger thus makes clear that the Ideas cannot exist in absolute isolation from one another. We have already seen in the *Phaedo* that particulars can participate in several Ideas at the same time. The question is now asked about the Ideas themselves. How far can they intermingle? Clearly it is impossible for all the Ideas to mix with one another, for then everything could be everything, any predicate could be applied to any subject and there would no longer be any objective laws in the universe. The Ideas themselves would lose all meaning. On the other hand, as we saw, they cannot be completely isolated from one another. It follows that some can be found in close relation while others can never come together at all (251e–252e). Just as certain letters can combine to make words while other combinations are meaningless, so (253*d*) :

' to classify things in accordance with the Ideas, and not to mistake the same Form for a different one or a different one for the same belongs to the science of dialectic, does it not?
—Yes.
—Therefore the man who can do this, who can satisfactorily perceive one Idea spreading everywhere over the many, while each remains a separate entity ; many others circumscribed by one from the outside, and again one spreading over the whole of many united as one, and many quite separate everywhere. To recognize, that

[1] p. 22 above and note.

is, where each can combine with others and where it cannot, this is to know how to classify according to the Kinds (i.e. Forms).' [1]

The word 'kind' (γένος) is throughout this passage used as an equivalent of Form,[2] as it is in the *Parmenides*. The five Forms or Kinds which Plato proceeds to use as illustrations are Ideas in the same sense as any others, and he expressly tells us that he uses them as examples only, because it is impossible to go through all the Forms. The only difference is that these five (being, rest, motion, same and other) have a more general application than most. Being indeed combines with every other Idea, since each of them *is*, and this being is the supreme reality logically considered. So every one of these five is the same as itself and different (other) from the others (i.e. it *is not* the others), and we are now no longer puzzled by the old problem of how a thing can both be and not be. ' Every one of the Forms contains a certain amount of being, and an infinite amount of non-being ' (256e), since it *is not* everything but itself.

Thus the *Sophist* clears up the old logical puzzle of the meaning of ' to be ' ; it follows up the criticisms of the *Parmenides* by breaking down the frozen isolation of the separate Ideas, by making them combine with each other, as they must in any abstract reasoning, and prepares us for a further working out of the relation between the gods and the Ideas by insisting that movement, soul and life must also find a place in the supra-sensual world.

The *Politicus* does not make any specific contribution to the theory of Forms. Their existence is, however, taken for granted. In the discussion of the proper method of division and classification Plato emphasizes once more that it is essential to divide ' according to the Ideas ' and that every class should correspond to a Form.[3] At the end of the dialogue, when contrasting moderation with courage, he speaks of the Form of each virtue.

---

[1] For a discussion of this passage see Diès, II, 110, n. 315.
[2] See 253b, c, d ; 259e, 260a and *passim*.
[3] e.g. 262b : τὸ μέρος ἅμα εἶδος ἐχέτω. In this dialogue too γένος is synonymous with εἶδος, 304e, 307d, 308b.

There is also a curious passage [1] in which he once more argues for the existence of objective truth, this time in the guise of an absolute standard of measurement. Things, he maintains, are not only bigger or smaller than one another, they are also too big or too small in relation to an objectively existing mean. You may therefore either judge excess and defect in relation to one another, or absolutely. I would illustrate as follows what I consider to be the meaning of this passage. I may touch Socrates, then touch Theaetetus, and say that Socrates is hotter than Theaetetus. This is a relative judgement. It is true, but it tells us very little about either man. I may on the other hand feel Socrates' temperature, compare it with what it ought to be, and say that Socrates is feverish. In this case I am comparing Socrates' temperature with an absolute standard. This is what Plato means by the absolute mean. He might even have said the Idea of man, for temperature of a definite kind, for example, is part of the Idea of man. But he does not mention the Ideas in this passage. He is content to establish the necessity for an absolute standard in every science, and to insist that to have any value a science must know this mean. Of the two kinds of measurement the second only has any value, it can produce good results because it only has in view ' the mean, the opportune, the necessary, the middle between both excesses '.

The difference to which Plato is here pointing is an undeniable fact : that Socrates feels hotter than Theaetetus (or hotter than usual) is not the same as Socrates having a temperature. And it is upon the proper and appropriate temperature that the doctor keeps his eye. So far Plato is right and the point was worth making ; it is in fact the difference between the empirical and the scientific. We may, of course, deny that the scientific standard is absolute, that it never changes in any century or climate. Even so, however, there are two standards. This point Plato was the first to see, and to express as definitely, if not as clearly, as his pupil Aristotle.

The *Philebus* is primarily a discussion of pleasure, but it

[1] For summary and interpretation of this passage see Appendix III.

raises incidentally, as Plato's manner is, metaphysical problems of the first magnitude. The old problem of the one and the many, of unity and plurality, comes up once more. In so far as it applies to the physical world, says Socrates, there is no difficulty and that the same particular can be considered both as a unity and a plurality need not disturb us. We know (we have seen it in the *Parmenides*) that the theory of Ideas will solve that. The difficulty is with the Ideas themselves (15*a*) :

'when one attempts to consider man as a unit (i.e. as one class), and ox as one, and beauty and the good. It is earnest concern with these units (ἕναδες) by means of division that brings doubt.'

Three problems arise, we are told, whether such 'monads' exist ; whether they continue to exist as units and are not subject to birth and decay ; how they can be present in many particulars and yet remain one. We recognize at once the difficulties of the theory of Ideas. That they are called henads or monads here creates no difficulty ; it is from this point of view that they will be discussed in this dialogue and Plato was never tied to any particular name for his Ideas. He seems indeed to have deliberately avoided using a consistent technical vocabulary : not only does he call his Forms by many names but he continues to use the words εἶδος and ἰδέα in their untechnical sense, a thing which a Greek would probably hardly notice but which not infrequently troubles commentators.

What is more surprising is that after this restatement of the difficulties inherent in his theory we once more expect him to deal with them and to expound the theory of Forms more or less *de novo*, but we get nothing of the kind. After a warning against a merely contentious use of the method of logical classification he introduces an 'ancient theory' to account for the existence of the physical world, 'those things which are always spoken of as existing' (τῶν ἀεὶ λεγομένων εἶναι, 16*c*), namely that everything is made by a combination of limit (πέρας) and the unlimited or indefinite (probably a Pythagorean theory). He then repeats that it is our duty always to search for *one* Form, or as few as possible. Thus in a classification we will pass from one to as few classes as possible, each embodying a Form, and not leap from one to infinity (the unlimited). We must not, for example, jump from the genus animal to particular specimens, but subdivide the animal kingdom into definite classes or species according to their common characteristics. It is quite clear that here at least the Forms are identified with the limiting factor.

A little later Plato returns to the formula of the limit and the indefinite and elaborates it into a general formula to account for the existence of things in the phenomenal world.[1] He now adds a third kind, the result of their mixture (συμμισγόμενον), and then also the cause or agent which provokes the process. In explaining these various factors he identifies the indefinite with the more-and-less, by which he means the old opposites of previous philosophers for which more-and-less is a general formula. Hot-cold for example, or more exactly hotter-colder, is a continuum capable of infinite extension in either direction, but every actual object has a definite temperature. As Plato puts it, limit or definiteness has been impressed upon the more-and-less. Everything that exists has a so-much (ποσόν) of each of its qualities. This is a point of contact with the passage from the *Politicus* discussed above, for the so-much is an approximation to the absolute mean which science keeps in view. The right combination of limit and the more-and-less produces health in the body, as it produces music out of a meaningless chaos of sound (26a).

We are once more studying, from a different angle, the old problem of the ' participation ' of particular objects in the Ideas. The whole formula of limit, unlimited, mixture and cause is but a general formula to cover every particular case of such participation. It is not meant to supersede, but to explain it. We also understand now why the Ideas were called henads or monads at the beginning of the dialogue. They typify oneness or unity as against plurality, and the one is definitely identified with the limit, plurality with the unlimited or indefinite.[1] We know from the passage on the human and the cosmic numbers in the *Republic* that the Ideas can, from one point of view, be looked upon as mathematical formulae. Any such formula or equation is essentially the

[1] See Appendix IV.

limit with which they are here identified, while the inchoate potentiality of what is unordered by number is the more-and-less. Hence also the repetition at the beginning of the dialogue that somehow—how, it is difficult to understand, but somehow it must be—the monad or Idea, though present in an infinite number of particulars, yet retains its essential oneness, remains an ever-same, unchanging, eternal unit.

It has been well said that ' causality through the indwelling presence of the Idea is to Plato a mere blank cheque, of universal dialectical application, but intended to be filled up whenever possible with concrete ethical and physical meaning '.[1] The *Philebus* gives a description of the general formula in accordance with which this cheque is to be filled in if it is to be valid. We have, for example, a number of potentialities indefinitely extensible in either direction, one for every quality of man, and we have the Idea man, itself a focus of other Ideas which here combine (as we have learned from the *Sophist* that they could) to form this Idea of man. The Idea is then impressed upon the mass of indefinite potentialities and the result is a man. This may be looked upon as a single operation, or a series of simultaneous operations if each combining Idea is considered separately, as logically it may, and in each case the operation consists of the impress of limit upon the indefinite more-and-less.

And each operation, being an act of birth and therefore an activity, needs an agent, the fourth factor, the making or moving cause.[2] This moving cause is later identified with mind ($\nu o\tilde{\upsilon}\varsigma$), naturally enough, for mind is the highest function of the soul, and the soul is the only thing which is capable of originating motion.

The *Philebus* does not then in any way supersede the theory of Ideas, but the whole argument is, on the contrary, built upon their existence. We find them in this dialogue, not only as the monads of the beginning of the dialogue, but later also there are ' those things which remain ever the same and

---

[1] By Shorey : *The Idea of Good*, p. 198.

[2] Clearly we have here three at least of Aristotle's four causes : Form (here limit), matter (the unlimited, or rather the indefinite, for it is not strictly substance to Plato), and the moving cause. It might be maintained that the mixture is the final cause, but that is a doubtful identification. The other three, however, are obvious.

unmixed ' (59a), ' justice itself which exists . . . and all those other things that really are ' (62a), and ' the good which cannot be tracked down as one Form but can be expressed in three : beauty, symmetry and truth ' (65a). All these are clearly Ideas in the same sense as they ever were.

In the *Timaeus* the Ideas are the pattern or model which the Maker has in view when he fashions the universe, and he makes the whole world as like them as possible. This pattern consists of the Forms of every kind of thing in the world, as well it may since there is, strictly speaking, a Form of every universal term, every genus, species, element or ethical value, perhaps even of all manufactured as well as natural objects. The relation between this ideal pattern and other kinds of reality will be discussed elsewhere.[1] Suffice it to say here that the Ideas are still the supreme reality after which the world is made.

The *Laws* is a treatise of practical politics. An Athenian discusses with a Spartan and a Cretan the foundation of a new colony. No doubt the Athenian represents the views of Plato himself, but neither of the other two is a philosopher in any sense. We do not therefore expect to find any very profound discussion of metaphysics, logic or psychology ; and the theory of Ideas is not directly referred to. There is no reason why it should be. But the general point of view is essentially the same as before : wisdom is still the highest good for man, truth the thing to be attained above all others, and we must still follow reason.[2] The priority of the soul is asserted and, when it is established by argument in the tenth book we find that it is knowledge that makes the soul like the gods. The order and purpose of the universe are insisted on.[3] What the knowledge may be which our rulers must have is explained very briefly at the very end : they must understand the one supreme aim of statesmanship, which is to encourage virtue and goodness. To do this they must

[1] When discussing Plato's gods, below p. 167.
[2] See e.g. 631c, 639b, 645a ; 688e, 696c ; 730c ff. ; we may also note that division is still ' according to the Forms ' in the case of music at 700a ff.
[3] See 726, 889e, 892a, 897b, and passim.

understand the nature of 'the one' and 'the many', how the virtues are four and yet one; they must be able to give a reasoned account of them, for then only can they have understanding (965*b*) :

'Therefore we said that the best craftsman and guardian must in every case be able to look not only at the many things, but also be able to press forward to the underlying unity and know that, and thus get a general view of all things and arrange them in relation to it.
—Rightly.
—And could there be any more precise examination and contemplation of anything for any one than to be able to look from many things unlike one another towards one Form.
—Perhaps.
—Not perhaps but certainly, my friend. There is no surer method for any man than this.
—I will take your word for it, my foreign friend. Let us proceed on that assumption.'

Clearly this is the knowledge of Ideas. The Cretan does not understand, and this was obviously not the place for a fuller explanation ; but Plato makes it quite obvious that he has not abandoned his belief that the statesman must have knowledge of the eternal values. For, he adds (966*a*) they must also understand the essential unity of all beauty and of all good, and this means to apprehend the Idea in each case. The statesman must also be able to give an account of everything of which an account is possible.[1]

We have now seen the Ideas slowly emerge from the Socratic definition, as Aristotle said they did, and then blaze forth in all their glory in the dialogues of the middle period. We have seen them remain, until the very end of Plato's life, the fundamental hypothesis upon which he based the rest of his philosophy, in spite of the fact that he was well aware of the difficulties which the theory implied. To make com-

---

[1] 967*e* : ὅσα λόγον ἔχει, τούτων δυνατὸς ᾖ δοῦναι λόγον. On the question of the Ideas in the *Laws* see Brochard's discussion (*Etudes*, 151–68) with which I fully agree. (He makes a slight mistake, however, when at 668*c* ff. he takes ὅτι ποτ' ἐστι and οὐσία to refer to the world of Ideas. They clearly refer to the phenomena which works of art imitate.)

pletely valid knowledge possible it was essential that there be some such universal realities not subject to change and decay, and that these should be apprehended by the human intelligence. And, since some such realities were necessary, Plato was satisfied to assert that there existed such a reality corresponding to what we are more apt to call every abstract concept. But to look upon the Ideas as concepts in any shape or form is a mistake, for a concept cannot by definition exist until the mind has conceived it, and this Plato quite deliberately refused to admit of his Ideas. They are rather the objective reality to which the concept corresponds, and they exist whether we know them or not. If the whole human race were senseless savages, the eternal Form of justice would exist as fully in any case, though it would be even less perfectly realized in the world. So that in the intelligible world there is no place for progress or evolution : the pattern is the same though the copy—the world of sense—may reflect it more or less closely at different times. That it progresses in this direction in a sure and certain manner is not definite ; if we are to trust the *Politicus* myth, the old belief in cycles of alternate advance and relapse had its attraction for Plato.

The Ideas are spaceless and immaterial. That is perfectly clear from the *Phaedo* on, and to press poetical expressions used in certain myths which would seem to assert the contrary, is childish and ridiculous. Ideas are quite independent of particulars : men may come and men may die, they may even all die, but the Idea of man, like that of beauty, goodness and all the rest, would still exist. In fact humanity does not die, and the problem of extinct species probably did not occur to Plato.

Considered as truth, the Ideas are the objective realities that general terms connote. It is from this aspect that Plato thought of them as mathematical formulae which governed the physical world and brought order out of chaos, laws that governed every human action as well as the movements of the stars and planets, the one right way of doing things in the moral sphere. For as a mathematician he dreamed of introducing mathematical accuracy even there. And as they make for harmony they are beautiful and are the objects of our passionate longing to see, to know and understand beauty and, by means of this understanding, to create further beauty. Again as the source of order, bringing harmony where chaos reigned, they are good, for harmony is the essence of goodness and usefulness (almost synonymous terms to a Greek) whereas what is discordant is not only ugly, but useless and self-destructive. They are also the truths of logic, for it is from them that both subject and predicate derive their meaning. But to regard them merely as logical entities and rules of thought is to deprive Platonism of all its inspiration and emotional appeal.

II

PLEASURE

THE second half of the fifth century is well known as a period of criticism. The old laws, the old traditions, were all vigorously called in question. The Sophists are typical products of this spirit and to some extent exploited it. The fundamental problem of all ethics naturally attracted their attention. When duty and pleasure clash, as they so often seem to do in life, why should the latter be sacrificed to the former? Several of the Sophists maintained that it should not, and they expressed this conflict as a struggle between nature (φύσις) on the one hand and law or convention (νόμος) on the other. It was then 'natural' for a man to seek only his own pleasure and happiness, provided that he were strong enough to rise above the legal obstacles and punishments which the weaker majority tried to put in his way.

In opposition to this view Socrates and Plato boldly asserted that any such wild beast behaviour is thoroughly unnatural and against human nature in the true sense. This position is consistently upheld throughout the dialogues, but there are interesting differences in Plato's attitude to the pleasure principle in man, from the puritanical anti-hedonism of the *Gorgias* —a very natural reaction against the apostles of pleasure for a young man with deeply idealistic and social beliefs—to the saner and more mellow teaching of the *Laws*. For we must not let the severity of the punishments decreed against certain types of crime in this last work blind us to the fact that Plato's philosophy is there more balanced, with a greater depth of understanding, and that he incorporates a great deal that he had rejected in his youth.[1]

---

[1] See Friedländer, II, 644-5. Ritter (II, 589-612) contrasts the attitude of the *Phaedo* with that of later works.

A discussion of Plato's attitude to pleasure will take us mostly to the *Gorgias*, the *Protagoras*, the *Phaedo*, the *Republic*, the *Philebus* and the *Laws*.

The *Gorgias* is formally a discussion of rhetoric and of its function in the state. Gorgias himself, the veteran teacher of oratory, would have been the last person to uphold a crude hedonism which he probably despised as heartily as Plato did, but, as Socrates points out, he is putting in the hands of his pupils a dangerous weapon which, unless properly used, may do far more harm than good ; Callicles, Socrates' chief opponent, is just such an irresponsible pupil. Polus on the other hand, like his master before him, has only failed to think out his fundamental assumptions.

In the first scene, which is comparatively short, Gorgias in fact admits Socrates' point, for he compares himself to a teacher of boxing, wrestling or fencing, and maintains that the pupil, not the master, should be held responsible for the use he makes of his newly acquired skill (456c ff.). This is a sound and reasonable position, but it is hardly consistent with the dignity of the great sophist whose vague pretensions were much wider. When pressed, he lightly admits that should any of his pupils be ignorant of right and wrong (τὸ δίκαιον) he would certainly teach them this also (460a). The contradiction is obvious, for he now accepts the very responsibility he was denying before, and, when this is pointed out to him he retires from the argument. This he can do with good grace, for he had been lecturing for some time before Socrates' arrival (447a), and is by this time somewhat weary.

Polus now takes up the argument. He sees quite clearly the weakness of Gorgias' position and frankly admits that the aim of rhetoric is pleasure (462c) ; pleasure to him is a good and a fine thing ; to which Socrates replies that rhetoric undoubtedly gives the power to do what one thinks fit (ἃ δοκεῖ) but this is of little use, for what a man really wants (ἃ βούλεται) is to do what is good for him, and the two are not necessarily the same (466e). He boldly states that it is better to suffer wrong than to do it. To this Polus will not agree, because, he says, the wrong-doer is clearly happier than his victim, which Socrates in turn denies. The discussion seems to have reached a deadlock, until Polus admits that, though it is *worse* to suffer than to commit a wrong, the latter is more ugly. This concession—that to do wrong is ugly—offers a common basis for discussion, nor is Socrates slow to take advantage of it. He makes Polus admit that a thing is beautiful (καλόν) when it is either useful or pleasurable or both, and ugly when it is painful or bad. If then to do wrong is uglier than to be wronged, yet less painful, it must be worse, i.e. more evil. Polus is forced to agree, and the rest is easy. To do wrong is now admitted to be worse than to suffer it, yet all men want what is good for them. If so they should prefer to be sinned against rather than to sin, and Socrates is free to develop at length his paradoxical, but profoundly sincere belief that happiness is to be found in righteousness only and that sinners ought to wish for their own correction.[1]

Here and there the argument seems to us purely logical and academic, all the more so because a good deal is taken for granted, as for example the equation of good with useful. This, however, was a common Greek idea which to Socrates' audience seemed self-evident. They made no difference between ' good ' and ' good for somebody or for something '.[2]

Callicles now comes upon the stage in full rhetorical panoply. Though not himself a sophist, he is a typical product of their education. He is the complete and uncompromising hedonist who is not to be shamed or browbeaten. The discussion between him and Socrates is one of the most dramatic in Plato. In it the two lives, that of the search for pleasure and that of the search for truth, hedonism and the love of knowledge, stand face to face, personified in the two protagonists. Callicles indeed cannot at first believe that this is anything but a clever debate, but, once he is persuaded that Socrates is in earnest, he launches upon a long speech which we may take to be typical. It is no parody, but a very fine specimen of real eloquence and consummate skill.[3] He certainly has not

---

[1] In the argument with Polus (466–81a) a certain confusion is introduced when Socrates, in defining ' beautiful ' (including the beauty of laws, institutions and music) as pleasurable or useful or both, fails to differentiate between the pleasure of the subject and that of a spectator (474d).

[2] See on pp. 217 ff.

[3] Note how carefully Plato has constructed this speech. It has four parts : (i) 482c–483a, introductory remarks ; (ii) 483a–484c, the anti-

studied rhetoric in vain. He goes over the weak points of
his two predecessors and rebukes Socrates for taking advantage of them. Clearly and unambiguously he puts before us
the contrast between convention and nature as he conceives
it. Polus' admission that to do wrong is ugly was purely
conventional, he says, and should have been understood as
such. Current morality is merely a convenient arrangement
by which the weak restrain the strong, whom they fear (484*a*) :

'But I think that, if a man is born with adequate natural endow-
ments (φύσιν ἱκανὴν ἔχων), he will shake off all those restraints,
break through them and escape, trample underfoot all our writings
and trickeries and charms, all law that is contrary to nature. This
slave of ours rises to be our master and natural right shines.'

Philosophy, he goes on, is all very well for youths and very
suitable for them. In middle age, however, it is highly ridiculous and prevents manly and virile pursuits. He then concludes with an earnest appeal to Socrates to put away such
childish things (485*e*) :

'You care not, Socrates, for the things for which you should care,
and you distort the noble nature of your soul to a childish form ;
you could not properly conduct an argument in court, nor is it
probable that you could make it convincing or give vigorous advice
to another.

And yet, my dear Socrates—do not be angry with me ; I speak
for your own good—do you not think it shameful to be in such a
position as I believe you are in, you and those others who pursue
philosophy too far ? If any one were to arrest you or some one like
you and drag you into prison, accuse you of a wrong you had not
committed, you know you would be at a loss what to do, you would
be dazed and gape and have nothing to say. In court you would
be condemned to death though your accuser be evil and inferior, if
he asked for the death penalty. How can that be a wise thing,
Socrates, an art which takes hold of a noble man and makes him
deteriorate, unable to help himself, unable to save himself or others
from the greatest danger ; which allows him to be robbed of everything by his enemies, to live quite without rights in his own city ? '

thesis between nature and convention ; (iii) 484*c*–485*e*, criticism of philosophy ; (iv) 485*e*–486*d*, personal appeal to Socrates. Contrast this, for
example, with the supposed speech of Lysias in the *Phaedrus* (231*a*–234*c*),
which is purposely lacking in construction.

Here at last is a man who does not shrink from the consequences of his convictions, who is, it seems, clear-headed
enough to realize them. Socrates welcomes him with a warmth
that is not altogether ironical, for with such a man you know
where you stand. Faced with this thorough-going hedonism,
how will Socrates proceed? In his characteristic way, by
making Callicles define his terms. Right, we are told, is the
advantage of the strongest. That is, stronger and better are
identical terms.

Very well, but who *are* the stronger? For in one sense the
majority are stronger than the few, so that they may be
right after all. With some irritation Callicles protests that
he is not referring to physical strength, else a mob of slaves
would rule us by virtue of their superior numbers. This first
limitation is, of course, important. And when he has further
somewhat lightly accepted the definition of the stronger as
the more intelligent (φρονιμώτεροι), we proceed in the same
way with his other term ' advantage ', literally ' to have more '.
More of what? Food? Drink? Clothes? Callicles protests (491*a*) :

' I have been telling you for some time. First of all by those who
are stronger I do not mean shoemakers or cooks, but men who can
intelligently manage the state, who are not only intelligent but
brave also, able to carry through what they intend, and not to
fail through softness of heart (διὰ μαλακίαν τῆς ψυχῆς).'

He indignantly rejects the notion that self-control (to rule
oneself) is a good thing. Self-indulgence, on the contrary,
is his aim and ideal. To say, as some do, that happiness
consists of having no needs or desires is to praise the life of
a stone, not of a man. At that rate a corpse would be the
happiest of men. To which Socrates replies, quoting Euripides and the Orphic sages, that perhaps it is. Answering
imagery with imagery he then compares Callicles' ideal to
a man trying to fill a sieve, a torture of hell, or a jar with
large holes, the filling of which is painful and interminable,
whereas your self-controlled man has a jar that will hold
what is put into it. Which is the better?

All this is myth, not argument, and Callicles remains unmoved : sieve, jar, torrent, anything you like, but the life

of pleasure is just that : to be hungry and to eat, to be thirsty and to drink. Also no doubt, Socrates adds, to itch and to scratch, and be happy in the scratching ? Does this apply to scratching the head only ? Need we go further ? asks Socrates. But Callicles will not be shamed, though he is disgusted at Socrates' vulgarity (494*d*).

We may pause here a moment to note that only the fear of contradicting himself makes Callicles continue to maintain, with obstinate courage, that pleasure and the good are identical. Socrates is perfectly justified in pushing the argument to its logical conclusion even at the cost of shocking polite society ; and the other's disgust is very typical of his sophistic surroundings. Squeamishness is ever the enemy of mental integrity. Callicles is all but beaten already, the simplest appeal to experience drives him to insincerity. His position is then attacked logically (495*c* ff.).[1]

He agrees that good and bad are opposites that cannot apply to the same thing at the same time : health and disease for example cannot coexist, one follows the other, one disappears as the other appears. On this general statement Socrates bases his refutation of the assertion that pleasure and good, pain and evil, are identical. For on this assumption thirst is evil, the pleasure of quenching it good. But you do not feel pleasure in drinking unless you are thirsty, the pleasure ceases when the pain is no longer present. Therefore pleasure and pain, since in this and other cases they coexist and are conditioned by one another, cannot be true opposites like good and evil, and it follows that the identity of pleasure with good, pain with evil, is untenable.[2] Further,

---

[1] In a compressed passage, which has no immediate bearing on the argument, Callicles is made to maintain that while pleasure and good are identical, knowledge is different both from good and from a virtue —courage. The point seems to be to emphasize the difference between him and Socrates, who notoriously identified knowledge with virtue and good. Incidentally, Callicles seems to have forgotten that knowledge is essential to his ' strong man ' since he has defined him as knowledgeable, φρόνιμος.

[2] The close relation of pleasure with pain is often emphasized in Plato. As Socrates, whose bonds have just been loosened, says to his friends in *Phaedo*, 60*a* : ' What a strange thing, it appears, is that which men call pleasure. How strange its relation to what is considered its opposite, pain, in that they refuse to visit a man together, yet if he pursue one of them and capture it, he is almost always compelled to have the other also,

Callicles had called his strong men wise and brave (φρόνιμοι καὶ ἀνδρεῖοι), but he now admits that the ignorant feel as much pleasure as the wise, the coward as the brave. But if pleasure is the only good, man is good in so far as he feels pleasure. What does he mean then by calling the wise and brave better men?

Callicles is now compelled to shift his ground, and does so in characteristic fashion (499*b*):

' I've been listening to you and agreeing with you for quite a while, Socrates, and reflecting how gleefully you hold on to any point one may concede to you in jest, just as if you were a boy. Do you really suppose that I, or any other man, would deny that some pleasures are better and others worse?'

Socrates does indeed grasp at this important concession, that some pleasures are good, and others bad, and this he at once, with the other's consent, takes to mean that some are useful, others harmful.[1] The former clearly do us good, and we seek them for the sake of that good. So also we will submit to beneficial pain. This gives us another criterion by which to choose our pleasures, and pleasure is no longer our ultimate aim. We do what is pleasant for the sake of what is good, and not vice versa (500*a*). To know what pleasures are good is a subject of study in which special knowledge is called for. Thus we get back to the fundamental Socratic position that knowledge is the aim of life and philosophy is vindicated.

Socrates now has little difficulty in forcing Callicles to agree to the whole point of view which the latter could hardly believe to be seriously meant when he first entered the lists; the ideal of self-indulgence is shown to lead only to disorder, disease and unhappiness. We should aim, says Socrates with some emphasis, not at pleasure, but to attain what is good: order, knowledge and self-control (507*d*):

' This seems to me the aim that we must keep before us throughout life. To this all our actions, both public and private, should tend,

like the two sides of an angle.' Wilamowitz (I, 173) arbitrarily emphasizes the difference between these two passages.

[1] Cp. *Lysis*, 221*a*, where Socrates speaks of good and bad desires as being useful and harmful respectively.

to endow with justice and moderation those who are to be happy. This is how we must act, and not allow our passions to go unchecked in an attempt to satisfy them, for it is an aimless evil to live a pirate's life like that. Such a man would be a friend to no one, man or god. For he is incapable of co-operation, and where there is no co-operation there is no love. The wise men tell us, Callicles, that it is co-operation and love and order and moderation and righteousness that hold together heaven and earth and gods and men, and for that reason, my friend, they speak of order of the universe (κόσμος) not of its disorder and turpitude. . . .'

I have dealt with the *Gorgias* at some length because it puts the essentials of the problem before us with a dramatic vigour that is nowhere surpassed, as well as the general attitude of Socrates and Plato towards it. It does not, however, attain any very great height of argumentation or depth of understanding. Callicles takes up a position so absolute as to be impossible, and once he is driven from it his defeat is all but achieved. It should be noted that throughout this dialogue Plato's attitude to pleasure is hostile, almost puritanical. It is true that some pleasures are admitted to be good, or rather to lead to the good, which is our real aim, the pleasure being presumably incidental. But the emphasis is definitely on the bad pleasures, the existence of which Callicles is forced to admit. The pleasure-seeker is constantly opposed to him who seeks the good—Socrates—and the two points of view are presented as definitely incompatible. The mention of the aesthetic pleasures of colour, sound, &c., at 474*e* is the only hint that there are higher pleasures than the pleasures of the body upon which the whole discussion is focused. We are left with the impression that the pleasure instinct is regrettable to say the least, hardly indeed that it is a natural human instinct at all except for Callicles and his like, who can only claim consideration because of their numbers. But Socrates admits that the true art of speech (which is none other than philosophy) should investigate the nature of pleasure (501*a*).

The same is true, to a lesser extent, of the *Protagoras*, to which we must now turn, and it is one of the many common traits of those two great dialogues of Plato's youth. The *Protagoras* takes up the problem exactly where the *Gorgias* left it : We have seen so far that pleasure and good cannot be identical, for while some pleasures are good, others are admittedly harmful, and from this Socrates concluded that our aim should be the good, not pleasure. But this, we now see, does not necessarily follow. Socrates examines with Protagoras the position of the man in the street ('the many') that some pleasures are good, others bad. And just as Callicles was forced to take up this position, so Protagoras in the dialogue that bears his name may be said to agree to it by default.[1] In the course of a discussion on the unity of virtue or excellence, and especially as to whether courage can be reduced to knowledge, Socrates introduces the problem of pleasure as follows (351*b*) :

'You agree, said I, Protagoras, that some men live well, others badly?'

He agreed.

'Do you consider that a man lives well, if he lives in pain and suffering?'

He said not.

'What if a man has lived pleasurably up to the time of his death? Would you not say in that case that he lived well?

—I would, he replied.

—Then to live pleasurably is good, the contrary bad?

—If, he said, one takes pleasure in the right things.

—What is this, Protagoras? Do not tell me that you, like the majority of men, call certain pleasures bad and certain pains good. For what I mean is, are things not good in so far as they are pleasurable, *unless indeed some other consequences follow from them*, and is not pain bad in the same way, in so far as it is painful?'

But Protagoras will not agree to this without qualification, and they proceed to examine the whole question. They agree in the first instance that men are ruled by knowledge and reason, not by impulse.[2] That being so, it is necessary to explain how men can be said to be overcome by passion, pleasure, love, &c., against their better judgement, and

---

[1] For proof of this see my article on 'The Structural Unity of the Protagoras' in *Classical Quarterly*, July–October 1933.

[2] Since they both agree to this, it is not necessary to argue the point here. It is a cardinal point of Socratic ethics which is discussed on pp. 216 ff.

Socrates continues his imaginary argument with the man in the street (353c) :

'And then again, I said, if they should ask us : " What then do you say is that which we call being overcome by pleasure ? " I would answer them as follows : " Listen, Protagoras and I will try to tell you : Do you say, gentlemen, that this happens in the following cases : often men are overcome by the pleasures of food, drink and sex and perform actions which they know to be evil ? "—They would agree—Then you and I would ask them further : " Why do you call those things evil ? Is it because each of them provides an immediate pleasure and is pleasurable, or because it leads to later diseases, and brings poverty, and many other things like that ? Supposing something does not lead to any such later consequences, would it still be evil because it in some way gives man intended enjoyment ? "—Must we not suppose, Protagoras, that they will answer that those things are evil, not because they give immediate pleasure, but on account of their consequences, diseases and what not ?

I think, said Protagoras, that the ordinary man would answer in that way.

" Then in causing disease they cause pain, and in causing poverty they cause pain ? " I think they would agree.

Protagoras thought so too.

" These things then, gentlemen, according to Protagoras and myself, seem bad to you for no other reason than because they end in pain and deprive you of other pleasures." Would they not agree ? We both thought they would.'

In the same way, ' the many ' are shown that if they say that certain pains are good, it is only because, like physical drill and surgical operations or military service, they lead either to further pleasures or to the avoidance of greater pain (354c) :

' This then you think to be bad, namely pain, and pleasure to be good, since you call pleasure itself bad at such times as it deprives you of greater pleasures, or leads to pains greater than the pleasure it contains. For if it was with reference to some other end that you called pleasure bad, and for some other reason, you would be able to tell us of it. But that you are unable to do.'

And the same is true, *mutatis mutandis*, of pain. It is clear now that the qualified hedonism of the masses and (by implication at least) of Protagoras can be reduced to hedonism pure, since the only criterion by which they judge the good is pleasure or pain, and no other. Socrates then goes on to prove that when people are overcome by passion or pleasure they are guilty of a miscalculation in comparing the pleasure immediately before them with the pleasure or pain that will follow later, in weighing pleasure against pleasure, pain against pain, and each against the other. Their contention that they do evil though they know what is good becomes absurd if for good and evil we substitute the, to them, equivalent terms pleasure and pain, for then we must suppose that they choose pain instead of pleasure. Immediate pleasure is more attractive only because it *seems* to be greater at the moment, and that can be rectified by more accurate measurement. Hence what we need is a more accurate science of measurement (τεχνὴ μετρητική). Once more we come to the conclusion that knowledge is our aim, even admitting the hedonism of the ordinary man.

With this we are not at the moment concerned, but we note that Callicles need not have let himself be driven so easily from his fundamental position that pleasure and good are identical, even if he had to admit, as every one must, that not all pleasures are desirable. For that need not imply any extraneous good with reference to which pleasure must be judged. The distasteful pleasures which Socrates so rudely brought into the discussion could have been admitted to be vicious because they lead to pain and for no other reason. If, then, in the *Gorgias*, Plato proved that hedonism in its crudest form is untenable, in the *Protagoras* he makes it clear that it is not enough to admit, as Protagoras did, that some pleasures are bad unless you are prepared to provide, which Protagoras was not, another criterion than pleasure by which to judge them. Failing that it is meaningless, with Gorgias and Protagoras, to dissociate oneself from hedonism as a philosophy.

Nor need we be shocked by Socrates' attitude in this dialogue. He does not in fact identify himself with the hedonistic calculus which is primarily an *argumentum ad Protagoram*, though he argues the point with great vigour and freshness, and with the zest of an explorer. Even if he never argued this side of the question in his lifetime (which can never be proved) there would be nothing shocking to a Greek in seeing the apostle of the useful in this rôle. The Greeks had been spared both a puritan revolution and a Victorian revival of Puritanism, and there was nothing shameful to them in lusty enjoyment. Nor, for all his austerity, was there to Plato, though in his earlier works, such as the *Gorgias* and even more the *Phaedo*, he expresses himself about the life of pleasure with a severity worthy of an ascetic. Fortunately his Greek common sense and realism were never far distant, and preserved him from puritanical excess.

Plato's early works are full of hints that will be developed later, and it is interesting to note the distinction made by Prodicus in the *Protagoras* between enjoyment and pleasure. It is rejected by Socrates later in the argument, and is indeed largely verbal : Enjoyment Prodicus defines as occurring ' when one is learning something, and taking a share of wisdom with the mind ' and pleasure is what one feels ' when eating, drinking or having some other pleasant experience with the body '.[1] With the exception of this hint, there is not, any more than in the *Gorgias*, any mention of the higher pleasures. It is eating, drinking and sex, the stock phrase for physical pleasures, that are first and foremost the subject of discussion in the passages on hedonism.

It is clear now that we must find some criterion by which to judge pleasure, if we are to avoid hedonism. Socrates had already said in the *Gorgias* that this was ' the good '. But unless that refers to the absolute Form of Good which we find in the *Republic*, and the theory of Ideas is at least not explicitly referred to in the work of this period, it is not very helpful, and in clear need of investigation. To put the same difficulty in another way, our problem is to find what it is that the good or useful pleasures have in common, what constitutes this quality of goodness which other pleasures do not possess ?

The problem is very clearly stated in the *Hippias Major*,[2] where a definition of beauty is sought. The attempt to define beauty is to Plato also an attempt to define goodness, and is thus in itself a search for the criterion we need, but there is one

---

[1] 337c. Note the sophist's *petitio principii* in including the word pleasant in the definition of pleasure.

[2] For Platonic authorship see note 1 on page 8.

passage which concerns us even more directly. After several
definitions have been found wanting, the beautiful is defined
as that which is pleasurable to eye and ear. This includes
pictures, sculpture, music, stories, and even laws and institutions.

The question then arises : what is the difference between the
beautiful and other pleasures ? What is their common characteristic which justifies us in putting them in a class apart ?
They cannot differ in being pleasures, for that at least they
share with all the others. Variations of intensity are here
irrelevant (299*d*), except that the most intense pleasures seem
to be the most ugly. Nor is pleasure of sight beautiful because
it is of sight, or of hearing because it is of hearing, for we are
seeking a characteristic of both classes, together or apart.
Nor is it the fact that they are pleasures of eye *and* ear, since
one class can be beautiful apart from the other. Finally, the
last and most vital suggestion is that the pleasures of eye and
ear are beautiful because they are the ' most harmless ' of
pleasures. This is then equated with ' most useful ' and the
definition of the beautiful as the useful had already been
rejected because the useful is ' that which causes good ', thus
establishing a difference between good and its cause, beautiful,
which is not acceptable (297*c*). The *Hippias Major* does not
indeed give us any criterion by which to judge pleasure, but
it puts the difficulty very clearly, and the last suggestion, though
rejected here, will reappear later : the ' harmless ' pleasures
we shall meet again as the ' pure ' pleasures of the *Republic* and
the *Philebus*. We are still concerned only with the pleasures of
sense, but some doubt is definitely expressed whether
certain things may not give pleasures which cannot be so
classified (298*d*).

This distinction between pleasures of the body and others
is carried further in the *Phaedo*. As is well known, there is a
very definite separation in this dialogue between body and soul,
and it is the philosopher's business to live as far as possible
removed from bodily passions and desires. But the pleasures
which he must avoid are qualified by some such phrase as the
' so-called ' pleasures (64*d*). In fact to him they are not really
pleasurable at all (ᾧ μηδὲν ἡδὺ τῶν τοιούτων 65a). The *implication* is that there are other pleasures for him to enjoy, but

these are referred to only once.[1] The word pleasure is still firmly attached to the body, and still primarily refers to eating, drinking, sex, and the like (64*d*). There is also a passage which is of special interest as repeating the hedonistic calculus of the *Protagoras*. Ordinary men are brave through fear of worse happening—their virtue is a fake (68*e*) :

'Because they are afraid that they may be deprived of other pleasures which they desire, they avoid certain pleasures because they are overcome by others. And yet to be ruled by pleasure they call depravity. But it is only because they are overcome by some that they overcome others. This is what we were saying just now : their self-control is due only to their depravity.

—So it appears.

—My dear Simmias, this is not the right way to goodness (ἀρετή) —to exchange pleasure for pleasure, pain for pain, fear for fear, the bigger for the smaller like coins—wisdom alone is the proper medium for which all should be exchanged. For with this, and with this alone, is courage real courage, and self-control and in a word true virtue, with wisdom, with or without pleasure and fear and all other such things.'

And he goes on to explain how a proper standard of conduct can be based only on knowledge. There are two ways of life then : the wrong way, that of the average man based on a careful weighing of pleasure values, and the right way, that of the philosopher, based on knowledge. And, in the *Phaedo*, good means the transcendental Form of Goodness. This is an object of knowledge, and it is in this knowledge that the philosopher will find the only reliable criterion in the choice of his pleasures. To physical pleasure he will attach little importance, but of any other pleasures we have heard practically nothing. We are left to conclude that the pleasure instinct plays little or no part in the life of the thinker, and this is quite in harmony with the complete divorce we find in this dialogue between the noetic and the physical world, reflected in an all but complete separation of the knowing mind from the rest of man's personality.

The *Symposium* leaves us with a very different impression.[2]

---

[1] 114*e* : τὰς δὲ περὶ τὸ μανθάνειν (ἡδονάς). There is also reward and punishment after death and presumably the reward is pleasurable.

[2] See pp. 129 ff.

There the satisfaction of the passionate desire for beauty leads to the greatest happiness and the greatest pleasure. This vindication of the emotions implies the abandonment of the pure intellectualism of the *Phaedo*, which it all but denies.

It is here that the *Republic* makes its great contribution to our problem, by a theoretical reconciliation of the two points of view. There is, however, little about pleasure in the earlier books.

In the introductory scene we find, it is true, a charming discussion of pleasure and old age, but it adds nothing to what we have seen hitherto. The pleasures discussed are still those of the senses, eating, drinking and sex, the privation of which old men deplore. But they are wrong, says Kephalus, in blaming age, they should blame their own incontinence which makes them wretched in age as it does in youth. The proper attitude is shown in the anecdote about Sophocles who, when asked whether he could still enjoy the pleasure of sex, replied : ' Hush, man, I am delighted to have escaped from that, like a slave who has run away from a wild and crazy master ' (329c). The rest of the first book is a discussion with the sophist Thrasymachus who takes up the same position as Callicles in the *Gorgias* ; to him also right is the advantage of the stronger. The attitude of Socrates is the same as before, and the general argument is on the same lines, though Thrasymachus is by far the more subtle and capable opponent. Throughout, the emphasis is on justice or right (δικαιοσύνη) rather than on pleasure, which is hardly mentioned specifically ; nothing new is contributed to the problem of pleasure.

This does not, in fact, enter the discussion in its own right until the fifth book, and then only for a moment. It is taken up in earnest only in the ninth. No doubt it is present by implication throughout, since the question put at the beginning of the second book, and answered in the ninth, is whether the just or the unjust man is the happier ; which life, that is, contains more pleasure. Whenever Plato treats of passion, the pleasure which comes from the satisfaction of it is obviously a factor in the discussion. Also, the scheme by which family life is eliminated in the fifth book is in a sense a scheme to subdue the violence of the sexual instincts to the needs of the state, and to create such a community of interests as will lead

to ' common joys and common sorrows '.[1] The desire to
obtain the pleasures of love more freely is recognized where
the rewards of the brave are homerically described, not without a touch of broad humour, as more kisses, wives, wines and
roasts as well as honour,[2] whereas the pleasures of love are not
specifically mentioned when the arrangements for marriage
and procreation are made.[3] An important addition is made
where, in the description of the philosopher, it is definitely
stated that he finds pleasure in the pursuit of truth, his love
for which is claimed to be as fundamental a passion as any
other.[4] The hint of the *Hippias Major* is followed out, and the
pleasures of the soul are definitely separated from those of the
body. Recognizing the philosopher's life as pleasurable in
the full sense, Plato can now admit without qualms that we
can only desire in any real sense that which gives us pleasure,
though he still frequently uses the word of the physical pleasures
alone.[5]

We are told in the fifth book that our guardians will need
knowledge of the good. But what is the good ? Some say
it is pleasure, others that it is wisdom. Both theories have their
difficulty : the believers in wisdom, when pressed, can only
define it as wisdom about the good, an obvious inclusion of the
term to be defined in the definition, while every hedonist must
admit that some pleasures are bad, an obvious contradiction.
Appealed to for his own opinion Socrates is persuaded to
describe, not indeed the good, but the offspring of the good,
and gives the famous simile of the sun, which is to the world of
sight what ' the Form of the good ' is to the world of knowledge.[6] What follows, the clearest exposition in Plato of the
theory of Ideas, is from our present point of view an elabo-

---

[1] See p. 270.   [2] 468c, d.

[3] For in 460b, the ' greater opportunities of lying with women ' are also
only considered as the reward of the brave. It should be noted however
that those who have passed the official age for child-bearing are to be
free in their sexual relations. This, evidently, is no longer the concern
of the state (461b).

[4] ἡδονὴ ψυχῆς in 485d. The love of truth as a real passion see 474d ff.,
and 485d.

[5] In the same way he goes on using the word 'passionate', ἐπιθυμητικόν,
of the lowest part of the soul, even after he has made it explicitly clear in
Book IX that every part has passions of its own. See pp. 136 ff.

[6] For explanation of this simile and that of the Line see pp. 23 ff.

ration of the answer given in the *Phaedo* to the problem of the *Protagoras*, a solution foreshadowed in the *Hippias Major*. The 'Form of the good' is the criterion by which pleasure can be judged. It is clear that in the simile of the Line the pleasures will be good in so far as they approach the highest point B, the Good, and that they will be so to the same extent as the objective reality and the functions of the soul which correspond to each section. Throughout the sixth, seventh and eighth books the interest is mainly metaphysical and political, though we should not forget that the whole discussion started from an attempt to determine the rival claims of pleasure and goodness.

When we come to the ninth book, however, the ideal city has been built, the philosopher and the ideal Forms have been described, as well as the different types of government and of individuals corresponding to them. We can now return to the question debated in the first book : who is the happier, the good man or the bad ? Here is the natural place for a further discussion of pleasure, and so we find it in the second and third proofs that the tyrannical man is the most unhappy. The first proof was an appeal to experience, a description of the tyrant's court as full of foes and flatterers, which convinces Glaucon that such a man cannot be happy (578–80).

The discussion of pleasure begins by an explicit and emphatic statement that each part of the soul has its specific pleasures and passions (580*d*) :

'As there are three parts of the soul, so it seems to me there are also three kinds of pleasure, a particular one for each, and so also with passions and ways of ruling the soul.' [1]

There are three kinds of life, that of the lover of wisdom which is actuated by a passion for truth, that of the ambitious which is actuated by a passion for honour and victory and the 'passionate' properly so called, whose main object is the gratification of physical desires, and the accumulation of wealth required for that purpose. Which gives the most pleasure ? (581*c*) :

'You know that if you were to ask each of those three men in turn which of the three lives is the most pleasurable, each would

---

[1] The psychological importance of this passage and of 586*d* which repeats the statement is discussed on pp. 135 ff.

praise his own life most. The money-maker would say that, compared with personal gain the pleasures of being honoured or of learning are worth nothing, unless something about them brings money.'

And the same is then true of the other two (581e) :

' When the pleasures of each kind and the life itself are in dispute, not as to which is the more beautiful or ugly, nor the better or the worse to live, but as to which is actually the more pleasant and less painful, how are we to know which of them is speaking the truth ? '

Socrates decides that three things are essential to a correct judgement : experience, knowledge, and the power of expressing it. Which of our three men can claim superiority over the others in these ? To take experience first : the money-maker knows nothing of the joy that comes from the discovery of truth, whereas the philosopher must needs have experienced from childhood the advantages of money and the physical pleasures ; honour comes with success to all three kinds of men, so that the philosopher also knows the pleasure it gives ; while with the pleasures of research he alone is acquainted. In experience therefore he stands first. As for wisdom and knowledge, or intellect, the very instrument with which judgements are made, it is his own special tool, and language is the instrument of knowledge.

Clearly then the philosopher alone has the experience, the wisdom and the power of expression required to make any true comparison ; his opinion therefore will be the true one. It follows that the pleasures of the mind are the greatest, those of honour inferior, and the physical pleasures come last of all. Plato does not say that physical pleasure is a delusion, or that honour is an empty thing. He merely gives it as his considered opinion that they pale into insignificance by the side of the pleasure one gets from the search for truth. We should remember that honour too was his in full measure, and that of those who have had experience of the three kinds of delights, he is by no means the only one to hold this opinion. That his contention was true for himself it is impossible to doubt.

It has now been established that the pleasures of the mind are the greatest, judged *qua* pleasures, both by an appeal to the outsider (Glaucon admitted from a description of the tyrant's court that he could not be happy) and by an appeal to the subject himself. Socrates now tackles the problem set in the *Gorgias* as to the nature of pleasure itself. And this he can now do because the theory of Forms expounded in the previous books has given us what was lacking before, an objective criterion by which to differentiate between good pleasures and bad ; and he proceeds to assert that the pleasures of the philosopher are the most *real*, that the other pleasures are not 'altogether true' (παναληθεῖς) and that they are not 'pure'.

There is such a thing as pleasure, and there is its opposite pain, but there is also a mental state which is neither one nor the other : 'Between the two is a state of rest of the soul ' (583c). It is pleasant after acute pain, as is a return to normal health after sickness ; so the cessation of an acute pleasure seems painful, but it is not really so. Pleasure and pain are both active states, κινήσεις, i.e. movements. And indeed there are pleasures that do not require previous pain, e.g. the pleasures of smell. We must imagine a higher and a lower region, and a point between them. Those who reach this point from below call it high, those who reach it from above call it low, like a man who compares grey with black and calls it white, because he has never seen the real colour. But it is not really white. And so it is with pleasure and pain. A modern image will probably help to make Plato's point clear.[1] As the mercury rises in a thermometer we feel warmer. Those who live in a very cold climate will speak of heat at a point which still feels cold to those who live in a torrid zone. The former do not know ' real heat ', the latter ignore ' real cold '. They mistake the mere cessation of their customary state for its opposite. It may well be objected that the words heat and cold are relative. That is so, and Plato's conception of a purely negative middle state is a doubtful one. Be as relative as you please, however, there is still a degree of 'real heat ' which is unknown to the Eskimo. So Plato maintains that there is a kind of real pleasure which is only known to the philosopher. It is also worth noting that by refusing the name of pleasure to the absence of pain, and vice versa, Plato asserts both

[1] Cp. the kindred concept of an absolute mean in the *Politicus*, where I have also used temperature as an illustration, p. 43.

pleasure and pain to be active states, and thus refuses to confuse happiness with the mere imperturbability, the absence of all desire, the negative, dead state which was to be the ideal of the Epicurean. But then no Epicurean could ever have written the *Symposium*.

The superior ' trueness ' of the pleasures of the mind is then supported by a more metaphysical argument. All physical pleasure is ' the filling of a void '—a notion that reminds us of the sieve and jars of the *Gorgias*—and so in a sense are the pleasures of the mind. But a void is more truly filled when it is filled with something that is more true, and when the receptacle is also itself more true and permanent. As the mind is filled with the Forms of true Reality, and is itself akin to them, it is more truly filled, and the pleasure it feels in the filling is also more true (585c). This argument, depending as it does on a metaphor, will not appear very convincing. A careful reading of the passage, however, shows that it is the stability and permanence [1] of the objects of knowledge, and hence the stability and permanence of the pleasures to which they give rise that Plato is emphasizing in perhaps too picturesque a manner. To this he will return, and also to the question of ' purity ' which he does not elaborate here, though the mention of pleasures not preceded by pain gives us the clue to his meaning (584b). It must be admitted, however, that his use of the word ' true ' or ' real ' (ἀληθής) and, without sufficient explanation, ' pure ', is very confusing. There follows one of those vivid paragraphs that abound in the *Republic* (586a) :

' Those who have no experience of wisdom and virtue, being ever occupied with feasting and the like, are carried down (i.e. to pain, conceived of as below the middle or neutral state) and then again to the middle state, and thus they wander throughout life, but they never reach beyond this to what is really above. They neither look up to it nor are carried thither, they are never truly filled with what truly exists, they never taste certain and true pleasure, but ever look down, with their heads bent like cattle to the earth and at the banquet tables they feed, fatten and fornicate. For the sake of an abundance of such things they kick and butt and kill each other with horns and hoofs of steel, because they are insatiable, because they

---

[1] e.g. 585c τὸ τοῦ ἀεὶ ὁμοίου ἐχόμενον καὶ ἀθανάτου etc., that which depends on the immortal and ever-same. . . .

have never fed upon reality that part of themselves which, existing truly, would give them satisfaction.'

He then makes an important concession (586*d*) :

'As for the desires of the greedy and the ambitious parts of the soul, if they obey the commands of reason and with its help seek and grasp such pleasures as wisdom dictates, they too will attain pleasures that are as near truth as is possible for them.'

So that in the philosopher's soul every part finds its own pleasure and its own satisfaction in perfect harmony. If not reason but another part of the soul is in command, it cannot even find what is best for itself. There follows a process of fanciful multiplication by which the tyrannical man is proved to be 729 times more unhappy than the philosopher king. The details of this are not meant to be taken over-seriously, it is the distance between the two that is mythically represented as immense.[1]

Clearly the *Republic* marks a considerable advance in Plato's theory of pleasure. Hedonism in its crudest form is here, as in the *Gorgias*, shown to be untenable. But the metaphysical theories of the central books have provided us with an extraneous and objective criterion by which to judge pleasure, namely the Forms, and above all the Form of good. We also derive some help from the tripartite division of the soul into passions, feelings, and intellect, and the intellectual pleasures are recognized as the most real and the most pure in the sense that they are free from pain. Those of the lower parts, on the other hand —and these include the physical pleasures upon which the attention was focused in the earlier dialogues—bound up as they are with the previous pain of physical need, are but a mixture of pleasure and pain and indeed little more than the middle state of rest or mere cessation from pain. But this,

---

[1] The mathematical leger-de-main is much simpler than is often thought. We have the following descending scale of merit : (1) the philosopher king, (2) the timocrat, (3) the oligarch, (4) the democrat, (5) the tyrant. Counting both ends of a series as the Greeks did, the oligarch is *third* from the king, and is three times more unhappy. The tyrant is *third* from the oligarch, he is 3 × 3, i.e. 9 times removed from the king in the matter of pleasure. But to represent life we need a number in three dimensions (cp. the Platonic number, p. 29), and so we cube the number 9 and we get 729 which represents (mythically and semi-humorously) the difference between the ways of life of the two extremes.

as it is a mere negative state, is not truly pleasure.[1] Then, almost as an afterthought, Plato admits that these lower pleasures have a function to fulfil and are capable of giving enjoyment when under the guidance of reason.

It is in the *Philebus* that we find by far the longest and most profound discussion of pleasure. At the beginning of the dialogue Philebus is just retiring from an argument that has been going on for some time, and the position is restated for the benefit of Protarchus, who takes up the discussion in his place (11*b*) :

' Philebus says that pleasure, joy and delight, and everything that goes with them, are good for all living creatures. Our contention is that it is not those things that are good, but knowledge, understanding, memory and what is akin to them, right belief and true reasoning. That whatever partakes of these is better than, and superior to, pleasure, for all who can share in it.'

Once more then we start from the extreme position which was shown to be untenable on either side. And as the central metaphysical books of the *Republic* emerged from an attempt to settle the question propounded here, it is not surprising that in the *Philebus* also there are some important contributions to the science of Being.

The first difficulty which arises is the manifoldness of pleasure (12*c*) :

' To hear the word used thus simply, pleasure is one thing, yet it takes on various forms that are somehow unlike one another. For consider : we say that the dissolute man feels pleasure, and pleasure also the moderate man feels in his very moderation. So also the ignorant man who is full of ignorant opinions and expectations, and the wise man in his wisdom. How then can one say, without deservedly appearing foolish, that all these pleasures are similar to one another ? '

The force of this is that to call all pleasures good is to attribute to all the so different forms of pleasure another fundamental quality in common besides the one—pleasurableness—which they all obviously share, and thus to postulate a greater similarity between them than seems borne out by experience. On the contrary, they may well be to a high degree opposites,

[1] Cp. *Phaedrus*, 258*e*.

for true opposites are found within the same genus, as is the
case with shapes and colours (12*e*). We need not, however,
be unduly dismayed by the multiplicity of pleasures, for the
same can be said of the other claimant, as there are different
forms of knowledge. This leads to a re-examination of the
proper method of division and classification (διαίρεσις), the
old problem of the one and the many.[1]

It is suggested that neither pleasure alone nor wisdom alone
can be identified with the supreme good which is something
beyond either of them, something which is complete and perfect
(τέλεον), adequate (ἱκανόν), and the final aim of all desire (20*d*).
This pleasure alone cannot be, for without mind, memory, or
opinion we could not even be conscious of any feeling, whether
pleasant or the reverse. Such may be the life of a mollusc,
it is certainly not that of a human being. As for mind, let
us see (21*d*) :

' whether any one of us would consent to live possessing wisdom,
understanding, knowledge and memory of all things, but without
any share of pleasure great or small, nor of pain, altogether without
experience of anything of the kind.'

To which Protarchus makes the only possible answer :

' I would not choose either life, nor I think would anyone else.'

Both claimants then have to renounce the first place. We
have already seen in the *Republic* that both extreme views lead
to contradictions, but here the life of pure intellect is more
definitely rejected as inhuman, undesirable and impossible.
The conclusion may seem obvious, but it was worth while
reminding fanatics—and in his earlier works Plato comes
dangerously near fanaticism at times [2]—that we would not,
and could not if we would, give up the world of feeling and
emotion for a pure intellectualism that does not exist, for us
human beings at least.

[1] See p. 44.

[2] Cp. Ritter, II, 446 : ' Der *Philebus* ist in seinem Urteil über die not-
wendige Lustgefühle entschieden weniger schroff als die *Politeia* ' and the
whole discussion ad. loc.
But although Plato sometimes speaks as a fanatic of the intellect, in his
calmer moments he always advised a well-balanced development of all
the ' parts of man ' ; e.g. *Rep.*, 410, where an excessive studiousness leading
to the neglect of physical culture is admitted to make a man ' soft '.

The good life then must contain an admixture of both knowledge and feeling, of intellect and of pleasure. It remains for us to see which of the two is more akin to the supreme good that is beyond them both, and thus deserves the second place. To do this we must know something of the supreme reality to which they approximate, and so we find here a metaphysical discussion : Reality consists of the Unlimited or Indeterminate upon which Limit or Measure is impressed, thus creating the mixture of both which is the thing itself, and to these three should be added the cause of the mixture, the agent.[1] When further he classes pleasure, abstractly considered, with the Indeterminate as capable of infinite extension, and intellect with the genus of Cause as the ' king of heaven and earth ' (28c), the superiority of the latter is once more established for all those who accept his metaphysical assumptions (31a) :

' Let us remember this about them both : Mind is akin to Cause and to that class, while pleasure is itself unlimited, and akin to that class of things which in itself has neither beginning, middle nor end, and is never likely to have.'

But actual pleasure, like every other phenomenon, is to be found in the third or mixed class of reality, for we cannot examine it apart from pain. Its origin is as follows (31d) :

' I maintain that when harmony is destroyed in living things, their natural state is dissolved and at the same time pain arises.
—Quite probably.
—When on the other hand harmony is restored and the natural state returns, pleasure must be said to arise, to put the matter in a nutshell.' [2]

Pressed to explain this somewhat cryptic statement, Socrates illustrates it by the case of hunger and thirst (31e) :

' Thirst is destruction, pain and dissolution, whereas the power to fill that part of the humid which has dried up is pleasurable. And again any unnatural separation or dissolving, for example in a

---

[1] For a discussion of the metaphysical formula see pp. 45 ff.
[2] This is clearly reminiscent of the fifth-century medical theories of health as balance or harmony between opposites, a theory usually associated with the name of Alkmaeon. The physiological side is worked out in detail in *Timaeus*, 64a ff.

drought, is pain, while cooling and return to the normal is pleasure
. . . see whether you agree with my argument that whenever a
living species, which has come to be from Limit and the Unlimited
in the manner I have described, is destroyed or corrupted, pain
arises, whereas the return to its own nature is in each case pleasurable.'

We have now studied the nature and origin of pleasure—the
problem set in the *Gorgias*—and we find that it accompanies a
return to normal and healthy functioning in the organism.
Essentially then it is no longer an enemy to be conquered or
denied, but an enjoyable companion of the good life, even
though up to this point in the *Philebus* as in the early dialogues
we have considered only physical pleasures. The problem still
remains as to how the pleasures of the wicked are going to fit
into this picture, and with this Plato will deal later. He must
now return to the analysis and classification of pleasure into
its various kinds.

This, the central part of the dialogue, is somewhat confusing because the problem is approached from four different
angles, and there are four different classifications, loosely
strung together and by no means mutually exclusive. It is
only later that the contribution which each division of pleasure
has to make becomes clear.

The first classification is a simple one into pleasures of the
body and pleasures of the soul, but with a difference. The
physical pleasures are indeed the same as of old, but Socrates
is now at pains to establish that even this type of pleasure
affects the mind or soul as well as the body. He clearly
distinguishes them from such minor physical disturbances as
remain unperceived, i.e. do not reach consciousness at all.
In other words, there is no such thing as purely physical
pleasure,[1] since all consciousness implies the soul. The so-
called physical pleasures affect the body primarily and through
it reach the soul or, as we would put it, the mind.

As against these there are the pleasures of memory and
anticipation, originating in memory and desire, both of which

---

[1] 35*e* : 'This argument denies that there is such a thing as physical
passion' ἐπιθυμία σώματος. Already in the *Republic* he spoke of : 'the
pleasures that reach the soul *through* the body ', διὰ σώματος. See La Fontaine, p. 38, with references. Cp. also *Theaet.*, 186*c*.

belong entirely to the soul, by which is meant that they are not caused directly by any sense perception. It should be noted that we are still only at one remove from food, drink, sex and the like, for this second class is merely due to anticipation of the first. Plato wants to establish that there are pleasures which do not come by way of the senses; and if he can establish this without departing too far from the ordinary pleasures and without introducing new kinds of delights not discussed hitherto, his argument is far more likely to gain acceptance. To advance thus step by step is a dialectically excellent way of preparing his readers for those other delights not of the body which will be introduced later.

Another point emphasized at this stage is the mixture of pleasure and pain which occurs when one is hungry but anticipating a feast, thus drawing attention once more to the fact that both can occur together, a fact, we well remember, which caused the downfall of Callicles. Use is also made of the existence of bodily disturbances so slight as to remain unperceived to prove that there is a neutral state which is neither one nor the other. The importance of this was seen in the *Republic* and will be taken up again later.

The pleasures of anticipation are then divided into *true and false*, but this classification, though formally only a further subdivision, is so important that we must consider it as a second aspect from which pleasure as a whole is analysed. We are familiar with it from the *Republic*, but it is here established in a different way. In attempting to label certain pleasures as false, the easiest point at which to start is clearly those based upon hopes of the future. Socrates tries to establish that, just as there are true and false hopes and expectations, so there are true and false pleasures based upon them. Now to speak of feelings as false or untrue seems at first sight an obvious fallacy, and Protarchus would dismiss it as such (36c–e). But if Plato refuses to dismiss it and treats the matter at considerable length, it is because he is emphasizing a distinction that, whatever the names we use, is very real. The feeling of pleasure, as a feeling, is of course real enough, even if it is based on false hopes, but then the false hope or wrong opinion is itself also a fact. That, however, does not prevent its being false;

' whether the pleasure be true or false, does not destroy the fact that pleasure is felt ' (37*b*).[1]

On the other hand there is a very obvious difference between a hope or expectation which corresponds to fact and one which does not :

' The images of true beliefs and sayings are true, those of false beliefs are false' (39*c*).

So we may rejoice in anticipation of things that will come to pass, and also of things that will not (40*a*) :

' Every man, as we said just now, is full of hopes.
—Quite so.
—And each one of us holds certain converse with himself, and this we call hope.
—Yes.
—And thus we have images depicted within ourselves. A man frequently sees himself as the possessor of a large fortune, and derives much pleasure from the sight. And he sees himself depicted within himself as greatly rejoicing.'

The mental pictures of good men correspond to fact, those of bad men do not.

' There are thus, according to our argument, lying pleasures in the souls of men, ridiculous imitations of the truth, and so also with pain,'

and we are forced to admit

' that it is possible for a man to feel pleasure in fact, though he do so at everything at random, at a present that does not exist, sometimes at a non-existent past, and often, perhaps mostly, at a future that will not come to pass ' (40*d*).

The conclusion is that just as hopes and opinions are bad when they are false, so there are false pleasures, and they are bad for the same reason. At any rate such enjoyment as is based on false hopes cannot be called correct or true. Socrates may well be accused of straining the meaning of the word ψευδής, lying or untrue, or, at the least, of using it in a very unusual context. Nor is the analogy with opinion altogether

---

[1] To indicate ' true ' pleasure Plato here uses two words : ἀληθής, true or real, and ὀρθός, right or correct. The latter is certainly a more appropriate term. See Ritter II, 443.

correct. We do not, as a rule, judge pleasure in relation to truth, though Plato's point is that we ought. However that may be, it should be noted that he defines his words very carefully, and that the distinction he is making is real. May we not call ' false ' pleasures those of the man who takes refuge from the troubles of life in the dubious joys of impossible day-dreams, the man who is ever thinking and talking of the great things he will do in the distant future, and ever neglecting the little things that he could, but will not, do to-day? [1] Plato no doubt goes farther, and in the last resort would brand as untrue most of what passes as the pleasures of life with the majority. He may be accused of going too far, but only a thoughtless reader will deny that there is much to be said against what he terms ' false ' pleasures, and not least the fact that they are out of touch with actuality. In this section also he takes up the ' measuring science ' described in the *Protagoras*, of which we must needs make use when faced with a mixture of pleasure and pain. He adds that we must beware of allowing the nearness of certain pleasurable images to throw our expectations out of focus, and to make us blind to the greater pains that may be hidden behind the little pleasures immediately in front of us.

The search for false pleasures leads Plato to classify pleasure as a whole from a third point of view, that of intensity. At the bottom of the scale, and indeed not to be included in our classification at all, are motions of the body too slight to be perceived (for is not our body in perpetual motion?).[2] As before, these are taken to prove the existence of a neutral state which certain thinkers identify with pleasure itself, a theory rejected here as vigorously as it was in the *Republic*. From the point of view of intensity, it is clear that the greatest pleasures ($\mu\acute{\epsilon}\gamma\iota\sigma\tau\alpha\iota$ $\dot{\eta}\delta o\nu\alpha\acute{\iota}$) are physical. The pleasures of sex, for example, obviously entail a greater shock to the system than

---

[1] The class described at *Rep.*, 458a, where Socrates humorously identifies himself with ' those lazy-minded people . . . who before they discover the means to make their desires come true, neglect this so that they may not get tired by deliberating on the possible and the impossible. They suppose that what they want is there, and proceed to arrange the rest ; they rejoice in making a list of what they will do when it has happened. Thus they make their otherwise lazy soul still lazier.'

[2] See also *Timaeus* 64b-c.

any intellectual pursuit, and it is for this very reason that they are usually reckoned to be the greatest. And here Plato pursues the subject further : if intensity is what we seek, we shall not find it in health or moderation. Drinking, he points out, is never so pleasant as when the body is tormented by fever, eating gives the greatest delight when we are all but starving. Yet surely such intensity cannot be our aim : mere violence of pleasurable sensation must be a poor guide, if it is found in disease and excess. These we all wish to avoid and rightly so, for intensity of pleasure is then accompanied by equally violent pain and suffering. That is what Socrates means when he says (45*d*) :

'Answer me, do you see greater pleasures—I do not mean the greater number, but those that are greater in violence and intensity —occur in a life of excess (ἐν ὕβρει) or in a life of moderation ? Think well before you speak.
—I see what you mean, and the difference I perceive is great. For moderate men are ever kept in check by the well-known proverb " nothing too much " which restrains them, whereas ignorant and profligate men are possessed by pleasure to the point of madness and wild shouts.
—Well said. And if that is true it is obvious that the greatest pleasures and the greatest pains are to be found in a bad state of mind and body, and not in excellence or virtue.'

All the pleasures discussed hitherto are mixed with pain, and this leads to a final analysis and classification of pleasures into mixed and pure, the word pure (καθαρός) in this connexion meaning, as before, free from pain. To take the mixed pleasures first : these may occur in the body, the soul, or in both body and soul.[1] The body may feel both hot and cold in a fever, and even where the two are not concurrent many physical pleasures lead to pain later on in the body itself. Or

---

[1] This seems at first sight to contradict the earlier statement that there is no such thing as purely physical pleasure, and that there is a verbal contradiction can scarcely be denied. But Plato is really taking his former classification for granted, and all mixed pleasures must be understood to affect the soul in some way, since we are conscious of them. Here however we are concerned with another difference : sometimes there are two opposite feelings *in the body*, such as hot and cold, &c., sometimes the pleasure is physical, the pain mental, or vice versa, and sometimes both pleasure and pain are mental. (46*b* ff.) See La Fontaine, p. 38.

the body may feel want where the soul feels the joys of anticipation. Thirdly, to the soul alone belong such mixed feelings as anger, fear, desire, sorrow, love, envy ; in a word, the emotions. To these are added the pleasures of comedy and tragedy in an interesting passage, the main point being that the enjoyment of tragedy is based on sorrow, and that the fun of comedy is bound up with envy and ignorance of self.[1]

The second main class, the pure pleasures, are those to which the whole discussion was meant to lead, and here we must quote at length (50e) :

' After the mixed pleasures we are naturally bound to proceed in turn to those that are pure.
—Well said.
—I will turn to them and try to describe them to you. For I do not at all agree with those who say that all pleasure is but cessation from pain, although, as I said, I take them as witnesses to prove that there are apparent pleasures that are not real, and many other intense ones that are only imagined. These are closely bound up with pain, and with relief from the greatest pains of the body and perplexities of the soul.
—But the true pleasures, Socrates, what is one to think of them ?
—They are caused by the colours that are called beautiful, by forms, by many perfumes, by sounds, by all things of which the lack is unperceived and painless, whereas their presence is perceived, delightful and free from pain.
—What do we mean by that, Socrates ?
—My meaning is not at once clear, I grant you, and I must try to make it plain. By beauty of form I am not trying to express what most people would suppose, namely living creatures and pictures made from them, but (so speaks the argument) I mean something that is the straight, and the round. From these are derived the many straight or round shapes that are made in two or three dimensions on the lathe, or by ruler and quadrant, if you follow me. They are, I say, not beautiful compared with something else, as other things are, but they are always beautiful by their own nature, and have their own peculiar pleasures which have nothing in common with the pleasures of scratching. And there are colours of this kind, also with similar pleasures. Do you understand ?
—I try to understand, Socrates, please try to speak still more plainly.
—I refer to the smooth and clear sound of such notes as express

[1] For a discussion of this passage see p. 195.

some pure and simple song, that are beautiful in themselves, and
to the pleasures that come from hearing them.

—Yes, such exist also.

—The pleasures of smell are of a kind less divine, but neither are
they bound up with unavoidable pain, and wherever we find this to
be true, we have a kind of pleasure that is opposed to the others.
For these, you understand, are two classes of pleasures.

—I understand.

—And to these let us add the pleasure of learning, if indeed you
agree that there is no hunger of learning, and that pain does not in
the first instance arise through a longing to learn.'

They agree that this is so, that ignorance is painful, not when
we have never known, but when we have forgotten. Such
then are the pure pleasures, the highest of which are to be
found in the contemplation of beauty and of truth. Every
step in the argument has prepared us for a better understanding
of them : they are pleasures of the soul only, or at least in so
far as they are pleasures of the senses, the bodily functions,
though necessary, are definitely secondary ; they are true
pleasures, and as they consist in the contemplation of truth
they cannot play us false ; they are, it is true, not as intense
as the more physical pleasures, but as they occur in health and
in a state of harmony, they will be the more lasting ; above
all they are not conditioned by previous pain, and so cannot
be confused with the mere relief from such pain. Clearly
then it is here that we will find the real nature of pleasure (53b) :

' We shall be right to say that a little pure white is both whiter
than much of it mixed with other colours, more beautiful, and more
true.

—Most certainly.

—What then ?   We shall not need many such illustrations for our
discussion of pleasure. It is enough that we should understand
from this that with every pleasure also, a little of it, if free from pain,
would be more pleasurable, more true and more beautiful than a
large and frequent amount mixed with pain.

—Definitely. Your illustration is sufficient.'

Once more Socrates proves that pleasure cannot claim to be
the good, for it is by nature ever changing and coming to be
while the good is a constant, unchangeable absolute. Having
thus terminated his analysis of pleasure, he proceeds to a

similar analysis of the different kinds of knowledge, in a passage which, though of great interest, does not directly concern us here.

We have seen that neither pleasure nor knowledge can claim to occupy the first place. A mixture of the two is the only good life for men, and in this mixture things will be accepted in so far as they show kinship with the supreme Good, which cannot be described more exactly than as one reality seen under three aspects, Measure, Truth and Beauty. This condition of acceptance is, in more explicit terms, the same criterion which we found in the *Republic*, by which pleasure (and indeed everything else) must be judged. Plato now finds that each of these, symmetry, truth, beauty, is more akin to knowledge than to pleasure, for do we not hide our greatest delights, our most intense pleasures, as something ugly to behold, and rather ridiculous ? [1]

In the final scale of goods will be found : first those things which show order and measure, second what is beautiful and symmetrical, third intellect and wisdom, as partaking of truth, in the fourth place come the particular sciences, crafts and right beliefs, as doing so to a lesser degree. In the fifth place we find pleasures, and then only those we have defined as pure because unmixed with pain. To these should be added (63e) the necessary pleasures, those without which we cannot live, the moderate satisfaction of our natural wants.

There is not much theoretical discussion of pleasure after the *Philebus*. A few passages from the *Laws* are, however, of the first importance as indicating not indeed any change of doctrine, but an even fuller reconciliation to pleasure and a fuller incorporation of it as a necessary and valuable ingredient of the good life.

Great stress is laid on the training of the pleasure instinct as an important factor in education [2] and in a later passage

---

[1] This point is also made in the *Hippias Major*, 299a. The explicit reference is to sexual pleasure. The argument is fallacious because it fails to distinguish between the pleasure of the spectator and that of the lover. Also, of course, a desire for privacy is not necessarily the result of a sense of shame. The feeling is sometimes traced nowadays to a fear of being defenceless and at the mercy of a possible enemy.

[2] See pp. 243 ff.

the hedonistic calculus of the *Protagoras* is so definitely repeated and explained that we understand why Epicurus might have made a unique exception in favour of ' the golden Plato ' in his general condemnation of previous philosophers [1](662*b*) :

' I would inflict almost the greatest punishment upon any one in the country who said that there ever are men who are wicked, yet live in enjoyment, or that there is any difference between what is advantageous and what is right.'

If it were not so, he insists in a passage that is highly reminiscent of the protests of Glaucon and Adeimantus in the second book of the *Republic*, neither parents nor lawgivers could ever ask or expect youth to follow the life of justice (663*b*) :

' For no one would willingly be persuaded to do anything in which there is not more pleasure than pain. Anything seen in the distance seems dim and uncertain to everybody almost, and especially to children. A lawgiver should correct this, replace darkness by light, and, somehow or other, by means of habits, eulogies and argument show how blurred is men's view of right and wrong, for to them unjust actions appear contrary to the view which the just man has of them : seen by an unjust man they appear pleasant and just actions most unpleasant, whereas by a just soul all this is seen to be quite the contrary in both directions.' [2]

This does not mean, as Plato carefully points out, that the life of justice does not require hard work (807*c*) but in the end, if we persist, the pure and lasting pleasures described in the *Philebus* will be our reward. And again, after a discussion of the several virtues and the lives corresponding to them, we find the following quite remarkable passage (732*e*) :

' We have discussed the ways of life one should follow, and the kind of man one should be, but we have restricted ourselves to what one may call divine, and have not spoken of what is but human. Yet we must do so, for we are speaking for men, not gods. It is pleasure, pain and passion that are by nature most human. From them every mortal creature depends and to them he is bound by

---

[1] See Diogenes Laertius, *Life of Epicurus*, § 8, though it may have been a derogatory reference.

[2] This, I believe, is the correct translation, understanding ὁρωμένῳ or some such word after τῷ τοῦ δικαίου, and ἑαυτοῦ after δικαίου in *c* 5. ' Seen from the point of view of an unjust and bad self—from the point of view of a just self. . . .'

most important ties.   So we must praise the finest life, not only
because it is most considered and brings a fine reputation, but also
because, if a man is willing to pursue it and does not desert it in
youth, it excels in the very best thing which we all seek, an excess of
pleasure over pain in the course of a whole life.   That this is certain
will readily and definitely appear if one pursue it in the right way.
But what is the right way ?   This too we must investigate in our
discussion, whether it is natural for us, or vain and unnatural we
must examine by a comparison of different lives, pleasurable and
painful, as follows.

We all want pleasure, pain we neither choose nor want.   What is
neither one nor the other we do not prefer to pleasure, but we want
relief from pain.   Little pain we choose if accompanied by greater
pleasure, greater pain with less pleasure we reject.   When the two
are equal we have no means of choosing between them.   In all these
our means of choosing is any difference there may be in amount,
number, intensity, or whether they are equal, in each case.

When faced with both to a great and violent degree, we will
choose the life wherein pleasure prevails, the contrary we reject.
Where pleasure and pain are equally balanced we must reason as
before :   we will choose whichever is more pleasant to a friend, not
to an enemy.   And so we must consider every kind of life in the
realization that we are naturally bound to pleasure and pain, and
reflect upon the kind of life that we naturally choose.

And if we maintain that we choose in a way different from this,
we speak in ignorance and inexperience of life as it is.'

The difference in tone between this passage and the *Gorgias*
needs no comment.   But for all that there is no essential
contradiction.   From first to last Plato has objected to the
shortsighted ethic that makes pleasure as such the aim of life.
Such a philosophy is of no value, for pleasure of a sort can be
had in every kind of life :   no one can honestly deny that even
vice may be pleasant.   The power of pleasure over the minds
of men is a problem which always interested Plato, as it must
interest any ethical thinker.   At first he is largely negative :
the position of an extreme hedonist like Callicles is untenable,
and though Socrates praises the good life, he does not work out
its relation to pleasure.   In the *Protagoras* he shows us that
many thoroughly honest people are unthinking if not professed
hedonists, and also that when we speak of being overcome by
passion and pleasure, we mean that we are blind to even the

pleasure-value of a particular act on the long view, that we are
ignorant in a very real sense ; and the remedy for ignorance is
knowledge. This calculation of pleasure-values has been
repeatedly said to be unplatonic. Wrongly. It does not
contradict his philosophy, but is merely a part of it. Just as
he accepts the perpetual motion of Heraclitus and the relativism
of Protagoras as far as the physical world is concerned, so he
came to accept hedonism as a natural way of life for the average
man, whom he knew very well to be incapable of knowledge
of the universal values which are the absolute Forms. All
we can do for him is to correct his calculations,—to make
him see, so far as is possible, that there are greater joys than
any he has dreamed of. And where he cannot be made to see
he must trust those who know better than he. Hence the main
thesis of the *Republic*, that the good man is happier than the
rascal. Hence a frank admission in the *Laws* that the desire
for joy is a natural and universal human instinct which we must
accept and take into account. Furthermore, even the greatest
men go through a period of infancy and adolescence when
reason and intellect are theirs in but a small degree, and, being
the best, they are capable of the worst if badly trained.[1] They
are during this period at the same level of existence at which the
majority of men always remain, and are terribly accessible to
bad, as fortunately also to good, influences. For such also
the hedonistic calculus is a sound and reasonable view of life,
provided that their guide be a good mathematician. Literally
so to Plato, since it is by way of the mathematical sciences that
we come to the realization of the universal Forms. But those
who define the good as pleasure mistake an incidental for the
essential. Whatever is good is pleasant, but only incidentally.
And the philosopher, who knows that pleasure is not the good,
will also know the reason why. He will know that because the
universe is based upon a harmony of universal Forms, unchanging and absolute, any even partial realization of them
and approximation to them must be pleasant to those who are
in tune with the purpose of the world, and it is his business
as an educator to make men so. He will know that any pure
and permanent pleasure-value is due to such an approximation,
to the realization of the orderly values that rule the world,

[1] Cp. the temptations of the philosophic soul in *Republic*, 490e ff.

though imperfectly, and that the more the phenomenal world ' shares in ' the absolute Ideal values, the more true, the more harmonious, the more beautiful it becomes, and at the same time the more pleasurable.

But most men, as they can know but little of all this, must needs follow their instinct for pleasure, and if they can only be persuaded to follow the good life, and not desert it before they have even tasted it, then on their own hedonistic premises they will remain faithful to it, for thus alone can their organism as a whole function as it was meant to do, and pleasure is a by-product of the return to health of any organism.

Such at least was Plato's belief.

III

EROS

It is well known that homosexual love alone was generally regarded by the Greeks as fulfilling the highest desires of men, and that the love of men for women was little more than a means of procreation. This fact we must accept without prejudice as to its naturalness or perversity, without emotional revulsion, if we are to understand the meaning of the Greek Eros.

It is probably an over-simplification to attribute it entirely to the inferior position of women in society. Cause and effect, in a case of this kind, are difficult to disentangle, and on the other hand the social inferiority of women can easily be exaggerated. It is however certain that women did not, in Athens, share men's education, men's intellectual or artistic interests, and that they could not therefore be associated with them in their general interests. Marriage could not be an association between partners who share their life in its every aspect, a partnership for better or for worse extending far beyond the limits of the home. This, the modern ideal, none too easy of realization in our own century, was quite impossible in the fifth or fourth century B.C. Not that the wife was despised or downtrodden; Xenophon, in his *Oeconomicus*, gives us a charming picture of a real gentleman's attitude to his young wife —his kindly instructions to her about her duties in the house, his respect for her place in the household, his gentle reprovings when she has failed, his teachings to her on the necessity for order, cleanliness, the way to rule slaves, &c. It is a picture against which a modern feminist would at once rebel, and rightly if it were taken as a pattern for all time; but if we remember that the husband is a middle-aged man of some standing, his wife a child of fifteen who has seen nothing of the world, we should rather be charmed by the delicacy, tenderness and restraint of one who is represented as the perfect Athenian gentleman. But for all its charm, Xenophon's description will make us realize even more clearly how impossible it was for an intelligent and educated Athenian to find in his wife an equal and a friend who could stimulate his mind as well as his senses. And their sound common sense did not allow that ridiculous chivalry which places woman either on a pedestal or in the gutter : motherhood was to them a noble yet an everyday function which deserved respect but not worship. At the other end of the scale prostitution did not merit execration. The prostitutes were also treated as human beings ; when successful they led a freer life, were more able to achieve some kind of education and could share to some extent the interests of men. Aspasia, the famous friend and mistress of Pericles, was renowned for her intelligence and wit, and there were others. But these were exceptional and the lot of the ordinary hetaira was far less enviable than that of the respectable wife and mother, however humble. Certainly, there were not enough Aspasias to make any appreciable difference to the emotional life of the Greeks. And though it is true that at Sparta the wife was more openly respected, at Sparta also homosexuality was, in the full sense of the word, more common than at Athens—due possibly to the excessively military life led by the men.

Plato was an apostle of women's rights in the sense that he wanted to give them, in the *Republic* and the *Laws*, equal political rights with men.[1] Their training and education is to be the same as that of men. They are to occupy all political offices for which they are fitted, even the highest ; men are thought of as on the whole more able, but there is to be complete equality of opportunity. In the *Republic* (457d ff.) all children will be brought up in state institutions and parents will know only that their child is one of a group. Marriages are only temporary associations at certain festivals for the purpose

---

[1] For a full account of Plato's proposed reforms in the position of women, both at home and in the state, see Ithurriague, who gives a brief account of the position of women in antiquity and discusses Plato's contribution in relation to it, especially pp. 116–42. See also Wilamowitz, I, 398–9, who says : ' Dahin konnte Platon aber nur so kommen, dass er von der Frau verlangte Mann zu sein, und sie, weil sie das nicht vollkommen kann, für unvollkommen erklärte.'

of procreation. This ' communism of wives and children ',
as it is often mistakenly called, for the wife and husband are
on exactly the same footing and their partnership soon dissolved, requires from the guardians, to whom it is applied as
a class, a quite unusual degree of continence, for although they
may, when allowed by the rulers, enter several such marriages
at different festivals, there are to be no other sexual relations
of any kind, as long as they are of an age to have children.
Thus women from twenty to forty, men from thirty to fifty-
five shall be completely continent except at definite times,
and even the most distinguished man or woman, by whom the
rulers will wish to breed as much as possible, will not have a
partner more than for a period of a few days three or four
times a year ! This unnatural control is lightened in the more
practical *Laws*, where the family survives and only the number
of children, as well as the manner in which they are conceived
and born, is the concern of the state.

Thus the relations of the sexes are considered throughout
purely from the political and social point of view. Of any
ennobling individual relationship between man and woman
Plato has no conception any more than his contemporaries.[1]
He does, it is true, assert the equality of the sexes, but he fails
to see that such an equality, by producing women of a very
different calibre than those he saw around him, would make
possible a very different relationship by which could be satisfied those higher cravings which a Greek could only develop
in his love for other men. For this Plato can scarcely be
blamed, since, even after the partial emancipation of women
we have witnessed in the last generation, the association of free
and equal spirits in marriage is still an ideal imperfectly and
infrequently realized.

We must then at the outset accept the fact that Plato seeks
the higher manifestations of love and affection in love between
men. That he deprecated physical intercourse, especially in
his later works, is true, but comparatively irrelevant to the
main issue.[2] Alcibiades tells in the *Symposium* how he tried

[1] Perhaps less, for as Wilamowitz has noted (I, 37) we have no record
of any woman playing a part in Plato's life.
  For the inferiority of women in Plato see Ritter, II, 452-3.
  [2] Plato certainly deprecates sexual intercourse between men, and forbids
it explicitly both in the *Republic* (403*b*) and the *Laws* (839*a*) but, except

to seduce Socrates, and failed. The story loses all point if we refuse to admit that Socrates was tempted. It is his self-control, not his indifference, that is being extolled. Socrates loved young men and, instead of the satisfaction of physical intercourse, he sought to make his many friends into better men, he loved their souls even better than their bodies. But when confessing the attraction that physical beauty in men had for him he is not being ironical, he is merely truthful. The irony consists only in substituting for the physical reaction they expect his advice to live a better life. The whole atmosphere of his encounters with young men is tinged with eroticism such as we—most of us at least—only associate with the presence of young women, he talks to them as in our own day an elderly man strongly attracted by feminine beauty but with perfect self-control might talk to pretty and intelligent girls. The thought of sexual intercourse would, as a rule, not even be present to his mind, but the erotic attraction—if he knew himself half as well as Socrates did and were half as honest —he would be the last person to deny. It is in this spirit that we must understand the scene in his prison where Socrates gently strokes Phaedo's hair, that in the *Charmides* where, coming back from the war, he asks who are now the young men excelling in beauty or intelligence, hears the praises of the young Charmides, and, seeing him the cynosure of all eyes, thinks : ' What a marvellous man he must be, if his soul be as fine as his body.' And in this spirit too we must interpret his remark that he is but a poor hand at measuring beauty for ' nearly all young men seem beautiful to me ' (*Charm.*, 154*b*).

For unless we so understand Socrates' attitude to manly beauty and youth, we miss a great deal of the charm of these encounters. One of the most delightful is to be found in the *Lysis*, which is also the first dialogue wherein love is the subject of the discourse. As so often, we find here in embryo many thoughts that will be developed later, and it will be necessary for us to deal with it in some detail : Socrates is invited by Hippothales to come into a new palaestra or wrestling school.

for the purpose of procreation, he forbids intercourse between the sexes also (see below). It is therefore misleading to say that he condemned homosexuality as such, for he did not look with favour upon heterosexuality either ; what he disliked was sexual relations of any kind.

He will see those who are there. 'Who is it, he asks, who is
the beauty?' Opinions vary. When Hippothales is asked
what he thinks, he merely blushes. And Socrates says (204*b*) :

'You needn't tell me whether you are in love or not. I can see
not only that you are, but that you have fallen pretty deeply in love.
For though I am a poor and useless person in other things, I have
received this gift from a god, that I can quickly recognize one who
loves or is loved. And when he heard this he blushed even more.
And Ctesippus said : It is pretty of you to blush, Hippothales, and
to hesitate to tell Socrates the name. But if he were to remain with
you for even a short time, he would be tortured by the number of
times you do mention it. For, Socrates, our ears are filled and
deafened with the name of Lysis. Even when he has been drinking he probably wakes us by calling on the name of Lysis. The
catalogue of virtues he goes through is bad enough, but not so bad,
only he then proceeds to deluge us with poems and writings. And,
even worse than that, he sings to his darling in an extraordinary
voice, and we must endure listening to it. But now, when you ask
him, he blushes.'

Socrates then inquires who this young Lysis may be, and when
he hears he congratulates Hippothales on his good taste. He
would like to see them together, to judge whether Hippothales
knows what a lover should say in such a case (205*a*) :

'Do you put any faith in what this fellow says?
—What, said I, do you deny you are in love with whom he says?
—No, he replied, but I don't compose poems or write about him.
—He is ill with it, said Ctesippus, he is mad and talks nonsense.'

Then Socrates asks how he· means to treat his beloved.
Ctesippus supplies the information : It is ridiculous to see a
man in love paying no attention to any but his darling. He
celebrates his ancestry, his wealth, his family's victories at the
games, descent from Zeus himself, and other old wives' tales
of that sort. Socrates protests that this is not the right way.
These poems really concern Hippothales himself : if he succeed in his love he will appear the finer fellow, if he fails he
will be the more absurd (206*a*) :

'a man who is wise in matters of love, my friend, does not praise his
love before he capture him (ἕλῃ), fearing things might not turn out

well.   And beautiful youths become high and mighty when any one praises and extols them.'

The prouder the more difficult to catch (δυσαλωτότεροι), and to write poetry to your own harm is hardly being a good poet ! And Socrates then promises that he will show him the proper way to act.

There is irony here, for the way in which Socrates ' catches ' young men is, of course, not the way of Hippothales, and this will only become clear in the sequel.   But the young man's love is throughout regarded as a natural and in no way a reprehensible thing.   No doubt it might express itself in unpleasant ways.   So can heterosexual love in our own day, but the feeling is natural, and the amused and slightly contemptuous words of Ctesippus could be paralleled from thousands of conversations of young men with reference to love for a young woman. There is a further difference, which jars even more upon us, namely that the object of this love is a boy of school age (208c), still under the care of his personal slave—παιδαγωγός— and who can therefore be no older than sixteen.   That too is a feature we must accept.

Socrates and his friends then enter the palaestra and are joined by the young Menexenus and then by the latter's friend Lysis, while Hippothales keeps himself shyly in the background to watch Socrates' display of how young beauties should be dealt with.   After some preliminary banter Socrates turns to Lysis :   To love [1] is to wish the person one loves as happy as possible.   Your parents love you, therefore they wish you happy.   Yet they do not allow you freedom in all kinds of

----

[1] The word for love in the *Lysis* is φιλία, which is a more general term than ἔρως (sexual desire) and includes the love of parents or that between two youths like Lysis and Menexenus here.   It is also the more natural word when talking to them.   But it must also include the passionate love of Hippothales or else the whole introduction is singularly irrelevant. ἐρῶν is used at 221b.   In the *Symposium* on the other hand we find φιλία used of the affection of the παιδικά for the lover, almost as the equivalent of χαρίζεσθαι (182c, 183c) ; and at 179c φιλία includes ἔρως.   We are therefore justified in tracing the development of Eros through the *Lysis* to the *Symposium*, as is usually done, in spite of Wilamowitz' assertion (II, 68) that they have little in common.   The very close parallels between the two dialogues make it quite clear that we are dealing with the same subject, or at least that the Eros of the later work is to be included under φιλία here.

things. You may not drive your father's horses, you are subjected to the dictates of slave and schoolmaster, &c., &c. —Lysis suggests that perhaps he is too young.—But, Socrates points out, there are many things you may do. Why this difference ?—Lysis at last hits upon the right answer : he may do that of which he has sufficient knowledge. Knowledge, not age, is the real test. Furthermore, every one will entrust us with things we can do, if they know we have the knowledge, be they our family, our compatriots or any one else. People will like us in so far as we are useful, and thus we shall be dear to them. And Socrates' final point here is the advice that, if he wishes to be loved he must acquire wisdom. This is the way to become dear to all men.

This preliminary conversation (207d–10d) takes place during a temporary absence of Menexenus. In it Socrates gives, for the benefit of the silent Hippothales, a compressed example of the improving kind of conversation which a lover should hold with his beloved. The theory, here completely taken for granted, that we value our friends only, or at least chiefly, in so far as they are useful, is somewhat startling to us, but it is really a corollary of Socrates' belief that a friend or lover should seek to make those dear to him as good as possible, a thing which Hippothales, for all his flattering verses, failed to do. It is part and parcel of Socrates' utilitarian point of view, and, when rightly interpreted, not as objectionable as, thus baldly stated, it would seem.

Menexenus now returns and the discussion on friendship continues. There is one thing, Socrates says, for which he has longed since childhood, something which he prizes more than any other possession : a comrade (ἑταῖρος) or friend. And he continues, with obvious irony, to say how happy he considers Lysis and Menexenus to be, for they have obviously found in each other what he has looked for all his life. How then does one man become another's friend, and what is a friend ?

The stage is now set for the search of a definition, in Socrates' customary manner, here a definition of φίλος—friend. Now the word could be used, like our own word friend, either of the lover or the beloved and the first thing to do is to be sure in what sense we are using it. Hence Socrates' question :

' which is φίλος, the lover or the object of his love ? ' The youth at first replies that it makes no difference. Yet obviously it does, for love is not always returned, and you may love some one who hates you. Shall we say φίλος can only be rightly applied to people who love each other ? Apparently, but that does not correspond to ordinary usage, for we speak of men who are lovers of dogs, horses, wisdom, &c. Shall we say that the object of love is the ' friend ' ? On the same principle the object of hate is the enemy, and we find that we may be the friends of our enemy and the enemy of our friends. Which is absurd.

This logical by-play fulfils two functions : it draws our attention to the different uses of the word and further it emphasizes the futility of paying attention to the words only (213d) instead of to their meaning. So we start afresh, this time with the old philosophical adage that ' like is friend to like '. On this principle the good must be friends of the good, the bad of the bad. But the bad—who are never constant in their likeness to anything, even to themselves—cannot be friends to anything.[1] The old saying can therefore be applied only to the good. But he who is completely good and self-sufficient needs no one to make him so ; and if love is based on need he cannot feel it. Such friends, being completely good and needing no one, cannot be of great value to one another.

But then, if friendship or love be based on need, the poor must be the friends and lovers of the rich, the weak of the strong, the sick of the doctor, &c., and love exists not between the like, but between opposites. Longing is for the opposite, not for the like. But here again we will be faced with all kinds of logical difficulties : just and unjust will be friends, good and bad, moderate and intemperate. This again is impossible. There is a third possibility : that which is neither good nor evil is the friend or lover of the good. And good is admittedly identical with beautiful. This we may reduce to

[1] 214c. This is a compressed version of the argument found in *Republic*, I, 351c ff. that badness (ἀδικία) means ignorance and discord, while goodness means harmony. That even rogues must be to some extent in agreement with one another to be successful even in their roguery. That a completely bad man could never do anything at all ; and the same argument is applied to the different parts of the individual soul. A completely bad, i.e. discordant, soul can do nothing.

the general formula that that which is neither good nor evil, because of the presence of evil but before it has become evil itself, loves the good. Body, for example, loves health because of the presence of disease. The lover of wisdom is not completely wise—for then he possesses wisdom and need long for it no more—nor is he so completely ignorant as to be unaware of his own ignorance. Being in this middle state between good and evil he loves the good, because of the presence in him of the evil of ignorance (218c).

That is really the end of the search for a definition of love. The remainder of the dialogue is concerned with a further difficulty : every object of love is loved for the sake of some further good ; we love the doctor for the health he gives us, but there must be some ultimate object of love which is loved for its own sake. And if it is the presence of evil that makes us love the good, then if evil were abolished we would no longer love the good. Perhaps we are wrong in calling evil the cause of this love. So we may correct ourselves and say that desire or passion (ἐπιθυμία) is the cause of love and that it loves that of which it is deficient. This must be what is naturally akin to itself (οἰκεῖον), so that friends in a sense are akin or belong to one another. But then if we interpret what is akin (οἰκεῖον) as what is like to (ὅμοιον), we are back to love as the desire of like for like which we rejected some time ago.

As usual at this period, the dialogue ends in perplexity and love remains unexplained. Yet many points are raised which will appear again. From the very beginning love is understood in the widest sense. The appeal to the Physicists' dictum ' like loves like ' shows that we are dealing with a universal natural force of which affection between human beings is but a particular application. This force is a longing for something we need, something which we know we do not possess. Already we catch a glimpse of the philosopher, the lover of the good and the beautiful, longing for perfection because of his knowledge of his own imperfection ; a glimpse too of an ultimate object of all desire, loved for its own sake, an ultimate good and beauty (the two are here identified). There is also the description of what we needs must love as something which, though akin, is yet not similar to ourselves. From all this there begins to emerge the Socratic conception of mutual love as a means to joint search for supreme truth.

Thus prepared we may go on to the two great Platonic expositions of love, the *Symposium* and the *Phaedrus*. The scene of the former is a banquet which is in process at the house of Agathon to celebrate the success of one of his tragedies. Some one suggests that, in view of the fact that most of those present did some heavy drinking the night before, they should spend the evening talking instead, a suggestion that is unanimously approved. Phaedrus has complained that Eros is the only god who has never received proper praise from poets or Sophists, and it is now proposed that each of those present should deliver a speech in honour of the god. We thus get a series of speeches on love, culminating in the famous speech of Socrates which he modestly attributes to the Mantinean priestess Diotima. There is deepening of thought as we proceed and the first encomia are fairly commonplace, yet each speaker has a definite contribution to make which is later taken up and developed by Socrates when his turn comes. Each also has his own style and tricks of diction, but that point we must here leave out of consideration.[1]

Phaedrus opens the series with quotations from Homer and Parmenides as witnesses that Eros is the eldest of the gods. As such he makes men feel shame and ambition. His influence is greater than that of any other feeling, family affection not excluded. Lovers will refrain from all meanness and cowardice in each other's presence and their love will inspire them to mighty deeds. Not only men, but even women are willing to die for their beloved; the examples of Alcestis and Achilles, and the punishment of Orpheus who, being a musician (ἅτε ὢν κιθαρῳδός) was too soft to face death, make abundantly clear how love is held in honour by the gods, especially when the beloved sacrifices himself to his lover.

This speech is a thin performance, and thus a good starting-point. The emphasis on military training and the slighting reference to music, as well as the admission that even a woman's love may have a certain nobility, seem to show that Phaedrus

---

[1] The reader will find an interesting analysis of the speeches from this point of view in the introduction to Bury's edition, pp. xxiv–xxxvi.

was an admirer of the Spartan ways of life, and such, as we know, were not uncommon in Athens. The only real contribution he makes is to represent Eros as an inspiration to noble deeds.

The next, that of Pausanias, may be summarized as follows : we must distinguish between two kinds of Eros, each the follower of a different Aphrodite : the elder goddess, the motherless daughter of Heaven, and the younger, the daughter of Zeus and Dione whom we call Pandemos (common, plebeian). So it is with every action, in itself it is neither good nor bad, but it must be judged after the manner of its performance. The Eros of Aphrodite Pandemos is that of inferior men who love women no less than boys, who love the body rather than the soul, whose only aim is to gain their end careless of the manner in which it is done. Their goddess partook at birth of both the male and the female nature. The heavenly Aphrodite derives from the male alone. Her followers turn to men only, their love is more lasting, they do not love young boys but adolescents. Their aim is a lifelong association, not the exploitation of the inexperience of youth. There should be a law to forbid the love of young boys, and good men make such laws for themselves. We try to make the vulgar type of lover conform to it and prevent him, if we can, from making love even to free women. For these men are responsible for the reproaches cast at love. Laws about (homosexual) love are easy to understand in other cities, for they are simple. In uncivilized places like Elis or Boeotia it is considered altogether good to yield to a lover, presumably to save men the trouble of persuasion, an art for which their lack of culture unfits them. In Ionia, on the other hand, and other countries under barbarian influence, Eros is forbidden along with philosophy and athletics, because despots fear anything which will make their subjects proud. But in Athens and Sparta the matter is not so simple, and this is quite right. On the one hand we forgive anything to a lover—many a meanness, flattery and even perjury are excused by gods and men—which would never be forgiven to any one else. On the other hand we must carefully protect the beloved and advise them never to give way. This is also right because we wish to protect our youth from the pandemian lover and his purely physical infatuation ; our

restrictions test the lover as time is made to elapse. To yield
for profit or honour is shameful. As in everything else, all
depends upon the way the thing is done, and the only worthy
association is that which has moral excellence as its aim. When
the physical association tends to educate the beloved in wisdom
and courage, then and then alone is it free from blame. It is
the motive that counts.

This is a remarkable speech, far more able and on an altogether higher plane than that of Phaedrus. For our modern
dislike of homosexuality should not blind us to the very important distinction it establishes between the pandemian Aphrodite
of mere physical infatuation and the heavenly love which aims
at a lifelong association in athletics and study (philosophy).
The distinction will recur in the *Phaedrus* ; in connecting the
higher love with philosophy or the love of wisdom Pausanias
prepares the way for Socrates, even though he uses the word
philosophy in a sense which Socrates would not ultimately
accept. The first speech failed to make such a distinction at all.

The main points of the next speech, that of the physician
Eryximachus, are the following : The distinction made by
Pausanias between two kinds of Eros is sound, but it has a far
wider application than the souls of men, it applies also to
animals, plants and indeed everything that exists. Medical
science teaches us that our bodies have this double Eros or
desire. Like desires like, and unlike unlike.[1] It is right to yield
to good desires and the good of the body is health. It is the
doctor's business to know which are good desires, to replace
one by another, and to reconcile them. The opposites, hot
and cold, bitter and sweet and the like must be harmonized
by means of Eros, desire. This is the aim of medicine, as
also of music to make harmony out of discords, and it requires
scientific knowledge. To reduce things to order we must yield
to the better kind of desire, and this is the love called heavenly.
This is true of all things human and divine, of things on earth
and in heaven, of seasons and climates, and of the relation
between men and gods by encouraging the desires that lead
to justice and piety.

This curious and somewhat pedantically professional performance is full of echoes of Pythagorean medical theories, and

[1] Cp. *Lysis* above.

of the philosophy of Empedocles who had made Love and
Hate the two causes of motion ; and the bad Eros in this very
wide application of the word seems at times to become the
mere negation of the good.   Its main contribution from our
point of view is to broaden the conception of Eros and to
insist on its essential kinship, if indeed not identity, with the
forces at work in the whole of nature, a step that can but deepen
its significance.

Aristophanes comes next.   True to character, he gives us a
piece of broad farce with an undercurrent of seriousness.   In
the course of it he uses medical and philosophical vocabulary
with humorous intent in a manner which along with many
other jests must be lost in any summary.   His main theme is
that originally there were three kinds of human beings each
with twice the number of limbs and organs we now possess.
Some were male, some female, some androgynous.   These
primeval humans, in their strength and power, conspired
against the gods.   Zeus was in a quandary because, if he did
away with the human race, the gods would no longer be worshipped.   So he cut them in two, instructing Apollo to sew
up the halves, turn round their heads and rearrange them
generally.   Since when men have looked for their other half.
Each half of an original man loves another man, every half
woman another woman, while the halves of the androgynous
kind are given to heterosexual love.   A marvellous thing it
would be if we could thus find our other natural half; in the
meantime we must do the best we can following the kind of
love natural to us, and worship the gods, lest they split us into
halves again.

It would be vain to look for any very deep meaning in this
very amusing piece of writing, but the general conviction it
leaves with one is the realization of the tremendous depth and
power of the instinct of love.   We also note that heterosexual
love is at least put on a par with the homosexual,[1] and that
men and women are in precisely the same state.   This however
naturally follows from the exigencies of the tale, and should
not be pressed too far.

[1] So Robin (*L'Amour*, p. 48).   Note also that Aristophanes' description
of Eros as a passionate desire for something that is akin to our own nature
and completes it, is reminiscent of the *Lysis*.   See above, p. 95.

Agathon is the last speaker before Socrates. He criticizes the others for not describing the nature of Eros, before praising him, and proceeds to do so in a delightfully poetical speech. He uses his words as carefully as he is careless of real meaning and proceeds to shower upon Eros a galaxy of glowing epithets that would be hard to match. Beauty, tenderness, youth, courage, moderation, wisdom and righteousness are all attributed to the god, and justified by a series of charming sophisms and plays on words. Eros is himself the greatest of the poets for he inspires poetry. He lives in the souls of men and violence is quite foreign to his nature. From him come all blessings to men.

This speech which says very little, yet says it so beautifully, must have been characteristic of the man. With its soothing calm, it makes an excellent transition between the uproarious-ness of Aristophanes and the emotional storm soon to be aroused. Many of the epithets applied to Eros by Agathon will be fully justified by Socrates. Two things are gently emphasized : Eros is always concerned with beauty, and it resides in the souls of men.

Agathon's performance is received with enthusiastic applause, as the successful young poet deserves. Socrates expresses his great admiration for his beautiful use of words, though not without considerable irony, and professes to be afraid that he cannot possibly match it, for in his innocence he had supposed that what was wanted was the truth (198*d*). There are one or two questions, however, he wants to ask Agathon, for he would like to ascertain the nature of Eros, which Agathon so rightly said should be done (but, of course, did not do). This he pro-ceeds to do in a dialectical passage of some length, the extreme importance of which is too easily overshadowed by the few magnificent pages of the speech itself.

Love always has an object and its relation to that object is one of desire. Now one desires what one does not possess, or else that one's possession of it should continue in the future. Eros always desires the beautiful and the good, and therefore cannot be either. This argument startles the company. We have already met it in the *Lysis*. Here Socrates introduces the name of the Mantinean priestess Diotima to whom he attributes the rest of what he has to say, for he professes to recount a previous conversation he has had with her (201*d*). To say, he continues, that Eros is not beautiful or good is not, however, to say that it is ugly or bad, only that it is somewhere between the two. In the same way Love is not a god, but somewhere between the immortal and the mortal—a spirit or daimon (202*e*) :

' Carrier and interpreter between men and gods, it brings human prayers and sacrifices to the latter, commandments and rewards to the former. Existing in the place between the two it completes and binds the whole together by means of itself. From it derive all prophecy, the art of priests that concerns sacrifices, ritual, prayer, all divination and magic. A god cannot mingle with man, but through Eros is all association and converse of gods with men awake or asleep. And he who is wise in these things is a man inspired (δαιμόνιος ἀνήρ), while the wisdom of other arts and crafts is but lowly. There are many such spirits of various kinds, and one of these is Eros.'

Socrates then tells how, at the birth feast of Aphrodite, Poros (Resource) was resting in the vineyard when Penia (Poverty) schemed to have a child by him. Thus Eros was born the minister of Aphrodite and took after both his parents, poor, harsh, needy, shoeless, homeless like his mother, and because of his father ever greedy of the beautiful and the good, brave, dashing and energetic, full of trickery, a clever hunter, eager for knowledge, loving wisdom his whole life long, a dread magician. Himself neither mortal nor immortal, he lives and dies and lives again, neither wise nor ignorant but somewhere in between. The gods and the wise love not wisdom, for they possess it. Nor the ignorant, for they know not it exists, and believe themselves beautiful, good and wise. But Eros is between these, and Eros loves wisdom (φιλοσοφεῖ). Beauty is the object of love, it is not love itself. Love aims at happiness, which is the aim of all men. Men love the good, and they wish to possess it always. Furthermore, Eros aims at creation in beauty, whether in the body or in the soul. That is its final object (206*e*) :

' Why love of creation (γέννησις) ? To give birth to something is to be everlasting and immortal as far as mortal can. We agree then that Eros must desire immortality along with good, if it desires to possess the good for ever. Thus immortality is the object of Eros.'

Thus what is mortal is yet preserved, not by itself lasting for ever like the gods, but by leaving behind another like itself. Hence also man's love for glory and renown, for he wishes to last for ever. Those who are pregnant in the body are lovers of women and they seek immortality and happiness in their children. But those who are pregnant in the soul seek to bring forth wisdom and other forms of excellence. Such are poets and inventors. But the finer kind of wisdom expresses itself in the management of house and state. And a youth pregnant with these, longing to bring forth, seeks for beauty wherein to give birth, embraces manly beauty allied with beauty of soul and straightway he has abundance of fine words regarding excellence, and tries to educate his beloved (209c) :

' For in contact with the beauty and in his company, he produces and brings to birth those things with which he was pregnant of old, and together they bring up their offspring, and such have with one another a far deeper communion than that found in producing children, and a far more stable affection (φιλία) for they are associated in offspring more beautiful and more immortal.'

And Socrates adds that every one would rather produce the poems of Homer and Hesiod, the laws of Lycurgus and of Solon, than mere children of the flesh.

Before we go on to the last sublime pages of Socrates' speech, perhaps the most famous in all Plato, let us consider for a moment how far Socrates has already taken us. First he has elaborated the argument we met in the *Lysis* : the lover, himself neither good nor bad, neither wise nor ignorant, neither beautiful nor ugly, longs to possess beauty, goodness, and wisdom. In the earlier dialogue this broke down because it meant longing for something which was akin to oneself, yet not like oneself (οἰκεῖον, not ὅμοιον). But since then the theory of Ideas has been elaborated in the *Phaedo*. We have learned to know Truth and Reality as a set of transcendental Forms to which the soul of man, or some part of it at any rate, is fundamentally akin. And surely in the Eros who is an interpreter between gods and men Plato is seeking for something that will bridge this gap between the noetic and the physical world and

will thus ' bind the whole together ' by providing a way for
man to apprehend the Ideas. Elsewhere this understanding
comes by severe intellectual study, but such study is an activity
and all human activity springs from an emotional motivation
or it cannot come to be.[1] This is provided by Eros, and it is
because Eros must provide it that Socrates so clearly insists
that he is neither of this world nor the other, but holds a
middle place between the two. Plato made many attempts to
explain the way to the Ideas, always by means of a psychic
activity. And, as Agathon says, Eros lives in the souls of men.

When he returns to consider Eros in the lives of individuals
and builds his ascending scale of loves, it is clear, however
unpleasant to our ears, that here too the love of women holds
the lowest place, suitable only for those who cannot be poets
or statesmen (or philosophers, as will soon appear). And if it
be objected that poets and statesmen, and even philosophers,
do have children, it is yet quite clear that in doing so they are
here supposed to live only according to the body and indulge
their desire for immortality only in its lowest form. When
Socrates puts above this the love of man for man which leads
to virtue and children of the brain, it may be argued that he
refers only to the philosophic lovers who, as is made clear later,
will refrain from physical intercourse, and that the relationship
extolled in Pausanias' speech is not here included. That may
be so, or he may be purposely vague, but we should remember
that Pausanias is present and that Socrates has said nothing
that could make him realize that *his* lovers, whose intercourse
he described in very similar terms as aiming at excellence and
philosophy, have been ruled out of court.[2] They have certainly not been dealt with, and if they are not here, where are
they ? I believe that any reader who compares this part of
Socrates' speech (209a–e) with the words of Pausanias without
prejudice must come to the conclusion that they refer to one
and the same kind of Eros. Socrates does not use phrases
unambiguous enough to point to actual sexual intercourse,
but neither does he use any word that would exclude it. That
is not unnatural, for we know that he would not advise it, and

[1] See also on p. 136.
[2] Cp. Wilamowitz, I, 366 : ' Platon, der den Pausanias ungestraft . . .
reden lässt.'

some may perhaps remain chaste even though they be not
philosophers. There is no absolute imperative, at this stage,
that they should.

Thus far we have followed Diotima without much difficulty,
but now she will rise to greater heights, as she herself makes
clear (210a) :

' So far, Socrates, perhaps even you might be initiated in matters
of love.[1] But the final and higher mysteries, from which these
derive the reason of their existence if any one rightly approaches
them, I do not know if you could follow. Yet I will tell you, she
said, and do my very best. A man who approaches this matter in
the right way must begin in youth by frequenting beautiful bodies
and, if he is guided aright, he will first love one such body and hence
produce beautiful thoughts. Then he will perceive that the beauty
of one body is akin to that of another, and if he must pursue physical
beauty it is very absurd not to consider all physical beauty to be one
and the same. Realizing this he will be the lover of all beautiful
bodies and he will relax his passion for a particular one and despise
it as something small. Next he will consider beauty of soul to be
more worthy than beauty of body so that if any one with a fair soul
have but small physical grace, it will suffice ; he will love and cherish
such a one and seek to utter such thoughts as make young men
better ; that he may further be forced to contemplate the beauty of
laws and traditions and see that this is all of one kin. He will then
consider beauty of body a small thing. From traditions he will be
guided to the sciences, that he may see the beauty of these, gazing
upon much beauty and no longer on that of one thing like a slave
who loves the beauty of his boy or of some one man or one institution,
an inferior creature of little worth. Not so, but turning to the vast
sea of beauty and gazing upon it he will utter thoughts both proud
and beautiful in the abundance of his love of wisdom (φιλοσοφία)
until he gathers strength there and power to look upon one such
science, which is the knowledge of beauty such as this :

Try, she said, to concentrate on this as much as you can. For he
who has been led to this point in love, looking upon beautiful things
continually in the right manner, as he comes to the goal of love will
suddenly see something marvellously beautiful in its nature, that

[1] This, of course, is just Socrates' customary modesty and plea of ignorance. To suppose that Plato means us to understand that he is now going
beyond his master (Ritter II, 58) is quite ridiculous. He means, if anything, that this is about as far as his audience will follow him. Which, to
judge by their speeches, is quite true.

very thing, Socrates, for the sake of which he endured all his previous labours. First, it is for ever, it neither is born nor dies, it does not increase or fade ; further, it is not in one way beautiful, in another ugly ; nor beautiful compared with this, compared with that ugly ; nor beautiful to some, ugly to others. . . .'

This final vision, the ultimate goal of him ' who loves boys in the right way ' (211*b*) is further described and is, of course, the Idea of beauty, or rather the supreme reality considered as the object of love. The way up, Socrates repeats, is step by step from the love of one beautiful body to that of two, to the love of all physical beauty, to that of traditions or institutions, to beautiful studies, finally to the one supreme study, the knowledge of beauty itself. Then the lover knows indeed ' what beauty is ', and in this contemplation he will create not semblances of excellence, but excellence itself. He is the true philosopher in love.

The *Phaedrus* is formally a discussion of rhetoric based on a speech of Lysias—whether a genuine speech of that orator or a parody does not matter for our present purpose—on the subject : that it is better for a youth to grant his favours to one who does not love him than to one who does.   This is a typical paradox to give scope to sophistical ingenuity. It is followed by a counter-speech on the same subject by Socrates himself as a specimen of what can be done. The speech of Lysias is, as Socrates well says in the sequel, an ingenious string of arguments without proper construction and full of repetitions.   Lysias tells us that lovers act under compulsion, that their passion is followed by remorse, neither of which is true of non-lovers, among whom there is a wider choice. Lovers, he tells us, are chained by passion as by a disease, they boast of their conquests and give themselves away, they are jealous of all other company, they love only the bloom of youth which will pass, whereas non-lovers show a friendship that will not be diminished by physical intercourse. Lovers need you more it is true, so do beggars need to be invited to dinner rather than your friend.[1] You should choose wisely, for promiscuity is inadvisable in either case. From all this

[1] Cp. p. 94 above.

I will quote one significant paragraph (233*b*), in which the non-lover says to the youth :

' If I persuade you, I will, in the first place, seek your company not with immediate pleasure, but also with future advantage in view ; not overcome by desire but master of myself. I will not become your bitter enemy because of some trifling incident, important matters only will move me to anger, and that slowly. If you err against your will I will forgive you, if willingly, I will try to prevent you. These are the tokens of lasting friendship. If you have supposed that a strong bond of friendship is impossible without passion, you must remember that we could then not hold our sons dear, nor our fathers or mothers, that we could not possess trustworthy friends whose affection arose not from such passion but from other common pursuits.'

This rhetorical farrago is obviously not devoid of a good deal of sense, but it leaves us very confused because the orator has failed to define his terms. There is a general antithesis between Eros, passion, and φιλία, friendship, but the difference is not clear cut and the denial that Eros may be good is very repulsive.

It is exactly this defect that Socrates, when he is at last persuaded to give a speech on the same subject, proceeds to remedy. The speaker is supposed to be one among several lovers who is clever enough to pretend that he does not love. This is not in order ' to safeguard his own character by abstaining from even a playful defence of a morally disgraceful thesis ' [1] for his thesis, as we shall see, is not at all disgraceful but simply because a man who is not the victim of the Eros as about to be defined is obviously, since he has the φιλία, which even Lysias granted him, a lover in a higher sense later to be explained. The speech begins, as a speech by Socrates should, with a very careful definition of Eros as understood in this at first sight strange performance : Eros is desire (ἐπιθυμία) but even those who have not Eros (i.e. in Lysias' sense) desire the beautiful. So we must find another difference between them. We have in us two leading principles ; an inborn desire for pleasure and an acquired capacity of judgement (δόξα) which aims at what is best. Sometimes these two agree,

---

[1] Taylor, p. 303. Friedländer (II, 488) and Lagerborg (66) remark on the importance of this definition. Wilamowitz (I, 476) points out that the first speech of Socrates is complementary to the palinode.

sometimes they differ. One or the other gains the day. When our judgement wins we have self-control or moderation (σωφροσύνη), when desire leads us to pleasure *against our judgement*, we have excess (ὕβρις). In the case of food this victory of hubris is gluttony, in the case of drink, drunkenness, and in the case of the pleasure to be got from beautiful bodies it is Eros.

Having thus carefully defined the Eros he intends to attack, Socrates, after a very short interlude which in itself should awaken us to the importance of the definition, proceeds to what should not, except as far as the language is concerned, be taken as a mere sophistical exercise upon an uncongenial topic, because it very obviously is a thoroughly sound attack upon immoderate physical passion, mere brute infatuation unsanctioned by reason, upon possessive, jealous, brutal Eros, the Pandemian lover condemned by Pausanias in the *Symposium*.

Such love, he tells us, is bad for the soul of the beloved because the lover, with his own pleasure alone in view, desires to keep his darling in a constant state of inferiority and dependence, prefers him to be ignorant, cowardly, inarticulate and slow. The opposite good qualities make for strength in the beloved and may deprive the lover of immediate and unquestioned satisfaction. He will keep the youth away from improving company and from the divine love of wisdom (θεία φιλοσοφία) because as long as he remains ignorant he will look to his lover for everything. Love that aims at pleasure before good is bad also for the young man's body. It will make him soft, not strong, make him lead an indoor and a pampered life where cosmetics will usurp the healthy tan of the sun, and lead to a physique the weakness of which will encourage his enemies but be a source of fear to his friends and even to his lovers themselves. Economic subjection too is this lover's aim. The poorer the beloved, the more pleased the lover. He would deprive him, if he could, of parents, friends and of all support. He is jealous of all his possessions and would prefer him without wife, children or home that he may the longer work his own sweet pleasure upon him. Such pleasure aiming only at immediate satisfaction, is an evil flatterer, a wild and harmful beast. And to the beloved youth the lover is not even pleasant. Youth should seek its pleasures with youth, for in the society of an older man it will only find satiety. To see, to touch, to hear no one but an older man night and day becomes terribly irksome, and the watchful jealousy of the lover a hard burden of compulsion. And when love has ceased and the lover regains his self-control he will avoid paying the price or fulfilling the wild promises he made and the youth pursues him with complaints, not realizing that the other has changed. For these reasons the youth should favour the non-lover—for like the wolf's affection for the sheep is a lover's affection for his boy (238d–241d).

Such is Socrates' indictment of Eros. Phaedrus desires him to go on to praise the non-lover, but this Socrates refuses to do, excusing himself by saying that the non-lover has all the corresponding advantages. This refusal is natural enough, for there is no such thing to Socrates as the affection of a non-lover. There is the Eros as defined above and there is the Eros of which he will speak later, affection without Eros is impossible. So instead of praising this he suddenly exclaims that he has blasphemed against the god of love and he must deliver himself of a palinode before harm come to him from the god. And here, as is not infrequent, Plato's humour has misled most of his commentators. The blasphemy was only in giving the name of Eros to the kind of passion described. Hence the palinode. Of the substance of his magnificent indictment of mere physical erotic madness which is ruthlessly possessive and profoundly selfish he does not need to retract a single word for it gives us an understanding of what real Eros is not, which is essential to the understanding of the true nature of the god of Love. So, he tells us, any one who heard him say that *lovers* pick quarrels with their beloved on the smallest provocation and that they are envious and harmful must have thought he was listening to a man brought up in the sailors' quarter (243c) among those who have never known the love of free men, and would not agree with the reproaches against *Eros*. Socrates does not mean, of course, that such lovers as he has described do not exist, but that they do not deserve the name of lovers.

His 'palinode' is the famous myth of the journey of the soul. As before, his first concern is to make us understand the nature of the very different Eros with which he is now dealing. And because this can only be properly understood against a background of psychology we get the description of the human soul and of the eternal Ideas. Love is a μανία, a form of madness that comes from the gods, one among several—prophecy, augury, and art are of a similar kind—it is μανία because it is unreasoning emotion, though it attains its highest level, the philosopher's love of truth and beauty, only when allied with reason. Or rather it is the emotion that motivates the philosopher's search, for the source of movement, the mainspring of action is to be found in the soul. The soul is here mythically represented as a charioteer with two horses, one obedient one obstinate and hostile.[1] At death the soul rises to the rim of heaven and catches a glimpse here and there of the eternal Forms beyond. In the crush of souls it loses its wings and comes back to earth, and the soul that has seen the Ideas most clearly becomes a ' lover of wisdom or lover of beauty, one who lives with grace ',[2] a lover of wisdom, (all of which refers to the philosophic life), also ' one who loves boys along with the love of truth ' (παιδεραστής μετὰ φιλοσοφίας, 249c). By recollection awakened by the sight of beauty, we remember the Idea of beauty and the other Ideas (250c) :

' As for Beauty, it shone, as we said, among the realities yonder.[3] And when we come hither we recapture it gleaming brightly by the clearest of our senses (for sight is the sharpest of our bodily senses) in a way that wisdom is not seen, for it would awaken marvellous love, if some such clear image of it were present to our eyes—and so with other lovely realities. But now this fate belongs to Beauty alone, so that it is the most manifest and the most beloved.

He who is not fresh from initiation, or who has been corrupted, is not quickly led hence to beauty itself that is yonder. He directs his gaze to what is called beautiful here below, so that he does not revere what he sees, but surrenders himself to pleasure ; he tries to go on all fours like an animal and beget ; in company with insolent excess he feels no fear or shame in the unnatural pursuit of pleasure. But the initiate, he who gazed at length upon the things above, when

---

[1] See pp. 131 ff.

[2] μουσικός (248d): Here only means a cultured man, an adept at the art of life. The artist in our sense is well below him.

[3] Beauty, as a Form, is of the same nature as the others here. It is because the sense of sight is the clearest of our senses that the perception of its images here below is clearer. So Robin, L'Amour, 221, though he seems to imply the opposite on pp. 51 and 180.

he sees some divine face, a fair imitation of Beauty, or a body of
fine appearance, at first he shivers and some of the fears he felt above
creep upon him, then he looks and reveres it as a god, and he would
offer sacrifice to his darling as to the statue of a god if he did not fear
to be thought quite mad. And as he looks he ceases to shiver, and
perspires from unaccustomed warmth. For as his eyes absorb the
stream of beauty, the roots of his wings are warmed and refreshed,
the hardness that sealed the wings away and blocked their growth is
melted, and as nourishment flows upon them, the tips swell and
start to grow from the root—in his whole soul. For the whole soul
was winged once. Then the whole soul of him whose wings begin
to grow seethes and throbs with an itching and irritation such as is
felt in the gums at the growing of the teeth, for as it grows wings it
seethes and irritates and itches. And as it looks upon the beauty of
the boy and particles come flowing thence upon it, which is called
desire, it is warmed and refreshed, it is relieved of its pain and rejoices. But whenever it is alone and in need, the lips of the passages
where the wing is pushing through dry and close and shut off the
growth, and the wing, imprisoned with desire, pulses like an artery,
pressing its way out so that the whole soul, goaded this way and
that, is crazed with pain, yet rejoices in the memory of the beauty it
has seen. Frenzied by the anxiety of both feelings together and the
perplexity of its strange plight, maddened by sleepless nights and
restless days, it is driven by its desire to where it thinks it will see him
who is beautiful. While looking on him desire now freed opens the
closed barriers ; the soul finds rest from stings and pains, and culls
the sweet pleasure of the moment. Thence it will not willingly
depart. Nothing is more precious than the beautiful beloved.
Mother, brother, friends are all forgotten, fortune lost through
neglect is of no account. Law and manners, in which it formerly
took pride, are all despised and it is ready to be a slave and to sleep
as near the object of desire as one allows it. And besides revering
the beautiful one it finds in him the only healer of its greatest
travail. That is the state that men call love. . . .'

Each man, we are told, reacts to love according to his character,
according, that is, to the god he followed on high. The
philosopher, as follower of Zeus, with more dignity; the soldier,
as follower of Ares, with more violence. The philosopher
wishes his beloved to be divine in his soul, a lover of wisdom—
he studies the character of his god and tries to make his beloved
as like to Him as possible. And so with the followers of the
other gods. Socrates then proceeds to describe the effect of

Eros upon the soul in another way, by means of the parable
of the soul as the charioteer and the two horses. The dark
horse does not wish to obey the goad of the charioteer but
leaps at the beloved. Dragged away against his will he leaps
forward again and again until he is tamed at last, and the
lover's soul, fearful and respectful, can safely approach the
beloved (255a) :

' Being cared for in every way like unto a god by a lover no longer
dissembling but quite sincere, the beloved himself naturally returns
friendship for care. If then he has been blamed formerly by his
fellows or any one else who told him that it is shameful to go near a
lover, and has thus sent him away, yet as time passes his age and his
need of him will lead him to accept his company. For it is decreed
that the bad will never be friend to the bad, or the good not friend
to the good. And when they thus come together and converse, the
goodwill of the lover fills the beloved with wonder when he perceives
that not all his other friends and relatives offer him any affection at
all, compared to his divinely inspired friend.
And when this has lasted for some time, and he comes near him
and touches him either in the gymnasia or at other times when they
are together, then the source of that stream which Zeus called desire
(ἵμερος) when in love with Ganymede, flows strongly upon the lover
and some disappears into him and some, when he is filled, overflows.
And like a breeze or the echo that leaps back from hard smooth
surfaces to whence it came, thus the stream of beauty makes its
way back to the beautiful boy through his eyes and naturally pene-
trates to his soul and causes his wings to grow, moistens the channels
where they sprout and the soul of the beloved is in turn filled with
love. Then he too loves, but he knows not whom. He does not
know what he feels and cannot explain it, like one whose eyes have
been infected through another, and he does not know the cause, so he
does not realize that it is himself he sees in his lover, reflected as from
a mirror. And when the other is present, his ache ceases as does
the other's, and in his absence he desires and is desired, for he now
feels the requital of love (ἀντέρως) which is an image of love itself.
This he calls, and believes it to be, not love (ἔρως) but friendship
(φιλία). Like the lover, but less strongly, he wants to see, to touch,
to kiss, to lie together. And it is likely that soon after this he does
these things. And when they sleep together the lover's undisciplined
horse has something to say to the charioteer and deems that he will
get a little delight for his many troubles. That of the beloved has
nothing to say, but embraces his lover in perplexity, and throws his

arms round him, clinging to him as to one who wishes him well, and
whenever they lie together, he cannot for his part deny anything,
if the lover ask for satisfaction. But the other horse and the
charioteer strain against this with shame and reason. And if the
better part of the lover's mind win through to the appointed way of
life and to philosophy, they lead henceforth a happy and united life,
masters of themselves and disciplined, having subjugated evil in their
soul, and freed virtue. And in the end, light and winged they have
won one of the three truly Olympian bouts, than which there is no
greater blessing which either self-control and moderation or divine
inspiration can give to men.

But if they live a commoner life, that of the lover of honour, not the
lover of wisdom, then it will easily happen when drunk or at some
other moment of carelessness that their two undisciplined horses will
capture their unguarded souls, lead them together, and take what
the majority call the blessed choice, and go through with it.
And when they have done so, they will continue this relationship,
though sparingly because what they do has not the approval of their
whole soul. These two live their lives as mutual friends, though they
are less so than those others, both throughout their passion and afterwards, for they deem that they have given and received the greatest
pledges which it is not right ever to transgress and become enemies.
When at last they leave the body they are wingless but they have
started on the road that leads to wings, and they thus get no small
reward for their erotic madness. For it is the law that those who
have started on the heavenly road shall not go the journey below the
earth, but they live on in the light journeying together and when the
time comes they will grow wings together because of their love.

Such are the divine gifts of a lover's affection, dear youth. But
intercourse with one who does not love, mixed with but human
moderation, leads only to a human and a small result ; it is conduct
unworthy of a free man and, though praised by the majority as
producing virtue in the loved soul, it makes this soul to roam upon
the earth or below it in ignorance for nine thousand years.'

Socrates ends his discourse with an invocation to Eros and the
rest of the dialogue continues the discussion of rhetoric. The
Phaedrus, unlike the *Symposium*, begins and ends with the love-
relationship between individuals, and as this is Plato's fullest
pronouncement on the subject, the above lengthy quotations
were inevitable. In this last speech Socrates has most carefully
explained the nature of the real Eros. Based upon a realization
of the eternal universal Ideas, awakened by the sight of physical

beauty in men, it aims at leading the beloved also to an understanding of beauty and truth, and the common search for these
can, in this dialogue at least, be successful only when motivated
by the joy of love requited.

We shall see that the *Phaedrus* makes important contributions
to the Platonic conception of the soul and the gods. We
also find Eros here more definitely linked with the Ideas by
means of the recollection of them which is quickened by the
contemplation of earthly beauty. This is very natural in a
later dialogue. But as far as Eros itself is concerned, the main
difference with the *Symposium* is that there is in the *Phaedrus* a
much fuller description of the working of the passion in the
individual soul ; its roots remain more firmly fixed in sexual
attraction between individuals, while in the earlier dialogue
this attraction is rather lost sight of. But it would be a mistake
to attach too much importance to this difference or to find in
it a development in the conception of Eros between the two
dialogues. The *Phaedrus* speeches are after all specimen
speeches on the definite topic of the love relationship between
individuals and this obviously accounts for the difference of
approach. And apart from this difference of emphasis, the
Platonic Eros is essentially the same in both dialogues. They
may therefore be discussed together.

In both we find the same three kinds of lovers. The lowest
kind, the victims of a selfish and purely physical infatuation,
are condemned with equal severity by Pausanias and Socrates.
Above them stand the better lovers of Pausanias ; these, not
being true philosophers, will indulge in sexual intercourse,
though sparingly. In both dialogues Plato treats them with
sympathy, not with contempt or ridicule. They are weaker
brethren no doubt, but then there are few human beings with
the self-control of a Socrates ; and Plato was the last person
to expect a great number. He admits that such love is inspiring and that it helps men to progress towards the life of philosophy, mythically expressed in the *Phaedrus* as the growing of
wings. These lovers must have moderation—as who must not ?
—in their passion, and, since all men aim at the highest, their
way of life cannot be entirely satisfactory, we are told, even
to themselves. But it was evidently not a contemptible
compromise for a Greek, caught, owing to the unfortunate

circumstances of contemporary life, between an ideal of almost impossible chastity on the one hand, and on the other love of women which could not, whether owing to woman's inferiority or his own instincts, be more to him than mere physical desire almost devoid of the psychological elements which every intelligent and civilized human being requires in his affections.

Well above him and supreme in the Platonic scale of lovers is the true philosopher in love. There is no question of physical intercourse here. We may call this ' Platonic love ' in the usual sense, provided we remember that the lovers belong to the same sex, that their aim is mutual inspiration in the search for truth and goodness, not mutual delight. There is also the difference that Plato does not deny the physical basis of this love. His lovers do desire physical intercourse but control this desire and transmute it into a passion for common study. That is the point of the tale of Alcibiades' temptation of Socrates, and the lover's resistance in the *Phaedrus* is described in terms which remind one of that episode. But a certain amount of kisses and embraces are allowed, which should be enough to convince us that Plato is sufficiently Greek not to be repelled by such expressions of homosexual affection.

And if he stopped short of allowing this Eros its full physical expression it is because such intercourse is unnatural in that it has no natural issue. Considered in this way it is useless and thus, to Plato, neither good nor beautiful. But there is little in his writings to suggest that his revulsion from full heterosexual intercourse was not equally strong. The reference to ' those who go on all fours and beget ' and the whole tone of the *Phaedrus* as well as the *Symposium* do not encourage one to think otherwise. Throughout, marriage is only a means of procreation ; only at the end of his life, in a passage of the Laws, does this stern disapproval show any sign of relenting.[1]

In another way too Plato's conception of philosophic love is difficult for us to accept. As we follow the philosopher on his upward journey we feel that something has gone wrong, that passionate oratory has somehow left love behind ; that in the contemplation of supreme beauty the philosopher may indeed find a sublime satisfaction, but we would hardly call this the satisfaction of love which must surely be limited to relations

[1] See note at the end of this chapter.

between individuals. If we look closer we shall find that the
point where we should part company with Plato is when
Diotima reaches the beauty of ' laws and institutions '. Love,
we feel, must have and retain some sort of physical basis and
Plato has here, though to a less extent in the *Phaedrus*, been
carried away on the tide of his own magnificent metaphors.
But before we thus lightly dismiss the metaphors it is important
to realize that they are still in common use in every civilized
language: We not only speak of love of country—which can
logically perhaps be reduced to love of one's countrymen but is
essentially something quite different—we also speak of love of
honour, of institutions ; and we speak of the love of God.
Such persistent misuse of words, if misuse it is, must point to
a very strong connexion between the emotions concerned.

Such a connexion Plato is ever at pains to emphasize. Indeed he insists not only on the connexion but on the identity.
We have seen the physical pleasures pale into insignificance
before the ' pure ' pleasures of the mind in the *Republic* and
the *Philebus*.[1] We shall see that the passionate love of truth
in the mind is the same stream of desire which expresses itself
in physical passions, redirected towards the attainment of
knowledge.[2] We cannot therefore say that Plato was carried
away by his own metaphors, for he very definitely asserts that
they are not metaphors at all. In this he was no doubt guided
by his own experience. It must have been true in his own
case that the longing he felt for mental discoveries was, if not
as intense, at least as real as, and more lasting than, any longing
for physical satisfaction. The two feelings seemed to him
essentially the same, and he called them both Eros. And this
may be true enough.

He knew physical desire of course. He also knew that affection for boys and men, friendship, which can be satisfied and
be a source of great delight with the minimum of physical
contact. Teaching always remained to him a communion
between master and pupil, research always a common quest
between friends. He knew that man cannot stand alone,
that he needs sympathy from, and interchange of ideas with,
congenial minds. And here the homosexual habits of his
contemporaries may have helped him to dissociate Eros from

[1] Pp. 70, 80.   [2] Pp. 135 ff.

all physical contacts. On the one hand the love of woman was debased to the mere physical level, on the other the love of man for man could, he thought and probably knew from experience, be uprooted from the physical plane altogether. And since this Eros led in intelligent intercourse to interesting discoveries through mental contact, he based upon it his conception of Eros as the motive power of all intellectual activities. It remained quite definitely rooted in sex attraction, homosexual attraction for the most part, and that he fully realized this the *Symposium* and the *Phaedrus* are there to prove. To those who still deny it, it is idle to attempt a proof of what Plato himself has expressed with crystal clearness.[1] This flight away from the physical raises a further question. How far are we to take each higher step reached as cancelling the one before? Is one who has reached the final goal, the perfect understanding of reality and the contemplation of it as supreme beauty, one who is producing perfectly virtuous actions, the perfect man in short, is he still to enjoy the sight of physical beauty?

It seems difficult to exclude the lower stages, even when the higher are reached. But they will lose greatly in importance. We know that Socrates could drink with the best, and it seems absurd to suppose that he did not enjoy it; so elsewhere Plato regards pleasure as the natural concomitant of the reasonable life in every part of the soul. What we do have to exclude, however, is any violent desire, any Eros, for physical pleasure. We also know that Socrates had a marvellous endurance and could withstand privations better than any one. That was because his longings were concentrated upon higher things, and though, being human, he had to feel the need of food, as long as he had enough to keep him well, the slight pleasure he felt in the process of eating did not interest him much—he knew of such far greater delights. And we must suppose that Plato's attitude was much the same with regard to sex. The physical urge might presumably be satisfied in

---

[1] As Wilamowitz (I, 44) has well put it : ' Diese Erotik aber wurzelt in Gefühlen der Knabenliebe, die uns fremd bleiben, weil sie wider die Natur sind, und die wir doch geschichtlich nicht nur begreifen, sondern nachempfinden müssen, sonst bleibt uns Sokrates schlechthin unverstandlich, und von Platon erhalten wir nur ein verblasstes oder verzerrtes Bild.'

marriage, but even that urge would be considerably weakened by concentration of desire upon the problems of dialectic.

That is why the philosopher, as we are told in the *Republic* (604c), when he loses one near and dear to him, will not give way to grief like other men but face the future bravely and get on with his work. And this will be made easier for him because the very intensity of his universal interests makes him less dependent upon others. But his entire soul, when governed by reason, still has pleasure in its every part, and thus presumably desire—for without desire there can be no pleasure—and the aim is balance and harmony under the control of guiding intellect. There is no need to read asceticism into Plato. In his post-*Phaedo* writings at any rate, it is not there, even though at times his passion for the blessings of the intellect drives him into forms of expression that come near to it. What he does say is that the intellectual life is so much more satisfying, so much more real, that those who have once known it will lose a great deal of the ordinary man's interest in things physical.

Up to a point this is undoubtedly true. The thinker does take less interest in his food than the common man, is less dependent upon his nearest and dearest, less enslaved to his physical passions, though he will still need the love and support of a friend and lover, whether man or woman. And in this he will be successful only if his universal interests, though they may have weakened his other passions, do not deny their existence, or try to stamp them out. The result, as Plato often said, must be balance and harmony, with intellect as a benevolent monarch, not a tyrant, in the soul. And it was Plato's belief that in a real philosopher or lover of wisdom, harmony would be the inevitable result. The disharmonious soul merely paid lip-service to philosophy, and the love of truth had not truly entered into his heart.

Such is the Platonic love, the love of truth and beauty quickened by mutual affection. It is regrettable, no doubt, that in his philosophy the love of man for woman had no place, that he therefore sought his higher Eros between man and man, and since, appealing to the animal kingdom, he realized that homosexual intercourse was unnatural, he was led to dissociate Eros from its physical basis altogether. But even those who, in a more fortunate era, may be able to make a synthesis of the mental and the physical in love (a synthesis which in his own way Pausanias also tried to achieve) where the circumstances of his time led Plato to divorce them almost completely, may well learn a good deal from him, were it only from his insistence upon the psychological and intellectual factors without which all love is only a rather tiresome animal instinct.

NOTE

THE passage in the eighth book of the *Laws* (836b–842a) which is Plato's last pronouncement on the subject, agrees with what has gone before except that homosexual intercourse is more definitely condemned than elsewhere (except in the *ideal* republic) and that he seems less hostile to love between man and woman. He begins by condemning sexual intercourse between men as unnatural, on the analogy of the animal world, and also because it does not lead to virtue.

There follows a division of φιλία, the more general term, into that of like for like, here equated with the good love, and that of unlike for unlike based on need, which he here equates with the wild infatuation condemned elsewhere also ; and a third kind mixed of the first two, which is at odds with itself : one part bids it take its fill of bodily joy, the other part prefers contemplation (ὁρῶν δὲ μᾶλλον ἢ ἐρῶν, 837c) and is in love with the soul. This last is the better lover of Pausanias and it should be noted that Plato is evidently thinking so far mainly or solely of homosexual love. He desires to rid his city of both the inferior loves by declaring them impious so that men shall refrain from them as they now refrain from incest.

The actual law which he proposes, in consequence, forbids homosexual relations altogether, and allows intercourse only with the woman by whom one intends to have a child. This will mean the end of excesses and further ' men will be friends to their wives ' (γυναιξί τε αὐτῶν οἰκείους εἶναι φίλους, 839b). He declares this not impossible since athletes have been known to practise continence.

Yet it is curious to find how much opposition he expects ; and indeed he goes so far as to propose a second-best law (841a). This is to make sexual pleasure shameful (presumably with the exception allowed above, though he does not say so) so that the practice will be difficult and infrequent. In this way, though we will not expect continence, men will be ashamed to be caught (τὸ δὲ μὴ λανθάνειν αἰσχρόν, 841*b*). He thus expects three factors to act as restraints : first piety, since sexual relations are now taboo except in marriage, as incest always was ; second, ambition, for men will lose their reputation if they are caught ; third, the higher love, where it exists.

This strange second best, by which Plato hopes to achieve a tolerable morality, bears a strong resemblance to the general modern practice. We may well doubt whether the advantages which Plato hopes from repression and hypocrisy are not likely to lead to worse evils than he is trying to avoid. His chief aim, however, is to eradicate pederasty, and adultery with it ; love between the sexes remains secondary.

Nevertheless it is interesting to find in this work of Plato's old age a glimmer of understanding of what love between the sexes might be, especially if we may include it under the heading of love between equals of which he approves at 837*a*. But I doubt whether he intended this. As so often, the suggestion of man and wife as ' friends ' is thrown out casually, and its possibilities left unexplored in the most tantalizing manner.

IV

THE NATURE OF THE SOUL

THE most common abstract words in any language frequently defy exact translation. *Ψυχή*, which as a rule we needs must translate by ' soul ', does not in fact mean the same thing at all. For instance, where Socrates argues at length that the soul is immortal, a modern thinker would rather argue for its existence and consider immortality to belong to it by definition. But the Greek word primarily means the principle of life in any being, and whatever is alive must possess it by that very fact. The word continued to be used in this vague sense both in everyday language, where such an expression as *περὶ ψυχῆς ὁ δρόμος* [1] means simply that 'it is a case of life and death', and also in philosophical discussions. We shall not be surprised, then, to find Simmias suggesting in the *Phaedo* that the psyche is merely the harmonious arrangement of the bodily parts. That theory is there rejected, but the point I wish to emphasize is that even in the fifth century the word ' psyche ' was not automatically linked with the conception of immortality. So towards the end of the *Republic*, after several discussions of the parts and functions of the soul, the subject of immortality is introduced as follows (608*d*) ;

' Do you not know, I said, that the soul is immortal and is never destroyed ? '
And he (Glaucon) looked at me in surprise and said : ' Heavens no ! Can you prove that ? '

It is true that we find a belief in immortality in very early times, and that the part of man which survives death is then called the psyche. But it is as well to remember that in Homer

---

[1] *Theaetetus,* 172*e*. For an interesting discussion of the word *ψυχή* see Burnet, *Essays and Addresses,* pp. 141 ff. (The Socratic doctrine of the soul).

life after death is but a shadowy counterpart of full-blooded life on earth. The souls fly to Hades shrieking like bats, they cannot speak to Odysseus until a draught of living blood has restored a little life to them, and the dead Achilles complains that he would rather be a servant to the poorest man on earth than king among the dead. There is no suggestion that the psyche is in any way man's highest or noblest part. There is nothing spiritual about Homer's souls and his dead would gladly come back to life, however painful.

The conception of the soul as the highest part of man seems to have been imported into Greece by those mystical teachers and prophets who are usually somewhat summarily lumped together as the Orphics. Their doctrines came from the East ; they seem to have taught an immortality that was no longer a pale reflection of earthly life, but a release from the body and a deliverance. The body to them was the prison or tomb of the soul—σῶμα σῆμα, as they pithily expressed it. Man then aims at the purification of this soul, and after many incarnations rises to perfection and is absorbed, or reabsorbed, into the divine. It was probably under Orphic influence that the Pythagoreans developed their way of life as a gradual process of purification. But to them this immortal psyche was the intellectual power of man and purification lay to a large extent through a strictly scientific, which to them meant a mathematical, training ; though some of them seem to have laid a great deal of emphasis on number-magic and on ritual. From them must have come the conception of the intellect as the noblest and immortal part of man, of salvation through knowledge, the conception so magnificently expressed in the *Phaedo*, and it remained with Plato to the end.

This emphasis on the intelligence as the most divine thing in man, the most essentially human because the only part of himself which he does not share with the animal kingdom, is one of the most important differences between the Platonic and the Christian doctrines of the soul and should be kept in mind throughout. But here again 'intelligence' is not a very happy translation, for the supremacy of the intellect did not to Plato imply the denial of emotion, as it is so frequently, if mistakenly, thought to imply it to-day. All this will become clearer as we study the texts, but we must be on our guard from the beginning

against the instinctive associations of the word soul with any
spiritual values which are quite separate from, if not actually
hostile to, intelligence and reason.   To Socrates and to Plato,
as to Aristotle, the activities of the soul culminated in the
intellect as its highest function.   So much so that ' mind ' is
at times a far more suitable translation of ψυχή.

Though the influence of the Pythagoreans on Socrates can
be exaggerated, it is well established ; and his theory of the
human psyche is a natural development of their general
point of view.   To him the soul was that which directs, or
should direct, men's lives by ruling over and controlling the
body and its passions.   This is the meaning of the famous
tendance of the soul, which he makes the aim of every individual
and every state.   The clearest and simplest statement of it is
found in the *Charmides*.   The beautiful young Charmides is
asking him for a cure for headache which Socrates professed
to know.   It is, says Socrates, a certain herb, together with
an incantation, which will cure far more than headaches (156*b*) :

' Perhaps you have yourself heard good doctors say to a patient
who comes to them for eye-trouble, that they cannot heal the eyes
alone but that it is necessary to treat the whole head before they can
effect a cure, and further that they believe it sheer ignorance to treat
the head by itself apart from the rest of the body.   Hence they turn
their attention to diet for the whole body and attempt to cure the
part along with the whole.   Or have you not noticed that they say
this, and that such is the case ?
—Certainly, he said.
—Do you think they are right ?   Do you accept their point of
view ?
—Most certainly, he replied.
—And when I heard him agree I was heartened.   My confidence
returned by degrees and I was keen.   I said :
Now this incantation, Charmides, is something of the same kind.
I learned it when on active service from one of the Thracian doctors
of Zamolxis, who, they say, even make people immortal.   This
Thracian said that when our Greek doctors spoke in the way we have
just mentioned, they were right.   " But Zamolxis, said he, who is
our king and a god, says that just as one should not attempt to treat
the eyes without treating the head nor the head without the rest of
the body, so one should not minister to the body apart from the soul.
That is the reason why the majority of ailments elude doctors in

Greece, because they neglect the whole which should be their care. For if the whole is ailing, the part cannot be well."

He said that everything good and evil in the body and in the whole man originated in the soul and spread thence as from the head to the eyes. The soul then should be our first and our greatest care, if the head and the rest of the body are to be well. And, my friend, he said the soul must be tended by incantations, and that these incantations are beautiful conversations. From such conversations self-control and moderation arise in men's souls, and once they are present it is easy to bring health to the head and the rest of the body.

Then when he taught me this remedy and incantation he said : " Let no one persuade you to treat his head unless he first submit to the incantation's treatment of the soul. For that is the mistake men make now : some try to be doctors without either moderation or health. They should have both." And he enjoined me not to allow any man, however rich, well-born or beautiful, to persuade me otherwise. I swore I would not and I must keep my oath. To you too, if you are willing to surrender your soul to the influence of the Thracian's incantations, I will give the cure for a headache. Without that we cannot help you, my dear Charmides.'

Here we have the Socratic doctrine in its clearest, its simplest and its most moderate form. Health and virtue—in this case the virtue of moderation—are parallel to each other, complete each other. Everything depends on the soul, but the ultimate aim is the health, physical and moral, of the whole man. This is, in the main, the attitude of the earlier short dialogues, though more emphasis is usually laid upon the soul and less consideration given to the body.[1]

It is the essential inferiority of the body and its pleasures which we also find insisted on in the *Gorgias*.[2] In that dialogue occurs the interesting parallel between different arts : just as the body is developed by physical training and its defects, once they have arisen, are cured by medicine, so the soul's healthy development is the object of law-making and its defects corrected by the administration of justice.[3] It follows that the health of the body and that of the soul are objects of knowledge and require systematic investigation.

That the soul is immortal appears from the myth of the day of judgement at the end of the *Gorgias*, but it should be clearly

---

[1] See e.g. *Laches*, 185e.　　[2] See pp. 52 ff.　　[3] See p. 209.

understood that Socrates' arguments for the good life are in
no way based upon it in the first instance and that, here as
elsewhere, his ethical system stands even if this immortality is
denied. The myth is an addendum, not an argument. At
least until in his later dialogues immortality followed from
premises he had by then worked into his philosophy, Plato
was inclined not to treat the belief in it as a main argument
for, but only as an added inducement to, the good life.

We find the immortality of the soul also in the *Meno*, though
still in mythical form.[1] It is emphasized in the course of the
discussion and is used to introduce the theory that knowledge
is only recollection, that learning is only remembering what our
soul knew before birth. This theory will be used in sober
argument elsewhere when immortality is the actual subject
under discussion. It at least illustrates very vividly the fundamental conception of education that is Plato's, that education
consists in drawing out, not in putting in (81*c*) :

' The soul then, being immortal, has come to birth many times.
It has seen what is here and in the underworld and all things, and
there is nothing which it has not learned. No wonder it can recollect
what it knew before about virtue and other things. For as the
whole of nature is akin and the soul has learned everything, there is
nothing to prevent a man—after first recollecting one thing, which
is what we call to learn something—from finding out all the rest for
himself, if he is courageous and does not weary of his search. For
all research and learning is but recollection.'

But the first dialogue to make a real contribution to our
present subject is, as we would expect, the *Phaedo* where
Socrates, on the day of his death, is attempting to prove the
immortality of the soul. Recollection appears again, this time
in connexion with the theory of Ideas, which enables Socrates
to express his belief in the essential kinship of the human soul
with the world of thought. We also find, in a form more
violent and more uncompromising than anywhere else in

---

[1] This is clear from the way it is introduced (81*a–b*). ' Poets and priests '
have said the soul is immortal, which is the regular way of introducing a
myth. The whole argument is meant to show that we need not believe
those who say that ' we cannot find out what we do not know ' (see p. 12).
And Socrates does not insist upon the details of the refutation (86*b*), only
that it can be refuted.

Plato, an excessive dualism, an almost complete divorce, between soul and body.

In the introductory part of the dialogue we are told that death is a boon to the thinker, indeed that the pursuit of philosophy is but a practice for death. Death is the separation of soul from body and it is the aim of the philosophic soul to free itself, even during life, from the obstacles, such as distracting pleasures and confusing sensations, which the body puts in the way of the soul's development. It is by reasoning, as far as possible without the help of the bodily senses, that the mind can reach truth and the apprehension of the eternal Forms. Socrates expounds this theory of purification from the body in a passage of great eloquence in which the word καθαρός, pure, and its derivatives—words strongly charged with orphic associations—occur with significant frequency (66b) :

' As long as we have our body, and the soul is confused with this evil, we shall never satisfactorily attain the object of our desires, which we say is truth. For the body keeps us busy in a thousand ways through its need of food. Further, disease may hinder us in the pursuit of truth. The body fills us with desires, passions and fears, all kinds of imaginings and nonsense, so that we can never understand by means of it anything in truth and in reality, as we call it. It is the body and its passions that make for wars, revolutions and battles. For all wars are due to the acquisition of wealth, and wealth must be acquired because of the body, enslaved as we are to its care. And because of all this we have no time for philosophy. Worst of all, when we have some respite from it and proceed to some investigation, it interferes once more at every point in our search, interrupts, disturbs and intimidates us, so that we cannot, because of it, contemplate the truth. We have in fact proved that, if we are ever to have any pure knowledge, we must escape from the body and consider things in themselves with our soul (mind) alone. Then, it would seem, we shall realize the wisdom that we desire and love, after death, as our argument shows, not during life.'

From this and many similar passages in the *Phaedo* we find that the soul is thought by Socrates to be that part of man by which he knows or apprehends those eternal objects of knowledge, the Forms or Ideas, and only that part. The soul is here a unity and it does not include anything beyond the reason or intellect. Pitted against it at every turn is the body as the seat of sense-perception, of passions and desires, of pleasure.[1] The way of philosophy is to withdraw oneself as far as possible from all these bodily affections, to ' purify ' oneself from them, to grant them no mercy and to keep them rigidly under control. It is the ' way of death,[2] since only after death can we find that wisdom which is the aim of life !

His belief in the immortality of the soul so understood Socrates supports by three main arguments :

The first is based on rebirth and runs as follows. There is an old belief that our souls from here go to another world and that from there they return hither. This is but a particular example of the general principle that all things are born from their opposite. Living souls then come from souls that are dead and the dead from the living. If this general principle is accepted we must have the double journey, from death to life as well as from life to death (72*b*) :

' for if things of one kind did not ever yield to the other kind as they come to be, travelling in a circle as it were, but one thing became another in a straight line to its opposite and did not turn back on its return journey, then everything would in the end be of the same kind, reach the same state, and cease to become '.

That is to say, all souls and indeed everything that changes would, if change were in one direction only, ultimately reach the same terminus and cease to be.

The second argument is based on the doctrine of recollection, and on the existence of Ideas which are the objects of recollection. If you admit that the Forms exist and that knowledge is the recollection of them, caused by sense perception—and this, after due explanation of Socrates' meaning, Simmias and Kebes enthusiastically do—then the existence of the soul before birth necessarily follows, and if it exist before birth it will also, on the strength of the first argument (opposite from opposite) exist after death.

The third and last argument is also based on the theory of Ideas. Granted the existence of these, we have two kinds of

---

[1] Wilamowitz (I, 341) says of the soul in the *Phaedo* : sie ist vielmehr durchaus eine Einheit, als Gegensatz zum Körper erfasst.
There is indeed a hint of higher pleasures, but only a hint. See p. 64.
[2] ' Weg des Todes ', Friedländer, I, 75.

existence ; the one of simple eternal, unchanging Forms, the objects of knowledge ; the other of particulars composite, mortal and ever-changing. The first is divine, the other is not. Which of the two does the soul resemble ? As its very nature is to rule over the body and to apprehend the Forms, it must surely be similar to the Forms and akin to the divine (78–80) Hence it must itself be simple and not composite (ἀσύνθετον). It is therefore more likely to be indissoluble or almost so.

Socrates then repeats with greater emphasis the doctrine of separation from the body and all its ways : some souls, through contact with the body, become heavy and body-like themselves. After death they wander as shadowy ghosts on the outskirts of the physical world until they are once more attracted into the bonds of the body, or indeed descend into animal life. The fate of those who are ruled by ambition rather than love of possessions is not so bad, and politicians perhaps become bees or ants. But high above them all the soul of the philosopher, freed from the pleasures and pains which nail body and soul together (84a), freed, that is, from the body

' following reason and concentrating upon this, it contemplates the truth and the divine, sees what is beyond belief, and is nurtured by it, thinks that in this manner it must live as long as life lasts, and when it dies it goes to that which is like unto itself and is freed from the evils of human life '.

Two conceptions of the soul are now brought forward by Simmias and Kebes. One, that the soul is a harmony, that the soul is to the body as melody is to the lyre, that as the body is stretched and held together by the hot and the cold, the dry and the moist, &c., so our soul is, as it were, ' the harmonious mixture of these when they are mixed in due measure '. The second suggestion is that, though the soul may exist before birth, it may perish when we do. The body may outlast the soul, but this proves nothing, for so a weaver might wear out many coats in the course of his life but his last coat will survive him (87). That the soul is essentially more lasting than the body has been proved, but it does not follow that the soul itself may not come to an end, after either one or several lives.

Dealing with the first theory, that the soul is a harmony,

Socrates points out that in that case it cannot exist prior to the body, and that if you believe in the soul as a harmony you cannot believe in Recollection. Further, a harmony cannot oppose its parts, yet a struggle between soul and body is a recognized fact (93a, 94b). Thirdly, if the soul is a harmony it must be harmonious or not exist at all ; it follows that men whose souls are not a perfect harmony have no soul at all. And what is to be the relation between goodness and the soul ? A harmony of a harmony ? That is absurd, and one must, since a harmony either is complete or does not exist, be driven to conclude that all men—since they all have a soul—are equally harmonious, that all their parts and functions are a perfect blend, and that all men are equally good. The soul cannot therefore be a harmony.

To the second suggestion (that the soul might outlast several bodies and yet perish) Socrates does not immediately reply, but interrupts the argument with an account of the development of his own thought and of his disappointment with the physical philosophers who confuse the how with the why (98c). He himself finds in the theory of Ideas, which he here further describes, the only satisfactory explanation of the why of things.[1]

Upon this theory, when he returns to the main argument, he bases what is not so much an answer to Kebes as a fourth attempt to prove the immortality of the soul. He has explained how a particular thing not only participates in its own Form, but also in some other Forms that are essential to it, and that it cannot be invested with a Form which is the opposite of any property it necessarily contains. Three, for example, not only contains the Form threeness but also that of the odd. It cannot contain the Form of the even. Fire cannot admit cold, and so on. In the same way whatever has soul has life, life is thus the inevitable concomitant of soul, so that the latter cannot admit death which is the opposite of life and is therefore deathless (105).

This is not the place to examine at length the validity of the four arguments for immortality. We will merely note in passing that the first is based on an extension of the principle that ' opposite is born from opposite ', that the other three

[1] See p. 18.

are based upon a belief in the existence of the Forms and of Recollection. The last argument further rests upon an ambiguity in the word ἀθάνατος, deathless.[1] Its proper conclusion is not that the soul is immortal but that a dead soul cannot exist, that soul and death are two mutually exclusive terms, and that when a man dies his soul goes on living or ceases to exist at all, a conclusion with which no one could possibly quarrel.

We have now learned, not only that Plato considers the soul to be immortal but that he considers it to be in some essential way akin to the eternal Forms, changeless, simple, without parts, ever the same. We have noted also that the soul as here described is essentially the mind and the intellect, that it stands in direct opposition to the body, its passions and its pleasures, and that it aims at being as completely separated from it as the world of Forms is from the world of sense. Clearly there is an implied contradiction in this, for if the philosopher has a passionate desire for truth he cannot be devoid of all emotion. But no solution is offered here. To regard philosophy as a training for death is a dangerously negative point of view in which no allowance is made for the development of the human emotions. There is good reason to regard the teaching of the Phaedo, splendid though it be, as pure intellectualism divorced from life, its final aim being the eternal preservation of the soul in the cold storage of eternally frozen absolute Forms.

But that is Plato's first word, not his last. He is putting before us in all their starkness the two extremes between which a synthesis must, and will, be made. From being intellect pure, which will always remain the master, (though even here it will be necessary to inquire with some care what Plato means by intellect and not to neglect the explanations he has given) [2] we shall find the soul gradually absorbing all of man that is not sheer physical matter. And in the Timaeus even that matter loses its solidity.

The emotional intensity of the Symposium reads like a violent

---

[1] Plato seems vaguely aware of this, and tries to equate ἀθάνατος and ἀνώλεθρος (indestructible) at 106b.
[2] See pp. 253 ff.

reaction against the all but complete denial of emotion which is characteristic of the *Phaedo*. It is possible to maintain that there is no contradiction between the theoretical position of the two dialogues and Plato certainly succeeded in making a synthesis between emotion and intellect in the psychology of the *Republic*. But the difference of approach, of emphasis, of general attitude, is clear and unmistakable ; it is the difference between repression and sublimation. In the *Phaedo* all the emphasis is on purity, death and immortality ; in the *Symposium* it is all on love, on beauty and on life. The philosopher's goal is no longer to cut himself off from all pleasure and desire but to rise by means of desire and love from the slavish infatuation for an individual to the adoring contemplation of supreme beauty ; and his ultimate aim is intellectual creation in that beauty (ἡ γέννησις καὶ ὁ τόκος ἐν τῷ καλῷ). Of death as a milestone on that road there is not a word. Immortality of the soul is not only not mentioned, it is all but denied.[1]

This vindication of the importance of emotion leads us straight to the problem dealt with in the later books of the *Republic*. With this dialogue and the *Phaedrus*, which probably followed it, we come to some very important developments in Plato's psychology. We saw that the *Phaedo* considers the soul as all but pure intellect, and immortal, and that the *Symposium* speaks of the offspring of a soul which is mortal. It may be to solve this contradiction that Plato came to examine whether the soul should not, indeed must not, be divided into different parts. He does so in the fourth book of the *Republic*. He has already established three classes in the state and, since goodness in the individual is the same as in the state, he concludes that there must also be three parts of the soul. This parallel, though he admits that it is not yet scientifically established (ἀκριβῶς 435*d*), is not a mere analogy to Plato, for he was deeply convinced of the close connexion between social and individual psychology. But he also argues from a common human experience, that of conflict in the mind. Now in accordance with the law of contradiction ('the same thing cannot act upon another, or be acted upon by it, in two contrary ways at the same time and in the same relation' 436*b*), which he takes some pains to explain, if it can happen that we

[1] See note at the end of this chapter.

feel thirsty and yet do not wish to drink, there must be something in our psyche that bids us drink, and something else that
forbids it. The latter is the reasoning or calculating part of
the soul (λογιστικόν), the former the passionate. And there
is also a third part that cannot satisfactorily be classed with
either. The story of Leontius (439e) :

' while coming up from the Piraeus on the outside of the northern
wall, he saw some corpses lying by the executioner. He both
wanted to look and at the same time was angry with himself and
turned away. For a time he struggled and covered his face, but,
overcome by his passion, he forced his eyes open and said to
them, rushing towards the corpses, " There then, you devils, have
your fill of the evil sight." '

proves that anger can oppose the passions and is therefore
different from them. We have then a third part of the soul,
the ' feelings '. This ' temper ' or ' feelings ' (θυμός) is found
to work under the command of reason and to be its ally. The
parallel with the state is now complete : reason in the individual corresponds to the ruler class in the city, the feelings to
the soldiers and the passions to the rest of the people.

The same tripartite division of the soul is found in the myth
of the *Phaedrus*,[1] and it will be most convenient to consider
the relevant passages at this point. The famous image of the
three parts of the soul as a team of two horses and a charioteer
is described as follows (246a) :

' To describe the nature of the soul is an altogether superhuman
and a long story, but it is a lesser task, and within human power, to
say what it resembles. So let us do that. The soul is like a team
of winged horses and a charioteer that have grown into one. Now

[1] The *Phaedrus* was most probably written after the *Republic*. See Ritter's
chronological tables, I, 254. Taylor (299 ff.) inclines to the same view,
though Shorey analyses it before the *Republic*. Robin (*L'Amour*, 62–120)
wants to date it near the *Timaeus*. He denies (144) that the tripartite
division of the soul in the *Phaedrus* corresponds to that in the *Republic*,
because the white and black horses follow the charioteer upon his heavenly
journey. How, he asks, can the lower parts of the soul be immortal ?
Plato himself raises this question at the end of the *Republic* (see below), but
the question is not raised in the *Phaedrus* and it is not necessary to press
the details of a myth in this way. In any case Robin's own equation of
the two horses with ' l'image de l'Autre ou de la Nécessité ' of the *Timaeus*
is completely unconvincing. The main point is that the soul is not looked
upon as a unit.

the horses and charioteers of the souls of the gods are all good themselves and of excellent lineage, but those of other souls are mixed. Our charioteer rules over the pair he drives ; one of his horses is beautiful and good and of similar parents, the other the opposite in both respects. Our driving is therefore necessarily difficult and troublesome.'

And the myth goes on to describe the journey of the dis-embodied souls, following the gods in groups according to their characters, lifted up by the love of beauty which causes their wings to grow. The gods, well above the rim of heaven, spend their whole time in the contemplation of the ideal Forms, and the human souls follow as best they can. In the clash and confusion of souls they too now and again catch a glimpse of the eternal Forms, but then lose their wings and drop back to earth. And here, through the love of beauty, the sight of earthly beauty causes them to remember the absolute beauty which they saw above, and thus the wings of the soul start to grow once more [1] (253c) :

' At the beginning of our tale we divided each soul into three, two parts like unto horses and one like a charioteer. So let it be now. Of the two horses the one we say is good, the other not. But we did not explain the goodness of the one or the badness of the other, and this we must now do. The right-hand horse is high of stature, with agile limbs, high neck, straight profile, white to look upon, dark-eyed, a lover of honour tempered by respect and moderation, a companion of true belief ; unafraid he needs no whip but is con-trolled by command and speech alone. The other is crooked, heavy, loose-jointed, with a short and thick neck, snub-faced, black in colour, grey-eyed and bloodshot, the companion of insolence and pride, shaggy about the ears, deaf and hardly yielding to the whip and the goad.

Whenever the charioteer looks into the eyes that he loves ; at the sight the warmth of love spreads through the soul and he is over-come by the goads of an itching desire—the obedient steed, now as always under the compulsion of respect, controls himself and does not leap upon the beloved. The other, submitting no longer to the driver's goad or the whip, leaps up violently and rushes forward. He gives no end of trouble to the charioteer and the other horse, compels them to approach their darling and to be mindful of the joys of love. . . .'

[1] See pp. 109 ff.

This division of the individual soul into three parts is a very great advance on all that had gone before.   In the *Phaedo* we find Plato distinguishing between three different types of men, whom he calls lovers of wisdom, lovers of honour and lovers of gain.   It has often been pointed out [1] that in this he was probably inspired by the Pythagorean doctrine of the three types of life open to men.   But those who interpret this Pythagorean doctrine as ' implying ' the tripartite division of the soul miss the whole point.   The difference is that whereas the *Phaedo* (and the Pythagoreans) speaks of three different types of *men*, in the *Republic* and the *Phaedrus* these become three *parts of the same soul*.   It is true that also in the *Phaedo* the philosopher has to overcome his passions, but these are not part of his soul.   By extending the meaning of ψυχή to include these passions and desires, Plato is brought to the notion of conflict within the individual mind or soul, a most valuable step and one of which he makes full use in the *Republic* and elsewhere.   We still have the three lives, but it is now a question of how the conflict has been solved, which part of the soul is in the ascendant.   The fundamental basis is the same for all men.   Far from being a ' primitive view ', this is very advanced ; one of the most startlingly modern things in Platonic philosophy is just this discovery of the importance of conflict in the mind.

We cannot, of course, prove that Plato had not his whole psychology worked out when he first put pen to paper, but for his readers at any rate this development takes place in the third and fourth books of the *Republic*.   In order to find justice in the individual we seek for it ' writ large ' in the state.

---

[1] Burnet (*Phaedo* on 68c ;   *Thales to Plato*, 42) Taylor, p. 281 and *Commentary*, p. 497 ; and Natorp (p. 527).   They all want to reduce the three parts of the soul to the three lives.   Natorp because he wants to make the *Phaedrus* the earlier work, Burnet and Taylor because here again they want to reduce Plato to the Pythagoreans.   Of course, even in the *Phaedo* the notion of conflict is present, but it is a conflict of soul versus body rather than a conflict within the soul.   Too much is made of a chance phrase in the *Gorgias* which seems to imply that the soul is not entirely homogeneous.   The actual words are (493b) ' that part of the soul where the passions reside ' (τοῦτο τῆς ψυχῆς οὗ αἱ ἐπιθυμίαι εἰσιν).   I agree with Wilamowitz (I, 231 n. ;   395) that these words should not be pressed. Burnet also relies on a quotation from Posidonius in Galen (*De Hipp. et Plat.*, p. 425, Kühn) and one from Iamblichus given in Stobaeus (*Ecl.*, 1, p. 369, Wachsmith) which attribute the tripartite soul to the Pythagoreans. It is quite likely that they too failed to see where the advance lay.

Not unnaturally we establish the three classes in the state to correspond to the three types of men, the three lives. Then, coming back to the individual, we follow the analogy of the state and are thus led to transfer the three types into the soul and they become three parts of the individual soul. And it is noteworthy that whereas Plato always refers to the three types of lives as common knowledge, he thinks it necessary to prove at some length the fact that there are parts of the soul. No doubt he saw the importance of the step he was taking.[1]

From then on the good life is the proper functioning of every part of the soul in its proper place and a man is master of himself when his feelings and [2] his passions are obedient to his intellect—the charioteer of the *Phaedrus*—as a state is its own master and happy when the councillors' commands are obeyed by the rest of the people and when each of the three classes is satisfied with its position (443c) :

' In truth then justice appears to be something of this kind. It is not concerned with external actions but with the inner state of a man and his several parts. He must not allow every part of himself to interfere where it has no business, the different kinds (γένη) of soul must not hinder one another. The just man puts his own house in order, thus ruling over himself, friendly with himself, harmonizing the three parts like the three notes of a melody —the high, the low and the middle, *and any others there may be between* —binding them all together so that from a multiplicity he becomes a unity, controlled and harmonious. In this manner he acts, whenever he does anything regarding the acquisition of wealth or the care of the body, or some public business or private contract. In all these he believes and declares a just and beautiful action to be that which preserves or achieves this state of harmony, and wisdom to him is the knowledge that presides over such deeds, whereas an

---

[1] See F. M. Cornford, *Psychology and Social Structure in the Republic of Plato* in *Class. Quart.*, 1912, pp. 247–65, who shows that the division of the state came first. He points to an interesting connexion with the three ages of man. Also Hackforth, *The Modification of Plan in Plato's Republic, C. Q.*, 1913, pp. 264–72.

[2] The middle part of the soul, θυμός, is often translated by ' spirit ', but the adjective spiritual, and the use of spirit in that sense, which has of course nothing to do with θυμός, make this ambiguous. The literal meaning is anger. Fear, indignation and the like belong to this part of the soul. I have therefore called it feelings, which in that sense are quite distinct from passions, as when we talk of saving a person's feelings. Perhaps ' sentiments ' (Cornford l.c.).

unjust action is that which ever destroys the harmony, and ignorance is the belief that presides over that.'

The division of the soul into three parts was never meant to be an exhaustive classification of all the soul's functions and the comparison with the notes of music hints as much in the last quotation. Nor does Plato lose sight for long of the essential unity behind the parts. On the contrary, he re-establishes this unity when, in describing the philosophic character he says (485d) :

' When a man's passions incline violently in one direction, they are, we know, weakened in other directions by this fact, like a stream that has been canalized.
—True.
—When they flow towards study and things of that kind and are concentrated upon the pleasures of the mind (psyche) alone, the physical pleasures are given up ; when a man, that is, is a true philosopher and does not merely pretend to be.
—Necessarily.
—Such a man will be controlled, and never greedy of wealth. . . .'

Nor is this an isolated illustrative passage, but it prepares us for the psychology of the ninth book. There, as we saw in our discussion of Pleasure,[1] Socrates tries to prove that the lover of wisdom is happier than the ambitious or the mercenary man. In so doing he makes it repeatedly clear that each part of the psyche not only has its own pleasures but its own passions and desires also (580d, 581c). Further, all parts of the soul have their function if they will obey the intellect (586e) :

' When the entire soul follows that part which loves wisdom, and is not rebellious, every part can fulfil its own function in other ways too and be good ; each can reap its own joys which are true as far as can be.'

These extracts point to another most important development in Platonic psychology. We saw how, by dividing the soul into parts Plato came to realize the importance of mental conflict. He now goes farther. Behind the very real diversity he rediscovers unity once more, and he pictures this unity as a

---

[1] See pp. 67 ff. For the metaphor used in the passage quoted cp. *Phaedrus*, 251e : ' canalizing desire ', ἐποχετευσαμένη ἵμερον.

stream of passionate desire which can be directed and canalized to different objects according to the character of the man. That the philosophic life had its own pleasures, and so must have its own desires, was more or less implied from the beginning. But there was, in the *Phaedo*, no explanation of how this could be. But now, by charging every part of the soul with its own passions, by insisting that the philosopher desires truth with the same passion as other men desire food, drink or sexual satisfaction (474*c* ff.) and making the difference one of direction, he makes clear once more that the aim is not repression but sublimation. If a man love truth as he should, the intensity of his physical passions will by that very fact be diminished. And in this weakened form they have their place. The accusation of anti-emotionalism, or at least of cold intellectualism so often levelled against Plato no longer holds. Intellect itself is now vivified by a stream of deep emotion. The three parts of the soul are now only three main channels along which this stream must flow.[1] This clear and explicit view should not be obscured by the fact that Plato still goes on speaking of the lowest part as the passionate. It always remains so, for the majority. All these desires are not the only function of the soul. They are, however, the one big vivifying factor which all parts have in common. And it is obvious that this stream of passion is no other than the Eros of the *Symposium* which rose from lower to higher until it became the passionate desire for creation in universal beauty. So that we have here a carefully propounded psychological theory which combines the uncompromising intellectualism of the *Phaedo* with the magnificent defence of emotion which is the *Symposium*.

There is a passage in the tenth book of the *Republic* which has, quite mistakenly, been interpreted as a correction of the tripartite division of the soul we have been discussing. Where he shows how far removed from the truth is imitative art, Socrates makes a distinction between ' that in the soul which perceives through the senses ' and ' that in the soul which knows '. The former is said to be full of confusion, the latter to bring order by the science of measurement. But this is in

---

[1] In the *Timaeus* (73*b*–74*a* ; 77*d*) a physical link between the three parts of the soul is provided by the marrow.

no sense a new twofold division. It is merely the usual division
of the cognitive faculties into perception and intellect, fully
explained before (523e ff.), which corresponds to the difference
between belief and knowledge (478), and their objects are
respectively the physical and the Ideal world as explained in
the central books. This antithesis is one of the most common
in Plato, indeed it is *the* Platonic antithesis. Of course, both
perception and reasoning are in the soul and part of the soul
but, unlike most of his commentators, Plato does not in fact
use the word part or form (μέρος, εἶδος) at all in this passage
(602c ff.). Not that it would have mattered if he had. He
does call perception inferior to knowledge, and he then proceeds to include the confusion of strong emotion as being also
encouraged by art and as being characteristic of the perceptive
stage of cognition.[1]

There are, at various points in the *Republic,* three separate
divisions of the soul : first the three parts, reason, feelings and
the passions ; then, in the simile of the line, two parts, each
again subdivided, understanding (νοῦς) and reasoning (διάνοια)
on the one hand, belief and imagination on the other ; [2] and
then in the tenth book the knowing and the perceptive parts.
This last corresponds to the main division of the line, and even
in the third book passion and feelings are contrasted with
reason, so that they naturally rely on perception and belief,
not on knowledge. That Plato easily passed from the cognitive
to the moral aspects of the psyche is not surprising, for the one,
to him, implied the other. Truth cannot be discovered unless
the main stream of desire be directed towards it. Hence the
confusion caused by unanalysed perception and that of immor-
ality go together and are corrected at the same time. These
various divisions of the mind or soul do not contradict each
other. None of them is meant to split the soul into separate
compartments and it is but natural that when a living continuum is studied from different points of view there should
only be a general correspondence between the different
divisions. At least it is natural for a philosopher whose aim is
to help us to understand the different sides of our nature, not to

---

[1] Note that both the δοξάζον and the λογιστικόν are said to be τῆς διανοίας
in 603b, 10.

[2] See p. 27.

create a fool-proof system of neat little compartments, which would nowhere correspond to the truth.

It is also in the tenth book of the *Republic* that we find a further argument in favour of the immortality of the soul. It may be summarized as follows :

Everything has its own good and its own evil ; the former benefits and preserves it, the latter corrupts and destroys it, and it can be destroyed by nothing else. So ophthalmia is the evil of the eye, disease the evil of the body, blight that of corn, and so on. If then we find something which cannot be destroyed by its own particular evil it will be indestructible. The evil of the soul is injustice, intemperance, cowardice and ignorance (the opposites of the four virtues, sin). But a man's soul cannot be destroyed by sin. A bad man continues to live (execution by law being, of course, an incidental and not a direct consequence of sin) ; therefore the soul is immortal, for physical disease, being the peculiar evil of the body and not of the soul, cannot kill the soul but only the body. He then repeats the argument from opposites which we met in the *Phaedo* and adds that the souls will always be the same. They have always existed for they cannot come to be from what is mortal (608d–611a).

This argument that vice cannot kill the soul is awkward in several ways. It implies a far more complete divorce between body and soul than we find elsewhere in the *Republic*, and though death does not follow from vice Socrates would have to admit that the soul is yet very definitely affected by it.[1] Further, we cannot but ask whether all the parts of the soul are now immortal or, if not, which part is. Plato realizes this difficulty but he does not solve it here. He says (611b) :

' That the soul is immortal is proved by our present argument and others. But its true nature we must not examine in its present state, harmed as it is by communion with the body and other evils, but such as it is when pure ; in that state it should be considered by our mind and to find that is to find also a clearer examination of the just and the unjust and all we have spoken of. Now we can only speak the truth about the soul as it appears to us, for we examine it in the

[1] e.g. the passage here quoted and 408 ff., where it is said that the judge must not have any personal experience of evil for it will affect his soul.

same state as Glaucus was when he rose from the sea. People could not recognize his original nature because some parts of his body had been torn off, he had been harmed by the waves, and accretions clung to him, shells and seaweed and pieces of rock, so that he appeared more like any kind of a beast than what he really was. So we see the soul affected by a thousand evils. But this is the way we must look at it, Glaucon.

—How?

—We should look at its love of wisdom, consider what associations it reaches out to and longs for, how it is akin to the divine and the immortal, what it would become if it followed this longing entirely and by that desire were lifted out of the sea wherein it now resides, after the stones and shells which cling to it now had been knocked off. For now it feasts upon the earth and many earthy, stony and wild incrustations cling to it as a result of those so-called happy feasts. Then might one see the soul's true nature, whether it has many aspects or only one (εἴτε πολυειδὴς εἴτε μονοειδής, cp. *Phaedrus*, 271*a*), or what its nature may be. Now, however, I think we have fairly described its forms and attributes in human life.'

Thus, when Plato comes to consider the problem of immortality in the light of his more advanced psychology, he is at once faced with the difficulty that, while the arguments for immortality in the *Phaedo* were largely based on the simple and uniform nature of the soul and its kinship thereby with the Forms, the soul has now been shown to be a multiplicity of parts and functions. Those arguments then no longer hold and the soul's kinship with the Forms is seriously imperilled. He brings a new argument forward—that of the characteristic evil of each thing—but he fully realizes that this does not dispose of the question : which part of the soul is immortal ? For them all to be so is clearly difficult. The problem is too large to be dealt with as a mere appendix to the *Republic*. It will be taken up again. Meanwhile he merely reasserts his belief that the essential part of the soul (its immortal part) cannot be the whole of what, in the *Republic*, has been included under psyche.

Nor is the problem tackled in the *Phaedrus*. The mythical representation of the charioteer and his team has already been quoted. Two further principles of some importance in this connexion occur in that dialogue. First that the soul is the

originator of all movement, and therefore of all life, a principle
of the greatest importance in the works of the later period.
The point is not argued, it is dogmatically stated and made
the basis of another proof that the soul is immortal (245c) :

'All soul is immortal. For that which is ever in motion is
immortal. That which moves something else and is moved by
something else, when its motion ends, then also ends its life. That
alone which moves itself, since it never fails, never ceases to move,
but is the source and beginning of motion for all other things that
move. For the beginning never came to be. And from the beginning all that comes to be is born, whereas itself it derives from none.
For if the beginning was born of something else, it would no longer
be the beginning.

And since it did not become, neither will it be destroyed. For if
the first principle were destroyed it could not again be derived from
anything else nor could anything else be derived from it, if indeed
all things are derived from a first principle. Thus the first beginning
of motion is that which moves itself.'

The immortality of the soul then, as the beginning or first
principle of motion, is here added to the theory that it is the
origin of all life, that without soul there is no life. Life and
motion are ultimately equivalent terms, and soul, which alone
has the power to move itself without external stimulus, is the
sole origin of them.

Further, the kinship of human souls with those of the gods
is also established, though in mythical form. Their souls too
are represented as a charioteer and a team of horses, more
perfect it is true, but the fundamental structure is the same.
And this kinship between men and gods is more closely woven
into the philosophy of the later dialogues.

The next group of dialogues : the *Parmenides*, *Theaetetus*,
Sophist, *Politicus* and *Philebus*, do not contribute very much
directly to the problem we are investigating, the nature of the
soul considered as a unit or a plurality and the relation of the
different parts to one another. From the *Theaetetus* we would
naturally expect something, since it inquires into the nature
of knowledge, but it concerns itself more with the actual
process of knowing and its objects than with the nature of the
mind that knows. It describes this process and the psychology

of sense perception and of intellectual apprehension. In its
attack upon the relativism of Protagoras it does, of course,
maintain the existence of a distinct individual soul as against
the conception of man as a mere aggregate of unrelated
perceptions and feelings ; it reaffirms the existence of the
Ideas which, as in the *Phaedo*, the soul grasps ' by itself ' (186a) ;
and it shows that all perception takes place not in the body but
in the soul via the body (186b–c). Clearly it is in the soul that
knowledge is to be found.

The *Sophist* makes important contributions to logic and
metaphysics but from our present point of view there is little
except that we may note in passing how ψυχή is used as an
equivalent of διάνοια (thought) as a sign of the way the soul
is throughout these dialogues taken to mean especially the
intellect. We may note also the expression ' the eyes of the
soul ' by means of which we see the divine, an unusual expression strongly reminiscent of the *Republic*.[1]

In the myth of the *Politicus* the world is presented as a living
creature (269d–273b) endowed with soul as well as body, yet
not completely able to move itself for ever (the real characteristic of soul) but dependent for the original impetus upon
the guidance of a god, and unable to carry on alone beyond a
limited time without heading for destruction. As ever, it is
dangerous to press the details of a myth too far ; Plato is
only emphasizing that the world is dependent upon some
power outside itself (as we understand the world). It is, however, attractive to suppose that he had not yet clarified his
conception of the soul of the world.

This ' soul of the universe ' we also find in the *Philebus*, where
the whole universe (τὸ πᾶν) is said to be body endowed with
soul (σῶμα ἔμψυχον), that is, in the last analysis, with life ; and
just as our bodies are nurtured by the matter of the outside
universe and are part of its body, the same is true of the
relation between our soul and the world soul. Soul is the cause
of motion and within it resides mind or νοῦς, which cannot
exist without it. Mind is the efficient cause of all that exists
in the physical world and must be prior to all phenomena.[2]

---

[1] 254a : τὰ τῆς ψυχῆς ὄμματα. See the interesting discussion of the significance of such expressions in Friedländer, I, 20 n.

[2] See p. 46.

In this dialogue also all pleasure and all perception is of the soul, not only bodily.[1] Here we trace the same process of broadening the conception of the soul, at least of the human soul, to include all aspects of life, and this has been made possible by the tripartite division explained in the *Republic*.

The whole theory of the soul is fully restated in the *Timaeus*. There too the world is a living being endowed with soul and mind (ζῷον ἔμψυχον ἔννουν 30*b*, &c.) and this soul is spread throughout the universe. It is prior to body, since without it the world cannot live, though this priority is logical only and there never was a time when the world was not ; soul once more is the beginning, origin or first principle (ἀρχή) of life. The creation of soul is described in some detail, first that of the world and then human souls from an inferior mixture of the same ingredients. The process is as follows : From Being in the physical and Being in the intelligible world the ' Craftsman ' makes a third, an intermediate kind of Being mixed from the other two ; he then proceeds in the same way to make a mixed kind of Sameness and one of Otherness, both of which constituents also exist in the noetic as well as the sensible world. These three preliminary mixtures he then blends into one whole, and this is soul.[2] The point of this curiously abstract procedure—which is, of course, mythical as is the whole dialogue, and Plato warns us again and again that it is only ' a probable tale '—seems to be this : all judgements which the mind makes can be reduced to three fundamental kinds, judgements asserting existence, e.g. ' This is ' ; judgements that point to similarity between two things ' A is similar to B (in some or all respects)' and judgements of difference ' A is different from B (in some or all respects).' [3] Hence, on the principle that like is known by like, which Plato had adopted from earlier philosophies, the mind must have within itself Being, Same and Other. But the soul can make such judgements both about the objects of sense and the objects of thought, about the physical and the intelligible world, and it is the function of the mind to act as a bridge between the two worlds.

[1] See p. 75.
[2] This seems to me the only intelligible account of the passage 35*a–b*. See my article in *Class. Phil.*, Jan. 1932.
[3] See 37*a–c*.

Therefore it contains within itself Being, Same and Other as they exist in both worlds.

The old notion of the correspondence between the microcosm and the macrocosm is then further developed. The soul of the universe is arranged in two circles, that of the Same which typifies the regular (apparent) diurnal motion of the sphere of heaven studded with fixed stars, and within it on a plane corresponding to the ecliptic the circle of the Other split up in a number of concentric rims to correspond to the orbits of the planets, the sun and the moon. Into the astronomical details of this we will not go.[1] Suffice it to say that all this is done in accordance with certain arithmetical and harmonic progressions which are the mathematical basis of Platonic astronomy. There is then a definite correspondence between the world soul and the souls of men. Not only are they made of the same ingredients but human souls also are divided into the circles of Same and Other (Being, of course, belongs to both) which have their spherical motions within the head ; and it is by the study and understanding of the motion and rhythm of the universe that we may best induce within ourselves the appropriate motions of our intelligence.

But all this only applies to the immortal part of the soul. For Plato here answers clearly the question he left unsettled in the *Republic*. The intellect alone is immortal as the most divine part of the soul. It is that which is akin to the gods and that alone which is the work of the Maker. To weld this immortal part into a human body by means of lower and mortal parts of the soul is a task that is left to the lesser gods that he himself has made, for his own work must be everlasting.

So here again we have first the most important division of the human soul into intellect which is immortal and another, a mortal, part. This latter is then subdivided into two parts similar to those we found in the *Republic* but with a wealth of detail appropriate in a myth, and each now receives a definite place in the body (69c) :

' Of divine things he himself is the maker, mortal things he orders his own offspring to bring about. They received from him the immortal first principle of soul and next in imitation of him

[1] For a full explanation of them see notes in Taylor's commentary.

fashioned around it a mortal body as a carriage for it and within this they built another part of the soul, which holds strange and compelling attributes within itself : first pleasure that greatest bait of evil, then pain escape from good, then rashness and fear, witless councillors, anger that is hard to pacify, hope that is easily misled. These they mix with unreasoning perception and desire that will grasp at everything. Thus of necessity they put together human-kind.

And because of this, fearing to corrupt the divine where not quite inevitable, they house the mortal away from it in another part of the body ; and that they might be apart they place the neck between as an isthmus or frontier between the head and the breast. . . .

The part of the soul that possesses manly courage and temper (θυμός) and is ambitious they put nearer the head between the neck and the diaphragm so that, as it is obedient to reason it should with it hold down by force the passionate part whenever the latter is not willing to obey reason and its commands. . . .'

There follows a description of the heart, the chief organ of the region of the ambitious part, and the way it helps to bring the passionate part to heel. The latter inhabits the part of the body between the diaphragm and the navel, the ' trough of the body ' where it is swayed by pictorial representations and images of the commands of reason upon the smooth surface of the liver ! We need not, however, take too seriously the physiological implications of this semi-humorous passage.

Thus constituted, the soul spreads from the highest to the lowest of living beings, and even plants possess the lowest part of it (77b) :

' For whatever has a share of life would rightly be called a living creature (ζῷον). And that which we are now mentioning (the vegetable kingdom) shares in the third form of soul which we say is established between the diaphragm and the navel, which has no part in belief, reasoning or mind, but in perceptions pleasant and painful along with passions.`

While on the other hand the highest part of the soul is almost more than human (90a) :

' As regards the most important part of our soul we must think this : that a god has given it as a spirit (δαίμων) to each of us, that which we say dwells in the top part of the body, to lift us from the earth to its kindred in heaven, for we are not of earthly but of divine nature. . . .'

In the passage immediately following we again have the two-fold, which is after all the important, division and we are once more told that it is necessary for each part of the soul to be active in its own way.

The *Laws* have not much to add to Plato's conception of the nature of the soul, though they repeat and amplify a good deal of what has been said before. There is, in the first book (644*e*), a splendid picture of the conflict of emotions within the human soul, and we are told that in this conflict we must follow ' the golden thread of the intellect, that which is called the common law in the state'. Soul must be honoured above all other possessions and second only to the gods. As the cause of all change and of all movement in the world it is prior to matter and to the body, and as that which has the power to move itself—the highest form of motion—it is the beginning of all things. All that has life has soul.[1]

So far there is nothing new. But the theory of parts or forms of the soul does not appear. This may be due to the fact that, in the tenth book where he combats the views of the ' atheists ' who believe in neither soul nor gods, Plato is primarily concerned (as he was also in the *Phaedo*) to establish the existence of the immortal soul so that its relation to the body is not his immediate concern. Having fully explained the different aspects of the soul in the *Republic* and the *Timaeus*, he can use the ordinary antithesis of soul and body without fear of misunderstanding by his followers, and therefore need not bring into this conversation an elaborate psychological theory which would be largely irrelevant and only confuse the more general public to whom the *Laws* are obviously addressed. But it is quite clear that, as in the *Charmides*, the thing to aim at is the health of the whole individual. As appeared from a study of the passages concerned with pleasure, the *Laws* seem to recommend control and synthesis rather than repression.

There is, however, one passage of the tenth book which brings a new and a somewhat startling development. It has

---

[1] See v, 726*a* ff. and the tenth book, especially 891*c*. ff. and 895*c*. For a discussion of the religion of this book see pp. 171 ff.

just been established that the soul is prior to the body and is the cause of all motion. The Athenian then continues (896*d*) :

'And after that we must surely agree that soul is the cause of things good and bad, beautiful and ugly, just and unjust, and of all the opposites, if indeed we are to make it the cause of all things. —Of course.

—And as soul resides in and controls everything that has movement it must necessarily control the heavens also ?

—Why not ?

—Is there only one soul, or are there more than one ? More. I will answer for you. Not less than two at any rate : one that does good and one that does evil.

—You are quite right.

—Very well. Now soul drives all things in heaven, on the earth and on the sea by its own motions which are called will (βούλεσθαι), investigation, care, deliberation, belief true or false. It feels joy and pain, boldness and fear, hatred and love and all that is akin to these. Original motions with the help of the secondary motions of the body bring everything to growth and decay, mixture and dissolution, and what follows from these, namely heat and cold, weight and lightness, hardness and softness, whiteness and blackness, bitterness and sweetness ; all of which the soul employs in its work. If it has acquired wisdom, god unto gods,[1] it guides all things to right and happiness ; but if it associates with ignorance it works the opposite in all things.'

This curious dualism is the result of following to its logical conclusion the theory that the soul is the origin of all motion and all life, for some human actions at least are not directed towards a proper goal and yet their origin must be traced to a human soul as their cause. As for the possibility of two warring souls in the heavens, that is soon disposed of : the regularity of the heavenly bodies' motions is a sufficient proof that the cosmos is ruled by one or more good souls gifted with wisdom (897*b*–898*c*) and that the various souls responsible for the motions of the sun, the moon and the stars have divine wisdom and are rightly called gods (899*b*). The bad souls therefore can only be the souls of ignorant men. It is ignorance, we are told, the absence of knowledge—which is after all a

---

[1] θεὸν ὀρθῶς θεοῖς : the meaning seems of the vaguest.

negative concept—that make some souls misdirect their powers, and this can be cured by teaching and education. The purpose of introducing these bad souls is somewhat vague, but it seems due partly at least to the desire, always prominent in Plato, to make man responsible for his own actions. When a man has not tended his soul as he should he is therefore not only useless, but an active source of evil.[1]

Thus from first to last in Plato we find that the soul is the highest and noblest part of man, the part he should primarily care for and develop. Throughout the emphasis is on the reason, the intellect, for virtue is always, to him, a matter of knowledge. But though there is no fundamental contradiction there is considerable development in the Platonic view of the nature of the soul. At first the word ψυχή is used without explanation as that part of man which should control his life and as such it is understood to be immortal. Once the Forms have made their appearance it is by means of the soul and its functions that Plato endeavours to bridge the gap between the two worlds, for the soul which exists in the body is yet able to apprehend the absolute Ideas. In the *Phaedo* we find the soul essentially akin to the Ideas ; so close is this kinship that the soul, there looked upon as pure intellect, is unduly separated from the body, its pleasures and pains, and is in danger of leaving it with a life of its own. In attempting to fill one gap Plato bids fair to make another.

The importance of emotion is then magnificently stressed in the *Symposium* and later in the *Phaedrus* ; in the latter dialogue the soul is, in the myth, closely linked not so much with the Ideas as with the gods. It is also said to be the origin of all movement. The tripartite division developed in the *Republic*,

---

[1] The ' bad soul ' may also refer to whatever principle of motion resides in matter, or rather in the indeterminate space-matter of the *Timaeus*, since in this also there is chaotic movement which the demiurge reduces to order (see p. 164). With this difference, that in the universe as a whole, though there may be a struggle (and even this is not certain) the victory of wisdom was always looked upon by Plato as assured. In human affairs on the other hand, at least in the affairs of an individual man or state, there is no such assurance. For an interesting discussion of this view of the bad soul see Wilamowitz, II, 316 ff. Robin takes it to refer to the principle of good and that of evil in the same soul. This is ultimately true, but I do not think Plato had it in mind in the *Laws* (*L'Amour*, p. 164).

by recognizing the claim of feelings and passions to a place in the soul, is intended to rejoin the mind to the body and thus to do away with an undue splitting up of the human personality. It also re-establishes unity behind the different parts by its image of a stream of desire which can be directed along three main channels and thus links up with the desire-philosophy of the *Symposium.* The parts of the soul once more come to the fore in the *Timaeus,* and Plato may now safely reassert his belief in the immortality of the intellect, and of that alone. The soul as the originator of all life is further emphasized in the *Laws,* as is its kinship with the gods, while the mythical process of the soul's creation in the *Timaeus* similarly insists upon this essential kinship. It also shows the soul as belonging to both the physical and the intelligible for it is made up of elements from both.

As for immortality, the human soul as a whole definitely does not attain it, since part of it is unequivocally stated to be mortal : neither physical desire nor ambition survives. So that the human personality as we know it ceases to be at death. It is however said with equal clearness from the *Phaedo* to the *Timaeus* that the highest part of the soul, the mind or intellect, the capacity to apprehend universal truth, does survive. It lives on, presumably, as a focus of soul-force, that is, of the longing for perfection, beauty and truth, which is the ultimate origin of all ordered movement and life in the universe. If we ask, further, how far this immortal mind keeps its individuality we must remember that from first to last the aim of the Platonic philosopher is to live on the universal plane, to *lose himself* more and more in the contemplation of truth, so that the perfect psyche would, it seems, lose itself completely in the universal mind, the world-psyche. Hence it remains individual only in so far as it is imperfect, and personal immortality is not something to aim at, but something to outgrow.

Such seems to be Plato's view. He does not anywhere describe more precisely, except in myths which must not be taken literally, the state of the soul after life, or between lives. But we can scarcely blame him for not attempting to describe the indescribable. Besides, even for him, as for all the Greeks of his day, the centre of interest is and remains neither heaven nor hell, but human life. And in life the soul is both active and complete. Its function is the fusion of the intelligible with the physical. It alone can apprehend the universal, it alone can initiate the harmonious and rhythmical motions that are life. The Forms do not depend, it is true, upon it for their existence, but without it they can be neither apprehended nor realized to any extent at all. Without soul the physical world on the other hand could not even exist.

NOTE ON *SYMPOSIUM* 206c–208c

THE passage may be summarized as follows : Love is the desire for reproduction (τίκτειν ἐπιθυμεῖ ἡμῶν ἡ φύσις). Man and woman unite and reproduce. This is the divine power of reproduction in living creatures, it is what is immortal in them (τοῦτο ἐν θνήτῳ ὄντι . . . ἀθάνατον ἔνεστιν 206c). It is the desire for immortal glory which makes men seek fame even at the price of death. Mortal nature (ἡ θνητὴ φύσις) seeks to be immortal as far as possible, and reproduction is the only way (δύναται δὲ ταύτῃ μόνον 207d). There are offspring of the body and of the soul. Whatever is subject to death (knowledge included) can only survive by reproducing another like itself, for only the divine remains altogether stable and the same. ' Thus the mortal shares in immortality in a different way from the divine ' (ἀθάνατον δὲ ἄλλῃ, 208b, 4 ; see Friedländer, II, 314 n, for justification of this, the MSS. reading). And Plato then goes on to describe the offspring of the mind and to place them high above physical offspring.

There is not a word to indicate that the individual soul is immortal. With the *Phaedo* before us we may no doubt say that Plato does not include the immortal intellect in the θνητόν that can only reach immortality by reproduction. But surely Homer and Solon who are mentioned as having left offspring of the mind behind them are not considered here apart from their minds ! The explanation is, no doubt, that Plato is using ψυχή in a commonplace sense, and is thinking of the whole man, and that he does not wish to bring in the controversial question of immortality. The important point for us here is that he does omit any mention of it, and that to make the passage at all compatible with the *Phaedo* we must include the intellect under the ἀθάνατον which is immortal ἄλλῃ. But certainly no one who had not the other dialogues before him would take this to refer to anything but the gods. What a difference with the *Phaedo* where the immortality of the soul is kept before us all the time !

V

THE GODS

THE Greek word θεός and the English word God are by no means equivalent ; their associations are obviously very different. The chief difference is perhaps best expressed by Wilamowitz[1] where he says that to a Greek, god is primarily a predicative notion. Where the Christian says that God is love or that God is good he is first asserting, or taking for granted, the existence of a mysterious being, God, and making a qualitative judgement about him. He is telling us something about God. With the Greek the order was frequently reversed. He would say that Love is god or Beauty is god ; he is not assuming the existence of any mysterious divinity but telling us something about love and beauty, the reality of which no one could deny. The subject of his judgement, the thing of which he speaks, is in the world we know, and in that world pagan thought was focused in classical times. By saying that love, or victory, is god, or, to be more accurate, a god, was meant first and foremost that it is more than human, not subject to death, everlasting. It is not for nothing that the Greeks ordinarily referred to their gods as οἱ ἀθάνατοι, the deathless ones. Any power, any force we see at work in the world, which is nòt born with us and will continue after we are gone could thus be called a god, and most of them were.

It was not only the adjective divine (θεῖος) that could be applied to anything greater and more lasting than man, but even the noun θεός was constantly used in such a vague way that it cannot be translated god without making nonsense. The Milesian philosophers, for example, called θεός the substratum of the physical world for which they sought, so that

---

[1] Platon, I, 348 : ' Denn Gott selbst ist ja zuerst ein Prädikatsbegriff.' The whole passage is very interesting in this connexion.

when Thales said the world was full of gods he may only have meant that it was full of water ! Indeed Euripides [1] goes so far as to say that to recognise a friend is 'a god'. Such a statement is unmeaning to us because to the modern mind the word god is definitely associated with a divine personality endowed with all but human emotions, mind and memory, and with purposes and desires that must be such as to secure our approval, with love and frequently with anger. Our modern conception of the divine is, in fact, more definitely anthropo-psychic than was that of the Greek.

It is true that these abstractions were clothed with a human form by Greek artists and poets. But this anthropomorphism, though it certainly affected the popular conception of the divinities, was, to the educated Greek at least, definitely symbolical. At times the symbolism was no doubt lost sight of by the ordinary worshipper and the anthropomorphism was very crude, but before we condemn it too complacently we should remember that the old white-bearded Lord of Hosts (a far less beautiful person than Zeus) has by no means been utterly expelled from our modern heaven.

Something of the earlier vagueness clung to even the most standardized of the Olympian super-humans, and this may help to explain why Greek religion had neither dogma nor creed. It may seem labouring the obvious to insist in this manner that there is no word in any modern language which adequately translates θεός, but I believe that a failure to keep the two distinct has been responsible for a good deal of confusion in discussions of Plato's God. [2] Our word God is a synthesis of two concepts which the Greeks kept distinct and which are clearly differentiated in Plato. The divine has two aspects : the static and the dynamic. God may be looked upon as the ultimate reality, the highest form of being, the eternal absolute. We also speak of God as the creator, the first link in the chain not of existence but of causation, the maker, an active force causing movement and life.

To ask what is the nature of Plato's god is therefore a question to which there is no single answer. It is not one question but

[1] *Helen*, 560.
[2] A good example of this can be seen in Ritter, II, 776 ff., and I think the same is true in Burnet, *Platonism*, pp. 113 ff.

two, and the answers are not the same. We should ask :
What is, to Plato, the ultimate and absolute reality ? and also :
What, in Plato, corresponds to the dynamic aspect of god, to the
maker or creator of life ? The first, the ultimate existence or
rather (not to force monotheism upon him) existences are the
Platonic Forms or Ideas ; and they remain supreme to the end.
In this sense we may say that the Ideas of goodness and beauty
are the god of Plato, in so far as this is one aspect of what we
designate by the word.[1] But Plato never calls his Ideas gods.[2]
That name he reserves for those more personal beings, those
more than human forces personified, in whom we may find
help and guidance in living the good life. These are the gods
of the myths who do not find a place in Plato's philosophy
proper until the last dialogues.

Only when we have studied the account which Plato gives
of his gods will it be possible to understand more definitely the
relation between them and the eternal Forms, but the problem
is put very clearly as early as the *Euthyphro* where the professional priest of that name has suggested a definition of the
right (τὸ ὅσιον) as that which is dear to the gods, and Socrates
asks (10*a*) :

' Do the gods love what is right because it is right or is it right
because the gods love it ? '

It is definitely established that the first is the case, and this is
of the greatest importance, for it gives in a nutshell a point of
view from which Plato never departed. Whatever the gods
may be, they must by their very nature love the right because
it is right. They must conform to it as we must, but more
rigidly because they are more perfect. The universe is not
ruled by the divine will, since he who must conform cannot
be omnipotent. He cannot love the right at his will, he *must*

[1] This is the answer I once gave in an earlier discussion in the Canadian
Journal of Religious Thought, April 1930. But it is a mistake to identify
the Ideas with the gods as is done by Wilamowitz (I, 589, &c.).

[2] There is an exception : In *Timaeus*, 37*c*, the living world is spoken of as
an imitation of ' the eternal gods ' (τῶν ἀϊδίων θεῶν ἄγαλμα). This must
refer to the Ideas, and it is just because they are *not* called gods elsewhere
that this passage has so much troubled commentators (see Taylor's notes
ad loc.), though this loose use of θεός as little more than the equivalent of the
adjective θεῖος is very natural. That this is the only place where the Ideas
are called θεοί is very remarkable.

do so. This separation of the dynamic power of god from the ultimate reality, this setting up of absolute values above the gods themselves was not as unnatural to a Greek as it would be to us.[1] It did not require any great mental effort or originality, for the Greek gods never claimed to have created the world. The gods who ruled on Olympus in historical times had obtained their power by conquest over a previous generation of gods, and even these were not creators but created beings. As in Homer Zeus must obey the balance of Necessity, so the Platonic gods must conform to an eternal scale of values. They did not create them, cannot alter them, cannot indeed wish to do so.

But before we set out to follow the gods through the dialogues, it may be well to consider briefly Plato's attitude to the Olympians themselves. There was much in the official religion of which he disapproved : he disliked the dogmatic way in which even Greek augurs and prophets expounded their stories and beliefs about the gods, the claim they made to knowledge where they obviously could only rely on faith or inspiration. They made no effort to explain their beliefs on rational grounds, a thing which even in the *Laws* Plato very definitely does. He also objected to the teaching that the wrath of the gods could be placated by prayer and sacrifice. And of course he disapproved of the tales told about the gods.[2] But in this he was attacking the popular conception of the gods rather than the gods themselves, for, though the people derived their ideas of the divine from the tales of poets and priests, there was no canonized version of these myths. A Greek was perfectly free not only to reinterpret but to reject altogether any one story about the gods, and indeed almost any number of them, without necessarily laying himself open to the charge of atheism, or even of heresy. In this vagueness and fluidity lay both the strength and the weakness of the Olympian religion. It could make a very different appeal to different individuals : the common man might well believe in the Zeus depicted by

---

[1] This point is well made by Brochard (*Etudes*, p. 98) : ' Façonnés par vingt siècles de Christianisme, nos esprits modernes hésitent devant une conception qui pourrait sembler impie et un peu choquante. Est-il rien pour nous de supérieur à Dieu ? Il n'en était pas ainsi pour les Grecs. Au-dessus des Dieux, les Grecs plaçaient le Destin.'

[2] For references on these points see below, pp. 158 ff.

Pheidias or even Homer, while to the educated man the
Olympians were pure abstractions to whom ' doubtful philosophers can pray with all a philosopher's due caution, as to so
many radiant and heart-searching hypotheses '.[1]

Nor had Plato much patience with those who tried to
rationalize the myths (*Phaedrus*, 229c) :

' But Socrates, tell me, do you believe this story (the rape of
Orithyia by Boreas) ?

—It would not be strange if I disbelieved it, like our clever men.
I would then in my cleverness say that the breath of the north wind
hurled her down from the rocks nearby while she was playing with
Pharmaceia, and that from her death in this way arose the story
that she was snatched away by Boreas either here—or from the
Areopagus.   For sometimes they say that it was from there and not
from here that she was snatched away.

Such interpretations are attractive, my dear Phaedrus, but they
strike me as rather too clever and laboured and not altogether
happy, if only because the interpreter will then be compelled to set
us right about the physical appearance of the Centaurs, the Chimera ;
a whole mob of Gorgons and Pegasus' will stream upon him, and
a difficult crowd of strange monsters.   If the disbeliever is to
approach each one of them with a probable explanation, he will
need plenty of time for this rather crude cleverness of his.

I have no time for such things.   And for this reason : somehow I
am unable to know myself, as the Delphic saying is.   Before I know
myself, it seems ridiculous to investigate other things.   That is why
I let those things be, and accept the traditional belief about them.
As I said just now, I examine myself, not them. . . .'[2]

Symbolic or allegorical interpretations do not appeal to
Socrates any more than the above rationalization as to the
origin of the story.[3]   Plato does not deny that there may be a
higher and deeper meaning than appears on the surface, but

[1] As it is well put by Gilbert Murray, *Five Stages of Greek Religion*, p. 99.
The whole chapter is very interesting in this connexion.

[2] This docile acceptance of the customary in such matters is rather surprising in view of the attack made upon similar stories in the *Republic*.   But
elsewhere too we find Plato content to use even the strangest common
beliefs when another subject is more important at the time (e.g. *Laws*, 913c).
It might on the other hand be just what the historical Socrates would have
said.   The contradiction is more apparent than real, for Socrates may
well want to reject stories and at the same time hold that ingenious methods
of explaining them away (and keeping them) were a waste of time.

[3] See J. Tate's interesting articles in *Class. Quart.*, 1929/3 and 1930/1.

only that the immediate harmful effect of an immoral tale is
not to be redeemed by any amount of allegory or symbolism
(*Republic*, 378*d*) :

> ' The binding of Hera by her son, the hurling of Hephaestus from
> heaven by his father because he wanted to protect his mother from
> a beating, the wars among the gods of which Homer tells us, these
> things we will not admit into our city, whether written as allegory
> (ἐν ὑπονοίαις) or without allegory.

For such subtleties Plato had no time. And apparently he
never did have the time to discuss the Olympians. In the
Republic he is content to leave all the details of religious obser-
vances to Apollo ; in the *Philebus* Socrates says he is afraid to
misuse the names of the gods.[1] So in the *Timaeus* Plato
suddenly, and rather awkwardly, finds an undefined place in
his hierarchy for the orthodox gods and then speaks of them
no more ;[2] the same is true of the *Epinomis* (984*d*) where one
can place them ' where one likes ' !

It is often said that this distant and non-committal attitude
towards the Olympian gods was due to a fear of prosecution for
impiety. This may be true, but it does not seem very likely
at the time the dialogues were written. There is another and
a better reason. That Plato did not believe in the Olympians
as persons any more than Euripides did is obvious. But once
the more objectionable myths were removed, he probably
thought it an unprofitable task to destroy the old gods (even
if such a task had been possible) when these old moulds might
still be used as effectively as any other to express new ideas,
new conceptions of divinity—in so far indeed as even these
were new. A Greek thinker could find himself opposed to
almost all the popular conceptions in the matter of religion
and yet say in all sincerity, as Socrates did, that he did not
teach men to believe in new gods. So a man in our own day
might be unable and unwilling to believe in by far the greater
part of any Christian creed ; he might, for example, consider
the Virgin Birth to be not only a childish but a dangerous

---

[1] *Republic*, 427*b*, 461*e* ; *Philebus*, 12*c*, where the point is that Socrates
would hesitate to identify Hedone with Aphrodite as Philebus does.
Plato's lack of interest in cult and ritual is noted by Wilamowitz, I, 39,
412-13.

[2] See p. 165 below.

myth, and yet hesitate to attack Christianity as a whole
because of much that he accepted in its teaching and because
he might hope that what he considers unworthy might yet be
supplanted within the framework of Christianity itself (or
even of the Christian churches).   In Greece, where there was
no creed, no dogma and no priesthood in any real sense, this
attitude was both easier and more probable.

But there is more than that.   When Plato makes the Olympian gods lead different groups of disembodied souls in the
myth of the *Phaedrus*, when in the same dialogue he attaches
the names of Apollo, Dionysus, the Muses, Eros and Aphrodite
to different kinds of inspiration, he is not speaking of what he
does not believe.   Eros and Aphrodite do represent for him
the love of truth and beauty which makes a man a lover of
wisdom, a philosopher.   They are real forces, real deities if you
will, and Plato believed in them in that sense.   If he refrained
from any criticism of the Olympians themselves (as distinct
from the stories told about them), it was probably because to
him they stood for something very real, and because he thought
them still capable of meaning the same to others.

We will now turn to the dialogues to find what enlighten-
ment they bring upon the nature of the Platonic gods.   The
earliest, those where the Forms have not put in any even
uncertain appearance, represent what might be called the
conventional stage of Plato's use of gods.   By this I do not,
of course, refer to exclamations such as μὰ Δία, the use of which
no more implies a belief in Zeus than the exclamation ' by
god ' implies a belief in God.   Nor do I refer to introductory
prayers whereby now and again Socrates calls upon gods to
help him in argument, for such a formula could be used in all
sincerity by any one with a sense of the power of such forces
as the gods represent.

By conventional I mean rather the use of the word θεός and
its plural to indicate whatever there be in nature beyond and
above humanity ;   that there were some kind of higher forces
which worked for good was Plato's belief from first to last.
These, without analysis, are called god or gods at this stage
and their existence is never doubted, hardly indeed questioned.
To know oneself is the advice of Apollo, and Apollo is one of

the gods, without any further question or analysis. But it should be noted that at this stage Plato does not base his ethics on his theology. That the life of justice is the happier life, that it is better to be wronged than to do wrong, is proved in the *Gorgias* without reference to an after-life or indeed to any further reward in this life. Only when this is fully established does Plato go on to the myth of the day of judgement. The myth is not the main argument, it is only a story with a merely corroborative force for those who believe in immortality. In this myth the Olympians appear to represent the forces beyond, and it was surely natural that Plato should turn to them. As personifications of the divine they will do as well as any other, better for a Greek for whom no others could have the same appeal. So in the myth of the *Protagoras* we have Zeus as the creator of man. There is no theological argument, nothing but a certain bowdlerization of the Olympians, a process that antedates Plato by several centuries. But in the actual philosophical argument, the gods scarcely appear.

The most suggestive of the short dialogues of this earlier period is, in this connexion, the *Euthyphro*, where we saw that the relation between the will of the gods and the supreme standard of right is introduced. This later becomes the relation between the gods and the Forms that are, it would seem, just struggling to be born. It is made clear that Socrates does not accept the stories of quarrels among the gods, in spite of his feigned respect for Euthyphro's professional opinion. Piety or right is also defined as service to the gods—a glimmering of a belief that will be developed later—but this is rejected, and we have some sharp criticism of the ritualistic conception of piety which Socrates condemns as a commercial relationship that, as between gods and men, is absurd.

The appearances of the gods in the *Phaedo* are also of interest. In the introductory part of the dialogue we are told that men have been placed upon this earth by the gods and must not desert their post ; that a god looks after us as his possessions, that the philosopher will join the gods after death ; that we must try in this life to purify ourselves as far as possible until a god deliver us by means of death.[1] Except for this

---

[1] *Phaedo*, 62*b*, 63*c*, 67*a*.

last statement the gods do not appear at all once the philosophical discussion has begun, and they have no part in the discussion of immortality until, the philosophical argument being at an end, Socrates proceeds to the myth. There the gods are our guides after death though they do not play a very prominent part. In other words the gods and the Forms do not appear together.

Up to the *Republic* we may say that the gods are used in a general way to refer to the divine powers, without any argument or analysis except to a small extent in the *Euthyphro*. When the Ideas are fully developed, we get the impression that they and the gods are never on the stage at the same time. They can hardly be said to be differentiated and they are certainly not identified ; they are just not mentioned together. Both are divine, of course, in the general sense of being above humanity. If we insist on finding a connexion between them we have to say that the gods appear to be the mythical representation of that eternal world which the Ideas describe in a different manner.

But certainly the Ideas seem the more firmly established, though the gods have not yet surrendered their supremacy, or at least not confessed their surrender. In the *Symposium* love, which is desire for a perfection as yet unattained, cannot be a god, for a god is perfect ; it is only a spirit. In the *Republic* the gods still seem to be on a par with the Ideas, but here again no explanation is vouchsafed of their relationship. And it is interesting to note that in the whole of the *Republic*, before the myth of the tenth book, the gods enter the discussion only twice in any real sense, both times in the course of a discussion on art. As art itself is concerned with myths, we get a strong impression of the mythical character of the gods. The first mention is in the third book where the poets' tales about the gods are criticized and rejected. Certain characteristics of the divinity emerge (379*b*) :

' The good is not the cause of all things, but only of those that are good, of evil it is blameless.
—Definitely.
—God then, since he is good, could not be the cause of all things as most people say he is. Of few things he is the cause for men, for most he is not responsible, since there are far more evil things

than good in our life. For the good no one else is to be held responsible; for evil we must seek other causes, not the god.'

Further, the god is perfection that cannot change, since it would be for the worse. The gods must not be described as changing their shape.[1] The god is truth and cannot lie or indulge in any kind of deceit. Nor do gods indulge in any excesses.

The second mention of the gods is in the passage of the tenth book which puts the painter at two removes from the truth because he merely copies an actual bed, while the carpenter at least has the Form of bed in his mind, and *this Form is the work of god.* When we realize the otherwise mythical character of the gods in the *Republic*, how they are not mentioned at all in the discussions of the theory of Forms, and further that the Forms were never created because they are eternal, it is easily realized that no importance is to be attached to this one appearance of the god as creator of Ideas, which would flagrantly contradict any account of their relationship that we find elsewhere.[2] Nor, at this stage, is it really unreasonable for Plato to speak in this way, for ' god ' and ' gods ' are still used to represent, as in the *Phaedo*, the whole of the suprasensual world, and when the gods come before us in the myth the Ideas are before us no longer. The two refer to the same more than human world, but the Ideas are hard facts to Plato before which the gods are beginning to yield the first place.

In the myth of Er itself we find no actual Olympians but the three Fates, Lachesis, Clotho and Atropos, and the goddess Necessity. No great importance is to be attached to this. Plato was not committed to any particular gods and the different divinities that appear were probably taken over from the same source as the myth he embellished. On the other hand he does not hesitate to anthropomorphize these goddesses fully. When it comes to the choice of their next life by the disembodied souls, he is at pains to emphasize once more that the

[1] This is not, of course, an attack on polytheism, for Plato, here as elsewhere, speaks of god or gods indifferently. It is simply a condemnation of stories of individual gods : Zeus as a bull or a swan, &c.

[2] That this is introduced by the words ' I suppose ' (ὡς ἐγῶμαι 597b) should not be stressed as it is by Natorp (pp. 218 ff.) who interprets this passage as an ironic reply to those who would ask the question : Where do Ideas come from ? Bovet, p. 68, interprets as above.

choice is free and that the responsibility lies with the individual :
' the fault lies with the chooser, god is not responsible ' (617e).
Indeed this point, that the gods are not responsible for evil,
emphasized as it is both here and in the third book, is the main
contribution made by the *Republic* to the conception of the
gods.

The myth of the *Phaedrus* is of special interest in this connexion. In Socrates' hymn of praise Eros, it should be noted,
is not a mere daimon or spirit as in the *Symposium* but ' may
well be a god or divine spirit ' (242e). This is not so much that
Eros has been promoted as that the other gods have been
demoted. For here the gods and the Ideas appear together
and the gods are definitely put below the Ideas in the contemplation of which they too find the happiness of their eternal
life. Indeed a god is only divine because of his relationship
with the Ideas.[1] The hint of the *Euthyphro* is taken up and
developed. The gods are here the Olympians and none other.
As in the *Symposium*, Plato is concerned not so much in vindi-
cating the existence of the Forms as in bridging the gap between
them and ourselves. In both dialogues he follows the emotional approach through love, and this is ultimately only
another aspect of the more intellectual approach of the
Republic, with a difference of emphasis. And as heaven is in
the myth the abode of the gods, he places the Ideas in a ' place
beyond heaven (ὑπερουράνιος τόπος 247c). Clearly this must
not be interpreted in a literal spacial sense :

' Those souls that are immortal, when they come to the summit of
heaven, travelling outside it they stand upon its rim, and as they
stand its revolution carries them round and so they contemplate the
things that are outside heaven. But of this place beyond heaven
no one of our earthly poets has yet sung in a manner worthy. . . .'

It is no accident that in the *Phaedrus* also Plato says some things
about the soul [2] which he has not said before, for it is by means

---

[1] At least this is implied in 249c : πρὸς οἷσπερ θεὸς ὢν θεῖός ἐστιν, even if
the words refer in the first place to the soul of the philosopher. Robin
(*Amour*, p. 51) wants to take it as a general statement that whatever is divine
is so in relation to the Ideas, but that is not an accurate translation. With
this ' place beyond heaven' we should compare ἐπέκεινα τῆς οὐσίας in
Rep., 509b. ; see also Brochard, p. 97.

[2] See p. 139.

of soul, divine and human, that he henceforth endeavours to
bridge the abyss between the eternal realities and the physical
world. Both gods and men have the capacity to apprehend
the Forms in common but the gods, immortal and perfect
beings as they are far beyond our mortality and imperfection,
have a clear and constant view whereas the confusion and earthi-
ness of our human souls do not allow us more than an occa-
sional glimpse. So the gods have come down one step, as it
were to help us, and they lead the choirs of disembodied souls
that seek to contemplate the truth. As if to emphasize again
this kinship between the human and the divine Socrates adds
the detail that man's character depends upon which of the
gods he has followed on high (252c). Where this subject is
treated again we shall see gods and men, the best in men that
is, get closer and closer until they all but coalesce in the *Laws*.

The *Parmenides* and the *Theaetetus* add but little to our knowledge of the gods. The *Sophist*, on the other hand, puts before
us very clearly the question of their relation to the Ideas,
which had only been touched upon in the *Phaedrus*. The
problem is two-fold : there is the difficulty of any relation
between the Ideal and the physical and also that of the relation
between the Ideas themselves. With the second we are not
here concerned, but both must have led Plato to be dissatisfied
with his earlier versions of the Ideal world as composed exclusively of separate unassociated Ideas ; and he has to face the
necessity of including some active principle in the world of
reality for, since activity can only originate in a self-moving
soul, soul must also have its place as an integral part of the
realm of true existence (ἐν παντελῶς ὄντι),[1] These eternal
souls will appear later as the gods and the soul of the world
(they are the same), but the gods are not mentioned here
where we have little more than a formulation of the problem.
Thus, by insisting on the necessity of including movement and
soul in the ' real ' Plato is opening the gate by which the gods
will enter his dialectical discussions and become an integral
part of his philosophical system. He says (248e) :

' By Heaven, can we be ready to believe that the absolutely real
has no share in movement, life, soul or wisdom ? That it does not

[1] For a discussion of this passage see pp. 40 ff., and Appendix II.

live or think, but in solemn holiness, unpossessed of mind, stands
entirely at rest ?
—That would be a dreadful thing to admit.

And he goes on to include both rest and motion in the completely existent. In other words, Plato recognizes that the
immovable Ideas are not the only inhabitants of the supra-
sensuous world.

We made a distinction at the beginning of our discussion
between two aspects of what we call God : the supreme reality
and the creator ; so that the Ideas correspond only to the
first. This, I believe, remained true to the last. But Plato
now realized that he must make a place, not only in his
myths but in sober philosophy, for the dynamic as also real.
And we are now prepared for a *modus vivendi* to be reached
between the Ideas and the gods who have hitherto (with the
exception of the *Phaedrus* myth) so successfully ignored each
other. From now on we shall not be surprised to find the
gods and the Ideas appearing together as they do in the
Timaeus.

The *Timaeus* is a creation myth. There we find the ' divine
craftsman ', the demiurge, who makes the lower gods, the
soul of the universe and the immortal part of the human soul.
The lower gods in turn make all that is physical, and therefore
mortal, in the universe. Whether this is to be taken literally
so that we have a creating god, or whether Plato is only putting
into cosmological form an analysis of the different factors and
forces at work in the world as it is (thus adopting a time-
sequence merely as a convenient literary device) is a question
on which there has been a good deal of debate from early
times. The latter is probably the case [1] for there is no proper
chronological order. The making of the soul, for example,
comes after a general account of the elements though they
explicitly presuppose it. The probable significance of the
whole scheme is to emphasize that the phenomenal world cannot exist without realities of a different order and is utterly

---

[1] See Taylor's *Commentary,* pp. 67–70. As he says, the tradition of the
Academy was that the time-sequence was not meant literally, and this was
accepted by most Platonists up to and including Proclus (A.D. 500). The
main exceptions are Aristotle and Plutarch. See also Ritter, II, 415 ff.

dependent upon these. The creator in that case is not to be taken literally, but as symbolizing the source and origin of all life, now and always.

But however that may be, it is important for us to note that even within the myth itself the demiurge or god is in no way the maker of the Ideas. Here, as often before, we have two kinds of reality, the one the object of knowledge, the other the objects of perception and belief (28*a*) :

' Everything that comes to be is necessarily due to some (moving) cause. Nothing can come to be without a cause. When the maker of anything has in view a model that is unchangeable and thus fashions the form (ἰδέα) and function of it, then the result must necessarily be well achieved. But when the model is something that becomes, the result is not beautiful.'

And Plato then argues that since the phenomenal world (the world of becoming) is beautiful and its maker good it must have been fashioned after an eternal model. It must have a moving cause,[1] and this cause is its maker. Maker or Craftsman (δημιουργός) is the name by which the supreme god is referred to throughout. This maker must have an eternal and ever-same pattern before him at the time of creation, and this pattern are the Forms. So that within the myth itself, even if we take the time-sequence literally, the Ideas are prior to god and exist before him. Their existence is independent of his.

From this passage also Plato's teleological outlook emerges very clearly (29*a*) :

' If this world is beautiful and its maker good, then clearly he had an eternal model before him. But if—but this it would be impious even to mention (οὐ θέμις)—a passing model. It is clear to all that the world was made after an eternal model.'

He does not argue about it. The world is beautiful and its maker good. That is the starting-point. We then have a further description of the nature and functions of the Craftsman (29*e*) :

' He was good, and, as the good is ever free from malice, he wished

[1] Brochard (*Etudes*, p. 57) rightly compares the moving cause of the *Philebus*, see Appendix IV.

all things to be as like unto himself as possible. This, the wise tell us, was the first principle that ruled creation. And we are right to believe them in this. The god then wanted all things to be good and nothing to be inferior, as far as was possible. So he took over the visible existent which was not immobile but in chaotic and discordant motion and reduced its disorder to order, thinking this to be altogether the better state. It is not right, and never was, that the best should make anything but what is most beautiful. On reflection he found then that of things by nature visible nothing which has not understanding (νοῦς) can, all in all, be more beautiful than that which is endowed with it, and that further, mind cannot exist in anything without soul. This led him to put mind in soul, soul in body, welding the whole together that his work might be the most naturally beautiful and good. So, following the most probable tale, we must say that the world (κόσμος) is a creature truly endowed with soul and understanding because of the god's foresight.'

In this Plato remains true to the old Greek principle that nothing can be created out of nothing and, within the myth itself, his Maker is not a creator in the strict sense. Above and beyond him are the eternal Forms, a pattern to which by the very nature of his being he must needs conform. At the other end of the scale of existence there is something, the visible (one cannot call it matter since Plato reduces it to something which we can only picture as unco-ordinated movements in space, a kind of indefinite potentiality) and the god's function is to bring order into this chaos, to replace undirected and erratic vibration by the rhythm and regularity which is life. This he can do only by endowing the universe with soul as the one reality which has the power to initiate movement and activity.

Since the god thus makes the universe into as perfect an approximation as possible to the model which he has before him, and there can be only one such model, there can be only one universe. If he made another, it would either be inferior, in which case he would not wish to make it, or similar, and then it would still be less like the model in that it would not be unique (31a–b, cp. 55d).

We are not here concerned with the details of creation, the work of the god and the inferior gods ; neither with the fashioning of matter from the elements nor with the later reduction of those elements to combinations of geometrical patterns in space. The making of the soul, cosmic and human, we have discussed elsewhere. Throughout the god is represented as doing the best possible, and the use he makes of the regular solids in the construction both of elements and the world as a whole proves him to be a very competent mathematician. The motion of the world is spherical rotation ; this to Plato was the most perfect type of motion because it combines movement and stability, it involves no change of place (33e–40a). The world-soul which partakes of mind and harmony is spread throughout the whole in a series of circles which correspond to the orbit of the sun, moon and planet according to the astronomical knowledge of the time (35b ff). It is these revolutions, together with the light of the sun, that make possible for men the conception of time, ' the moving image of eternity ' (37d), and enable mortals to acquire the science of numbers and to reach understanding of the principles that govern the world.

More immediately relevant is the fact that the Maker is referred to as mind ($\nu o\tilde{v}\varsigma$). And now we must turn to the other divine inhabitants of the universe. The fixed stars are divine creatures endowed with mind and soul, so is the earth— ' the guardian and maker of night and day, the eldest of the gods that have come to be in the universe '—and the planets. Then, with startling suddenness, the Olympians are introduced in a passage that is obviously ironical (40d) :

' To narrate and understand the birth of the other divinities is beyond our power. We must believe those who have spoken of these things before us, for, as they said, they were descendants of the gods and clearly knew their own ancestors. It is impossible not to believe those who are the children of the gods, even though they speak without probability or compelling proof. As they are speaking of their own, we must obey the law and believe them.'

And that applies to the whole Pantheon. The function of these secondary divinities is explained to them by the maker himself (41a) : What he himself has made no one but he can undo. What is well made he will not wish to destroy. An example of this is the secondary gods themselves. They are not eternal as he is, but they are everlasting at his pleasure.

But mortal creatures have to be made or the world will be an imperfect copy, and if he made them himself they would be everlasting like the gods. To make what is mortal is therefore the duty of the secondary gods, and they too must do the best they can. Only one thing he will make himself, the immortal part of the soul of living creatures.

So from what remains of the constituents of the world-soul he blends a second and a third, necessarily less pure, mixture which are those souls. They are as numerous as the stars and the god explains to them the laws of their being : They will be fashioned into mortal bodies ; they will all have the same opportunities at the first birth (at the first incarnation all will apparently be men !) and if they live a good life they will return to their star seemingly for ever ; otherwise in their next life they will be women, then animals, and sink or rise according to the way they live. He then hands them over to the minor gods who set to work to make the body and the mortal parts of the soul by means of which the immortal part is bound to the body during life. Here again Plato is at pains to emphasize that the god is blameless of evil. That the second and third mixture was less pure is presumably an inevitable result of the material at his disposal. That men are mortal at all is presumably due to the same cause, though the Idea of mortality must be present in the model. This non-responsibility of god for evil, the old dilemma of the omnipotence of god and man's independence, freewill, and moral responsibility, implies many difficulties. One cannot claim that Plato solved them. But the essential point is surely his profound conviction, mythically expressed, that men have only themselves to blame (whether individually or collectively) for their own vices and the evils of the world.

We may now approach with a little more confidence the difficult question of the meaning and place of the demiurge in the scale of existence. As different grades of reality we have : the model or Ideas, the Maker, the soul of the universe, the other gods, human souls (to whom may be added other living creatures, animals at least, since they are, in the story, only degenerated men), and finally the receptacle or matrix endowed with erratic motion of its own, within which and by means of which the physical world is somehow constructed.

That the eternal model is the supreme reality, the highest point in the ladder of existence, is obvious. It is the sumtotal of all the Forms which, conceived as a whole, are this model, so that the Ideal pattern contains within itself the Forms of all that is. Hence, though it does not move or change, and therefore does not, strictly speaking, live, it must contain also the Form or formula which defines such life and may without straining the meaning of the word too far be called a ζῷον, a creature endowed with life. This name was perhaps the more easily given to it by Plato because the Greek word ζῷον could also be applied to any figure in painting or tapestry, even when they did not represent living creatures at all. So that the word is applied both to the physical world which is a living creature in the full sense and also to the eternal pattern which is, as it were, a picture of it. In any case, the separation of the two is only logical since the model is not conceived as having any separate spacial existence. The question also arises how far there are meant to be, in any but a strictly logical sense, Platonic Forms or Ideas of such abstractions as life and death. It is an obscure problem ; Plato did not attempt a solution (he never really separated the logical from the metaphysical aspect of his Ideas), nor indeed is one possible. But it seems certain that he did not think of the Ideas as endowed with any movement or activity beyond the passive capacity of being the objects of knowledge. Activity is restricted to the knowing subject, the soul.[1]

It is important to grasp this, the essential difference between the Forms and whatever partakes of them. Men die, but the Idea of death, the meaning of death, never dies and never changes. So the intelligible ζῷον, the model of the *Timaeus*, is conceived as containing within itself the meanings, the λόγος, of all the things and creatures of the earth as a picture or pattern which the divine intelligence of the Maker ' sees ' and understands, and then tries to realize in the material universe. It is not a picture in two dimensions, nor indeed in any dimension since it is not in space at all. It cannot live, move or change, but eternally is and is eternally the same, independently of the physical world and independently of the god himself.

[1] See Appendices II and IV.

For if the Forms remain thus absolutely objective they must remain also prior to the god, though not in time. This is obscured by those who consider the gods as a mere mythological equivalent to the Ideas.[1] That was true in the earlier dialogues, including the *Republic*, but we have seen the gulf between the gods and the Ideas widen ever since they were first mentioned together in the *Phaedrus*. The Ideas and the gods represent two quite different principles of the supersensuous world, the ultimate reality and the first cause of motion, which Plato kept distinct by continually reasserting the priority of the first. And those who would look upon the Ideas as the thoughts of God are guilty of the same confusion.[2]

It is true that the god (the article should not be omitted) thinks the Ideas, apprehends them as our minds also apprehend them, but more perfectly. Being soul, the god is more akin to us, or the best part in us, than he is to the Ideas. When a carpenter makes a bed he has before his mind the Idea of bed, an objective reality which exists not only in his mind ; so the creator of the world has before him the complete pattern of Ideas, and in the same way. Plato definitely refuses to regard the Ideas as concepts in the *Parmenides*. Nowhere does he say anything that would justify us in regarding them as concepts of the divine mind. As was said of the right in the *Euthyphro*, so here we must realize that the god thinks the Ideas because they exist, they do not exist because he thinks them. The distinction is important : the fundamental values and laws in accordance with which the world is made and governed are ultimate and absolute ; they are not at the mercy of any personal will, be it the will of the god or gods. Whatever men believed about the gods, the Ideas would remain unaffected by their religious beliefs.

It follows that any explanation of the Ideas as emanations from God is also quite unplatonic. Nor can any Idea be god, the supreme Idea of beauty or of truth is not a god, and it is a

---

[1] Wilamowitz, I, 589, 603 ff.

[2] e.g. Lutoslawski, p. 477 ; Ritter, II, 280 ff. and 749 ff., *The Essence* 374 ; Bovet, 160 ; Mugnier, 134 ff. ; Robin, *Physique*, 73. Diès (II, 550 ff.) takes the Ideas as the objective and the god as the subjective aspect of the same reality and thus seems to identify them though he later insists on the priority of the subject. My view is in the main that of Brochard, *Etudes*, 57 and 96 ff.

mistake to identify the two,[1] a mistake which Plato never made, for he never called his Ideas θεοί even in the *Republic* or the *Symposium*, at a time when he had not yet worked out the relation between the two.[2]

Who then is this mysterious creator? How does he fit in the general Platonic scheme, or even in this very dialogue? We have seen that the time-sequence of creation must be taken as a myth, a convenient literary artifice to facilitate analysis, for the world has always existed; that if the creation is interpreted literally it leads to several absurdities. If there was no creation, what becomes of the creator? As a creator he has no claim to existence at all, as would be more readily admitted if Christian commentators were not so eager to read their own conceptions of the divine into Plato. Taken literally, he is a mere stage device. Poetically and mythically, however, he is the personification of the active principle of movement and causation, of the love of good which belongs to all the gods, as to all good souls. It is natural therefore that once the other gods have been created by him the distinction between them and their 'maker and father' is apt to become dim. The divine nature as a whole is said to possess perfect wisdom (νοῦς), which man has only to a small degree (51e); the power to understand, as man cannot, the passage from unity to plurality and vice versa (53d). Not only a god, but even the god, in the singular, is spoken of as doing work which should obviously belong to the secondary deities; [3] plural and singular are used in the same sentence (92a). Only once, when the general purpose of the universe and the primary function of the divine are reaffirmed (68e–69c) do we again meet the supreme god in his proper function as he who of set purpose brings order where no order was before. And even that passage seems rather to summarize the method of work of the divine as a whole (τὸ θεῖον, 68e), for surely the minor gods also must be associated with him as the cause of all that is good. We are told that 'he himself makes all that is good in all things that become' but what becomes or at least that which also passes away they alone, and not he, should make at all.

The two kinds of divine nature then seem to come very close

---

[1] Zeller, II, 718, where see references.   [2] See p. 152 n. 2.
[3] See 46c–e; 44e; 73b; 75d; 78b; 80d; and ὁ κηροπλάστης in 74c.

together as the tale proceeds and to all but coalesce. The secondary gods are pure soul ; the demiurge himself must also be soul, since he has, or rather is, wisdom, and wisdom as we have been repeatedly told (30*b* ; cp. *Sophist*, 249) cannot exist without soul. And here we see quite clearly into what absurdities we are led if we press too far and take too literally the details of the myth. The god must be soul as the other gods are, yet it is he who is the creator of all soul—which is absurd. It is characteristic of Plato to express the divine principle as both a unity and a plurality, for he was a Greek and a pagan for all that later interpreters seek to impose monotheism upon him and insist in looking in his work for traces of their own supposedly higher religious conceptions, instead of explaining him in terms of his own.

As for the relation between the gods, the soul of the world and the human souls, there is but little to say if we would avoid pointless subtleties. The gods are very definitely part of the world-soul and indeed, together with the eternal in human souls, *are* that soul for they are, considered individually, the different foci of the soul-force which, considered as a whole, is the soul of the universe. And we may therefore, in view of what has been said before, identify this world-soul in turn with the demiurge who is mythically represented as creating it. And if it be asked why then Plato did not start with the world-soul as such, it must be because he wanted to give an analysis of its different aspects or components, an analysis which is of some importance psychologically, and this could only be done within the cosmological framework by describing the process of its creation. Then the exigencies of the scheme required a moving cause to account for it, and this cause or maker had to come into the picture.

Below all these active souls in the scale of reality is that which makes their activity possible in the physical world, the receptacle, room or matrix, the ἐκμαγεῖον. This is not the place to enter into the difficult question of the nature of this receptacle. Suffice it to say that it is conceived as pure potentiality devoid of form and that Plato seems to have thought of it rather as he pictured the more-and-less of the *Philebus*,[1] namely as an indeterminate background for qualities rather than for

[1] See Brochard, p. 106.

matter. It has, as we saw, a kind of unco-ordinated movement
of its own which is probably to be identified with the resistance
that prevents the Ideas from being perfectly realized and the
world from being perfect. But whatever it is, it is not matter.
It is rather a fusion between sheer space and the indeterminate
qualitatively considered.

We are thus left with the Ideas, an eternal and unchangeable
pattern of all the meanings of the world, which reminds us
once more of the Socratic definitions. Then the gods, perfect
souls working for the good, which together with the same love
of good in the souls of men make up the world-soul in its
totality, while this love of good, considered abstractly and
allied to wisdom which it everywhere aims at, is *the* cause of
life, the maker or demiurge. And below them all the mysterious matrix within which the gods and the divine in men strive
to realize a physical representation of the supreme Ideas.
That men and gods thus have a common aim naturally leads
to the idea of co-operation between them, a conception
elaborated in the *Laws*.

For with religion as with so many things, it is in the *Laws*
that we must look for the fullest discussion and for Plato's last
word on the subject. It should be noted that this is the first
time that the gods appear in a dialectical and not a mythical
discussion. Not that any very great interest in ritual is evinced
even here. Men should worship the gods in accordance with
their city's laws (κατὰ νόμους, 885c), as Apollo said they should,
for this will prevent all kinds of impious deeds. Plato never
attached much importance to the manner of worship ; what
he desired was worship, and worship of the right things.
Hence it is with the fundamental assumptions of the impious
that he is led to deal at some length, and these can be of three
kinds : either men do not believe in the gods at all ; or they
believe that the gods exist but take no thought for the affairs
of men ; or finally they think that the gods can easily be
placated by prayer and sacrifice.[1] Each of these errors he tries
to refute in turn, special attention being paid to the first.

The Spartan does not think it will be difficult to prove the
existence of the gods ; are not the order of the world and the

[1] Cp. *Rep.*, 365d–e.

prevalence of belief in gods a sufficient proof? But the
Athenian points out that we have to deal not with men whose
atheism is merely an excuse for depravity, but with a long line
of scientists and writers ancient and modern. Do they not
say that the sun, the earth, the moon and the stars are no more
than earth and stone?

Those who will not believe the tales they have learned at
their mother's knee Plato attacks (887c) with a violence that
seems strange in one who disbelieved so many of those stories
himself, until one realizes that there is an undercurrent of
irony about the details of this passage, as is but natural from a
cultured Athenian towards the much less cultured Dorians.
This however in no way militates against the seriousness of the
main contention that the gods exist because every one believes
in them, an argument repeated once more in an appeal to
the young unbeliever to suspend his judgement till later, for
of those who disbelieved in youth none has kept this disbelief
in old age, though the other fallacies may remain. All this is
no serious argument, and we soon turn to a full discussion of
the unbelief of scientists and philosophers, and of their account
of the world.

They say that things come to be either by nature, chance,
or purpose (τέχνη). Nature and chance to them both imply
the absence of a directing mind, so that purpose can only exist
in human affairs and therefore arose definitely later in time.
On this assumption the world has come to be mechanically
through the accidental mixture of the elements. To purpose
and mind, they say, can be due only such things as men have
made : arts of various kinds, laws and constitutions, all of
which are only conventions without warrant in nature itself.
So also they maintain the gods have been made by man in his
own image and are purely a convention. This discussion of
the atheistic position takes us back once more to the double
standard, the natural and the conventional, the difference
between which had been such a favourite topic of discussion
among the sophists. This ' natural ' philosophy, by destroying
any justification in nature for man's ethical ideals, led to the
life of the mighty rascal so vividly depicted by Callicles in the
Gorgias.[1]

[1] See pp. 53 ff.

To this position (890) Plato addresses himself after insisting at some length upon the need for persuasion rather than direct command to believe. His main argument rests upon the previously established theory that the soul is the only thing that can initiate its own movement, so that all motion must ultimately derive from it. This being so, soul must be prior to body everywhere and comes first also in the world as a whole ; it cannot be made out of the elements (892–896). These indeed cannot exist unless soul does, for all bodily movement is due to external force, as body cannot initiate movement. Since the universe is orderly, the soul which rules the world is one that is endowed with wisdom (897–8). It is clear that Plato here envisages a number of these ruling souls. The soul of the sun, which he then mentions, is only one example : it is endowed with mind, it moves with a spherical motion, which, as the most regular, is the typical movement of the mind always. So that it is the soul of the sun, whether it reside within or outside the physical body we see in the heavens, which is responsible for the sun's movement and so is a god. The same is true of the moon and the stars. The unbeliever must either disprove the premise that the soul is the origin of all motion or else accept the conclusion which follows from it, that the gods exist.

The second error, that the gods do not care for humanity, is more easily disposed of. It is sometimes due to a realization of the great amount of evil in the world allied to a conviction of the goodness and perfection of the gods, so that a man feels loth to hold them responsible for it. And rightly so. But it should be easy to prove that the gods care for the small as well as the big. We know they are good, that they cannot have any evil in their composition and thus cannot be lazy or careless ; since they know all they know that the part, however small, is important to the whole. Further, man and every creature endowed with soul is the possession of the gods as is the whole of heaven. They must therefore care for him as a doctor or any other craftsman will care for the detail as well as the whole. The gods cannot surely be worse than they. Every part exists as part of a whole and its function is in relation to that whole even if we, who cannot see the whole, do not always understand it (903*b*) :

' Let us persuade the youth that he whose care is for the whole has arranged everything for its preservation and excellence so that every part does and endures what is suitable as far as it is able. Governors have been assigned to them unto their smallest deed or affliction, achieving the ultimate aim unto the smallest fraction. And one of these parts are you, reckless man, and small though that part is it tends towards the whole it has in view. But you do not see that everything comes to be to realize this aim so that the nature of the whole may live happily. Not for your sake does it come to be, but you for the sake of the whole. For so every doctor, every skilful craftsman makes all for the sake of the whole, not the whole for the part. But you are angry because you do not know how best you will agree with the whole and with yourself according to the force of common creation. And because a soul joined with a body suffers all kinds of changes now this way and now that, either on its own or through contact with another, the Draughts-Player's work is only to move a character that has become better to a better place, a worse to a worse place, each according to his deserts so that he may have a suitable fate.'

He then further elaborates this picture : the world, itself a compound of body and soul, is everlasting though not eternal, it moves the pieces of the game which are ourselves up or down according to our way of life. And every individual soul is thus responsible for its own little province. Thus the vigilance of the gods is vindicated and man must bear the responsibility for his own life (905*d*).

It follows from this that the gods cannot be tempted from the path of justice by prayer and sacrificial offerings (905*e*) :

' One might also compare the gods to doctors who watch over the war of diseases in the body, or to farmers who fearfully expect the usual difficult weather for their crops, or to cattle-herds.

We have agreed that the world is full of many good things, full also of many things that are not good, and that the latter are more numerous. This makes for an eternal struggle, one that needs marvellous watchfulness. In this fight the gods and spirits are our allies while we are their property. We are destroyed by injustice and excess and folly, saved by justice, moderation and knowledge, all of which latter dwell in the living power of the gods. To some extent, clearly, they are also found among ourselves. But some souls that inhabit the earth are of evil character and bestial. Coming in contact with other souls (whether of watchdogs or shepherds or mighty masters) they persuade them by flattery and the charm of attractive wishes that they may give way to excess upon earth without suffering for it. And this error that we are now mentioning, excess, is in the body called disease, in the cycle of the seasons it is pestilence, whereas in cities and governments it is called —as the name implies—injustice.'

Clearly such gods as these cannot be bribed by prayer and sacrifice, for they cannot be worse than honest men.[1]

The Athenian then proceeds to describe the type of punishment suitable for these three kinds of impiety; and even though he makes a difference between the unbeliever of good, and the one of bad, character, the penalties of imprisonment and death which he contemplates seem to us terribly severe, and call to mind the horrors of the Inquisition. But it is important to remember that Plato had no experience of a persecuting religion, and could not foresee the abuses to which such a system is open.

How much does Plato require from his citizens in the way of belief? They must believe that gods exist, that they care for humanity, that they cannot be bribed by prayer and sacrifice. These gods must be worshipped in accordance with the laws, which means that all citizens must take part in the public religious festivals dedicated to certain not very clearly defined powers that are on our side in the fight against evil. Private rites are forbidden. Further than this Plato does not go; there is nothing more in the way of dogma, no creed to which the citizen is expected to subscribe, no sign that these gods will interfere at every turn through their appointed priests with the ways of life of the ordinary man, no definite way of approach or of prayer is specified. The ' atheist,' then, is the man who does not believe that there is any order or purpose in the universe, no powers outside man and greater than man that make for good; or the man who may say he believes in gods but that they are not concerned with humanity, which really comes to the same thing: that man can find no help outside himself; or again the man, and this Plato considers the worst of the three, who believes the justice of the gods can be interfered with by human prayer. Of this third form of disbelief

[1] Cp. *Rep.*, 364c–e.

the orthodox religion was, of course, always guilty. Granted
these three points, however, the individual is left free.

There is a tendency in the *Laws* which also appears in the
Timaeus and reaches its highest point in the *Epinomis*, namely
the identification of the gods with the souls of the sun, the
moon, the planets and other heavenly bodies. This should be
taken quite literally. It is a natural consequence (the law of
gravitation being, of course, unknown) of Plato's belief that
only soul could originate motion. For then a soul, whether
immanent or not, must be responsible for the motions of such
bodies as moved along a regular path in the sky. We know
that astronomical researches flourished in the Academy and
that one of the problems which Plato set to his students was
to account mathematically for the apparent irregularities of
the planets. If, as is thought, the problem was solved at the
time the *Epinomis* was written and the planets had been proved
to move in accordance with mathematical laws after all, there
must be minds that control such motions (or so it would appear)
and the enthusiastic identification of the gods with the different planets which we find in that dialogue, whether written by
Plato or not, would seem to follow naturally from Platonic
premises. This is not proposing a new religion instead of the
old [1] but rather is it putting new life and new meaning into
an ancient formula, the formula being quite Olympian.

As we look back over Plato's works as a whole we find that
his belief in an order and a purpose in the universe is the same
throughout but that the meaning of his gods deepens and
develops from one period of his life to the other. The keynote
is already struck in the *Euthyphro* where the absolute unchanging
reality of moral values, not subject to any personal will, is
definitely established. These values and other realities later
become the Ideas, and they remain prior to the gods and ultimate to the end.

The words god and gods—θεός, θεοί—are used from the
earliest works up to and including the *Republic* and in many
later passages where the nature of the gods is not the subject

[1] Harward, pp. 19 ff. For the genuineness of the dialogue see pp. 27–58,
and Taylor, *Plato and the Authorship of the Epinomis.*

of the discussion, in what I have called the conventional sense, to indicate anything eternal and more than human and the sum-total of such things ; and this is also true of the myths of this period. Of these passages it is true to say that the gods are the mythical representation of the Ideas in so far as the two never appear together while both seem to describe in turn the whole of the supra-sensuous world.

It is when the gods and the Ideas have appeared together in the myth of the *Phaedrus* that the static and the dynamic aspects of the divine are clearly differentiated and the gods are definitely restricted to the second. The urgent problem now was to work out the relation between the two, which is part of the larger problem of the relation between the Ideas and the world of sense. The germ of the solution was present from the first, for great emphasis is laid on νοῦς or mind in the *Phaedo* itself. Intellect is a function of the soul, human or divine, and so the gods become explicitly souls, and thereby a definite kinship is established between them and mortals. We find the same problem in the *Sophist* where Plato insists that somehow mind and soul must be part of the absolutely real. The soul apprehends the Ideas and the soul is the originator of movement and life as the only thing which can move itself and thereby lead to movement (activity) in the world.

Even though there was never a time when the world was not, the creation-myth of the *Timaeus* is a convenient way of explaining the relative priority and importance of the different forces at work in the world. The creator as a creator is pure myth, but he represents soul in its perfect state (intellect and the power to move), a force at work in the world through a multiplicity of souls human and divine, and upon which everything depends.

Hence it is not surprising that Plato speaks at times in imagery which is very similar to that of Christian writers : he too can speak of the gods as helping us, of the god as the king, the Father and the Maker of the world. But the similarity is very superficial and we should beware of making false identifications.[1] For example, when the demiurge is called the Father, he is so only as the cause and origin of things, the creator. He is nowhere a father in the sense of one who loves

[1] Ritter, II, 771 ff. is guilty of many such hasty identifications.

his children. We love the gods, or rather the Ideas which the
gods love also. But the gods do not love us. Eros, in Plato,
looks ever upwards and the love of god can only be the love
we feel for him (or them). But though the gods cannot love
us they can help and direct us [1] and we in turn can draw
strength from the knowledge that we are at one with the
purpose of the universe and that powers greater than ourselves
are also striving to realize the good.

Nor is Plato ever fully monotheistic, even if he shows a strong
tendency in that direction now and again. As the world to
him must have a purpose, that purpose must be one. But it
always works through a plurality of divine souls. Just as his
ultimate reality in the domain of logic is both a unity and a
plurality in the *Sophist*, so his divinity is and remains god and
yet gods at the same time, and he continues to use the singular
and the plural with an indifference which seems to us, accustomed as we are to regard monotheism as the higher religious
conception, thoroughly perverse.

There was never, for Plato, any antagonism between his
religion and his philosophy though at first they may be said
to have ignored each other. The only beliefs he insists on are
those he thought he had dialectically established : that there
is order and purpose in the universe, that the divine forces
are at work through the whole world and its every part, and
that the universal purpose is inexorable.

---

[1] So the philosopher loves only what is higher than himself. If he must
return into the cave to help those who are still in darkness, it is only as a
duty. He himself would be happier if he remained on the plane of contemplation (*Rep.*, 519c–521b). He is never actuated by love for those below
him. His only urge to help others is due to his love of the good and his
desire to realize it. Here Plato's desire to make his philosopher independent
of the world leads him to an undue avoidance of anything that might make
his happiness depend on the success of his dealings with it. This was probably due to Plato's own revulsion from political life (see pp. 259 ff.).

VI

ART

I. The Arts

When Plato opened the Academy and claimed that philosophy alone could lead men to acquire that wisdom upon which the goodness both of the state and of the individual soul was ultimately based, he was offering himself as a teacher of goodness. Before him there were two classes of men that were so recognized : the poets and the sophists.[1] The latter loudly proclaimed their capacity in this direction, but to expose these claims, which were by no means universally admitted, was a comparatively easy matter and one which caused Plato himself no heart-burnings and no perplexity. The case of the poets was different. It was not so much that they themselves claimed to be teachers of wisdom, as that they had for centuries moulded the religious beliefs of Greece and that men still turned to them for guidance and support as to the arbiters of conduct and of truth. It was therefore inevitable that Plato should deal repeatedly with poetry, and nearly always in connexion with education. This does not mean that the philosopher's motives were selfish or his attitude warped by prejudice. Himself a great artist as well as a philosopher, art was naturally a subject very dear to him, and it is in his own mind, we may well believe, that the quarrel between art and philosophy had to be fought out in the first instance. The philosopher won the day, and was eager to justify his victory to the artist and the world. We shall see how far he was successful. Meantime it is essential to remember, especially when Plato's theory of art will seem at times to narrow down to a discussion of poetry, that the word ποιητής means ' maker ' and was currently used to include every kind of creative artist,

[1] On this point of view see Wilamowitz, I, 478, and Finsler, 220.

and indeed every kind of craftsman as well. So that even where it is used in the more restricted sense of poet,[1] a wider connotation is often vaguely present. Further, Greek poets composed their own music and supervised the dance of the chorus in the performance of their plays, so that even when ποιητής means poet it includes a great deal more than its English equivalent. The same is true of the word μουσική : at times it means music and little else ; at other times it includes all the arts, everything connected with the Muses, as when Plato speaks of education in mousikê where the only correct translation is ' education in the arts '. Even then it is difficult for us to get the proper association, as this ' education in the arts ' was that of every Athenian boy.

Every one remembers how Socrates, in the *Apology*, after hearing that the Delphic oracle had said that he was the wisest man in Greece (21*b*), set out to test the truth of this pronouncement by going to those who had a reputation for wisdom in Athens, expecting to find them wiser than himself; how he found that they did indeed know certain things of which he was ignorant, but that they were quite unaware of the limits within which this knowledge applied ; and how he finally came to the conclusion that the god had regarded him as the wisest because he alone was aware of his own ignorance, because, as he puts it, he did not think he knew what he did not know. In this way he visited the poets among others, and confronting them with their own works, he would ask them to explain their meaning to him, but found that almost any one of the by-standers could do this better than the poets themselves. So he soon came to the conclusion ' that the works of the poets are not the product of wisdom, but of a natural gift, and that they are inspired like prophets and oracles ' (22*c*). They said many beautiful things, but they knew nothing about that of which they spoke.

The *Ion*, a short dialogue in the usual Socratic vein, is a fuller statement of the same theme. Ion is a rhapsode of some dis-

---

[1] Socrates himself explains this in the *Symposium*, 205*b–c*. In the *Phaedo* the expression ποιημάτων ὧν πεποίηκας 60*d*, apparently refers only to Socrates setting to music certain fables of Aesop.

tinction who claims not only to recite, but to 'talk about' Homer better than any other man. Yet he admits that a discussion of any other poet sends him to sleep (532c). But how, Socrates asks, can he know about Homer, unless he knows about the other poets also, since they all write on the same subject : war, peace, and the life of men ? No one makes such a claim in other arts such as painting or sculpture, where it is recognized that criticism of the work of one artist cannot be sound without knowledge of the work of others. Ion is frankly puzzled. Socrates solves the dilemma by saying that it is not knowledge, but inspiration that Ion possesses : (533d)

'It is not a craft (τέχνη) which enables you to talk well about Homer but some divine power which moves you, such as resides in the stone which Euripides calls a magnet, though it is usually called the stone of Heraklea. The magnet not only attracts iron rings, but invests them with the power to do as the magnet does, to attract other rings, so that sometimes a great cluster of iron and rings are hanging one from the other. And all these derive their power of attraction from the original stone. So the Muse herself inspires with divine power, and through those possessed a cluster of others hang on their inspiration and are inspired in turn. All good epic poets utter those beautiful poems not through their craft, but as men possessed by some other power. And the same is true of good melic poets : as corybants dance when beside themselves, so the melic poets are beside themselves when they make those beautiful songs. After they have embarked on harmony and rhythm they are like bacchanals possessed. . . .'

Because they rely on inspiration, poets can only write one type of poetry, whether it be tragedy, lyric or any other, and thus also the rhapsode, as the next link in the chain of inspiration between the poet and the audience to whom he communicates the divine possession to some degree, can perform well only over a restricted field, and the same is true of the actor. Ion is made to insist (535c) upon the violence of his emotions when he recites, and upon his success in communicating these emotions to his audience. We have here a fundamental belief of Plato's, and one which lies at the very root of his attitude to art, namely that successful art depends upon a stream of emotion which flows from poet to actor, and from actor to audience.

Ion is, of course, not quite convinced, and still maintains that he understands [1] Homer better than any one. But what in Homer does he understand so well? The passages about harnessing a chariot? Surely not he, but a charioteer, is the proper authority there, as of the descriptions of fishing a fisherman, and so on. The rhapsode makes a last stand on questions of war and battle, and for a while professes to be the best general in Greece. But he finally abandons this ridiculous claim, and with it any claim to knowledge, while he rests content with the ' divine inspiration ' which Socrates granted him from the first.

Not only the inspiration of the poet, but the beauty of the work he produces, is freely admitted in the *Ion*,[2] and there is here no quarrel between philosophy and poetry, so long as poetry does not, like the poets in the *Apology*, lay any claim to knowledge. In short it is the business of the poet, as Socrates tells us in the *Phaedo* (61*b*) to tell stories (μύθους) and not to give, *qua* poet at least, a logical account of things (λόγους). And when he adds that, in spite of dreams that bade him follow the Muses, he has hitherto neglected the practice of poetry and music to any extent because he is not ' story-minded ' (μυθολογικός) there is more than a hint surely that his is the higher calling, that it is not for nothing that he was the wisest of the Greeks.

When we turn to the *Republic* we find art discussed entirely from the point of view of the educator and the statesman. There is here no mention of inspiration from the gods, nor is the artist considered in himself. We are not concerned with the excellence of a work of art, but only with its social value. That this was its main value to Plato, or at least that any other it may have must be subordinated to this, is clear. But he seems to hint here and there even in the *Republic* that there may be another method of approach.[3] Plato considered art

---

[1] His actual claim is that he can ' talk about ' Homer (536*e*, &c.) better than any one. His power of oratory is, however, not in question, but the content of his criticism, which implies a claim to knowledge.

[2] Note the frequent use of καλός throughout and especially in 534.

[3] Not only where he admits that the art he condemns might be a source of great pleasure to ' the many ', but his condemnation is definitely not on the score of bad art (cf. οὐχ ὡς οὐ ποιητικὰ καὶ ἡδέα τοῖς πολλοῖς ἀκούειν ἀλλ' ὅσῳ

as a most important factor in the state and was very alive to its immense influence upon the lives of men, as well as deeply sensible to its beauty.[1] One quotation on this point should suffice (401*b*) :

' Is it then the poets only whom we shall command and compel either to represent the image of good character in their poems, or else not to practise among us, or shall we give orders to the other craftsmen also, and forbid them to represent, either in pictures or in buildings or any other work, character that is bad, unrestrained, mean and graceless. The man who cannot do this must not work among us, that our guardians may not, bred among evil images as in an evil meadow, culling and grazing much every day and little by little from many things, collect all unawares a great evil in their souls. We must search for such craftsmen as can excellently pursue the nature of the beautiful and the fitting, that our young men may be benefited on all sides like those who live in a healthy place, whence something of the beautiful works will strike their eyes and ears, like a breeze that brings health from salubrious places, and lead them unawares from childhood on to love of, resemblance and harmony with, the beauty of reason (καλῷ λόγῳ).

That is Plato's fundamental position, a general principle with which, in the last analysis, even the purest exponent of art for art's sake will hesitate to disagree.[2] And it is on this solid basis (cp. 395*c*, 391*e*, &c.) that we must examine his remarks and criticisms throughout, without, as is so often done, distorting scattered passages here and there, and completely losing sight of the wood in the contemplation of one perchance too austere and gnarled tree.

In the third book of the *Republic* Socrates has just been discussing the qualities required from his guardians—at this stage little more than professional soldiers [3]—and then passes

ποιητικώτερα, τοσούτῳ ἧττον ἀκουστέον, i.e. the more poetical the more dangerous, 387*b*, cp. 390*a*). Note also the phrase : ' such things may be well with reference to another standard ' (387*c* : εὖ ἔχει πρὸς ἄλλο τι) ; and the even more curious qualification that a good man will not wish to ' imitate ' what is unworthy of him ' except for the sake of amusement ' (ὅτι μὴ παιδιᾶς χάριν 396*e*). For if this amusement were entirely bad, surely the good man would not enjoy it. This question is taken up in earnest in the *Laws* (see below).

[1] See e.g. *Philebus*, 62*c*, where μουσική—the arts—' though full of guessing and imitation ' is admitted into the good life for man ' if our life is to be life in any real sense '.

[2] See p. 205.   [3] See p. 267.

on to their education. As always he emphasizes (377*b*) the importance of early training, and this brings us at once to a discussion of the kind of stories that should be told to them in childhood, and to the question of censorship of art, especially poetry. Many examples of tales about the gods that should not be allowed are given. The gods must not be described in an unworthy manner and, as our guardians must not fear death, we must avoid tales of horror about the underworld.

Noble heroes must not be pictured as giving way to excessive emotions, whether tears or laughter. But any further statement of what are proper subjects of art must beg the question, since goodness or virtue has not yet been found. So Socrates pulls himself up (392*b*), and passes on to a consideration of style and metre. He distinguishes three methods : narrative (διήγησις), impersonation (μίμησις, i.e. imitation), and a mixture of both. Lyric belongs to the first class, drama to the second, and epic, where the author speaks now in his own person, now as one of the characters, to the third. But a man cannot ' imitate ' (i.e. impersonate) many characters alien to his own, indeed we see that the same man cannot even write both comedy and tragedy, for human nature is extremely specialized, and is incapable of doing, or even of ' imitating ' many things well (395*c*) [1] :

' If what we have said before is to hold, that our guardians must be freed of all other duties, if their craft is to make a free city and if they must do nothing that does not tend to this end, then they should neither do nor imitate anything else. If they do imitate, it should be, from childhood on, what is suitable to their work, namely courage, self-control, righteousness, liberty, and everything of that sort. Whatever is slavish they must neither do nor cleverly impersonate, nor anything else that is shameful, in order that they might not, after impersonating them, enjoy the reality of such things. Or do you not realize that imitation, if it persist from childhood, moulds a man's customs and nature, whether in body, voice or thought ? '

[1] So in the *Ion* (p. 181 above) poets can only work in a restricted field. Yet at the end of the *Symposium* Aristodemus woke up to find Socrates arguing with Agathon and Aristophanes that the same man *ought* to be able to write both comedy and tragedy. No doubt the two poets had claimed to write with knowledge. If that is so, Socrates would have argued, knowledge of the comic implies knowledge of its opposite the tragic. But in fact poets rely on inspiration and therefore have only one kind of talent.

I have, in this extract, translated μίμησις by imitation and impersonation indifferently because I wanted to keep both meanings before the reader. The word is of the very first importance and it is essential to be clear as to its meaning before we proceed. It has two ; the general sense is to imitate, the particular sense, carefully defined by Plato himself in this book, is to imitate in a particular way, by impersonation.

Now in this discussion of style μίμησις is not used in the general sense at all. To introduce it here causes a great deal of confusion. For the confusion which results Plato's avoidance of a technical vocabulary and his careless use of words in several senses are no doubt partly responsible. Yet he is less to blame here than in other cases. The word does occur, it is true, in its general sense when he speaks of the ' hunters and imitators ' for whom he must find a place in the second, the feverish, city.[1] But this is before the discussion of style. In the third book at least, the primary meaning remains ' to impersonate ' throughout. The author, inspired by the Muses, identifies himself emotionally with his character, and in direct impersonation this emotional identification is, of course, most complete. The actor or rhapsode, as the next link in the chain, goes through a similar process, and, inspired by him in turn, the audience does the same. This process takes place to a certain extent in simple narration, but when actual impersonation takes place it is far more intense and, so it seemed to Plato, more dangerous. It is not restricted to art only, for we impersonate to a certain extent any one who spurs us to emulation. Plato firmly believed that we become like what we impersonate, and hence the more general statement that his guardians should not be indiscriminate impersonators, but, at the most, ' imitate ' what is good and suitable to their calling. He will not have them exposed, in the theatre, to emotional identification with evil characters. For that reason he will not admit those arts, especially the drama, which rely entirely upon impersonation, and deplores the realism of contemporary art which ' imitates ' not only unworthy characters, but even the sound of wind, storm and torrent, and seeks thereby to affect us

---

[1] 373b, also 388c. Once defined in 392d as impersonation, it is used in this sense only, with such slight change as is needed when applied to other arts.

emotionally to an undesirable degree. Where evil must have its part, it should be given in narrative only.

He admits that pleasure, and that in plenty, can be derived from other kinds of art—but not in our city for ' with us a man will not be double or manifold, since each man has one job to do ' (397e), and he decrees that (398a) :

'If a man who in his cleverness is able to take on many personalities and to impersonate all things, should come to our city with his poems and want to exhibit them—we would it seems bow down before him as before one holy, wondrous and sweet. We would say that there exists no such man in our city and that it is not lawful for such to be there. We would pour myrrh on his head and crown him with wreaths, and send him away to another country. We ourselves would employ a more austere and less pleasurable poet, teller of stories for our own good, one who would " imitate " the speech of a good man, and tell his tale in accordance with the principles we laid down when we were first undertaking the education of our soldiers.'

In this manner does Plato cast out the poet from his ideal state, not all poets indeed, that is at present quite clear, but such as are given to excessive impersonation, for these are dangerous. That tragedy and comedy as we know them come under the ban there can be little doubt, but a good deal of lyric poetry remains, a good deal of epic, and a kind of mixed narrative and drama which is to take the place of the rejected drama. We may suppose this to be not unlike a Greek tragedy in which the messengers' parts would be much extended. Any evil action would take place offstage and be narrated, as is the case with murder in actual Greek tragedy.

The same general principles are then applied to music and metre. Plato is careful not to commit himself as to detail, but makes it quite clear that we shall retain only the simple modes which ' imitate ' the life of brave men in war and noble men in peace. All the orgiastic rhythms and many-stringed instruments that had become the fashion must go.[1] The

---

[1] One may compare the desire of some producers to-day to return to more simple stage settings and to discard the complicated stage machinery and lighting effects which, many now think, only serve to distract the audience's attention.

style [1] is conditioned by the state of the poet's soul, from which the content directly derives, rhythm and music will follow style, and the keynote of the whole is simplicity. And the same rules, as we saw above, will apply to all arts and crafts (400).

Real art, he considers, is impossible without a study of goodness and of life, for one is but the representation of the other. Artistic appreciation is a necessary part of education (401 ff.), but living goodness and beauty is superior to that of any work of art that can only be a preparation for it. In fact Plato extends the meaning of μουσικός, artistic, cultured in art, far beyond art itself, to apply to the lover of all beauty, who (we may supply the thought from later passages) is again none other than the philosophos, the thinker. Such a one, were he an artist, Plato would accept and indeed welcome. There is nowhere any description of the type of work he could create beyond the general principles mentioned already. That such works however are not impossible, and that they would be far more than a mere copy of things, we gather from scattered references : the artist could in the first place combine differently what he sees in nature,[2] though one doubts whether any great art could result from this. But he can do much more. When challenged to prove the practicability of his ideal republic Socrates is made to say (472d) :

' Do you think a man any the less a good painter if he paint a model such as the most beautiful man would be, and having made an excellent picture could not prove that such a man can exist ? '

And again, when defending the philosopher-king (484c) :

' Are such men in any way different from the blind, those who are deprived of the knowledge of every true reality, who have no clear model in their soul, and cannot, as a painter can, with their eyes fixed on that which is most true, using that as a criterion and examining it as exactly as possible, thus establish our laws and traditions about beauty, justice and goodness, when necessary.'

[1] There is no clear differentiation between style and content, and λέξις seems to cover both.
[2] This is clear from 488a, where Socrates, in introducing the parable of the ship, compares himself to ' the painters who draw goat-stags and mix things up in this way '.

Not too much must be made of this passage, where after all
the reference may only be to the way a painter uses his model.
But the same metaphor is used in a far more elaborate manner
(500e–501b) : the philosopher is compared to a painter
because, using the city and the ways of men as his canvas and
the divine as his model, he makes a rough sketch first, and then,
carefully mixing his materials, he perfects the foundation of
his city.[1] On the kind of art which Plato rejects we get further
light in the powerful description of the force of public opinion,
and of the sophists who cater for it. So does the man who
merely studies the passions of the crowd, and reflects them in
his writings, making them, the ignorant, the judges of his
art (493d).

The discussion in the tenth book is somewhat confused
because Plato here seems to be using the word μίμησις in both
the general and the particular sense. We shall do well, however, to hold fast to the meaning of uncritical impersonation
from which he himself starts. For Socrates begins the discussion by recalling that they have previously rejected ' as
much of poetry as is imitative '.[2] This is a quite correct
reference to the third book where all poetry is rejected which
makes too free use of direct impersonation. Under this heading comes tragedy, comedy and Homer whose fondness for
impersonation (direct speech so that the rhapsode speaks in
character) of good and bad men earns him the title of ' the
first of the tragedians '. And throughout book ten the meaning remains very close to this. In impersonation we do not
use our critical faculties, but merely make ourselves as like as
possible to that which we impersonate. This lack of any
critical sense of values, which when poets bring a character
on the stage is impersonation, becomes in the painter a slavish
copying of a particular object and indeed of only one aspect of
that object. Plato is not laying down the rule that artists
should hold the mirror up to nature, but blaming them because that is, in fact, all they do.[3]

[1] Cp. also Cratylus, 424d.
[2] αὐτῆς ὅση μιμητική : this very definitely implies that there is some
poetry that is not imitative.
[3] The usual view, that Plato in the tenth book excludes all poetry from
the Republic is entirely mistaken, as is conclusively proved by J. Tate in his
articles on ' Imitation in Plato's Republic ', C.Q., January 1928 and July–

He condemns this kind of art first by means of the theory of Ideas and then on psychological grounds. The first argument may be summarized as follows (596*d* ff.) :

You can make or represent a large number of things by going around with a mirror and reflecting them into it. The work of a painter is of the same kind. He represents, not the Idea of bed as such, which is the work of god, but the actual bed itself, which is the work of the craftsman who has the eidos of bed before his mind as a model.[1] We have three beds therefore, the eidos, the actual bed, and the picture of it. The painter takes third place as regards truth, for he ' imitates ' the particular bed, and indeed not even that, but only one aspect of it. This ' imitation ' does not require knowledge, and the works of all poets since Homer are of the same kind.

It is idle to say, as many people do, that Homer always knows what he is talking about, or to follow him as a teacher. Indeed, he cannot even, as the sophists can, point to followers who believed in his knowledge. The poetical imitator has no knowledge of that about which he writes, he is a mere ' impersonator '. Stripped of the charm of music and rhythm, the words of such a poet are ' like the visages of the youthful who have no beauty, after the charm of youth has left them '. He can ' imitate ' in word or picture any craft, any art, but he knows nothing about them and has not even the instrument-maker's right opinion which comes from following the instructions of, and consorting with, those who will use the instrument. Hence he will ' imitate ' that which gives pleasure to the multitude, and that only.

This passage implies that ' all poets since Homer ' and all painters are excluded from the ideal republic, and commentators and artists have rushed to censure Plato for this. Too hastily, for what they have forgotten is just that it is an *ideal* republic for which Plato is legislating, ' a city which is not anywhere on earth ', one that is to be for us ' a pattern laid up in heaven ' (592*b*). In such a state no one has ever claimed a place for Pericles, Themistocles, or Solon, or indeed for any statesman that has ever lived. Why should an exception be made for the poets? Even Homer was far from

October 1932. I do not agree, however, that Plato uses ' imitation ' in two senses, one good and one bad, in the *Republic*. I believe the meaning to be essentially one, and such as I have described above.

[1] No doubt the carpenter does, in a sense, ' imitate ' the eidos. But Plato does *not* use the word here when speaking of him.

perfect, and Plato states quite definitely where he found him deficient.

We should be quite clear, however, that poetry as such is not excluded, but only that which is imitative. And Plato is very careful to qualify his references all the time, for he speaks of ' the tragedians ' (who, of course, are impersonators in the full sense of the third book) and the ' imitative poets '.[1]

The exclusion of painting, which is not qualified in this manner, is more startling, especially in view of the illustrations quoted above where it was implied that it was possible for them to imitate the Ideas directly. Note, however, that here also the painter is used to illustrate Plato's point. And to draw conclusions from illustrative passages about what is not the main point under discussion is, in Plato, notoriously dangerous.[2] We may, if we wish to press the point, say that Plato had an unfortunately low idea of that particular art. But what he probably means is that painters *did* in fact copy particulars (as indeed did poets), and he would include all actual painters under this charge, just as he included all actual poets under the ban—so would all actual statesmen be banned, and all orators.

But another kind of painting is no doubt possible, and another kind of poetry, as there is another kind of rhetoric than that practised by Lysias and Gorgias. In every case the good artist ' must have knowledge of what he creates, if he is to create beautifully ' (598e), but his knowledge will be of a very different kind from that which most Greeks so readily conceded to their poets. It will be on the same level, indeed of the same kind, as that of the philosopher.[3]

---

[1] In 600e and 601a he uses the expression οἱ ποιητικοί, where μιμηταί follows or is understood, i.e. the poetical (sc. imitators). The adjective ποιητικοί is not used by Plato for ' poets ', i.e. for οἱ ποιηταί. That all poetical imitators since Homer includes all poets since Homer may, however, be readily conceded. Why not ?

[2] In the very passage summarized above ' the god ' makes the idea. This is quite unprecedented and completely unparalleled elsewhere. See p. 159.

[3] In 598e Plato makes ' some people say ' that good poets who write beautifully have full knowledge of that about which they write. This was the ordinary Greek view. He, of course, agrees that they should, but he does not agree that the so-called ' good poets ' like Homer have any such knowledge. But then a poet good enough to be accepted in the ideal Republic would be a very different thing.

That the products of imitative art are 'at the third remove from the truth' is not the only argument to be brought
against them. They are bad also on psychological grounds.
Sense perception is confused (i.e. a straight stick appears
crooked when dipped in water, &c.,) and it is the business of
intellect to restore order by solving these apparent contradictions. But 'painting and all imitative art'[1] only increase
this confusion and give us no help towards its solution. It is
their nature to copy men in all kinds of actions, pleasant or
painful, voluntary or forced, in all kinds of emotions, quite
indiscriminately. But a man meeting with sorrow must try
to put up a good countenance before his fellows, the value of
human life being a doubtful quantity anyway (604). We
must not kick against the pricks, but must seek to heal our
soul and make it strong, for to concentrate on painful memories
is both cowardly and unreasonable :

'The *imitative poet*[2] has no natural connexion with the controlling
intellect. His wisdom is not concerned with it, if he is to have a
reputation with the multitude, but with the emotional and varied
parts of man because they are a good object of imitation (impersonation).
—Clearly.
—We should be right to attack him then, and place him on a par
with the painter, both because his works contain an inferior truth,
and because he associates with a part of the soul that is of the same
kind, not the best, and is made like to it. And so we were right not
to accept him in a city that is well-governed, because he rouses this
part of the soul, nurtures it and makes it strong, thus destroying
reason. It is as if in a city one were to make the bad men strong
and surrender the city to them, destroying the good. In the same
way we shall maintain that the imitative poet makes for bad government in the individual soul, pandering to that which is unintelligent
and knows not the bigger from the smaller but believes the same
things to be both big and small—a maker of images, far distant from
the truth.'

[1] 603a. One wonders whether the etymology of the Greek word for
painter—ζῳόγραφος, lit. one who draws living things—may not have in-
fluenced Plato in using the painter as an illustration of purely 'imitative'
art.
[2] 605a : ὁ δὲ μιμητικὸς ποιητής : clearly the adjective qualifies the noun.
Not all poets are necessarily included.

When we see a noble hero giving way to excessive emotions on the stage we share his emotions and we praise the poet if he can communicate them to us, though we would consider them unworthy in real life ; our controlling reason relaxes and we ourselves soon become uncontrolled. That is what Homer and the tragedians will do for us—we may well agree that he is the greatest and most poetical of writers of tragedy —and we shall reject such work, but admit hymns to the gods and in praise of good men. The Muse of pleasure we must cast out, lest pain and pleasure rule our city in the place of law and reason (607).

It is hard, Plato admits, to reject *such poetry as this* (607b), and we will gladly listen to any defence that can be made on its behalf, but until it is proved useful as well as pleasant it must go, for fear we should fall back into a state of mere childish passion and emotion.

The whole of this discussion in the tenth book, then, largely supplements what has already been said in the third and is an attack, somewhat enlarged, upon the same kind of art as was there rejected, with the possible inclusion of painting. It is an attempt to prove the condemnation of imitative art on metaphysical and psychological grounds, and though it seems to reject from the ideal state the most cherished Greek poetry it does not really introduce any new theory. To represent it, as is commonly done, as a condemnation of art as a whole is clearly mistaken, and definitely contradicts the commendation of good art, that of the philosopher-poet which is found in this very book as well as elsewhere.

When we come to the glorious myth of the *Phaedrus*, it would seem at first as if inspiration were praised beyond knowledge, for the whole myth is in praise of ' madness ' (μανία) which is but another name for inspiration and pos-session. A contrast has been drawn between madness and moderation (σωφροσύνη, 244a), and men speak, we are told, as if madness were simply an evil. They are wrong, says Socrates, for it is the cause of many blessings : the ancients will bear witness that ' madness which comes from god is a finer thing than the moderation which is from men '. This is in itself an important qualification, but it is true that (245a) :

' the man who approaches the threshold of poetry without the Muses'
madness, convinced that by his skill he will make a good enough
poet, is imperfect in himself, and the poetry of the sensible man will
be set at nought by that of those who are mad.'

Madness is a strong term, but it did not seem too strong to
Plato to describe the power of emotion which expresses itself
in passionate desire (ἔρως), coupled with the feeling of possession by some external power that comes upon men in their
moments of highest inspiration.

But as we proceed we find that there are different kinds
of madness : prophecy, which comes from Apollo, mystic
ritual which comes from Dionysus, poetic madness, from the
Muses, and the madness of love, from Eros and Aphrodite.[1]
And we find ourselves on familiar ground again when we are
told that this erotic madness, the highest of all, is none other
than the love of beauty and of truth, the passion that makes a
man a philosophos, a thinker, and which, here as in the
Symposium, leads one to the contemplation of the eternal
values, the Platonic Forms.   Once more the philosopher stands
well above the poet, and, here as elsewhere, Plato insists that
the philosopher's passion for truth and knowledge is as inspired, as profound, as the madness of the poet, who is thus
beaten on his own ground.   Socrates was no teller of stories
but he was inspired none the less ; indeed to Plato he was so
the more.   And it is not surprising that of those souls that
have lost their wings and fallen to earth, the best, that which
has seen most clearly the eternal verities on high, becomes a
' philosopher ', a lover of wisdom and of beauty, the true
artist [2] (μουσικός) while the poet occupies but the sixth place,
before the artisan,[3] the farmer, the sophist and the tyrant it is

---

[1] 244a–b, 265b. The identification with the different gods is merely a
convenience, and must not be pressed. In particular the separation of
Apollo from the Muses is somewhat artificial.

[2] μουσικός applies to the philosopher. He is a true artist at the art of life.
This conception of life as an art recurs more explicitly. See Laches, 188d;
Philebus, 50b ; Laws, 817c ; and Ritter, II, 800.

[3] That the poet is here placed before the artisan should be remembered, for
too much has been made of the illustration in the Republic where the order
was reversed. Though here the artist is called an ' imitator ', he is clearly
not an imitator of manufactured articles at least. Between the thinker and
the prophet (the second madness), the ruler, the politician, the tradesman
and the trainer of the body all, we must suppose, do at the best share some-

true, but after the law-abiding king, ruler or general, after the politician and the tradesman, after those who train our bodies, after the soothsayer (248*d*).

The second part of the *Phaedrus* is a treatise on rhetoric, and expounds a method which the ' true orator should pursue. Indeed the whole dialogue might well be called a lesson in the higher rhetoric '.[1] Socrates' main point of attack is that oratory as practised aims at pleasure where it should aim at making people better, and that, even on their own low estimate of their craft, orators must have knowledge of the subject of their orations. Even to deceive, knowledge is useful.

The distinction between good and bad art which we found in the *Republic* is supported by the *Sophist* but with interesting differences. The word ' imitation ' (μίμησις) is there used in its general sense, but that need not mislead us. First the imitative arts are included among those that produce something (219*b* ff.). Later, the Eleatic stranger insists on the importance of the imitative arts in education : the danger is, he says, that those who in youth mistake the imitation for the real thing have, when they grow up, to unlearn all the opinions they based upon this error (234*d*). Painters and rhetoricians are explicitly mentioned among the imitators and finally (234*b–c*) the imitative crafts are divided into those which make a faithful copy which looks out of proportion at a distance, and those that merely imitate the appearance of things so that the result looks right at a distance but is, on a closer view, seen to be untrue to the model. This latter class includes painting and the other imitative arts. This is a very suggestive approach and one is forcibly reminded of the care with which Greek artists made their columns, metopes, &c., so that they appeared in the right perspective at a distance. But Plato does not pursue the subject and appears to condemn the practice.

thing of the ' true vision ', or in other words are guided in their life by the vision that is theirs to some degree. *After* them come the prophet, the poet and the tradesman, and last of all those perverters of truth, the sophist and the tyrant.

[1] Diès, II, 418 : ' une leçon de rhétorique supérieure '. He also calls the *Phaedrus* ' le discours programme de la rhétorique platonicienne '. His whole discussion of Plato's attitude to rhetoric is highly suggestive and of the greatest interest. See pp. 208 ff.

Of special interest to us is the passage where the productive crafts are classified all over again into those that make something themselves and those that merely make an image of it. There is a cross division of human and divine. The divine art is responsible for natural objects and their reflection in water, &c. Leaving out the divine we get the following division :

```
productive ⎧ (a) making actual
crafts :   ⎨     object
           ⎩ (b) image making : ⎧ (a) exact copy
                                 ⎨ (b) apparently correct ⎧ (a) by those who know
                                 ⎩     copy :             ⎪     what they copy.
                                                          ⎨ (b) by those who have
                                                          ⎪     no real knowledge
                                                          ⎩     of it.
```

Now art is included under the making of an *apparently* correct copy. There is an express reference there to ' any one who makes his appearance or his voice like yours ' (267*a*), which obviously points to actors and rhapsodes.[1] It is interesting, therefore, that this imitation can be based on knowledge, or merely on opinion, even though the reference be only to the object imitated. As so often in the *Sophist*, the point occurs by the way and is not elaborated. It is worth noting, however, that we have here two quite distinct kinds of artist ; and the one who knows what he imitates has at least a chance, if his knowledge is of the right kind, to produce works of art which Plato approves.

The inferiority of art to philosophy is established from another point of view, the nature of the pleasure it gives, in the *Philebus* (48*a* ff.). The pleasures we derive from seeing tragedy and comedy are there classed with those that are inferior, as being impure, in the sense of being mixed with pain.[2] As Homer said of anger, ' it brings pain even to a wise man, yet flows more sweet than honey '. That the spectacle of tragedy causes such a mixture of pleasure and pain is obvious enough, ' we feel pleasure, yet we weep '. The case of comedy is not so clear, but it is found on analysis that comedy is always bound up with a feeling of envy or of grudge (φθόνος), which is a painful emotion. Ridicule is ever bound up with ignorance

---

[1] So Finsler understands it. (p. 24, where he discusses this passage).
[2] See p. 80.

in the object of it who, in the words of the oracle, does not know himself. Self-ignorance may concern one's property, one's physique or one's mentality (κατὰ τὴν ψυχήν), and it is especially the mentally self-ignorant who are a proper target for ridicule provided only that our butt be not too powerful, for then laughter yields to fear. But to rejoice at the misfortunes of one who is not your enemy [1] is surely bound up with the painful emotion of envy, so that in comedy also our feelings are mixed, and our pleasure impure in that sense. The pleasures of tragedy and comedy therefore, to which dirges are here added, are inferior to those attained in the pursuit of truth. And this is true, Plato continues in a remarkable sentence, ' not only on the stage, but in the tragedy and comedy of life '.

By far the most mature, as well as the most complete, discussion of art is to be found in the *Laws*, where it should be noted we are no longer dealing with an ideal state. In the second book we find that art fulfils two functions : not only are the young to be educated by a proper appreciation of art to have the right feelings, to take pleasure in the right things before the age of reason and ' the first education is through the Muses and Apollo ' ; [2] but this training may get relaxed as we grow older and (653*d*) :

' the gods, taking pity upon the race of men and its labours, established as a rest for them the round of divine festivals, and gave them the Muses and Apollo their leader and Dionysus as compánions at the feast that they might be restored, and the sustinence that is theirs at the festivals with those gods '.[3]

Art, that is—and as always Plato has the dramatic festivals mostly in mind—is also refreshment and recreation for grown men, as well as education for the child. It has its

---

[1] This seems to endorse the common Greek notion that it is right to rejoice at the misfortunes of an enemy, which would seem to contradict the morality of *Republic*, 335*d*, where the just man will harm no one. But as so often, Plato, when not arguing the point, accepts the current morality when it does not affect his argument.

[2] Cp. *Timaeus*, 47*d*, where the importance of music in education is also recognized.

[3] This presumably is the explanation of the ' except for the sake of amusement ' in *Rep.*, 396*e*, quoted p. 182 note 3.

origin in the instinct to move which we all possess, and which is so evident in the inability of young animals and babies to keep still. But while we share this instinct with all living creatures, to man alone has been given ' the perception of order in movement which is called rhythm and harmony '. Education, then, consists in the introduction of order and rhythm into the song and the dance, that is into movement and speech, that one may be able to discern the beauty which will follow. This beauty, however, is not only a technical skill to perform, but a proper appreciation of the meaning of the performance, a tendency to take pleasure in the right things. Content is still more important than technique (654*b*) :

' if we can know the beautiful in song and dance, we shall know rightly who is educated and who is not ' (654*d*).

The song and the dance of the *Laws*, where the words are to be taken in the widest sense, include not only the poetry of the *Republic*, but almost the whole of ' the tragedy and comedy of life '.

Plato once more insists on the necessity for censorship. The beauty of art must represent such things as good men do, such words as good men say, and the connexion between artistic beauty and the good life is as close as ever before (654*e* ff.). Clearly, bad art has the same effect upon a man as bad company, for ' we become like that which we enjoy, even if we are ashamed to praise it ', and the education and play (παιδεία καὶ παιδιά) of the Muses must be restrained ; the poet's pleasure in creation is no excuse for his exhibiting his work before the young. Ideally, we should be able to find out the fundamentally beautiful types of art and to give them the force of law from which no one may depart. The example of Egypt (656*d*), where art has been stereotyped for centuries, shows that some general principles can be established. We must avoid at all costs the craze for novelty which is now (the Athenian says) so widespread (657*b* and 660*b*).

But the next question takes the discussion farther : Why is it that all men do not take pleasure in the same works of art ? Most people say indeed that art must be judged only by the pleasure it gives, and this contention we proceed to examine : We all enjoy representations that are congenial to our nature and habits, and if the two be in agreement, we praise and enjoy the same thing, whereas (655e) :

' those whose nature is good, but their habits the opposite, and vice versa, express praise that is at variance with their pleasure. They say that certain things are pleasurable, but evil. Before men whom they consider wise they are ashamed of the reactions of their flesh (κινεῖσθαι τῷ σώματι), they are ashamed to sing such songs because they would thereby explicitly signify their approval, but privately they delight in them.' [1]

Suppose you had a contest of all kinds of art where pleasure was the only criterion. What would happen clearly is that there would be great differences of opinion between those who differ in age or sex, as they all delight in different things.[2] Art must be judged by pleasure certainly, but it must be the pleasure of the right people. Not by the pleasure of the mob, as is the case in Athens, where the judge is swayed by the noisy approval of the audience. The judge should be the teacher, not the pupil, of the people (659b). In short, popularity is no proof of beauty in art, and pleasure is no guide, since we all find it in different things. ' We rejoice when we think we are doing well, and we think we are doing well when we rejoice ' (657c), and it is the business of the lawgiver to see that it should be ' well ' indeed.

After a passage in which he ensures that the whole city, young and old, men and women, shall take their part in ' the song in chorus ' and a discussion of the good life which the poet must represent (659–667b), Plato sets out to find a kind of art that shall be more beautiful than that of the common theatre, for as in the *Republic*, tragedy and comedy as we know them must go, and he now discusses how a right judgement on matters of art can be arrived at, in a passage that is of the greatest interest (667b–672b).

There are three aspects of a work of art : its charm (the pleasure it gives), a certain correctness of technique, and the good it does (χάρις, ὀρθότης, ὠφελία). Pleasure is found in

---

[1] We may remember that in the *Frogs* Dionysus refuses to choose between Aeschylus and Euripides because he considered the one wise but enjoyed the other (1411).

[2] (658c–d) Children would prefer conjurer's tricks, older children comedy, young men and educated women tragedy, old men the epic (the last being the mixed style of the third book of the *Republic*).

many things, but it is only a by-product : food is pleasant, but we judge food by its health-giving powers ; learning is pleasant, but it is its truth and usefulness that make it what it is ; so also with a work of art. If there be any work of art which does neither good nor harm (which is implied to be very improbable) it can be judged purely on its pleasure value, and this indeed would be ' pure play ' (667*e*).

Now every imitation must be judged by the standard of truth, and art comes under this head without exception.[1] To judge a work of art, therefore, we must know the nature of that which the artist is trying to represent (τί βούλεται), that of which his work is an imitation. *For example*, to judge a picture of a man, you must know what a man is, the propor- tions and relations of the limbs to one another. Thus alone can we judge if a work is technically correct.

In fact any judgement on art will be in two stages : first, having decided what it is that the artist is trying to represent, we shall draw upon our knowledge of the model to decide whether the representation is correct. Then we shall decide, Plato continues, whether it be well done in the sense that it will have a good effect upon those who see and hear it. It should be unnecessary to emphasize here that the painter is once more taken as a clear example only, in the other arts also we must find out ' what the artist is trying to do ' and whether he has succeeded in his aim before we proceed to give a moral judgement. Indeed technical correctness is explained as follows (669*c*) :

' The Muses would not be so mistaken as to make the words those of a man, the attitude and tune those of a woman, they would not ally the tune and bearing of a free man with a rhythm proper to the slavish and the mean, or again to a rhythm and bearing free join a song and speech quite the opposite, and they would not join the utterances of beasts and men and instruments and confuse every noise in one as if they were imitating one model. . . .'

That is, under ' correctness ' Plato includes consistency and characterization. ' Every song is correct (ὀρθῶς ἔχει) which contains what is suitable, mistaken if it does not ' (670*c*).[2]

---

[1] Art is ' imitation and imagery '. See below.

[2] Cp. *Cratylus*, 430*c* : where προσῆκον καὶ ὅμοιον is what is called ὀρθότης here, and also the passage from the *Sophist* discussed above.

The last stage, the judging of the good or evil that a work of art will do, the majority cannot hope to attain, nor indeed need the poet, but the judge must. Just as in a symposium, while others are more and more intoxicated and free in their speech, the master of the feast must remain sober and keep the revellers on the path of decency and decorum ; so the judge of drama must remain sober also and his orders must be implicitly obeyed. He must not, that is, allow himself to be swept off his feet by the wave of emotion that will pass over the audience, but keep his eye upon the good or bad effects of the performance.

It is interesting to note that Plato, though he insists that the poet must obey the lawgiver, admits here that the moral value of his work is not the poet's business. In a sense he is giving up his ideal of the poet-philosopher which we found in the *Republic* and the *Phaedrus*, and he admits that the poet and the audience will both derive pleasure—aesthetic pleasure presumably—from the realization of the ' correctness ' of a work of art, by which he means technical perfection in the widest sense. But in cases where the moral effect of the work is bad, this pleasure will be denied to them, as the performance will be banned. Thus he explicitly differentiates between an aesthetic and a utilitarian standard though he still insists that the latter must be supreme.

We should also note that the ability of the lawgiver to judge a work on moral grounds is but a last stage, and that to be a competent judge of it includes the previous stage : the realization of the aim of the artist and of its technical or aesthetic value. Presumably these factors must be taken into account.

Art naturally comes up again in the course of the next ten books, always in close connexion with education. Plato repeatedly condemns the amorphous confusion of contemporary art, and especially music. There at least, in the old days, he tells us, the different kinds were clearly distinguished. A man wrote a hymn to the gods, a dirge, a paean or a dithyramb, with appropriate rhythm and melody. Now everything is mixed and confused. Every kind of thing is done at once, all noises must be represented and poets, intoxicated by pleasure, lose sight of what is right (700*a*–701*b* ; 800*d*, 812*d*). Everything is done to please the mob and we have a ' theatrocracy' instead of an aristocracy—the rule of the crowd instead of the rule of the best—in all forms of art (701*a*).[1] It is to avoid this that he wants the different kinds of art fixed (799*a*; 801*a* ff. ; 816*c*) so that innovations will be avoided. Always the artist must obey the law-giver, and the Board of censors which will consist of the minister of education, the guardians of the law and some other citizens over fifty years of age, must be supreme (800*a* ; 802*b–c*).

There is an interesting passage where the Athenian is asked to give an example of the kind of art he would recommend. Elsewhere he answers : selections from past authors that are representations of the good life (812*b*), hymns to the gods and praises of the great dead (801*e*) and the compositions on these subjects by the elders, even if less artistic than others (828*d*). Here, however, he quotes his own work as an example (811*c*) :

' I am not altogether at a loss for an example. For now, as I look at the things we have said (λόγοι) since daybreak, they seem to me to be very like literature of a sort (ποιήσει τινι). And perhaps it is not strange that I should feel pleasure when I consider as a whole, as it were, arguments spoken after my own heart (λόγους οἰκείους). They seem to me to be, more than most of what I have known or heard in poetry or prose, most fair and suitable for the ears of the young. I do not think I could recommend a better model to guardians or educators. . . .'

Plato was probably over eighty when this was written, and his emphatic words surely apply to more than the *Laws*. Is it fanciful to suppose that he is answering those critics who accused him of doing away with ' poetry' altogether by pointing to his own works?

He condemns also the common Greek habit of learning large sections of poetry and even whole poets by heart without discrimination and without paying sufficient attention to the contents. Such learning by rote, he tells us, leads to superficial and discursive knowledge—polymathy as he always calls it (810*e*).

There is a last word to say about drama. Tragedy must submit to censorship or go elsewhere. The case of comedy was always more difficult for him (816*d*) :

[1] Cp. *Theatetus*, 173*c*.

' If a man is to acquire wisdom, he cannot learn what is earnest without knowing what is laughable, for the knowledge of anything implies the knowledge of its opposite. On the other hand, he must not write both if he is to share in goodness even a little, which is the very reason of his wanting both kinds of knowledge, in order that he should not because of his ignorance do or say something laughable when he ought not.

We must decree that only slaves and hired foreigners must represent such things. No one should ever take them seriously. Clearly any one who learns such things cannot be counted among the free, whether man or woman ; something unfamiliar ought always to be felt about them.'

We may now try to understand more clearly the meaning of the Platonic theory of art as ' imitation '. We have seen that the word is used in a general and, in the *Republic*, in a more restricted sense. General statements that art is imitation can be found not only in the *Laws*, but throughout the dialogues.[1] It is possible to argue that this does not mean very much, since the whole physical world is, in a sense, an imitation of the world of Forms. Why should not works of art be imitations in the same sense, expressing the Ideas in the physical world, without the intermediate model of that physical world itself? There is nothing in Plato's conception of the relationship between the two worlds which precludes such an escape out of the difficulty. There is, however, a very definite objection, namely that he himself never says a word to indicate anything of the kind. Quite the contrary. Not only in the *Republic*, but in the *Sophist*, and indeed wherever art is mentioned, we get quite the opposite impression. This being the case we are reluctantly driven to the conclusion that when Plato classes all artists as imitators he means quite definitely that they have the particular phenomena of the world of sense as their model.

References to art as imitation and imagery occur in Xenophon also. They may go back to the historical Socrates, though it is improbable that he worked out their implications. As so often, that task was left to Plato. After him it is a

[1] e.g. *Laws*, 668a. Cp. *Phaedrus*, 248e, *Politicus*, 288c, *Sophist*, 234b (quoted above) *Cratylus*, 429. This conception of art as imitation does not seem to have originated with Plato (see Finsler, pp. 11 ff.). As so often he takes over a rather vague doctrine, discusses it and deepens its meaning.

commonplace. Now it is worth noting that this first thought-out theory of Art does definitely establish a connexion between the artist and life. It does not look upon him as a mere teller of idle and empty tales. It recognizes his claim as an educator, thus giving theoretical expression to the general Greek feeling, and justifies respect towards poetry as a help to the good life. It further extends this respect to all the other arts on the same terms. Instead of loudly blaming Plato for reducing poetry to mere imitation of life, we should first praise him for recognizing its connexion with life.

Reverence for the poets of old had led men to look upon them for guidance. Plato emphatically agrees that they should guide, but he is eager to point out that they are not, in themselves, infallible guides. They do not possess knowledge, and knowledge alone is infallible. He does deny that imagination, poetical intuition or whatever we like to call it, is a faculty superior to thought. Like every other ' maker ' the artist must submit to the dictates of those who have the good of the state at heart and who know how to pursue it.

When he attacks the exaggerated claims of the artist in the *Republic*, it is with this in mind. They have not knowledge of good and evil, they do not adopt a critical attitude. Relying merely on inspiration they represent human life and identify themselves emotionally with their characters. And it is here that he restricts the word μίμησις to impersonation. By which he means that poet or actor or rhapsode identifies himself with a character, becomes that character for the time being, for we ' become what we imitate '. Applied to the other arts, especially in book ten, the word broadens its meaning, but its essential content is still the same : uncritical copying of an object, being quite uncritically affected emotionally by it. The ' imitative poets ' of the *Republic* are just those who do this. This class includes all actual poets since Homer in parts of their work at least and they are all banished from the ideal state. But that is, I repeat, the *ideal* state.

All imitative poets are bad, the word imitative being used in the restricted sense explained above. But the existence of other poets is implied. In the more general sense all poets are imitators. The passage from the *Sophist* on imitation quoted above allows of two kinds of imitation : the first is based on knowledge, the second not. In discussions of art in the *Republic* the word imitation is used to refer to this second kind of imitation only. Such loose terminology is quite like Plato and can be paralleled in other fields.[1] The philosopher-poet would not be an imitator in the bad sense, and would not have been called an imitator in the *Republic*. But he would elsewhere, in the general sense. The matter is further complicated in that Plato seems to have given up hope of the philosopher-poet—who would need no supervision, because he is one of the supervisors—by the time he wrote the *Laws*, as he had all but given up hope of the philosopher-king.[2] Hence in that dialogue *all* poets must submit to censorship, and he does not even expect them to be concerned with the moral effect of their work. That is the statesman's business.

I have said that Plato would have called every artist an imitator, and that by this he meant an imitator of physical objects. Even the perfect artist would be that. This putting of the artist below even the artisan in the scale of reality is repellent to the modern mind. Where Plato does this explicitly he is, it is true, referring to the kind of art he condemns. But an imitator the artist remains. Few would agree with this, few would admit that the artist is incapable of expressing the abstract directly. And Plato himself could be convicted of inconsistency for do not his myths represent, however dimly, truth which the human intellect, or that of the particular audience, cannot reach scientifically ? Even if we grant that he is right in his belief that the artist's imagination is a faculty inferior to the intellect, and that imagination is never a short cut to God ; that he would have been right to despise those who prefer his myths to his mathematics ; even so, is not the educative value of art, in which he himself so ardently believes, justified because the artist can, however dimly, grope towards truth which intellect cannot reach and not merely because he reproduces the lives of good men which are not always available as a pattern for the young ?

[1] An exact parallel is the use of ἐπιθυμίαι or desires. The word is freely used to mean the third and lowest part of the soul. Yet in *Rep.*, IX, we find that *each* part of the soul has its own desires. And the same word ἐπιθυμίαι is used in both senses. See pp. 135 ff.

[2] See pp. 279, 284.

There is no doubt that Plato is mistaken here, and inconsistent. The artist must, if confusedly, represent, or (to use Plato's language) imitate, the universal Forms as well as the particulars. Yet it should not be denied that his theory of imitation does contain a great deal of truth, for in his imagery at least the artist must copy nature. Plato was surely right to say that you must know what a man is before you can make a picture of him, that you must know life before you can write a tragedy. And there must be some correspondence between the model and the work of art. If there is not it ceases to be the intended picture of a man or a dramatic representation of life, and probably ceases to be a work of art. The parable of the ship of state in the *Republic* could not be drawn by some one who knows nothing of either ship or state. Is not the vividness of the picture directly due to the close correspondence to an actual ship at sea? Is not the whole point of the myth of the day of judgement lost upon one who has no idea at all of the functions of an earthly judge? In this way all painting, poetry, sculpture, and perhaps all art, must draw their imagery from actual life. And we should remember that to a Greek music was closely connected with eurythmics and was thus a much closer 'imitation' of the rhythm and movement of the dance. Even to-day a case might be made for the point of view that music, when it rouses in us certain emotions, is thereby re-creating and in a sense 'imitating' the emotions current in human life and the rhythms that cause them. Plato even thought of architecture as reproducing human character and feelings in its edifices.

Certainly no one ever more profoundly believed in, or more emphatically expressed, the powerful influence that the arts possess over the development of the human soul. It is the very strength of this belief that makes him insist upon the necessity for censorship. In this again he may have been mistaken, but every civilized state has adopted his main principle. No doubt the line is drawn differently, though who shall say if more wisely? To ridicule or condemn particular applications of the principle is at this interval of time, and in a different civilization, rather a foolish pastime. With the principle itself we can only disagree if we deny the need for censorship altogether. It is not enough to take refuge behind common law and to say that the law of libel, blasphemy or indecency is sufficient, for that is still censorship.

Plato had the dangers of excessive freedom so vividly before his eyes in this as in other things that he reacted to the other extreme, and enounced for the first time the theory of censorship of art. We, with the evils of repression brought home to us in a hundred ways every day of our lives, are likely to think him wrong.

Essentially, however, the principle of censorship means the subordination of art to the good. Such expressions as art for art's sake would have seemed to Plato absurd. Revolt against an unenlightened censorship has little to do with the question : many books now banned in most civilized countries would obviously be beneficial, many films [1] now shown are clearly bad. But those who denounce Plato's subordination of art to what he considered good for the state must be prepared to defend the rights of pornography as well as those of great art. And even if they do so they are probably actuated by the belief that there would be a balance of advantage to the community, which leaves the good supreme, and the beautiful still the useful, as it was for Plato.

One problem remains. We may admit that there is a great deal of truth in his theory of imitation, that censorship of Art has been generally adopted, that intellect is a higher function than imagination ; all this does not explain why Plato did not develop the hints he gives us here and there of what great art might be. Why did he so obstinately refuse to say that an artist might imitate the Forms direct, even if his imagery had to be drawn from actual life, as must the material for anything that man can make ? There was nothing in this that would have conflicted with any part of his philosophy and it would have helped to justify his own profound belief in the educative value of works of art. That contemporary art had degenerated, and that he had no sympathy with the modern tendencies of his day is not a sufficient reason, for he ruthlessly condemns Homer and the great tragedians. The ' Muse of pleasure ' must go, but why does he come so near to banishing all the Muses ?

[1] The cinema is the only form of art which has as wide an appeal as the drama had at Athens, and we should think of it in those terms.

The reason is probably to be found in the development of the philosopher's personality.[1] We are here on very slippery ground, so that I make the following suggestion not as a statement of fact but merely as an indication of the direction in which I believe the ultimate solution to lie. That he was sensible to the beauty of art is obvious, more especially so in his earlier works. Himself one of the world's supreme artists and supreme thinkers he must have found ' the tragedy and comedy of life ' of far more absorbing interest than any drama performed on the stage, and derived far greater pleasure from the contemplation of it. For, as Socrates tells us in the *Protagoras*,[2] thinking men do not need artists to explain the world to them.

As a man with an unsurpassed zeal for the betterment of human society—and to this his anger at humanity's stubborn stupidity and the underlying vein of pessimism and despair so frequent in his later works bear sufficient witness—Plato's centre of interest was human life itself. When he became a mathematician and a philosopher, the discoverer of the eternal Forms, the keenest of all pleasures must have been to him, especially as he grew older, the discovery of a new concept, the establishing of new relations, the solving of abstract mathematical, logical, or astronomical problems. Not so intense perhaps as the physical pleasures or even the contemplation of a work of art, yet so much more lasting, to him at least so much more *real* than those.[3] Until at last he grew impatient of his own art. There are magnificent passages even in the *Laws* which prove him a great artist to the end, but there can be no doubt that the dramatic verve of the *Protagoras*, the unique magnificence of the *Symposium*, the soaring imaginative splendour of the *Phaedrus*, are not found in the works of the last period. As he kept his own art in check—or perhaps we should say in undue subjection to his reason (mere carefulness of language, such as avoidance of hiatus in the later works, is a quite different thing)—as he ruthlessly subordinated form to matter in his own works, so he was led to relegate art as a whole to the education of the

---

[1] I have developed this suggestion in my article on ' Plato's Theory of Beauty,' *Monist*, 1927.

[2] 347c.   [3] See p. 78.

young and the relaxation of adults, as something which contributed much less to the life of men, something which uncontrolled—for are most men not children to him?—would
lead them astray, something of immense influence upon men
who had not reached the age of reason, but which like the games
of children, which were also important, must be arranged
for them by the philosopher-statesman who had a mature
sense of values such as neither they nor the artists could hope to
attain.

II. RHETORIC

Rhetoric was for the Greeks an art, and the one with which
the educated man came in closest contact. Poets still wrote
for recitation or performance on the stage ; the speeches
of orators, including Isocrates, however carefully prepared,
were meant to be spoken. Even historians, at least before
Thucydides, meant their words to be read aloud.[1] It follows that rhetoric, the science of the spoken word, was to
Plato far more intimately related to poetry, and to literature
generally, than it would seem to us. Hence it is not surprising that in the *Gorgias* he passes from the condemnation
of rhetoric to that of poetry without any conscious change of
subject and that the discussion of the art of speaking in the
Phaedrus is continually broadening out into a discussion of the
whole of literature at least. For it is in those two dialogues
that rhetoric is dealt with at some length.

In the first, Gorgias, himself the founder of the art for the
Greeks, sophist and speaker of great repute, insists that it is
the finest of all human pursuits and enables men to govern
the state, for it gives them the power to persuade judges,
councillors, indeed any assembly, even when they do not
possess special knowledge. It is then, says Socrates, the art of
persuasion. There are, however, two ways of persuading men.
You can teach them a thing is true, or you can make them
believe it, without giving them any real knowledge of the
subject under discussion. The latter is what rhetoric does.
Further, it can only be used among those who do not already
possess the knowledge themselves. Is it necessary for the
orator himself to have knowledge, of right and wrong for

[1] On this point see Friedländer, I, 126 ff.

example, things he must needs discuss continually? Gorgias
contradicts himself on this point and retires from the argument
which is then taken up by his pupil and admirer, Polus.
We have here the main points of Plato's aversion to rhetoric
as taught and practised. It does not impart knowledge, nor
require it in the speaker. It has therefore no firm foundation
and, as he goes on to prove to Polus, who has admitted that
rhetoric aims at pleasure (462c), it is only a form of flattery.
This theme Socrates pursues with gusto by giving a list of four
crafts or sciences. which care for the body or the soul, each of
which has its counterfeit that tries to supplant it, as
follows (464a) :

BODY			SOUL
	Sciences		
Physical culture	Medicine	Law-making	Corrective justice
	Counterfeits		
Cosmetics	Cookery	Sophistry	Rhetoric

The four sciences are based on knowledge and use this with a
view to secure good or well-being in body and soul, that is
health and moral goodness. The four counterfeits are based
only on unanalysed experience, on unrelated perceptions.[1]
They aim only at pleasure. This vivid classification gains
greatly in point if we remember that orators were fond of
claiming that they were doctors of the soul and that Gorgias
himself, in a fragment still extant, boasts that ' the ability to
speak has the same effect in bringing order to the soul as
orderly medicines have upon bodies.' [2] Socrates is putting
the rhetoricians in their place with a vengeance. Far from
being on a par with medicine, they are not scientists or craftsmen [3] at all. Far from being doctors of the soul, they are its
cooks, and bear the same relation to the judge as the cook to the
doctor. How annoyed those superior teachers of rhetoric must
have been when they read on and found Socrates explaining

---

[1] This is the meaning of ἐμπειρία in 462c, and αἰσθομένη, οὐ γνοῦσα in
464c.
[2] This point is made by Diès (II, 45) who quotes Gorg. Helen 14 (Diels)
Gorgias' word is τάξις, and it is interesting to note the emphasis on τάξις of
the soul later in the dialogue (504 ff.). See Protagoras' similar claim in
Theaet., 167a.
[3] τέχνη. On the meaning of this word see p. 223.

that their popularity was of the same kind as that of the cook among ignorant children who would assess his merit much higher than a doctor's ! The picture calls to mind Socrates' refusal to appeal to the pity of his judges in the *Apology*. Like the doctor before the imagined jury of children, he too was put to death. That is rhetoric as taught and practised. There may, Socrates admits, be another kind which would try to make the souls of citizens as good as possible, which would always fight for what is best, whether this pleased its hearers or not. There may—but it has never yet been seen (503*a*). Not even the most illustrious statesman, not Pericles or Themistocles, not Miltiades or Cimon have practised it. The word ῥήτωρ to a Greek always had primarily political associations, and the transition from rhetoric to politics was very natural. So is the transition to art, and Socrates naturally includes music as one of the pursuits that cater for the pleasure of the crowd, and from music he goes on to poetry in general and tragedy in particular (502*b*). Like the orators, poets do, in fact, aim only at pleasure, and tragedy too is a kind of flattery.

In the *Phaedrus* Socrates puts the problem as follows (259*e*) :

' Is it not essential to a good and fine speech that the speaker know the truth about the things he intends to discuss ?
—This is what I hear on that point, Socrates : that it is not necessary for one who intends to be an orator to learn the truth about right and wrong, but only the opinions of the crowd that will judge his case. He need not know what is really good or beautiful but only what will seem to be so. For it is this that leads to persuasion, not the truth.'

This was, as we also saw in the *Gorgias*, the opinion generally held by the recognized teachers of rhetoric. They regarded it, the more thoughtful of them, as a science which had the means of persuasion as its province, and had nothing whatever to do with philosophy, metaphysics, or ethics. Let us see how Socrates deals with this pseudo-scientific point of view (260*b*) :

' —If I were to persuade you to get a horse to repel an enemy attack, but neither of us knew a horse, and I knew this much about

you : Phaedrus thinks that the tame animal with the longest ears
is a horse.

—That would be ridiculous, Socrates.

—Wait a moment. If I were earnestly to persuade you, by
making a speech in praise of the donkey, which I would call a horse,
and to say that this animal is most valuable at home or on a cam-
paign, that he is good to fight on, able to carry equipment and useful
in many other ways.

—That would be altogether absurd.

—But is it not better to be ridiculous and popular rather than
clever and disliked ?

—One would think so.

—Well then, whenever the orator who does not know good from
evil undertakes to persuade a city equally ignorant, he is not indeed
praising the shadow of a donkey as being that of a horse but he is
praising evil as being good; for, being versed in the opinions of the
crowd, he persuades them to do evil instead of good. What sort of
a harvest do you suppose rhetoric will reap from the seed it has
sown ?

—Not a good one.

—But perhaps we have insulted the art of speaking more than it
deserves. And it might answer : " What sort of nonsense are you
extraordinary people talking ? I do not compel any one who is
ignorant of it to learn to speak the truth ; but, if my help counts for
anything, he will acquire the truth first and me afterwards. This is
what I boast of : that without me he who does know the truth will
not be able to communicate it scientifically." '

He then proceeds to equate oratory with the art of speaking
generally, whether in a crowd or in private conversation and
makes the interesting point that even if oratory consists in
misleading people into mistaking one thing for another, i.e.
in making them think that A is B, you will do this most successfully by emphasizing some characteristic that A and B
have in common, and to do this properly you must yourself
know the real nature of both A and B.

It follows that the orator must know what he is talking about
even if his intention is only to deceive. In the speech under
discussion [1] Lysias, by not defining his subject, did not make
clear what he meant by a lover (the implication being that
he did not know it himself) ; he took it for granted that we

[1] For summary of the speeches see pp 100 ff.

all know.   But in fact this is the sort of thing people disagree
about.   We all know what we mean by gold or silver, but not
what we mean by right and wrong.   Men are easily deceived
about such things, and it is therefore the special field of rhetoric.
That is why we must first study these things and know the characteristics of each.   Socrates gives as examples of good rhetoric
his own careful definition of the kind of Eros under discussion
in each of his two speeches (265e) and points out that these
definitions were arrived at by a sound method of division
' in accordance with the Forms ' that is in accordance with the
different kinds of love existing.   This method the rhetorician
must learn.   He must therefore be acquainted with dialectic
and ultimately the best orator is the philosopher who has
acquired technical oratorical skill also.

Another criticism of Lysias is that his speeches have no form
or structure.   Everything is pell-mell and any one thing might
be said before any other. As in the verses on Midas'
tomb (264d) :

    ' I am a brasen maiden, on Midas' grave I lie
    Till stop the flowing waters, and tall trees cease to grow
    Forever here remaining, on this lamented tomb,
    To those who pass by saying : Midas lies buried here.'

wherein the order of the lines is quite immaterial.   That is bad
art.

Without knowledge of dialectic, without analytical knowledge, little is left for the teachers of rhetoric to do except to
invent new technical terms for the different parts of a speech,
and this they did in abundance.   Plato scornfully gives a
number of examples no doubt culled from text-books on rhetoric
for different kinds of praise, proof, imagery, tautology, and
different ways of arousing this or that emotion in one's hearers
(267).   But these refinements are little more than preliminary
to the real art of speaking, and ignore the most important part
of it :   knowledge of the subject discussed.   The man who
thinks himself a rhetorician because he knows all those technical
names is like one who would go to a doctor and say (268a) :

' I know what medicine to give to heighten or lower a man's
temperature.   If I like I can make a man vomit or evacuate and

many other such things.   As I know all this I consider myself to be
a doctor, able to make others so by communicating my knowledge.'

The real doctor will naturally ask the fellow whether he also
knows when, to whom, and in what doses, the remedies are to
be applied and our man will answer :

' Not at all, I presume that any one who has learned these medicines from me will himself be able to do what you ask.'

The doctor will think such a person a madman : the knowledge
he possesses he could pick up from a book or a chance acquaintance with a druggist.   Though he thinks himself a doctor,
he has no understanding of medicine at all.   Again these self-
styled rhetoricians, Socrates continues, are like a man who
would go to Sophocles and Euripides and call himself a
tragedian because he knows how to make long speeches and
short speeches, pitiful speeches, fearful and threatening speeches,
whenever he likes ; and say to them that he is going to teach
tragic poetry.   They would only laugh at him ' if he thinks
that tragedy is anything else than the putting together of
these things in a manner consistent with each other and with
the whole play '.[1]   Pericles [2] was perhaps the greatest of all
orators just because, besides natural ability, his friendship
with the philosopher Anaxagoras gave him the breadth of view
and the interest in the laws of nature which are ultimately
necessary to all the higher crafts and sciences.

[1] $τῷ$ $ὅλῳ$ 268d : the whole, means the whole work of art.   It might, however, mean the whole of nature, in view of $τῆς$ $τοῦ$ $ὅλου$ $φύσεως$ in 270c which
is usually so translated.   I think, however, that commentators have been
misled by the reference to $μετεωρολογία$, the study of things on high, in
270a.   In 270c we are concerned with the study of the soul, and Plato means
that the nature of the soul cannot be properly studied except by a study of it
' as a whole ' (lit. apart from the study of the nature of the whole thing)
i.e. in its every part.   And this is the statement he quotes from Hippocrates
about the body, that it must be studied as a whole, a method the relevance of
which to medicine is obvious.   This interpretation is put beyond doubt by
the use of $τῷ$ $ὅλῳ$ in 268d above.
[2] This high commendation of Pericles does not really contradict the attack
upon him in the Gorgias (see below, p. 262).   There he is condemned along
with all other statesmen-orators.   Here he is only said to be the first among
them.   Plato does not mean that he was essentially different.   He comes
a little nearer to the ideal in so far as he has come into close contact with a
philosopher !   The case of Sophocles and Euripides is similar.   They were
in any case more than mere technicians.

Socrates now draws the parallel between rhetoric (of the right kind) and medicine as he sees it. Which is different from the way the orators themselves saw it. Rhetoric is to the soul what medicine is to the body. And just as medicine must—as Hippocrates maintains—study the body as a whole, so must rhetoric study the soul as a whole and in its every part. It must, as one must when studying anything, consider first whether it is one or manyfold, and if the latter then study the force it possesses for action and response (εἰς τὸ δρᾶν καὶ τὸ παθεῖν) in all possible relations. This is what we expect to find in a manual on rhetoric, but do not find in fact. Surely such knowledge is essential to the study of the different means of persuasion.

I give the next passage, which recapitulates the whole method, in full, because it is, in all essentials, the method which Aristotle actually follows in his treatise on *Rhetoric*, (271*d*) :

' Since the power of speaking is in a sense a guiding of the mind (ψυχαγωγία), it is necessary that he who would be an orator should study the parts (εἴδη) of the soul : that they are so and so many, of this and that kind ; therefore some men are like this, others like that. When he has done this classification he must analyse the different modes of speech, that they are so many, and each such and such ; that this type of men will, for a definite reason, be easily persuaded by this kind of speech on a certain subject ; others will be hard to win over for other reasons. Now he who has acquired a sufficient grasp of these principles must then observe these things in practice, and be quick to follow up his perceptions, else the theoretical knowledge he learned from his teacher will be of no use to him. When he can thus give a satisfactory account of the kind of man that is amenable to any particular kind of argument, and is further able to recognize in practice the kind of thing he was discussing when it occurs before his eyes, and can fit his speech and method of persuasion to it, when he has learned all this he must learn when to speak and when to be silent, when is the moment for brevity, when for an appeal to pity or fear and all the things he has learned. Then, and not until then, has the art of speaking been well and fully acquired. But whenever any one who falls short of this in speaking, teaching or writing, boasts that he is an expert, we shall be right not to believe him.'

Oratory, then, should be based on psychology in the first place : the speaker must learn the parts of the soul, their number and the nature of each. He must then classify the different kinds of argument, when each is appropriate and why, thus relating his technique to his psychology. In the third place he needs to watch others at work, relate their success to his theories and learn to apply those theories himself. Lastly he must decide when to speak and when to be silent. Special natural gifts are also essential : ' if you are naturally gifted for oratory, you will be a famous orator, if you add knowledge and practice ; but without these you will be but second-rate (ἀτελής, 269d) '. The method here outlined is not unpractical, and rhetoricians could follow it for some way at least. What they could not know without being philosophers who know good and evil is presumably when to speak and when to be silent !

What does this somewhat lengthy discussion of rhetoric contribute to Plato's theory of art ? His attack is obviously the same at all points : by detaching itself from philosophy, from a knowledge of ultimate values, from the apprehension of the Forms and especially the Form of beauty and of good, rhetoric and every other art fail to fulfil their proper function in the state. Instead of helping to make men better by persuading them to do what they know is good or by putting examples of right conduct before their eyes, rhetoricians and other artists lose sight of the moral aim of their craft and the immediate pleasure of their audience becomes their only aim. The rhetoricians become mere technicians, inventors of new styles and newfangled labels, as the dramatists lose themselves in meaningless novelties. Technique is important, but only as a first step, as a preliminary, to real art. Indeed it bears the same relation to art as mere pharmaceutical knowledge does to medicine. Both medicine and art are a great deal more. The former makes for health in the body, the latter is a ' guiding of souls ' by the power of the written or spoken word towards goodness and happiness. That is art as it should be, but there has never, we are told, been an actual statesman-orator who made this his primary aim, nor (the *Republic* adds) an actual poet of all those we know.

VII

EDUCATION

I. Virtue as Knowledge

THE belief that goodness is a matter of knowledge can, more certainly than any other, be attributed to the historical Socrates. He wished to reduce all excellence to some kind of knowledge and was profoundly convinced that ' no man does wrong on purpose ' because no man is willingly ignorant. Plato also maintained this apparent paradox throughout ; it is asserted in almost every one of his works and repeated in the *Laws* with peculiar emphasis.[1] It is therefore idle to dismiss the theory lightly by pointing out that it ignores the importance of character building and the problem of will-power ; Plato was fully aware of both difficulties. Even Socrates must have been aware of them ; how far he dealt with them we cannot tell, since any line drawn between the two philosophers can only be arbitrary. We shall therefore trace the evolution of the virtue-knowledge relationship in the dialogues, and try to understand the nature of the knowledge referred to, encouraged by the reflection that the connexion between knowledge and goodness is at least very close, or else why should any one hope that more and more education will make the world a better place, and may save humanity from chaos and self-destruction ?

The Socratic doctrine is expressed by two formulae : ' goodness is knowledge ', and its corollary ' no man sins on purpose ' ; closely allied with these is, as we shall see, the advice of Apollo at Delphi : know thyself.

The simplest expression of the close relation between knowledge and goodness is found in the *Lysis*,[2] where the youth of

---

[1] 862 ff. See also *Timaeus*, 86b. Cp. *Prot.*, 345d ; *Gorg.*, 509e ; *Rep.*, 351a, &c.

[2] The *Lysis* is probably later than most of the early dialogues. The passage referred to here is given as an example by Socrates of how one

that name has had to admit that though his parents love him they forbid him many things and is led to the conclusion that they trust him to act alone only where he possesses the necessary knowledge, and this is then shown to be the case with every one. As Socrates says (210*b*) :

'Every one—whether man or woman, Greek or foreigner—will entrust us with the things of which we have acquired knowledge. In such matters we shall do what we please and no one will want to hinder us ; we shall ourselves be free and rule over others. It is our province, and there we act with benefit. Where we do not possess understanding (νοῦς), no one will allow us to do what we want, every one will hinder us as much as possible, not only strangers but our own father and mother, or anything nearer to us still.[1] We must then obey orders. Such things are not our province, we can derive no benefit from them.'

It follows, then, that where we have knowledge we are useful. Any craftsman (τεχνικός) possesses a certain skill, he knows how to do something or make something, he is *good at* his job. The Greeks always tended to identify the useful and the good, and the word ἀρετή was used to indicate both a particular excellence and virtue in general. The ἀρετή of any craftsman was just this being good at his craft. So indeed do we speak of a good carpenter, but we do not go so far as to speak of the 'goodness' of a carpenter in this sense. The Greeks did. Hence the Socratic formula arose in a perfectly natural way ; its first meaning was : 'to be good at something is a matter of knowledge' and then it came to mean 'to be good is a matter of knowledge'.

In working out the implications of this remarkable formula Plato was naturally led to consider how far particular virtues could be reduced to knowledge. Hence those shorter dialogues which try to define one or other of them. The *Laches* deals with courage [2] in the typical Socratic manner, giving us by the way a delicious pen portrait of those two very different generals, Nicias and Laches. We find the latter characteristically

should talk to a beloved young man and is a good introduction to our present subject. See p. 93.

[1] εἴ τι τούτων οἰκειότερόν ἐστιν. Presumably ourselves, or something within us, hence the neuter.

[2] ἀνδρεία, a word intimately connected with ἀνήρ, man. It is the quality that makes one a man. For a good discussion of it see Wilamowitz, I, 61.

suggesting that to be brave or manly is to stand one's ground in battle. When this too simple definition is rejected, we find that courage is a kind of steadfastness of soul (καρτερία ψυχῆς). But this is not enough unless it is accompanied by knowledge, for you may be steadfast in a wrong cause. So knowledge makes an unobtrusive appearance, and it has come to stay. But what kind of knowledge? Surely not the technical expertness in the use of arms? On the contrary, a man who does *not* possess this expertness is all the braver for standing his ground. Here Nicias intervenes to say he has often heard Socrates maintain that we are good in so far as we are wise, i.e. that we are ' good at ' whatever we know. If so, courage is knowledge of a kind, possibly of what is truly to be feared and what is not. Laches protests that courage and wisdom are very different things, but he only succeeds in proving that courage is different from a great many kinds of wisdom.

If courage is a kind of wisdom, neither children nor animals can possess it since they do not possess reason, and it must be distinguished from mere recklessness, which often results in similar actions. The difference is that the brave man knows what is to be feared, e.g. he will face death because there are things he fears more than death. All this offers no difficulty. But to know what is to be feared ultimately implies knowledge of the future and of good and evil. This in turn implies *all* the virtues, so that we have failed to differentiate courage from the other virtues.

The *Charmides* attempts to define sophrosyne, moderation or self-control. Several tentative definitions, such as gentle quietude (ἡσυχιότης) and to mind one's own business, are declared unsatisfactory and Critias finally suggests that sophrosyne is to know oneself (164d ff.). If this is the true definition, sophrosyne, being some special kind of knowledge, is a τέχνη, a craft or science requiring special knowledge, namely the knowledge of self. But how can a science be its own object? (This step may seem illogical, the difficulty should be stated : can the knowing subject be the object of his own knowledge? As such it is real enough.) Then the moderate man, endowed with the science of science (ἐπιστήμη ἐπιστήμης) will be able to recognize knowledge both in himself and others. Seemingly turning away from the difficulty of knowledge being its own object, Socrates attacks it from another angle : how can we tell whether a man be a good doctor, i.e. that he knows medicine, unless we know medicine ourselves ? How can we, that is, know *that* a man knows without knowing what he knows ? For surely it is not much use knowing that this man knows something. That will not enable us to make use of him. This difficulty will reappear in the *Euthydemus*. If there is a super-knowledge that directs the special sciences, what can its object be, since it cannot be either itself or the special sciences ?

And yet, even though Plato seems unable to give a logical account of such a science, clearly he believed it to exist. For is this not precisely what his master Socrates claimed : that he knew his own ignorance and that he recognized both knowledge and ignorance in others ? And was Socrates not an illustrious proof that this wisdom did lead to goodness ? That is the fact which the *Charmides* fails to explain. When speaking of this science of science Plato seems to be feeling his way to two things : a system of logic,[1] i.e. a method of clear thinking and reasoning which he was to find in dialectic ; and also an objective reality towards which this super-knowledge can be directed.

The old Delphic advice, Know thyself, is discussed from another angle in the *First Alcibiades*, with which it will be convenient to deal here for it continues the search for the object of such knowledge, namely the self. After some previous discussion Socrates urges the necessity to ' care for oneself' (128a). By this he explains he does not mean to care for one's body, for this is the province of gymnastics ; nor for one's clothes. But just as we cannot look after shoes until we know what a shoe is, so we must know what is meant by ' oneself'. Now in every case the workman must be distinguished from his tools. A cobbler not only uses instruments in making shoes but also his hands, eyes, &c. They are his tools, and he is different from them. Man uses the whole of his body, and must not be identified with it. The man himself is something different, and that something is the soul. There are, Socrates recognizes, further difficulties, but this will do as a working definition (130c–d). When, therefore,

[1] Ritter, I, 353 ff.

the god commands us to know ourselves, he means that man should study his own soul.

The unsuccessful search for a definition of piety in the *Euthyphro* belongs to the same line of investigation. There too some attempt is made to reduce this particular virtue to knowledge, namely knowledge of ritual, &c., but with little success.

Three separate virtues have now been dealt with. But if each tends to reduce itself to knowledge, the question naturally arises whether this knowledge is everywhere the same, whether the commonly accepted virtues are not really one. It is not surprising, therefore, that we find in the *Protagoras* a discussion of the unity of virtue as well as an attempt to reduce particular virtues to knowledge. Socrates puts the whole problem afresh : Can virtue be taught? Which, of course, is the same as asking whether goodness is knowledge. Then, accepting on Protagoras' authority that it can (329*b*), he passes on to ask whether virtue is one or many (329*d*) :

' All virtues (says Protagoras) are part of a whole, which is virtue.
—But (asks Socrates) are they so in the same sense as the parts of the face, each of which is different from the others, or are they homogeneous parts of a whole, like bits of gold that are all gold ?
—The former . . . for men can be brave without being righteous (δίκαιοι) and righteous without being wise.'

Any such essential difference between the different forms of goodness Socrates proceeds to refute by trying to reduce them one by one to some form of knowledge. His arguments are purely logical, because he does not here discuss the nature or object of this knowledge. They are even at times fallacious, and one gets the impression that he is rapidly going over ground he had previously covered.

He first attempts to force upon Protagoras the identity of piety with justice by a fallacy, the well-known confusion between a predicative judgement and one of identity, which was not finally cleared up till the *Sophist* (piety, you say, is not like the just, it is then like the not-just, it is therefore unjust 331*a*–*b*). Protagoras sees through this, though he is forced to admit that the two virtues have a good deal in common. With moderation Socrates' case is a little better, though his argument is still verbal, for it depends largely on

the common root in the Greek words for wisdom and moderation (φρόνησις and σωφροσύνη) and its contrary (ἀφροσύνη).
To act with moderation is to act wisely, moderation and
wisdom have but one opposite : folly. They are therefore
the same thing. Again, this does prove that the two words,
wisdom and moderation, are in Greek used at times indifferently
so that the two virtues cannot be very distinct. Further, Socrates proceeds, no one will assert that a man who sins against
justice acts with moderation or control, so that justice and
moderation (the latter having already been proved identical
with wisdom) are identical. Courage in turn, after some
considerable delay, is reduced, as in the *Laches*, to knowledge
of what should or should not be feared.

In the course of this argument occurs the famous passage on
hedonism which has already been discussed in connexion
with Plato's theory of pleasure.[1] What is of interest here is
that it once more points to the close connexion between goodness and knowledge already found in the *Gorgias*. There,
when Callicles had admitted that some pleasures are good,
some bad, so that ultimately they must be judged by another
criterion than pleasure itself, Socrates asked (500*a*) :

' Can any man choose which pleasures are good, which evil, or
does it require special knowledge in each case.'

Even Callicles must agree that a proper choice of pleasure
requires special knowledge and is therefore the work of an
expert (τεχνικός) a specialist in his own craft or science. So a
little later it is definitely hinted that goodness is such a science.[2]
So also in the *Protagoras*, where the good life is reduced to the
search for the greatest amount of pleasure, it requires the art
of measuring one pleasure against another and this is a special
kind of knowledge. Once more goodness is a τέχνη, a special
craft or science.

But if goodness is a matter of study, what does it study ?
This question, already raised in the *Charmides* (how can we have
a science of science ?) comes up again in the *Euthydemus*. In
the passage which concerns us (278*e*–282*d*) Socrates is giving
a specimen of the right kind of reasoning in contrast to the

---

[1] Pp. 59 ff.
[2] 506*d* where ἀρετή is due to τάξει καὶ ὀρθότητι καὶ τέχνῃ.

methods of the two logic-choppers Euthydemus and Dionyso-
dorus. The argument is therefore short and compressed, but
it gives an excellent picture of the supreme science and of the
main difficulty that remains unsolved. Knowledge, says
Socrates, is essential to happiness. For to ' do well ' (εὐτυχεῖν)
in anything we must know how to act. Possessions are useless
unless we know how to use them, and then only are they
properly called blessings.[1] Wealth, health, and even beauty
are of no value unless properly used, and to do this requires
knowledge or wisdom (σοφία). Only then can we be truly
said to fare well. In themselves these things are neither good
nor bad ; they become good when wisely used. It follows that
only wisdom is good, only ignorance evil. The question is :
what is the special kind (or kinds) of knowledge required.
Reverting to this argument a little later (288d), Socrates adds
that we must clearly practise philosophy, since it is the acquisition of knowledge. But only of certain kinds of knowledge,
for it is useless to know where to find a mass of gold, unless we
know what to do with it, and the same is true of all the other
arts and crafts. What we seek is not medicine, it is certainly
not oratory, or hunting, or fishing. It is not even geometry,
astronomy or arithmetic, for they too find things out of which
others must make use, and their results, if they are wise, they
hand over to dialecticians (290c). So also generals capture
cities but hand them over to statesmen to administer. What of
statesmanship itself? The difficulty here is that, while all the
other arts are subordinate to it, we cannot find that statecraft,
or the kingly art, has any reality apart from them. It appears
as merely the sum of the others, and to be, as it were, its own
object (292d).[2] No positive result is obtained. We still do
not know what kind of knowledge is required. But it is certain
that wisdom and happiness are closely related. What we need
(as in the *Charmides*) is a science that will make use of all the
others as a statesman makes use of all the other subordinate
crafts and this is here called dialectic.

We may pause a moment to consider how far Plato has
taken us in his exposition of the doctrine that goodness and

---

[1] Plato often insists on this point. Cp. Pausanias' insistence upon manner
in *Symp.*, 181a. Cp. also *Laws*, 661b, &c.
[2] See p. 264.

virtue are a matter of knowledge or wisdom. He has shown that to be good at anything requires knowledge (*Lysis*), and so we must have knowledge to be good at the art of living. He has tried to reduce goodness in its different forms, the virtues, to some kind of knowledge (*Laches, Charmides, Euthyphro, Protagoras*) and to show that all virtue is essentially one (*Protagoras*), that even if pleasure be our aim, we must have the knowledge necessary to choose between pleasures (*Gorgias, Protagoras*). He has examined whether this knowledge be of oneself, inquired how such a knowledge can be (*Charmides*) and decided that self means the soul (*Alcibiades*). Finally he has drawn a picture of this supreme knowledge towering above all others and making use of them all (*Euthydemus*).

The word τέχνη is the general name for any kind of craft or skill and the use made of it in all these discussions is in conscious opposition to the sophists. Gorgias despises τέχναι, and so does Protagoras [1] and it is characteristic of Socrates to claim this title for the science of life. Just as in the *Apology* we find him going to the craftsmen and artisans as to men who definitely possess a special kind of 'wisdom' to test how he, who knows nothing, can be wiser than they, so when he is persuaded that goodness is wisdom, he calls it a τέχνη, thus using for it a name which the man in the street understands, and which implies a definite kind of knowledge such as every one recognizes to exist in daily life. And so far he has not differentiated between the two kinds, except that their objects are different, as are the objects of every craft. Nor does he do so in the first book of the *Republic*, where he discusses with Thrasymachus the nature of justice (δικαιοσύνη), here used as a general name for virtue. For the whole argument hinges on the fact that this virtue or excellence is a τέχνη in the same sense as any other. If we keep that point clearly before us the whole discussion with its emphasis on the nature of technical knowledge (that it cannot ever err and that strictly speaking (ἀκριβεῖ λόγῳ), an expert can never make a mistake, that knowledge of a thing implies knowledge of its opposite (334)) becomes perfectly logical and justified. But it is rather unsatisfying, just because there *is* an essential difference between an ordinary craft and the knowledge that implies virtue, and this is made abundantly

[1] *Gorgias*, 450b–c ; *Protagoras*, 318d–e.

clear in the *Hippias Minor*. The genuineness of this little work is established by a reference to it in Aristotle.[1] It reduces the identification of virtue with τέχνη, in the ordinary sense, to absurdity.

The whole point is that the very knowledge which enables one to do something well also enables one most surely to do it badly. The man who can do a sum correctly is also the man who can, if he pleases, be certain to give the wrong answer. And this applies to every pursuit : the best liar in every case is the man who knows the truth ; the man who knows the way to do a thing right is also the one who knows most certainly how to do it wrong. Now if, as Socrates maintains, knowledge is good, the man who possesses it is a better man than the ignoramus. A man who sins knowingly is thereby a better man than one who does so unwittingly. Hippias quite rightly objects that this is not the view which the law takes of wrong-doing, but he cannot upset the argument. Granted that the power given by knowledge is virtue, then the more of such power we possess the better we are, irrespective of the way we use it. And the dialogue ends on this absurdity.

Now it should be noted that this ambivalence of knowledge is true in the domain of ordinary arts and crafts : a famous doctor who lets a patient die, though he knows how to save him, is none the less a *better doctor* than the ignorant practitioner who accidentally hits upon a cure without knowing the reason of his success. Instances could easily be multiplied, but the general truth is quite established : technical or scientific skill can do harm or good, according to the way it is used, but this does not affect the quality of the knowledge.

Now we know that Socrates said that ' no man does wrong on purpose ', implying that the knowledge of what is right is enough to ensure right action. Indeed as much is implied, even in the *Hippias*.[2] But why should this be so ? He can only avoid the absurd conclusion of the *Hippias* if he recognizes that goodness is not knowledge in the same sense as other kinds, that ethics or the knowledge of good and evil is not a science in the same sense as medicine, engineering, carpentry are

---

[1] *Metaphysics Δ*, 1025 *a*, 6 ff.

[2] 376*b* : εἴπερ τίς ἐστιν οὗτος—' if there be such a man ' implying that there is not. For this sense of εἴπερ cp. *Euthyphro, 8d.*

sciences. To say that virtue is a τέχνη is not enough, for it must be something more. And if we continue to maintain that goodness is knowledge and that no one sins on purpose, as Plato did, we must discover in what way this knowledge is different from the others, since it quite clearly cannot be used for an evil purpose.

Wisdom does, however, detach itself from goodness in one sense. While it is still impossible to be wise without being good it becomes possible to be good without being wise, because a distinction is established between knowledge and right opinion or belief. Though the latter has no guarantee of permanence and can give no account of itself, yet good conduct can be based upon it ; and so we are not surprised to find, in the *Republic*, that moderation, self-control and courage can exist without wisdom. Of the three classes in the state— the rulers, the auxiliaries and the people—only the first, who are by far the least in number, possess wisdom, the nature of which is as yet undefined. The others must possess right belief : the auxiliary guardians, for example, whose duty it is to defend the state in the field, must have courage. This, for them, is defined no longer as the *knowledge* of what is the proper thing to fear (e.g. death rather than the shame of deser- tion) but as the *right belief* as to what should be feared (429). They will acquire this belief through an education in physical culture and the arts which will be designed by the rulers. The rulers on the other hand, to do this, must *know* that which the others *believe*. And they alone have knowledge. The equation of virtue with knowledge is thus considerably modified since virtue of a kind can exist without it. But only virtue of a kind definitely inferior : not only is the virtue of the rulers, based as it is upon their knowledge and directly derived from it, more perfect and more stable, but the virtue of others is based upon the ruler's knowledge, since they devise the system of education and persuasion by which such right belief is acquired. The knowledge of the rulers is, as the central books of the *Republic* tell us, the knowledge of the Forms,

For this is the answer we have been seeking. The knowledge of the eternal Ideas is the supreme knowledge foreshadowed in the *Euthydemus* and the Ideas are the object of the science of science. It is not immediately obvious why such knowledge ensures goodness, and to this point we will return after the study of Plato's system of education.

Before we pass on to this, however, we shall follow the fate of the Socratic formula ' no man sins on purpose ', in the remaining dialogues and see how Plato remained faithful to this paradox.

Great importance is attached in the *Republic* to order and harmony in the soul.[1] This is necessary, not only to the philosopher for whom all virtues are truly one since they all inevitably follow from his wisdom and knowledge of the Forms, but even the lowest class must possess sophrosyne and δικαιοσύνη (justice) which both imply it. We thus have two kinds of virtue, that of the ordinary man, and that of the philosopher. Both have harmony in the soul, but the former also has knowledge. To these two kinds of virtue must, of course, correspond two sorts of vice.

So in the *Sophist* 227e–228e, Plato establishes a clear difference between two kinds of evil (κακία) in the soul : the first is like disease in the body, it is discord between ' opinion and desire, feelings and pleasure, reason and pain ', for in inferior men these different parts of himself are at variance. Cowardice, depravity, sinfulness (ἀδικία) are of this kind. The other kind of evil is far more fundamental and is rather like ugliness than disease : it is ignorance. All men want the good, but whenever they set out to attain it, their lack of knowledge causes them to miss their aim. Now men generally recognize the first kind of evil, the disorder in the soul, as wickedness, but they fail to see the far more fundamental evil that is ignorance : this they do not speak of as evil at all. Yet clearly it is far more important. And there is a proper way of dealing with each kind : crime due to perturbation of soul (i.e. to lack of self-control, of mastery over self) must be punished, but the proper way to deal with ignorance is teaching the truth. And as ever the worst form of ignorance is that which believes it knows.

The subject is not further pursued in this dialogue. The notion of moral evil as a disease of the soul is quite common in Plato.[2] Here, however, it is restricted to disharmony between the different parts of the soul, to the vice therefore which is the opposite of that sophrosyne which we saw that every man

[1] Cp. *Gorgias*, 506d–e.   [2] e.g. *Rep.*, 444d ; *Tim.*, 86d (see below).

(even those incapable of knowledge) should possess. Ignorance is far more fundamental : it is generally the lack of philosophic knowledge, and like ugliness this is an evil that most men cannot mend ; though it also includes that worse ignorance of those who think they know what they do not know, of those, that is, who have *wrong* moral beliefs. Both kinds of ignorance are to be cured by teaching and Plato is asserting that education is a far more powerful fighter against evil than mere corrective justice. The whole passage occurs by the way in the course of an attempt to define the sophist by a process of division. The two different kinds of vice are not fully analysed or explained. For our purpose it is the distinction between them that is important.

A similar distinction is found in the *Timaeus* (86a ff.). As so often in Plato, the terminology is quite different. *All* vice is here called disease of the soul, and *all* evil is ἄνοια or lack of wisdom. There are, however, two kinds of ἄνοια, madness and ignorance. Madness is again the lack of balance in the soul, e.g. the excessive desire for sexual intercourse and other passions. Ignorance remains unexplained. The interesting point about this passage, however, is that the vice which is called madness is definitely attributed to physiological causes : an excess of semen or of bitter phlegms. This very close connexion between physical disease and lack of balance in the soul is one which is not pursued in Plato. We should perhaps remember that it is (like the whole creation myth) put into the mouth of Timaeus, the Pythagorean, though the whole question of the influence of bodily states upon the mind or soul is one which remains obscure.

In the *Timaeus* too (86d) it is emphatically asserted once more that all sin is involuntary. And the same is true of the ninth book of the *Laws* (86od ff. cp. 731c), where the Athenian stranger is considering the problem of evil from the legal and judicial aspect. A most important distinction is first made between inflicting injury (βλάβη) and sinning (ἀδικεῖν). Injury can be done accidentally or on purpose. Note that Plato does speak of injury done on purpose (861e) but not of sinning on purpose. This is because the word ἀδικία, which I translate sin or sinfulness, implies a depraved state in the soul, which no one willingly incurs.

About unintentional injury there is little discussion. It is a class recognized in law and by men generally. Intentional injury is the debatable class. In both cases the concern of the law is primarily to estimate the injury done and to compensate it, but as the lawgiver is an educator also, he will, says the Athenian, try to heal the injury into friendship, as sinfulness is due to 'disease in the soul'. He will teach men to love justice, and where both persuasion and correction fail, the sinner will be put to death, as an example to others. The penalty of death will be restricted to such hopeless cases. Plato then establishes three causes of intentional injuries : temper, i.e. anger, fear and other feelings corresponding to the second part of the soul of the *Republic* ; pleasure, corresponding to the lowest, the passionate part ; and ignorance. The latter is, as usual, divided into simple ignorance, and that worse kind which thinks it knows. The former does but little damage ; the latter, when accompanied by strength and power, does a great deal. Now temper, pleasure and ignorance each seek their own satisfaction, though these may lie in opposite directions. And the Athenian proceeds (863*e*) :

'And now I would define for you, clearly and simply what I mean by the righteous and the sinful (δίκαιον καὶ ἄδικον). The tyranny in the soul of temper, fear, pleasure, pain, envy and desires, whether it does harm or no, I call sinfulness in any case. But when a city or some individuals have any belief as to what is best, wherever it be among those emotions that they think to find it, and if that belief rules in their soul and regulates the whole man, then, even if they are mistaken to some extent, any action so performed is right. Whatever in each individual is ruled by this conviction is right also, and is best for the whole life of men. But men generally call injury thus inflicted unintentional sin. We will not, however, quarrel about words, but as we have found three kinds of error, we must fix them in our minds.'

And after recapitulating them, he proceeds to establish at length the punishments for various crimes.

We have then first unintentional injuries, which are not hard to deal with. Then intentional injuries which can be due to temper, pleasure or ignorance. The first two of these can be classed together in contrast to the third : they are the direct result of civil war in the soul between the various desires and fears, and they correspond to what is called 'disease in the soul' in the *Sophist* and 'madness' in the *Timaeus*. They are involuntary, for all sin is so, and it is these that Plato defines as ἀδικία. He does not here say why he refuses to call them voluntary, but he has made it clear enough, from the *Gorgias* on, why he considers that no man would willingly harbour such disturbance in his soul. In the *Sophist* he quietly restricts the word ἀδικία to this class. Here he emphatically asserts that the other class of errors, those due to ignorance, should never be called sin, ἄδικον, at all, though they do the greatest damage (863 *e*). Whatever is done by a disciplined soul, under the influence of ignorance and wrong opinion, is not a sin at all. Here indeed men speak of 'involuntary sin', but they are wrong. A mistaken fanatic does more harm than any man, but he is no sinner. Indeed Plato goes so far as to say that this ignorance is only man's desire for knowledge about the good, misdirected.[1] He is here not so much defending the Socratic doctrine of involuntary sin, for men will agree that offences due to ignorance are involuntary. He is emphasizing, in forcibly paradoxical language, two things : first, that discipline in the soul is in itself a good thing, that it is better that reason should mislead than not lead at all ; in the second place that what does most harm in the world is not sinfulness but ignorance, and, as he tells us in the *Sophist*, this should be remedied ultimately not by punishment, but by knowledge and education—which brings us back once more to Socrates' belief that goodness is knowledge.

We thus find the Socratic formula reasserted to the very last in Plato's works. We find also a division of wrongdoing into two classes. The names applied to them are not always the same, indeed the terminology is inconsistent. But the difference between the two classes is quite clear : the first is the lack of any kind of balance between passions, feelings and intellect or the usurping of the intellect's place as ruler or governor by either of the others. It is the vice which is the

---

[1] 864*b* : ἐλπίδων δὲ καὶ δόξης ἀληθοῦς περὶ τὸ ἄριστον ἔφεσις τρίτον ἕτερον. 'The urge towards hope and true opinion about the best is another, a third (cause of error),' i.e. the desire for truth, when mistaken and allied to force of character (863*c*) causes great harm. But this is not ἀδικία. The text is sound.

opposite of self-control, σωφροσύνη, and righteousness, δικαιοσύνη, in the *Republic*, the two virtues that belonged to all classes. The second kind of vice is ignorance, and if Plato refuses to call this ἀδικία or sinfulness in the *Laws* it is to emphasize that corrective justice, δίκη, is no help here. The only way to remove this, and here the *Sophist*, *Timaeus* and *Laws* agree, is not by punishment but by education.

II. SYSTEMS OF EDUCATION

An excellent outline of the Athenian methods of education is put in Protagoras' mouth in the dialogue that bears his name (325c) :

' As soon as a child can understand what is said to him, the nurse, the mother, the attendant slave, and the father himself, vie with each other to make him very good.   By every word and deed they teach him and show him that this is right, that wrong, this beautiful, that ugly, this pious, that impious, that he must do this and avoid that.   And it may be that he willingly obeys their advice.   If not, like a sapling that is becoming crooked and twisted they attempt to correct him by threats and blows.   Later they send him to school, with instructions to the teachers to pay more attention to the orderly behaviour of the children than to writing or music.   The teachers look after them, and when they have learned to read and are now coming to the point where they understand what is written, as before what was spoken, the works of great poets are put by them on their benches and they are forced to read and learn them.   There they find much advice, many stories, much praise and eulogies of the good men of old, so that the child becomes zealous to emulate them and to become such a man himself.

The same is true of the music teachers : they too pay attention to moderate conduct, that the youths may do nothing wrong. Besides this, when they have learned to play the lyre, they are taught the works of other good poets and the tunes of lyric poetry. The rhythm and melodies are made to dwell in the souls of the children that they may become gentler, and as they absorb rhythm and melody they become the better able to speak and to act.   For the whole life of man needs good rhythm and harmony.

Then furthermore they are sent to a teacher of gymnastics, that their stronger bodies may be the servants of useful thought, lest a bad physique might make them cowards in war or elsewhere.

All this parents do to the best of their ability, and the most able to do it are the rich ; their children start to go to school earlier, and

leave it later.   Once they have left school, the state compels them to
learn the laws and to take these as patterns to be followed in life lest
they act rashly for lack of guidance.   Just in the same way as a
teacher teaches letters to those who are not yet good at them by
making an outline upon the slate, and compels them to write by
filling in the outline ; so the city also has made its laws as tracings,
which are discoveries of good lawgivers of old.   In accordance with
these it compels men to govern and be governed, and punishes any
one who transgresses.   The name of this punishment, in your city
and many places elsewhere, is correction, because justice corrects.

When so much care is taken about goodness (ἀρετή) both publicly
and privately, are you at a loss to know whether virtue can be
taught ? ʼ

This rapid picture, slightly idealized perhaps, of Athenian
education shows us how it appeared to other thinkers before
Socrates.   The idea that virtue and moderation were the aim
of education was not new ; we find it also in Aristophanes.
But Socrates wondered whether the educators themselves had
any clear idea of what they taught, and further, who were the
right teachers ?   When he raised the question : can virtue
be taught ? [1] he was really emphasizing that if it could be
taught, it must be knowledge of some sort.   Nor was he satisfied as easily as Protagoras regarding the competence of the
teachers.   As long as children were learning to read and write
and play the lyre, there was no difficulty ; men knew who could
teach these things.   But beyond this ?   Protagoras' answer is:
the parents and the city, the latter presumably being the
ordinary citizen, in assembly and in private, and the politicians.   To these the sophists must, of course, be added.

The claims of these various teachers of goodness are examined
in the *Meno*, just at the moment when Anytus happens [2] to
join Socrates and Meno.   Who teaches goodness ?   There is
no difficulty in deciding who teaches handicrafts or sciences
such as medicine.   Nor is it difficult to find claimants in this
case, for goodness and citizen virtue is just what the sophists
profess to teach.   Are they, then, the teachers we are seeking
to find ?   The democrat's reply is surprisingly violent (91c) :

[1] e.g. in *Meno*, 87c, *Protagoras*, 329b.
[2] *Meno*, 89e ff.   This sudden appearance of Anytus is probably the worst
piece of dramatic technique in Plato, all the more curious in that the *Meno*
is a very vivid work.

'By Herakles, Socrates, don't be blasphemous. May no member of my household, no friend, fellow-citizen or guest-friend of mine, ever be mad enough to expose himself to the harm those fellows do, for they obviously harm and corrupt their followers.'

Socrates expresses some surprise : do the sophists not make a good deal of money by their teaching ? They cannot be as bad as that.[1] But he does not pursue the subject before Anytus' fury, except to make him admit that he never has had anything to do with any sophist ! They are lightly dismissed with the words : 'there may be something in what you say '. Plato's own attitude towards the sophists is perfectly clear from the *Gorgias*, the *Protagoras* and the *Sophist* : even the best of them have not examined the implications of their own position, they either teach mere rhetorical technique, or else they cleverly express the prejudices of the mob. They do not know what knowledge is, or the object of knowledge, and they are teachers of falsehood. The next claimant, the ordinary man, is put forward by Anytus. Asked for the name of a teacher of virtue he replies (92e) :

'Why must you have the name of one man ? Any good and true Athenian will make a boy better than the sophists can, if he will obey.'

and the Athenians good and true learned from those before them. Since the best Athenians, for Anytus, are obviously the great political leaders, Socrates wonders why, if they can teach so well, they did not teach their own sons better, an argument also used in the *Protagoras*. Exasperated beyond endurance, Anytus, with an ominous warning to Socrates that he had better be careful—which reminds us that he was to be one of his accusers—withdraws. But in fact, says Socrates, turning again to Meno, politicians do not all even profess to be able to teach civic virtue. He explains this by saying that they only have right belief, not knowledge. Hence they cannot be teachers at all. They have no more knowledge than poets or priests. Thus Socrates attacked the system depicted by Protagoras : those professed teachers, the sophists, statesmen, poets or ordinary citizens are no teachers in any real sense, for

[1] The ironical intent here is presumably that money should appeal to Anytus, the son of a self-made man (see 90a).

they have no certain knowledge. They promise virtue and excellence, but cannot even tell us what virtue is ; they promise reputation and success in public life, but what are these to a man who does not know what to do with them ? The most important thing that man can learn is surely to seek happiness not in mere trappings and externals, but within his own mind or soul. The first duty of a citizen is to be a good citizen, of a man to be a good man. And what is goodness ? It is surely to be sought within and the first duty of a man is to look after himself, and his real self (as he said in the *Alcibiades*) is his soul. It is his duty, therefore, to know himself, as Apollo commands. Not to absorb, as the sophists would have him do, the prejudices of his environment, but to examine them for himself for, as he tells us in the *Apology*,[1] the uncritical life is not worth living. A quite new factor, self-education, thus makes its appearance.

This setting up of the private individual's conscience as the ultimate arbiter, is hedged in and obscured by Socrates' intense conviction that a man must obey the laws of his city —or take the consequences. And when Socrates set himself against the government, as he did not hesitate to do under the Thirty, or opposed the clamorous desires of the multitude, he was always prepared to face the punishment. He did not, apparently, consider the possibility of a clash between his inner convictions and the laws of Athens, but he did not hesitate to disobey the law as interpreted by his fellow-citizens, even if he respected their verdict and refused to run away.

This ' tendance of the soul ', this personal attempt to become as good as possible, Socrates interpreted as a search for the truth in moral questions by men actuated by love of wisdom (φιλοσοφία) ; and to develop this love was for Plato the supreme aim of education. He was very clearly aware of the difference between education and instruction. And the doctrine of Reminiscence emphasizes that man possesses a special capacity for this search after Truth : that there is in the human mind something that will ' see ' the truth if only it is ' turned in the right direction '.

In the *Meno* we have a practical application of this principle. Meno's slave, who is totally ignorant of geometry, simply by

[1] 38a : ὁ δὲ ἀνεξέταστος βίος οὐ βιωτὸς ἀνθρώπῳ.

answering Socrates' questions and without being told a single
fact, discovers that, to construct a square double the area of a
given square, one must build the second on the diagonal of the
first. He makes mistakes but corrects them himself, and this
striking passage (82*b* ff.) might well be taken for all time
as a pattern of the proper method to teach even the facts of
mathematics.

The fundamental principle of education is clearly expressed
in the *Republic*. Socrates has just described, in the well-known
parable of the cave, how men rise from the darkness of the
world of phenomena and the uncertainties of belief into the
radiant land of knowledge (518*b*) :

' Education is not what some people declare it to be. They say
that they put into the soul knowledge that was not there before, like
putting sight into blind eyes.
—They certainly say so.
—But our present argument shows that this power is present in the
soul of all, the instrument wherewith every one acquires knowledge.
It is as if a man could turn his eyes from darkness unto light only
by moving his whole body towards it ; so with his whole soul he
must be led from the world of becoming, until it is able to endure the
contemplation of reality and of that in reality which shines most
brightly, which is the good.
—Yes.
—And the art (τέχνη) of education is then concerned with this
very question : how the man shall most easily and completely be
turned around. It is not a matter of giving him sight. He
possesses that. But he is facing in the wrong direction and does not
look where he ought. That is the problem.'

But I anticipate. The educational programme of the *Republic*
is divided into two parts. The first, which is described in the
second and third book before the theory of Ideas has made its
appearance, is the education of the whole guardian class, rulers
and soldiers. It is the Platonic counterpart of the training in
physical culture and the arts which was common at Athens.
The second, the higher education of the philosopher-rulers, is to
lead them to an understanding of the eternal verities, and is
restricted to them.

It should be realized that from beginning to end Plato
insists, with as much emphasis as any modern psychologist,

upon the supreme importance of training in the earliest years
of life. Already in the *Euthyphro* we find Socrates asserting,
not without irony, that Meletus, in accusing him of corrupting
the young, is putting first things first 'just as a good farmer will
be right first to look after the young plants, and only later
after the others' (2*d*).[1] In the second book of the *Republic*
he says (377*b*) :

'Do you realize that the beginning of any thing is most important,
especially for something both young and tender? For it is then
especially that it is shaped, and takes on any mould that one wants
to impress upon it.' [2]

and it is upon the tremendous influence of the stories told by
nurses and mothers to small children that he, in the first
instance, bases his argument for the censorship of art. But
he does not, here, enter into any details of infant education.
It would seem that a sense of its importance grew upon him,
for the subject is treated at some length in the *Laws*. Education in the arts is discussed first. The important place given
to poetry and music is no novelty, and Plato is fully Greek in
believing that they have tremendous power in moulding
character. But the lengthy discussion of art, and the ruthless
rejection of the most revered poets, or at least of a great deal
of their work was, as was pointed out in discussing art,
thoroughly revolutionary. He seems to indicate that further
discussion is required by the statement that one cannot be
completely cultured (μουσικός) until one knows and can recognize the different 'forms' (εἴδη) of moderation, courage, &c.,
both in themselves and in their images, and goes on very
briefly to discuss the incompatibility of pleasure and self-
control, ending with a prohibition of homosexual intercourse.[3]

---

[1] The *Apology*, of course, shows that Meletus did not deserve the credit.
There, too, Socrates is fully aware of the difficulty of dispelling prejudices
against himself which had been acquired in childhood and adolescence.
[2] Cp. 424*e*.
[3] This whole passage 402*c*–403*c*, consists of rapid references to topics which
Plato does not wish to discuss in detail till later. Nor could he do so until
the central books of the *Republic* were written. In view of this, though the
reader who was not familiar with the Platonic Forms could understand εἴδη
σωφροσύνης in the usual way as kinds of virtues, and 'images' as nothing in
particular, Glaucon who knows all about the theory (475*e*) and any reader
in the same position is warned that the real μουσική will come later and is

There was nothing very startling, to an Athenian, in the section on gymnastic training, though Plato insists, more than most of his contemporaries would have done, that the real aim of physical training is to enable the soul to do its part unhindered. A good soul, by its own excellence, will bring about the excellence of the body, not vice versa. The Platonic guardian must keep fit, but he knows why he keeps fit. Drunkenness must be avoided. The guardians will not train like professional athletes, for these are a sleepy race and easily upset by the least disturbance of their diet, while our soldiers must be ready to face privations. Hence the key word to their athletic, as to their ' musical ' training, is simplicity, ἁπλότης. Their diet will be homerically simple and they will avoid courtesans, cakes and all highly spiced dishes. Simplicity in mousikê makes for self-control as simplicity in physical culture makes for health. Such a man will be as far as possible his own judge and his own doctor.

Plato then—410c—tells us that both mousikê and gymnastics are needed in education, and both have the welfare of the soul in view. Neither alone leads to a satisfactory result, for gymnastics alone makes a man rough and quick-tempered, while mousikê alone makes him too soft. What we should aim at is a proper balance of those two elements, temper and love of learning. These are the main principles of education, and there is no need, says Socrates, to go into further detail. The details will follow naturally enough if the main lines are sound. The whole of the system here described aims at implanting in the young right habits and ways of thinking, that is ' right beliefs ', for the virtues of the (auxiliary) guardians simply consist in their ability to hold on to these beliefs in spite of temptation, throughout life (412e). The health of the state as a whole depends upon the right education of the guardians, and we must beware of too frequent innovations.

not forgotten. To him εἰκόνες αὐτῶν—images of virtue—must mean these virtues as they appear in particular acts. I do not think these ' images ' can be works of art. The artist as a ' copyist ' and a maker of images three times removed from reality belongs to Book X. Hitherto he has been an ' impersonator ' only (see pp. 185 ff.). The plural εἴδη should offer no difficulty. There is, of course, only *one* εἶδος of each virtue. The whole passage betrays the haste of a man who is conscious of having spent a very long time on one topic and is hurrying on to the next.

We must not be 'revolutionaries' in gymnastic and 'musical' training (424*b*). The whole state is affected by changes in the arts. Lawlessness in art leads to lawlessness in general. Children must therefore be taught to play in an orderly and lawful manner. This hostility to change, and the importance of early play-habits will receive fuller treatment in the *Laws*. Given education, there will be fewer lawsuits, more honesty in business and also far less petty legislation which men are so apt to mistake for the best (425 and 427*a*).

When he comes to the higher education of the rulers, the real lovers of wisdom, Plato makes the distinction between the two quite clear. Gymnastic gave them health, while mousikê (522*a*) :

'educates our guardians by habituation (ἔθεσι παιδεύουσα), giving them a certain harmony by means of music, not knowledge, and by means of rhythm a certain balance (εὐρυθμία). The stories of literature, whether in fact true or not, make for kindred qualities. But there is no learning there which leads to what you are now seeking.'

For what he is now seeking is the certain knowledge of philosophy. The earlier education is necessary for all guardians who must in the first place be trained to good habits and beliefs. Most of them indeed will get no farther. But those who possess the appropriate qualities, so frequently described in the intervening books, namely memory, intelligence, greatheartedness, grace, who, being by nature akin to them, love truth, right, courage and moderation,[1] those philosophical souls are capable of more. They must acquire the supreme science referred to in earlier dialogues, the science which is goodness, they must be led to apprehend the Ideas. What education will lead them on their way?

Plato's answer is well known : the mathematical sciences provide the studies propaedeutic to philosophy. Arithmetic comes first. The science of numbers in its widest sense is at the very root of all scientific thinking, and of all practical arts as well : for, as Plato said, if we cannot distinguish unity from multiplicity we cannot think, and scarcely act, at all. Our

---

[1] e.g. 487*a* : μνήμων, εὐμαθής, μεγαλοπρεπής, εὔχαρις, φίλος τε καὶ συγγενὴς ἀληθείας, ἀνδρείας, σωφροσύνης, cp. 489*e* ff., 535*b* ff.

perceptions are frequently contradictory. Whenever we get beyond simple perceptions such as ' this is a finger ', whenever we try to understand size, weight, width, hardness, we at once find ourselves tied up by a number of contradictions. The qualities of particular things are relative to those of other phenomena. The same object is both hard and soft, big or small when compared with one thing or another, and our mind is at a loss. It is here that the science of numbers comes to the rescue : it teaches us the meaning of unity and plurality. It teaches us how all these qualities, though a plurality in so far as they appear in many phenomena, are yet in a sense *one*, (523*b*–525*b*) and thus help us to reach the truth. This science of numbers also has some practical applications in trade and war and these may be useful if we have to persuade men to accept our laws. What is important to the educator, however, is that it leads men, more than any other science, to an understanding of the truth. It is a difficult science, but it is essential. In this way does Plato include under the science of numbers a good deal of what would seem to belong rather to the province of logic.

Having thus vindicated the function of arithmetic he goes on to geometry, the science of two dimensional things, or rather, as he would put it following the Pythagoreans, of number in two dimensions. This too has its practical applications, but the proper object of geometry is not bodies at all but hypothetical perfect planes, for actual matter nowhere, of course, exists in two dimensions. Stereometry, or the science of the third dimension, comes next (and Socrates complains that this science has scarcely been invented yet), to be followed by astronomy. Just as stereometry is not the science of material bodies, but of perfect, i.e. hypothetical, shapes in three dimensions, so here the stars, being material, are not the proper objects of this science. In fact, what Plato has in mind is not astronomy at all, but kinetics or dynamics : i.e. the study of the laws of motion, how perfect mathematical bodies (which do not exist in the physical world) would move in mathematical space.[1] Lastly, harmonics or the science of sound.

---

[1] There is no need to suppose (with Adam, notes ad loc.) that Plato ' conceives of a mathematical οὐρανός of which the visible heavens are but a blurred and imperfect expression '. Surely in such a non-spatial heaven

Here again, Socrates maintains that the science concerns itself with the mathematical proportions and ratios which produce harmony. The Pythagoreans had reduced the different notes of the tetrachord to numerical ratios : i.e. the ratios between the different lengths of a single string that would produce them. That (says Plato) is the proper way, as against experimental investigation by purely empirical means whether another note could be found in any interval.

These are the sciences which, if pursued to the point where their essential kinship becomes clear (ἐπὶ τὴν ἀλλήλων κοινωνίαν), will lead man on to the realization of truth. But they are only a beginning, for we need, above and beyond all this, the science of dialectic : of giving and receiving an account of things (531e—δοῦναί τε καὶ ἀποδέχεσθαι λόγον). As to the nature of this dialectic, it is clearly the power to think and express oneself logically. And as he has insisted that the objects of logical thought—the universals, the Forms—exist, he can speak of dialectic as the discovery of these Forms. But it is also the study of scientific method itself—which would bring us back to the old difficulty of the *Charmides*, how can a science be its own object ? For the present we may therefore consider dialectic mainly as the power of apprehending the Ideas, of thinking logically, so that the content of one's thought corresponds to Reality.

Dialecticians will thus grasp the Forms and finally the supreme Form. They will be able to classify things in accordance with those Forms, and will discuss (ask questions and answer them 534d) with perfect truth and perfect logic : dialectic is the ' keystone of the whole structure of science ' (534e). And so later, when in the *Sophist* we find that the Forms themselves are interrelated, the dialectician, who sees and knows these Forms, will also be the only one able to understand and to formulate these relations. He will also be the man who sees truth as a whole, and can make correlations

there could be no movement at all. The curious expression at 529c : ' the speed or slowness of true shapes in true measure ' refers to the study of the laws of motion, only imperfectly realized in the physical heaven. This is not ' an undue extension of the methods of pure mathematics to Astronomy ' ; it *is* pure mathematics, and not astronomy, in our sense, at all.

between different parts of it.[1] Having explained the nature of the sciences which are to be part of the higher education and, one may presume, of the plan of studies he attempted to follow in the Academy, Plato returns to his educational legislation (535 ff.). He once more gives a catalogue of the qualities the would-be philosophers must possess. And if they are to pursue this course of study successfully, they must start young. No compulsion must be used for, as he says, anticipating once more the most modern theories of education, ' a free man must not learn anything by slavish compulsion . . . learning forced upon the soul does not remain. . . . Children should learn in play ' (536e).

So in play the propaedeutic studies must be tasted in childhood besides the ordinary education in mousikê and gymnastics. The last two or three years of adolescence are given over almost entirely to physical training, including some military service. The youths have been watched from the very first with a view to selecting the future rulers : at the age of twenty the selection takes place, and special honours are paid to the successful. The somewhat scattered and erratic scientific knowledge they have acquired is now taken up in earnest and taught scientifically till their interconnexion becomes clear. This will last for ten years.

A further selection is made at thirty ; it is especially strict, for the course of dialectics which follows, being a questioning of first principles, is fraught with danger for any but the most balanced,[2] and many precautions must be taken. Those who pass this stringent test follow a five-year course in dialectic. After this they must take part in public affairs and fill the offices of state so that ' they may not be behind the others in practical experience ' (539e). This period lasts fifteen years. At fifty they are allowed to retire from active life if they have justified themselves. They are now rulers in the full sense and spend most of their time in contemplation of the good, except when they must take turns in governing the state. This is not a pleasant task for them but they must do so for the sake of the state and to bring up others like themselves.

---

[1] 537c : ὁ μὲν γὰρ διαλεκτικὸς συνοπτικός, ὁ δὲ μὴ οὔ.

[2] 539a. Plato comes very near to admitting that Socrates' teaching may well have done harm to some.

At their death the greatest honours will be paid to them. All that has been said of men applies to women also.[1]

There is no further complete discussion of education before we come to the *Laws*. But there are a few passages which help us to understand Plato's ideal of education and his criticisms of the Athenian system.

We saw above that Plato distinguishes between two kinds of evil, of which the greater is due to ignorance. He then makes a most interesting distinction between two kinds of moral education and in this context he is clearly thinking mainly of the inculcation of ethical principles. The first is (*Sophist*, 229e) :

' The old ancestral method, which the majority of people even now use towards their erring sons : sometimes they are angry, sometimes they more gently exhort them. And this whole method may be called the hortative (νουθετητική).

This is, though Plato does not say so, the method depicted by Protagoras in the passage quoted above, the method of Anytus and the ordinary man. Its fault, as Plato proceeds to explain, is that once we realize that all ignorance is involuntary, and that as long as a man thinks he knows he will not be willing to learn, we see clearly that : ' for all the trouble it takes the hortatory kind of education achieves little '.[2] What is needed is obviously different. There follows a simple yet excellent description of the other, the Socratic, method. Those who realize the difficulty (230b) :

' when any one believes himself to be saying something worth while on a certain subject, ask questions about it. As men wander without consistency in their beliefs, they do not find the examination difficult : they gather these beliefs together in conversation and place them side by side. And they show that these beliefs contradict each other on the same aspect of the same subject. The pupils, realizing it, are angry with themselves, but gentler to others, and in this manner they get rid of proud and fixed beliefs about themselves.

[1] At the end of this account of higher education, Socrates reaffirms his belief in the importance of early training by remarking that if such a city is ever to be realized, it would be advisable to exile everybody over ten to begin with.

[2] Cp. *Laws*, 729b : where the Athenian says example is far more effective than any amount of exhortation.

This kind of deliverance is very pleasant for the hearers and lasting for the victim. Just as doctors think that the body cannot profit from the nurture provided for it until the inner obstacles are removed, so in the case of the soul those who bring the process of purification about think that no benefit can be got from any knowledge that is brought forward until the man who tests the opinions of another has led him to feel a sense of shame and removed the beliefs that stood in the way of knowledge. In this way a man is made pure and no longer thinks he knows more than he actually does.

—That is a very excellent state to be in.

—For all these reasons, Theaetetus, we must say that this test, the elenchus, is the greatest and most powerful of all purifications. The man who has not undergone it, be he the Great King of Persia himself, is corrupt (impure) in the way that matters most. He is uneducated and ugly in the things in which any one who is to be really happy should be most beautiful and pure.'

This Socratic elenchus, this test of beliefs, was to Plato an essential preliminary to any real education.[1] He believed in it with the same kind of passionate conviction as some modern psychoanalysts believe in the process of analysis as a cure and a way to happiness. The elenchus was as new in Athens then as is psychoanalysis to-day, and it is important to realize the quality of Plato's feelings on this question. The purpose of this education is to make a man see for himself, to teach him what Plato, with his eye always on the life of society, calls the kingly science. For its particular characteristic is that the man who possesses it has sufficient knowledge to be his own master, while people with inferior knowledge can only fulfil the commands given them by others.[2]

To understand fully Plato's system of education, as with so much of his philosophy, we must turn to the *Laws*. We must remember, however, that the *Laws* is a practical treatise. We shall therefore hear but little of the higher education of the philosopher. On the other hand the earlier education which the *Republic* (except for the discussions on art) treats only in a very general way, is here fully elaborated. At the very beginning of the dialogue the Cretan Cleinias praises the laws of his

---

[1] Cp. also *Theaetetus*, 177a : where the only way to teach a sense of moral values is said to be by personal intercourse and discussion.
[2] *Politicus*, 260d, e.

country which aim at preparedness for war, since struggle is
the natural condition both of city and individual (626*d*) and
self-mastery is the first victory. But the Athenian wants to
reverse the order : surely it is self-control, not war, which is
the ultimate aim, harmony, not discord. Nor, he continues,
should lawgivers concentrate on courage and bravery at the
expense of the other virtues, as Spartans and Cretans do.
Indeed courage itself consists not only of resisting fear but also
of resisting pleasure and desires (633*c*). Mere prohibition, as
in Sparta, is no real solution (637*d* ff. ; cp. 729*b*). To make this
point clear Plato elaborates at perhaps surprising length the
function which wine-drinking, for example, can play in education. Properly conducted, a symposium is an excellent test
for youths, for under the influence of wine they will show most
clearly how deep-rooted is their proper sense of shame. This
insistence on the power to resist pleasure as well as endure
pain is of some interest and corresponds to the increasingly
sympathetic attitude of Plato towards the pleasure instinct.

It naturally leads to a discussion of the nature of education
as a whole. Once more, as throughout the *Laws*, the importance of forming the right habits early is emphasized (643*b*) :

' I say then that if a man is to be good at anything, he must
practise it from early childhood, and spend his playing as well as
his learning time in pursuits suitable to the subject. As for example :
he who is to become a good farmer or a good architect must play at
building some toy edifices or with a toy farm. And the person who
brings up children must provide them with the tools of their trade in
miniature, copies of the real things, and they must learn early the
essential teachings of their trade—a carpenter must learn to measure
and weigh, a soldier to ride, all as a game, and so with other occu-
pations. We must try in play to direct the pleasures and desires of
children towards the goal that they must ultimately attain. And
the principal part of education is the training that will lead the
mind of the playing child to desire that which will make him, when
he has grown up, excel in his profession. Consider whether you
agree with what I have said hitherto.

Cl. Of course.

Ath. Let us see then that we do not leave the meaning of education vague. For now, when we approve or censure men's upbringing, we say that so and so among us is educated—yet we call
uneducated some of those who are thoroughly trained to commerce

or navigation and other such pursuits. Our discussion would seem to indicate that education is not the pursuit of those things, but is concerned from childhood with moral excellence, and fills one with desire and passion to become a perfect citizen who knows how to be a just ruler and a just subject. It is this upbringing and this alone, or so it seems to me, that our argument now tends to call education, while that which aims at wealth or strength of some kind or other, or at some other cleverness unconnected with justice or intelligence, is base and slavish and unworthy of being called education at all. But let us not quibble about words : let us agree to this definite conclusion : that those who are properly educated become good men ; that education must never be despised, for it is the most precious asset of the best men. And if it ever goes astray, and can be corrected—every man throughout his life must do so, as far as he is able, always.'

Education is here contrasted with technical skill, just as we saw that in the early dialogues the knowledge that was virtue was found to be different from it. This knowledge is still the ultimate aim, but the *Republic* made it clear that the goodness of the majority of men was based on right belief only, though it ultimately derives from the knowledge of others. Education must show most men the way to victory in the moral struggle which is the lot of all (644*d*).

And a little later the purpose of education is defined once more (653*a*) :

' I say that the first perception of children is pleasure and pain. It is by way of these that goodness and evil first enter the soul. As for knowledge and right belief, even the man who attains them in old age is lucky. The complete man (τέλεος) is a man who has achieved these and all the good things that go with them. Education then is the goodness that first comes to children : if the right things provoke pleasure and affection, pain and hatred, in the soul of those who cannot as yet grasp things by reason, and when they achieve reason, it agrees that they have been rightly habituated by proper habits— this agreement as a whole is virtue (goodness).

It is right, to my mind, to divide off from this double process the proper nurture in pleasure and pain, so that the child hates what should be hated from beginning to end, likes what should be liked, and to call this education.'

Plato makes it quite clear that he is not renouncing higher education. But for the majority it was always unsuitable, and

it is with the majority that we are here concerned, so he restricts
the word education to this general kind.

This right habituation, however, is apt to be corrupted as
life proceeds, and the gods have therefore given us festivals
with their artistic representations.   The very young can never
keep still, they have an irrepressible desire to move, jump,
dance and cry.   This is true of animals too (653e) :

' But other animals have no sense of order or disorder in movement, which is called rhythm and harmony.   The gods whom we
said had been sent to join us in the dance, are those who have
granted us the pleasurable sense of rhythm and harmony. . . .'

' The first education ', as he forcibly puts it, ' is by means of
the Muses and Apollo ' ; a point which is elaborated at 659d :

' For the third or fourth time we come to the same conclusion :
that education is drawing and guiding children to follow the right
and reasonable discourse (λόγος) uttered by the law, which the
elders' experience has shown to be truly right.   What we call song
is really an incantation to the souls of children and its purpose is
that the soul of the child should not become accustomed to rejoice
and suffer in a manner contrary to the law and to that of those who
obey it. . . .   Song earnestly aims at that harmonious agreement
(συμφωνία) we mentioned.   And because young minds cannot
endure what is serious, the performance is called play and song.
So also when men are ill and physically weak we try to give them
the sustenance they need in pleasant food and drink, and make
unpleasant to the taste what is bad for them, that they may
welcome the one and come to have a proper dislike of the other.
In this way then the good lawgiver will persuade the artist—and
indeed compel him if he will not be persuaded—to express rightly
the deeds of self-controlled, brave and good men in beautiful
words of praise with appropriate rhythm and music.'

Thus far the first two books of the *Laws*.   As for what follows,
the details of the different officials in charge of the different
departments are of no very great interest (764c–766b) except
for the fact that the minister of education (if we may call him
so) is ' by far the greatest of the important officers of the state ',
for man, though gentle and capable of being the most divine
of all animals if rightly trained, becomes if brought up badly
the ' wildest of all creatures that live upon the earth ' (766a).

To this important office the best man in the state must be elected, and his election by the other magistrates takes place under conditions of the utmost solemnity. His term of office is five years.

When we come to the seventh book we find the longest and fullest discussion in the whole of Plato's works of the education that is suitable for the majority of the citizens. More attention is also paid to the education of very young children. Indeed the attention paid to it is in itself no small tribute to Plato's insight. Most of his advice is sound, and a great deal of it is startlingly in accordance with modern theories, as the following summary will show.

The care of children is a matter for advice and exhortation rather than law, for it takes place within the privacy of the home. To legislate to the smallest detail would only bring the law itself into disrepute,[1] and after all it is unwritten law and tradition that govern the citizens' lives. Now the aim of nurture and education is to make both body and soul as good and beautiful as possible, and we agree, do we not, that ' the early growth of all plants and animals is the most important and the greatest ' ? At twenty a man is scarcely twice the size he is at the age of five. During this early period proper physical exercise is of the greatest importance. We should, indeed, begin with the ' gymnastic of the embryo ' (γυμναστικὴ τῶν κυομένων). Shall we brave ridicule and decree (789e) :

' that a pregnant woman must take walks, and fashion the child like wax while it is still pliable. He must be in swaddling clothes till the age of two. We shall compel our nurses, under threat of punishment by law, always to carry the child about either to the country, the temple, or to visit relatives until it is able to stand up sufficiently well, even then to be careful lest standing up while still small twist the limbs, and to take the trouble to carry him till he is fully three years old.'

Movement, he continues, is very beneficial. Therefore mothers always rock their children to sleep and sing to them. This fits in with Plato's views on the confused motions within the soul in infancy, external movement helping to allay the chaos within. At this time also fear plays a great part in life (791b)

---

[1] For Plato's dislike of too many laws see *Rep.*, 427a.

and children must learn to overcome the terrors that come upon them. But all this is a matter for advice rather than official legislation (790*b*).

A child should not be spoiled or pampered, but neither must he be harshly treated. The first will make him grow up into a difficult and bad-tempered man, the second will make him too humble and reduce him to a condition fit only for a slave. Babies start to cry loudly as soon as they are born (791*e*) :

' Nurse wants to know what he wants, and she can only find out by bringing things to him. If something is brought and baby is quiet, she thinks that is right ; if he cries and yells, that is wrong. Infants can only show what they want or don't want by cries and tears—not at all a fortunate way of showing it. But this lasts for three years, and three years is a long period of life in which to form good or bad habits.'

Hence it is very bad for a baby to have his every want satisfied all this time, in fact it is the worst thing that could be done to him and permanently undermines his character. The good life does not consist in grabbing at every kind of pleasure and avoiding every kind of pain. And at this early age above all others, character is formed by habit (ἦθος διὰ ἔθος 792*e*).

Children from three to six need to play. They also need to be punished to avoid them being self-willed (τρυφή), but the punishment should be such that the child will not resent it. Between those ages they can be left to amuse each other and devise their own games. They will do so in common and will be taken to spend their day together in the temples of the district under the supervision of a member of a women's board who will punish them when necessary (794*a*). The temple thus fulfils the functions of our nursery schools.

At six another stage is reached. The sexes will be segregated and the time to learn has begun. The boys will learn riding, the use of bow and sling, and the girls also. The development of the right hand at the expense of the left will be avoided, for men are naturally ambidextrous, a quality useful in war. They will learn recitation and eurythmics, dancing in full armour, and wrestling, but not in the tricky way now fashionable (796).

We thus come once more to education in mousikê and

gymnastics. With solemn emphasis the Athenian declares that children's games (presumably after six) are of the greatest importance for the formation of character. For that matter change in what one is used to, even if it is not perfect, is generally a mistake unless one's habits are definitely bad (797d ff.). For such changes are apt to make trouble in the soul (798b) :

' As we said before, people think children's games trifling things, and that changes in them can do no great harm and are of no consequence, since they are but games. Children are not prevented from changing them, they are rather encouraged. Men do not take into account that inevitably children who make innovations in their games will grow up into men different from those who were children before them ; that, being different, they will look for a different life and that, in their search for it, they will want different laws and habits. Thus continual change, that great evil we mentioned, will come upon the state, but none will fear it.'

We said, he goes on, that art represented the deeds of good and bad men. Bad art our children should not want, and no one should tempt them to enjoy it. The manner of celebrating festivals should be fixed, with its dances and ritual (799a).

There will be public gymnasia and schools. Three within the city, three, for riding, archery, &c., outside the walls where the youths can practise. Our gymnastic teachers will be foreigners paid for the purpose. Education will be compulsory and no parent has the right to keep his child away (804d). Boys and girls will have the same opportunities to learn, for women must serve the state as well as men. Though our citizens are relieved of all menial tasks and will have leisure, it is a mistake to think that a life devoted to virtue is an easy life. We must, of course, have schoolmasters (808d), and indeed supervision,[1] first by mother and nurse, then by attendant slave and schoolmaster, is needed at all stages, for ' a child is the most difficult of all animals to deal with ' and he must be bridled. Every citizen who sees a child misbehave should correct him, indeed is compelled to do so.

When the children, at the age of ten, have gone through this

[1] Plato is here following the usual Greek custom. Perhaps the greatest fault of Greek education was that, like some modern schoolmasters, they thought that a boy left to himself would at once and inevitably get into some mischief.

course of largely physical training in the gymnasia they will begin their letters and all that this leads to : reading, writing and the more practical side of the mathematical sciences. Three years will be spent on learning to read and write, and they will attain such proficiency as they can in that time. Neither parent nor child can demand a longer period of time for this. And the same rule will hold for the next three years, from thirteen to sixteen, which will be occupied by music, learning to play the lyre, and the study of literature in prose or verse, carefully censored as before. Their music and dancing, as well as their reading, are carefully organized and as far as possible fixed within definite limits by the board of education, the members of which are selected by the chief magistrate whom we put in charge of the whole system.

We have come to the end, says the Athenian, of education in mousikê and gymnastics. But what of the sciences ? There are three things a free man should learn : calculation and the science of numbers is one ; geometry plane and solid is another ; astronomy the third. Clearly even the ordinary citizen should know something of these, or he will not be able to count at all. But how much ? The danger is that a mere superficial acquaintance with those sciences will only lead to polymathy (to thinking one knows what one does not know) and that those who have learned them badly are rather worse off than those who have not learned them at all (819a). Our citizens therefore had better approach these sciences in a practical way, like the Egyptians (819b) :

'First in arithmetic, things are found which children can learn simply, pleasurably and in play, the distribution of apples or garlands to greater and also to smaller numbers, so that the same totals correspond ; or the arranging of boxers and wrestlers, as happens in competitions, so that each plays in turn and passes a round. In play also the teachers mix up bowls of gold and silver and bronze and other metals, while others arrange them in whole sets of one kind. Thus, as I say, they teach in play the uses of the essential numbers. They benefit their pupils and fit them to make arrangements for a camp, raising troops, making expeditions, and again for household duties. Altogether they make men more useful to themselves and wider awake.'

That is, mathematics will be learned with a view to their practical applications. But this is not quite enough. The Athenian asserts that Greek ignorance of geometry is shameful. Solid bodies and planes can be measured and studied in relation to one another. Some knowledge at least of irrational quantities is desirable and can do no harm (820c). So with astronomy : our citizens must know enough not to blaspheme against the gods by believing that the sun and moon are just wandering stars without fixed paths. The contrary has been proved to be the case, and they must know that much at least.

Thus the Athenian brings his account of education to an end. It is important to be quite clear that there is no question here of the higher education of the *Republic*. We are dealing exclusively with the majority. There is no lowering of standard for the rulers themselves : as we shall see they are dealt with very briefly in the last book. But there is a very definite raising of standard for the average man. Not only does he get the mousikê and gymnastic training of the guardians in the *Republic*, which is more fully dealt with in the *Laws*, but a certain modicum of scientific education is also granted him, though it is a very different sort of science, which does not rise above particular phenomena. He will learn, by force of habit and entirely under instruction, to count apples, wreaths or anything else, but he will have no conception of the meaning of unity. He will be told how to do it and obey, just as he will be told that the sun and moon follow regular paths in heaven and he will believe it, without knowing why. Not only will he not study dialectic, nor be expected to go behind and beyond the fundamental hypotheses of any particular science, but within the limits of the particular sciences themselves he will not be taught in anything like the same way as the budding philosopher of the *Republic* at the propaedeutic stage. Plato is rather vague and uncertain on this point, but it is doubtful whether the ordinary citizen will be taught as well as Meno's slave, by question and answer and by finding things out for himself, though the dialectical method, in the earlier sense of question and answer, can be used at all stages. At any rate he will not reach the stage where the interrelation of these sciences is studied—which must be reached long before dialectic, in the higher philosophic sense, can be begun. One can only conclude that with his bowls and apples the child reaches only the stage attained by the philosopher of the *Republic* before the age of twenty, when the propaedeutic sciences began in earnest. Beyond that point all the mathematical sciences have abstractions as their object, and where they use concrete diagrams, these are only images of the realities they study. To the ordinary man the apples and the stars are and remain the only reality he knows. His is only a certificate of general information.

As we look over Plato's exposition of his educational system, which is remarkably consistent from first to last, we see two main stages, and then, more accurately, three. The function of each is best understood in the light of his psychology : there too we have the human soul divided into three ' parts ' or ' aspects ', of which the lower two easily group themselves together in contrast with the third.

To understand fully the meaning of the first stage in the educational process, infant education, we must call to mind the passage of the *Timaeus* wherein Plato describes man's first contact with the world. The human soul, like the world soul, consists of the intertwined circles of Same and Other, which have motions of their own. But when the gods place this in a material body, and add the mortal parts of the soul to it, a great confusion arises. The immortal intellect is suddenly linked to unreasoning feelings and passions and with these is tied down into a body which has motion of its own for, being matter, it is in a state of perpetual flux.[1] On top of this, sensations pour in from without and cause further disturbance. All this chaos has to be reduced to order before man can develop. It is here that we find the explanation of Plato's otherwise strange insistence upon the important part which continual movement plays in the first three years of life. No wonder the baby is afraid ! No wonder it must be rocked and carried so that the soothing motion from without may still the mad storm within (791*a*) ! That is, in fact, the first duty of the child, to master the inner chaos and to adjust himself. The process will go on throughout life, but it is most violent at the first. The unregulated movements of infancy must be

[1] Being composed of four elements each of which is trying to regain its own place in the universe. See *Tim.*, 43 ff.

tamed, and the main development at this stage is purely upon the perceptual plane. The child must learn to perceive accurately. He must also gain mastery over his immediate physical desires such as hunger and thirst, and here comes the point of contact with the lowest part of the soul where such desires have their being.

The second stage is to a larger extent concentrated upon the outer world. The child has by now gained some mastery over the unruly confusion which greeted his entry into the world. Some sort of order reigns in his own house and he begins to want other pleasures. He wants to possess things and has to face the temptations and ambitions which come with a turning of his attention upon objects outside himself. His feelings must now be trained by the influence of the arts and by the inculcation of sound beliefs as to which pleasures are to be sought, which to be avoided. This is effected by mousikê and gymnastics. Healthy development of body and soul is the aim. But the ' part ' of the soul most directly concerned is undoubtedly the θυμός, the spirit or feelings. This is as far as most men ever get. They have, of course, thought of a kind, but not what Plato calls knowledge. By proper training of desire or Eros in its widest sense man is gradually ascending to the philosophic love of truth and beauty. But imperfectly, for his intellect is trained only in practical science, and does not, as yet, reach beyond.

Above both these lower grades, and *possible only if they have been successful*, comes the higher education of the philosopher-king. Quite obviously it is with the intellect, the highest part of the soul, that we are here mostly concerned.[1] This higher education is not in any way given up in the *Laws*. Apart from scattered but emphatic statements that wisdom is still the ultimate aim and that the organization of the state must be based on it ; that real virtue means agreement between character and reason which only comes to the best men in old age, and other similar statements ;[2] Plato, in the very last pages makes it abundantly clear that the whole success of the state depends on the rulers possessing the same wisdom as the philoso-

---

[1] It includes, of course, ἐπιθυμία of a kind, the philosophic Eros. See pp. 135 ff.

[2] 710a–b ; see also 818e, 688b, 692c, 730c, &c.

pher of the *Republic*. Every art, he tells us, must know what it is aiming at, as medicine knows health. So the statesman must know the goal of statesmanship—σκοπός πολιτικός—and without this the whole city can neither see nor understand. The aim of statesmanship can only be one : goodness. This the guardians must know, as well as the differences between the different kinds of virtue. We need therefore a ' more exact education ', for they must reduce the one to the many and the many to the one ; they must grasp the one Form behind the many particulars. And as they know this, they must know also Beauty and Goodness and everything of importance. While other men merely obey the voice of the law they must be able to account for the existence of the gods, and indeed for everything which admits of reasonable explanation.[1]

III. The Knowledge that is Virtue

We have seen that the conviction that men sin for lack of knowledge remained with Plato to the end ; we have studied the kind of education he advised. We may now attempt to elucidate more exactly the nature of this knowledge.

It is often referred to in general terms, but where it is specifically distinguished from other kinds it is called νοῦς or νόησις. Νοῦς, mind, was also the directive force in the universe of Anaxagoras, but he only used this to account for the beginning of motion, and thereby disappointed Socrates [2] who felt that if the universe is directed by a purpose, this should be taken into account to explain its every part. Men cannot then know the why of anything unless they can explain how it accords with the universal purpose of things. If only men could acquire this knowledge they would inevitably act in accordance with that purpose. And that if the world was thus directed, it was directed towards the good, Plato never doubted.

It will simplify our search if we first eliminate those things which Plato definitely tells us that Nous is *not*.

We have already seen in the dialogues of the first period that it is not technical knowledge. So in the first book of the *Laws* we are told that a good general must possess not only the science of strategy, but must also be able to overcome fear (639*b*).

---

[1] See 961 to end, especially 961*e*, 962*a*, 962*d*, 963*a*, 965*b*, 966*c*, 968.
[2] *Phaedo*, 97*c*–98*c*.

He must, that is, possess not only the technique of his craft, but also virtue, in this case the virtue of courage. Now a man may be able to do this, like the auxiliary guardians of the *Republic*, if he possess right belief. But this right belief in turn depends on the knowledge of the real rulers. Nous then is different from any or all particular crafts and sciences, and uses them all, as the *Euthydemus* told us.[1]

Nor is the wisdom that is Nous necessarily an indiscriminate desire to know things which may only lead to acquiring a large number of unco-ordinated bits of information. This is made clear in an amusing passage of the *Republic* which distinguishes between the real philosopher and those who, ever eager for novelties, rush around to all the latest dramatic or choral performances in their passion to know about them (475*d*). They love to see and hear things it is true, but what they wish to see and hear are only particular things. So too those who love beautiful sights and sounds are unlike the philosopher who investigates the nature of beauty itself. He is concerned with the Idea of beauty and with sights and sounds only as expressions of this.

Again, wisdom is not mere cleverness (δεινότης) divorced from a standard of ultimate ethical values. This is what we usually mean by ' brains '. Nous, however, is a great deal more than brains. Clearly put in the *Theaetetus* (176-7), this difference is emphasized again in the *Laws* (689*c*) where the Athenian, after explaining that disharmony in the soul when the passions refuse to obey the reason is what he calls ignorance, continues :

' This then we believe and will repeat : citizens who are ignorant in this respect we shall not entrust with any power in the state. We shall blame them as being ignorant even if they are very clever (λογιστικοί) and are versed in all the accomplishments which make for quickness of mind. Those who are in the opposite case we shall call wise even though, as the saying goes, they can neither read nor swim, and we shall give them power, for they are wise.'

Plato is here emphasizing the need of harmony in the soul. Without this no amount of brains or cleverness will give people the wisdom that is goodness. He does not mean, of course, that

---

[1] *supra* 222 ff. Cp. *Laws*, 643*d*, *e*.

the supreme wisdom can be attained without being able to read, but only that some accomplished people are further removed from it than rustics who are willing to follow their betters. This is important. Nous definitely means more than mere capacity for mental gymnastics. Those who use their brains solely for private profit are not wise men but villains (πανουργία ἀντὶ σοφίας, *Laws*, 747c). What more is required we shall learn shortly, but we may note in passing that it is this realization that a little knowledge is a dangerous thing which led Plato to see the danger of questioning first principles unless one goes far enough to establish a new and firmer basis for the good life. Hence the extraordinary care with which those who are to be taught dialectic are chosen in the *Republic* ; hence also it is at times implied that Socrates' indiscriminate teaching may in some cases have done harm (e.g.*Philebus*, 15e).

The supreme wisdom then is not technical knowledge, it is not an indiscriminate desire to know, it is not mere brains. To find what it is we may approach it from three angles : the metaphysical, the logical and the psychological. We may study it, that is, in its object or content, as a method of thought and as a psychological process.

The object of the supreme knowledge is clearly the Ideas. And a knowledge of the Ideas means not only an understanding of Truth, of the structure of the world, but also of the moral and aesthetic realities in it, of its purpose and the reason why in all things. It then includes what we should call a sense of true values ; the knowledge of good and evil, of beauty and goodness as well as of truth. Its relation to cleverness or brains we may suppose to be similar to the clear distinction Plato drew between the apothecary and the doctor in the *Phaedrus*, or between the mere technician and the artist.[1] Technical knowledge may tell us how to do something, the philosopher knows why and when things should be done. The knowledge of supreme reality as truth is the knowledge of the laws of nature, to know it as goodness gives a sense of moral values.[2] All this belongs to the philosopher through his

---

[1] P. 213 above.
[2] Therefore the well-known type who is very clever at his own job (be it engineering or classical studies) and a fool in other departments has not Nous.

knowledge of the eternal Forms. Plato did not believe that he had solved all the mysteries of the universe, that perfect knowledge of reality was his or any man's, but he did think he could point the way along which it should be sought. As a method of thought Nous is scientific method, including both induction and deduction in its application. You investigate the evidence, make a hypothesis and examine its consequences, for every assumption must be such as not to clash with facts. Then you examine this hypothesis itself and seek to account for it along with others by another more fundamental hypothesis of more universal application. For we must ever be prepared to cancel any hypothesis that does not fit the facts on the one hand and the higher truths on the other (ἀναιρεῖν τὰς ὑποθέσεις). Every particular science starts from one or more axioms, and is not concerned to go behind them. This process of reasoning within limits Plato calls διάνοια : it is reasoning power or, in this limited sense, science. The philosopher, however, must go behind these fundamental axioms, test them in the light of further understanding of higher truths, and never rest until he reach one supreme truth, in reference to which everything could be explained. It may be that Plato thought all mathematics could be logically derived from a proper understanding of the meaning of unity, all ethics from an understanding of the good. And ultimately these, and the ultimate object of aesthetic contemplation, beauty, were to him but different aspects of one reality.[1]

Hence Plato's insistence that dialectic is essentially synthetic. It is so at every stage. For it gathers together particular phenomena under one Form, one kind ; and, as explained in the *Sophist*, it will grasp the possible relations between the Forms themselves, thus bringing classification into the noetic world. Any classification is, of course, also a division, for any synthesis implies the rejection of the irrelevant. Hence the process can be looked upon either as a bringing together into groups or a separation into groups (διαίρεσις). This process of dividing, by dichotomy if possible, is fully elaborated in the *Sophist* and the *Politicus*, and already adumbrated in the

---

[1] See F. M. Cornford, 'Mathematics and dialectic in the Republic, VI–VII', in *Mind*, vol. xli, N.S. 161, pp. 37–52 and 173–190, for an excellent analysis of Nous in its three aspects. See also p. 27 above.

Phaedrus. The secret of its success is that each class must have some common quality, some Form which justifies its members being put together. And since the Forms are to Plato the only positive reality and the success of the method depends on the apprehension of them, he naturally emphasizes the synthetic aspect when he describes the essential qualities of the dialectician.

His descriptions of the psychological process involved in the grasping of the Forms is vague and metaphorical. Indeed it could not be otherwise. We have seen that he clearly distinguishes Nous from the ability to reason from given premises. And in this he made a valuable contribution to the psychology of the mind. For it is well known that the faculty of deductive reasoning is essentially different from the faculty of induction. Gather what evidence you may, the perception of the universal does not follow : it is not enough, as Socrates says in the *Meno*, to gather all the bees in the world into one place. That will not in itself give a definition of a bee. One must *see* what their common properties are. So also the mathematician sees the premises implied in a conclusion. In both cases there is a jump or leap of the mind. This is to ' *see* ' an idea. And it is always by the metaphor of light and sight that Plato expresses the process of grasping a Form. He was the first to use the expression ' the eyes of the soul ' and to follow up its implications. We find it in the magnificent analogy between the supreme good and the sun, in the parable of the darkness of the cave, and scattered in a hundred places throughout his writings.

We may call this process intuition—it is the nearest equivalent. But it will not come to those who have not followed to the end the painful road of scientific education. It is not a cheap and easy alternative to intellect, it is the culmination of intellectual research, the flash of insight that comes to those, and only to those, who have made a thorough study of their subject. That seems to be what Plato meant by Nous, the supreme knowledge which I have called understanding for lack of a better word : the grasping by the mind of the universal above and beyond the particular and with it a knowledge of ultimate moral and aesthetic values, the power to think clearly and logically and to see universal relations in the phenomenal world, the faculty of leaping to a right conclusion based on a full knowledge of the facts available.

But why, we may still ask, can such knowledge not be misused ? Why is it impossible, when in possession of all this wisdom, to act with evil or selfish intent ? Our study of Plato's conception of education and of Eros gives us his answer. Unless a man's emotions have been properly trained, unless, that is, his primitive passions have been redirected into the channels of desires that flow towards truth, he will never have within himself the necessary motive-power to urge him forward on the hard path of scientific achievement, or to press on along the hard road that is lit up now and again by the flash of understanding which is the apprehension of ever higher and more universal Forms and values. And if he has this knowledge of real values, if he knows what is true and good, if he understands the purpose of the world, he cannot act against it for his own ends because this purpose is beautiful as well as true and good, because its beauty gives supreme satisfaction to that Eros, that very love of beauty without which he could never have come so far. He cannot but desire that the world of sense should approach the Ideal beauty he now contemplates, and he must needs do what he can towards its realization. Living above petty interests in the loving adoration of supreme truth, himself a harmonious being who has risen above all conflict in his own soul, the Platonic philosopher will inevitably seek everywhere to impose harmony upon chaos, which is to change evil into good. His knowledge is goodness indeed.

VIII

STATECRAFT

THE philosopher in Plato triumphed over the 'poet', as we
have seen. But, though he subordinated his art in practice as
well as in theory, he remained one of the world's great writers
to the end. No such happy solution was unfortunately possible between two other aspects of Plato's versatile nature, the
teacher and the statesman. It is only because he could not,
in the Athens of his day, play a useful part in politics—or so
he thought—that he became a teacher. And though the
theorist won in this case also, he was never happy in his
victory. Indeed, he used it to proclaim that in a sane
world there should have been no conflict or incompatibility
at all.

We have Plato's own account, in the seventh letter,[1] of the
reasons why he turned away from public life. He was about
twenty-three when the thirty tyrants, with his uncle Critias
as their leader, came to power in 404 B.C. Every one expected
a young man of his aristocratic birth and training to carve
himself a public career, and he tells us that his relatives and
friends in the government called upon him to do so under their
régime. At first he was willing and eager to believe them
when they claimed that their sole aim was to correct the evils
of democracy. But he was soon disgusted by their repressive
measures and especially by their attempt to implicate Socrates,
along with others, in their murderous designs. So he turned
away from public life. When the democracy was soon afterwards restored, hope returned. The democrats showed com-
mendable restraint in dealing with their late enemies and Plato
seems to have been on the point of entering politics once more.

---

[1] 324c–326b. The seventh letter is almost unanimously accepted as
genuine. See table in Harward, *The Platonic Epistles*, p. 76.

Then came the trial of Socrates. The death of his revered friend plunged the young Plato into despair. There seemed no hope of sanity or moderation, either from oligarch or democrat. Once more he turned away in disgust, and this time he never recovered. He saw the wrong men in power all round him, laws multiplied and were openly flouted. Political life seemed no place for an honest man and he came to the conclusion that all the states of Greece were badly governed by ignorant men and that the only hope for the world lay in ' the right study of philosophy ', that only wisdom and knowledge could provide a way out. So he devoted himself to the study and teaching of this wisdom.

In this seventh letter also we read the pathetic story of his journeys to Sicily when, late in life, he was called upon by his friend Dion to attempt the belated education of the young Dionysus, tyrant of Syracuse, into the type of wise ruler he had by then so vividly described in the *Republic*. He made the attempt on two separate occasions. At no time did he have any great hope of success, and when he started out for the second time at the age of sixty-seven he knew that failure was all but certain. Yet he who had dreamed as a young man of leading his own country dared not reject, when old, the only chance, however remote, of putting his political theories into practice. He tells us himself that his chief reason was an intensive feeling of shame lest he should find himself to be a mere builder of theories.[1] The point of special interest for us is not that he failed, but that he went at all.

But to a man of his birth and later of his reputation, the way to public life can never have been closed in Athens itself. There, however, it was not a question of converting one man, but a whole people. And the people would listen only to what pleased them. They would not tolerate him, and he would not deceive them. One is reminded of Socrates' words in the *Apology* (31*d*) :

' You know full well, gentlemen, that if long ago I had tried to engage in politics I should have been executed long ago and of no use either to you or to myself. Do not be angry with me for telling

---

[1] 328*c* : αἰσχυνόμενος μὲν ἐμαυτὸν τὸ μέγιστον, μὴ δόξαιμί ποτε ἐμαυτῷ παντάπασι λόγος μόνον ἀτεχνῶς εἶναί τις.

you the truth : no man can remain alive who genuinely opposes
you or any other crowd and prevents you from doing many wrong
and unlawful deeds in the state.   If a man really fights for justice
he must lead a private, not a public, life.'

It is not the danger but the futility of the attempt that must
have held Plato back.   Is there not an angry echo of his bitter
disappointment in the passage of the *Republic* (496*c*) where he
says of the genuine philosophers :

' those who have tasted philosophy and know how sweet and blessed
a possession it is, when they have also fully realized the madness of
the majority, that practically never does any one act sanely in public
affairs, that there is no one in whom one might find an ally in the
fight for justice, and live—then like a man who has fallen among
wild beasts, neither willing to join the others in doing wrong, nor
strong enough to oppose their savagery alone, for he would perish
before he could benefit his country or himself, of no use to himself
or any one else—taking all this into account, he keeps quiet and
minds his own business.   Like a man who takes refuge under a wall
from a storm of dust or wind-driven hail, the philosopher is glad,
seeing other men filled with lawlessness, if he can somehow live his
present life free from wrongdoing and impiety and thus reach death
with grace, goodwill and a beautiful hope.'

And yet, though its greatness had gone and its splendour had
faded, the Athens of Plato's day was not so outrageously
governed or so completely degenerate.   The fault lay in the
philosopher's character.   His aristocratic background, allied
to his intellectual power, made him, we may be sure, a man
who could not suffer fools gladly.   And if he blamed his disappointment on the ignorance and crass prejudices of his
contemporaries, he himself was temperamentally unfitted to
lead men in the mass, for he was incapable of those compromises
and small diplomatic deceits which even the best democratic
politicians,   all statesmen in fact, except perhaps an all-
powerful despot, must of necessity practise.

Only with this personal experience of Plato's before us can
we understand his attitude to politicians, if not to politics, and
his bitter and scathing criticisms of them.   These are especially
violent in his earlier work, up to and including the *Republic*.
Essentially, his treatment remains the same throughout, and it

might be said that the only development in his general attitude is that anger comes to be replaced by despair. But, in Plato, even despair is never sterile or vain. And if he must give up his ideal he will still try to show the way to improve the nations as they are.

There is no very complete political theory in the dialogues of the early period, though the keynote is struck from the first : politics is a science (τέχνη) and it aims at making the citizens better men. It therefore is a form of knowledge, namely that of good and evil. Politicians are then bitterly attacked for their ignorance. This position is put very clearly in the *Gorgias*. It will be remembered that Callicles, the complete hedonist of that dialogue, is himself an aspiring politician ' a courtier of Demos ' (481*d*). Socrates points out to him that the price of success in politics is to be as like the people as possible, for ' everybody likes to hear speeches after his own character ' (513*c*). The result is that the people will be master of your soul rather than you rule the people. But the true aim of politics is to make better citizens (515*c*, 517*c*). This no statesman has ever done, not even Pericles or Cimon, Miltiades or Themistocles. This attack upon the most respected names of Athenian history is sheer blasphemy to Callicles, and Socrates goes on to prove his point not without a touch of broad humour. It was Pericles' job to look after men. But it seems he did not do his job well, for they treated him worse at the end of his life than ever before, so that we may conclude that he fanned their evil passions rather than checked them. Reverting to his earlier distinction between doctors and pastry-cooks,[1] Socrates compares the great Athenian statesmen to the latter. They provided the people with sweetmeats in the shape of harbours, arsenals, money, &c., quite regardless of the use made of them. For goodness they cared not at all. And although it would be unfair to hold them responsible for all present misfortunes, they must bear their share of the blame. Socrates concludes his attack with the statement that he himself is perhaps the only true politician, for he alone tries to make men better (521*d*).

Criticism of the same kind is found in other dialogues of this

[1] See pp. 209 ff.

period, always on the score of ignorance, of not realizing that politics is a science. This science politicians seem unable to teach any one, thus showing they do not possess it ; indeed some of them do not even realize that it is a science.[1] So Alcibiades is taken to task in the first dialogue that bears his name. Socrates points out to him that ambition is no qualification for political life. When asked what he will advise the Athenians about, the young man naturally answers : about things he knows better than they do. This on investigation turns out to be when it is right to do this or that, the knowledge of right or wrong. Alcibiades, to his own very considerable astonishment, does not, it seems, possess it. A point worth noting also is the statement that the main thing needed in a state is goodwill and common aims (φιλία, ὁμόνοια).[2] The full force of this is brought out in the *Republic*.

Protagoras professes to teach this very thing, political science (πολιτικὴ τέχνη). But it should be noted that he divorces it from all truly scientific education. Arithmetic, astronomy, geometry, music (the propaedeutic studies of the *Republic*) are, he says (*Prot.*, 318e), quite unnecessary. He thus claims to teach one particular type of excellence or virtue. Socrates attacks this position from two angles. First he asks Protagoras to deal with objections made to its being a subject of teaching at all : the Athenians allow any one to advise on matters of general policy, politicians can't teach their sons, &c. The creation myth by which the sophist answers does not really solve the difficulty since it maintains that virtue is inborn and also teachable. But Socrates professes himself satisfied and, turning to the question of the unity of virtue, forces Protagoras to agree that they are all one. It is thus implied that to teach one kind of excellence is impossible and we see later, in the *Republic*, that the scientific education which the sophist rejects is an essential part of a statesman's training.

The *Meno* established a difference between knowledge and right opinion or belief. We have seen that this enables the guardians to be good without being necessarily wise.[3] This possibility is here granted to the politicians who may then

[1] See *Protagoras*, 319e, *Alcibiades*, 118d, *Meno*, 93 ; cp. *Laches*, 179d.
[2] *Alc.*, 126c ; cp. *Cleitophon*, 409d–e.
[3] See p. 225.

also do what is right without knowing why. But the extreme instability of belief is emphasized when speaking of them.

In a specimen argument in the *Euthydemus* Socrates briefly seeks to define the supreme ethical knowledge. He calls this ' the kingly science ' as well as dialectic. It is the science that makes use of all the others, and no difference is made between ethics and politics.[1] This identity, as is well known, is not peculiar to Plato. It was implied in the teaching of the sophists and was the general Greek point of view. They made no difference between a good citizen and a good man, and Plato's saying that the aim of statesmanship is the moral welfare of the citizens would not sound strange to the inhabitants of a city-state that was the focus of religious, social and artistic, as well as political life. And, whatever our modern political theories, it should not be forgotten that all modern states act upon the Greek theory to some extent. Opium and other drugs are forbidden because of the deleterious effects upon their victims ; homosexuality is a crime in English law even when it is based on consent and mutual affection ; the use of alcohol is restricted in one way or another. Examples could be multiplied from every country to show that the state still concerns itself with the moral welfare of its citizens, the only difference being in the extent of the interference. It may be said that no state can be counted healthy unless it is composed of individuals morally and physically healthy. That is exactly the Greek view, and it brings ethics and politics very close together.

Thus far the early dialogues : statesmanship aims at making men good, and for this purpose it requires the knowledge of good and evil. This the politicians do not possess ; when they act rightly it is at best only because they make, as it were, a lucky guess. To be a statesman in the true sense it is necessary to acquire the ' kingly knowledge ' that directs all the others. Further, as Socrates tells Alcibiades, it is essential to have self-

---

[1] See p. 222. Yet at the end of the dialogue he speaks of those who are half philosopher, half politician and are worse than either. Both philosophy and political science are good, and spoken of as two different things. This, however, is not a discussion of either but only a way of describing Euthydemus and his confrère. We need not therefore attach much importance to it. After all, they are different pursuits in practice, whatever they ought to be. But it is an unusual distinction.

knowledge also, as in this way only can one arrive at real knowledge of right and wrong, settle one's own conduct, and give
good advice to the state.

We soon find ourselves on the political plane in the first book
of the *Republic* when the sophist Thrasymachus defines the
right or just (τὸ δίκαιον) as that which is to the advantage of
the stronger (338c). He interprets the stronger to mean those
in power in the state ; they make laws to their own advantage
and it is right for the ordinary citizen to obey these. But,
pressed by Socrates, he soon finds himself in difficulties. For
Socrates points out that rulers may be in error as to what is
their own advantage. Are we to obey them then ?
But Thrasymachus is not caught so easily. He meets the
objection with a subtle argument which, however, plays into
Socrates' hands, namely that when a ruler makes a mistake he is
not a true ruler any more than a doctor who prescribes a wrong
remedy is, strictly speaking, a doctor, for he is not acting in
accordance with the science of medicine (340d). This implies
that politics also is a science, a kind of knowledge. Now
according to Thrasymachus the aim of political science is to
benefit its possessor, but Socrates shows that this is not the case
with any other art or science. Each has an object or product
towards which its care is directed, and so has politics : it looks
after the subject and aims to make him as good and happy as
possible. True, a doctor or a politician may make a fortune,
but this is not due to their excellence in their own craft, they
also possess a quite different one, that of making money (346e) :

' Clearly, then, Thrasymachus, no craft or rule contrives its own
advantage but, as we said a while ago, that of the subject. It seeks
to benefit him, weaker though he is, not to benefit the stronger.
That is why I said just now, my dear Thrasymachus, that no one
is eager to rule and attempt to put in order the affairs of others. He
wants remuneration because the man who intends to govern well
and expertly never acts or commands to his own advantage but to
that of his subjects as his art requires.'

Actual remuneration, whether in cash or honour, may not
attract the good man, but his refusal to rule will be punished
by his being governed by those who are worse than he. If

we had a city of good men, they would all try to avoid governing, for they would no longer be exposed to misrule.[1]

Thus does Socrates disprove the sophistic thesis of government by the strong man to his own advantage. The selfish
ideal of a Thrasymachus or a Callicles is not the real art of
government, but its opposite. Their primitive ideal can only
lead to strife and discord as evil conduct always does (352a–c) ;
we get a glimpse of government based on consent and mutual
goodwill, and also on a real knowledge of what is good for the
citizens as a whole.

When, in the second book, Socrates proceeds to found his
ideal state, the first principle he enounces is that a political
organization is based upon the need of men for one another
(369b) :

'A city or state (πόλις) comes to be because none of us is sufficient
unto himself (αὐτάρκης). We stand in need of many others.'

Men thus need one another. First of all we require food,
shelter and clothes. Let us therefore admit a farmer, a builder,
a weaver and a cobbler. How are they to divide the work ?
Must each provide for all his own needs, or will one man do the
farming, another the building, and so on, for the whole ?
Clearly the latter is the better alternative, and that for two
reasons : first, because men are born with different capacities,
so that one man will do a certain job better, another another.
And even if this were not the case a man who specializes at one
job can do whatever must be done at the most convenient
time. In farming, for example, he obviously has to wait upon
the weather and the seasons. Thus Socrates adopts the principle of division of labour and of specialization, explaining it in
the simplest terms as being more adapted to men's nature and
more efficient. This point is important, and he will make ex-
tensive use of it when his first idyllic picture of the simple life
is rejected by Glaucon as no better than a ' city of pigs ' (372d).

For if we are to have all the refinements of civilization, we
must admit into our hitherto small band of essential workers a
whole crowd of ' hunters and imitators, musicians, poets,
rhapsodes, actors, dancers, contractors, furniture makers of
every kind and beauty specialists ' (373b). We must have

---

[1] Cp. *Rep.*, 489b ; 519c–d ; see also p. 178 note.

more traders, nurses, barbers, cooks, swineherds, cowherds, &c.
(the simple life was vegetarian). In this ' feverish state ' we
shall find that the land no longer suffices to feed the population
once men have started on the greedy path to unlimited accumulation of wealth. They will covet their neighbours' land
and we shall have war (373*e*) :

' Let us not say now whether war produces good or evil results,
but only this : that we have found the origin of war, the source of
all evils in the state, whether public or private.'

War, that is, has its origin in a greed for private possessions,
which is the chief source of all social ills. This conviction of
the evils of private property is a cardinal point of Plato's
social philosophy and to this we shall have occasion to return.
If our city is to be in danger of war, we must have an army
and, in accordance with the principle of specialization already
established, it must be a professional army. Only thus can it
be efficient, Socrates insists, overruling Glaucon's old-fashioned
desire for a citizen army.

It is the duty of these professional soldiers to guard the city
against attack, and guardians (φύλακες) is a natural name for
them. But it is equally important that they should not use
their power against their own fellow-citizens. Great care is
therefore to be taken over their education, which is described
at considerable length.[1] Its chief aim is, by a combination of
gymnastics and mousikê, to develop both spiritedness and gentle
self-control, to attain a balance between two sides of human
nature which at first sight seem incompatible.[2] Such a mixture is found in young dogs : they are quick-tempered against
strangers yet love those they know. Our guardians must also
achieve this. The second quality Socrates by a humorous
play on words equates with the love of wisdom (φιλομαθής,
loving the known—loving to know—loving knowledge,
φιλόσοφος 375*e*).

Thus playfully introduced, philosophy has come to stay
and we gradually find that the professional soldiers have
become ' guardians ' in a much wider and deeper sense than
was obvious at first. They have become a superior caste in
the state. One may wonder that Plato thought fit to give

[1] See pp. 234 ff.   [2] Cp. *Politicus*, on p. 284 below.

so much power to the army in his ideal republic. But it is not an army in the usual sense and he never speaks of it as such. Their education secures that. Besides, a Greek army was a citizen body, indeed the citizen body organized in a special manner, and it was always honoured as such. So Plato's guardians are citizens in the full sense, with a particular duty, a very important one, to perform. This was not true of the navy, and it is an interesting reflection of current Athenian prejudice that the navy is not included in the guardian class and that the *Laws* (706*b*) speak of it in no complimentary fashion. No doubt Plato had the example of Sparta before him, but even there all citizens were soldiers. One might say that he was not awake to the dangers of a military ruling class were it not for the pains he takes to make his guardians live in a way that will annul those dangers. And it is worth noting that there is no military ruling class in the *Laws*. It could only be trusted in an ideal republic.

But we need rulers as well as soldiers, and even greater care will be taken with these. Their education is a matter of even greater moment and is described in the later books.[1] For the moment we are satisfied to select the older, wiser and more reliable from among the guardians. So that we have not two, but three classes in the state : the rulers, the other guardians, now called auxiliaries, and the rest of the citizen body. The hierarchy is illustrated by the myth of the earth-born which Socrates wants his first generation of citizens to believe : they are all born of the earth and must love the soil that gave them birth (415*a*) :

' All of you in the city—so we shall tell them the story—are brothers. But when the god made you he put gold in the mixture for those who are capable of governing, which is why they are held in the highest esteem. The auxiliaries he made with silver ; the farmers and other workers with iron and brass. You are all akin and for the most part will produce offspring like yourselves, but it may sometimes happen that a silver son is born from a golden parent, a golden son from a silver parent and all classes can thus produce each other. Now the first and most important command from the god to the rulers is that they must above all things carefully examine the metal mixed in the children's souls. If a son of their own is found to have

---

[1] See p. 237 above.

a brass or iron nature they must in no way pity him but value him as he deserves and cast him out to join the workers or farmers. If the latter in turn have children of gold or silver, they must bring these up to be guardians or auxiliaries. For there is an oracle to the effect that the city will be destroyed when it comes to be ruled by a guardian of iron or of brass.'

Such is Plato's aristocratic view of human nature, aristocratic in the real sense since merit, not birth, is the only recognized test. He is under no delusion that men are all born equal, he knows they are not. His main concern is that the best shall rule. Although, generally speaking, a ' golden ' father will have a ' golden ' son, there must be equality of opportunity based on merit. Even this qualified belief in heredity was, we may be sure, as unpalatable to an Athenian as to any modern democrat. We shall hear little more, in the *Republic*, of the ways of life among the lowest class in the state, but we should not forget this clear assertion that the capacity to learn and to rule is to receive recognition wherever it arises.

It is essential in such a system that the guardian class should not abuse their privileged position and use their power to their own advantage. They must be neither rich nor poor, for wealth and poverty are equally destructive of efficiency. A potter, says Socrates, who comes into a fortune inevitably becomes lazy and careless of his work, a worse potter in fact. But his work suffers also if he is too poor to buy the proper tools (421d) ; and this is true of every kind of work. Both excesses are to be avoided. We can see clearly how most cities are divided within themselves into two warring factions, the rich and the poor ; they are almost like two cities instead of one (423a). Our guardians must remain the real protectors of the people, ready to suppress lawlessness within as well as attacks from without. To ensure this Socrates makes them live on a communistic basis, without any private property whatever (416d). They will live in barracks where their meals are provided by the community and receive sufficient remuneration to pay for their equipment and the necessaries of life, but not enough to allow a surplus at the end of the year. With moneymaking pursuits they must have absolutely nothing to do. But that is not all. They are not to have a private family either, and this Socrates hopes to achieve by his famous scheme of communism of children, wives and husbands (457c–464b). This strange scheme is frequently misunderstood, and the first point to realize is that it enforces rigid sex control upon all those of an age to have children. By means of a ballot, faked by the rulers, a certain number of young people will be ' married ' at definite festivals, and only for the few days of the festival. After that the marriage is at an end. Several such marriages were possible for any one so healthy that the rulers wish to breed from him or her. But at best the favourite would only be ' married ' for a few days now and again. The children are to be brought up at the public expense, the parents will not know which is their child ; at best they can know only that it belongs to a certain age group, if still alive. Great care is then taken to avoid possible incestuous ' marriages ' with those in the direct parental line but not, apparently, between brothers and sisters.[1]

Almost any reader of the *Republic* will feel that such a scheme is both impracticable and undesirable ; impracticable because of the unnatural continence required, the faked ballot, the fact that physical resemblances will betray the parental relation in most cases ; undesirable because it does violence to the deepest human emotions, entirely ignores the love element between the ' married ' pair, and deprives the individual of the security of his family circle. Why then did Plato desire it, even in his ideal state ? Partly because he wants to control the size of the population and these *ad hoc* state-controlled unions are a certain way of doing this. But the chief reason is that he realized that the family is the point at which private property and all the evils that go with it are centred. He therefore attacks it in a characteristically provocative manner. Family interests are in practice frequently at variance with those of the whole community ; a man labours to amass wealth in order to give security to his wife and children and in so doing he comes to look upon the rest of the citizens as his opponents if not his enemies. The Platonic condemnation of the family as a ' centre of exclusiveness '[2] no doubt goes too far, but it cannot be denied that such a conflict of loyalties does exist, that it does often lead to anti-social acts, that family affec-

---

[1] See my article in *C.Q.*, 1927/2. [2] As Barker puts it, p. 219.

tion is frequently blind, selfish and possessive. This we should recognize as an evil even though we would not accept Plato's way of dealing with it. Not that he wants to destroy parental or filial love ; on the contrary he wants to spread it over the whole state, to make his guardian class into one big family with common aims and interests, devoted to each other and to the common good. But we feel that, although family affection thus far-flung will indeed have lost that intense possessiveness which Plato rightly condemned, it will have become so ' watered down ' [1] in the process that it will no longer have the power to unite the guardians as Plato desires it should.

The city is nearing completion. It is, of course, a Greek city-state. Its size must not reach the point where the state ceases to be a unit, and Socrates makes a tentative suggestion of one thousand men for its fighting force (423a–b) which would mean a guardian class of about five thousand men, women and children. Again he insists on the supreme importance of early upbringing to form right habits. If this is achieved there will be no need for laws on points of manners and conduct, or for a detailed code of law regulating transactions as long as the laws we have already established are preserved (425e) :

' if not, they will spend the whole of their lives ever making such regulations and correcting them, and think that by so doing they will attain what is best '.

This picture of legislators losing themselves in a mass of law which loses effectiveness as it gains in extent because they have no conception of the ultimate goal they pursue or of the general principles which should guide them, is as striking as it is true. From first to last Plato maintained that education was more important than law. In any case the *Republic* was not the place for an elaborate code. The task he left for his somewhat more patient old age.

In the completed city the virtues must be found (428a–434e) : wisdom, courage, moderation or self-control (σωφροσύνη), and justice or righteousness (δικαιοσύνη) to define which is the

---

[1] The adjective (ὑδαρής) is Aristotle's, *Politics*, II, 1262b 15.

formal purpose of the whole dialogue. Socrates finds that wisdom belongs essentially to the rulers, for a city is wise if it is wisely governed. Courage clearly belongs to the auxiliary guardians as well as the rulers, while even the third class must have moderation. Justice also belongs to all. Moderation is described as selfmastery (αὐτοῦ κρείττων), mastery that is over passion and desire, justice as 'doing one's own work' (τὰ αὐτοῦ πράττειν). The distinction is not very clear but, in the state, moderation seems to mean that each should be satisfied with his share and his position and should hold in check the desire for greater power than he is fit to exercise ; this produces harmony (συμφωνία) and a common purpose (ὁμόνοια). 'Justice' adds to this the positive desire to do one's own job well, the active co-operation of every citizen in doing the work and living the life of the city.[1]

To produce such a state is the aim of statecraft, which is thus more fully described than in the earlier dialogues. And it is when he is asked whether this can ever be realized that Socrates utters the most famous of all Platonic paradoxes (473e) :

'Cities will have no respite from evil, my dear Glaucon, nor will the human race, I think, unless philosophers reign as kings or those who now bear the name of king or ruler genuinely and adequately study philosophy, unless political power and philosophy become one. For now they go their separate ways and many of those who follow one or the other find fulfilment barred to them.'

Paradoxical this statement certainly is, and it is received as such. But we need not make it into an absurdity by thinking of pale metaphysicians ruling the world from the remoteness of their study. The Greek word means a lover of wisdom, and Plato is thinking of philosophy as practised by Socrates ' the only true politician of all the Athenians ', and also, no doubt, by himself. And the next two books are an elaborate explanation of the nature of this lover of wisdom whom he wishes to rule mankind. He will have knowledge of the eternal Ideas which, as we saw elsewhere, implies a true sense of values, an understanding of the principles that rule the

[1] 433e : ἡ τοῦ οἰκείου ἕξις τε καὶ πρᾶξις.

world, a love of truth and beauty and a highly developed faculty of reasoning besides. These can only be acquired by an exacting education of the thinking mind, and this to Plato meant the study of mathematics, the one highly developed science of his day. Can we deny that a thorough mental training is necessary for a statesman? Protagoras did indeed deny it, and it is just on this point that Plato attacked him. Many have denied it since without the same frankness. The denial is absurd none the less.

In fact, what Plato is asserting, in his usual provocative manner, is that no statesman is worthy of the name who is not also a thinker, a man of philosophic outlook with an eye for fundamentals, with a knowledge of dialectic, that is, a capacity to see universal relations between things, to come to correct conclusions from given premises and a readiness to revise his premises if his conclusions do not agree with given facts.[1] The essential truth of Plato's position properly understood no one will really dispute except perhaps professional politicians who do not come up to his demands.

These will prate of practical capacity. But the philosopher king will not despise practical ability. His is the kingly craft of the *Euthydemus* which makes use of all technical ability, and his task is to direct their activities towards the right goal : the true happiness of the citizens, a happiness based on right conduct. We may indeed believe that any such complete knowledge is impossible, Plato himself came to doubt its possibility more and more. But that does not relieve the statesman of the duty to search. Also, a philosopher for Plato was a man who had resolved the conflicts of his own mind. Perfect harmony may be another impossible ideal, but deliberate encouragement of man's baser instincts of hatred and cruelty by hysterical rulers is surely to be avoided at all costs, and here too Plato is clearly pointing in the right direction.

To Adeimantus' objection that surely philosophers are no use in politics, Socrates replies with that magnificent piece of political satire, the famous parable of the ship of state (488a) :

‘ The owner (i.e. the demos) surpasses all others on board in size and strength, but he is hard of hearing and also rather shortsighted,

---

[1] See *Rep.*, 533c : τὰς ὑποθέσεις ἀναιροῦσα κ.τ.λ.

and his knowledge of seafaring is of the same kind. The sailors are quarrelling with one another about the steering, each thinking he should be entrusted with it, though he has never learned the art and cannot point either to one who has taught him or to a time when he was learning. They even maintain that navigation cannot be taught, and are ready to cut to pieces any one who says it can. They are ever rushing around the master, begging him and trying to influence him in every way to entrust the wheel to themselves. Sometimes they do not succeed. Then they either execute or throw overboard those who do, and overpower their noble master with drugs or wine or by some other means. They rule over the ship and enjoy its stores ; drinking and feasting they sail as such men would. Further, they praise the man who is clever at devising how they may rule, whether by bringing persuasion or force to bear upon the master. Such a man they call a pilot and an expert navigator, any other they blame as useless. They do not even realize that the real pilot must study the stars, the seasons of the year, the winds and all that appertains to his craft to be in truth the ruler of the ship. Nor do they think it possible for him to acquire the art and practice of navigation, and the pilot's craft, whether they wish him to practise it or not. Do you not think that when this is what happens on board ship, the real pilot will be called star gazer, prattler and good for nothing by those who sail in ships thus equipped.'

The nature of the philosopher who should be king is the main subject of the central books. He is both the ideal ruler and the ideal man, he also possesses knowledge of the supreme reality ; and the whole discussion is a perfect blend not only of ethics and politics, but of metaphysics as well. This unity of outlook also shows itself in the close connexion between politics and psychology. Indeed, Plato is the founder of political psychology. When, in the third book, he passes from an analysis of the virtues in the state to those of the individual soul he states quite clearly that there must be a direct correspondence between the spiritedness, love of learning or greed of a state and that of the individuals composing it (435e). He selects the qualities that will lead him direct to the tripartite division of the soul, but surely the same applies to all qualities. As he says, ' where else could they have come from ? ' The Greeks are so often accused of considering the state as an abstraction apart from the citizens and of sacrificing the individual to the whole (in spite of the fact that the subject was much freer in Greece than anywhere else)[1] that the point, though obvious, needs emphasizing. So when Socrates answers Adeimantus' complaint that the guardians' life will not be happy by saying that our aim is not the happiness of one class but of the whole (420*b*), he means, of course, that the happiness of the other citizens must not be sacrificed to that of a single class, whether farmers, guardians or philosophers (cp. 519*d*), and he can mean nothing else.

The qualities of the state then, are but those of its individual citizens ' writ large '. And the kind of government will depend entirely upon the type of citizen that predominates. Hence the classification of the different kinds of state is paralleled by a description of the type of individual that conditions them, either by being in the majority or by being in power. Plato begins with the best and traces a gradual degeneration to the worst. This is a convenient arrangement for the purpose of exposition. It is, of course, not meant to be an historical picture. How could it be, since the perfect state has never existed ? It is true that these parallel descriptions lead Plato into metaphors that imply at times an artificially close resemblance between the internal constitution of states and individual souls. That was inevitable in an imaginative writer with a sense of humour. But there is no reason to believe that his tripartite division of the soul is entirely due to the fact that there are three classes in the state. It may have been the other way round or, more probably, the parallel arose spontaneously and was then effectively embellished. But the underlying assumption of a direct connexion between the form of state and the type of individual is sound and important.

This is not the place to go into the details of Plato's picture (544*c*–579*d*), which loses all effect by being summarized, and should be read as a whole. Aristocracy, the rule of the best, the ideal republic, comes first and the corresponding individual is the philosopher already described. It is the rule of wisdom in the state and the individual. Next comes timarchy, the rule of a guardian class no longer directed by wisdom, and the timocrat. Ambition is now supreme. After this, oligarchy, what we would call plutocracy, the rule of the rich. Cor-

[1] See Barker, p. 2.

responding to it is the oligarch, the money-lover whose only desire is to accumulate wealth. This reign of money, both in the state and the individual, is described with a wealth of detail and a vehemence natural in one so alive to the evils of self-interested money-grabbing. Then democracy, and the democrat, where the watchword is liberty and equality between all individuals and all passions and the result is the complete loss of any stability or any sense of values. And Plato uses to the full this opportunity for a desperate satire of the Athenian democracy he hated so much. Lowest of all, tyranny, the irresponsible rule of an ignorant and passion-ridden despot, where cruelty and brutality are dominant. In the tyrant himself we now find the completely successful wrongdoer who was, according to the plan laid down at the beginning of the *Republic*, to be opposed to the just man, the philosopher. And Socrates is free to turn to the solution of the problem he set out to solve : which of them is the happier ? At this point the discussion returns more definitely to the ethical plane.

It is quite obvious that the *Republic* marks an immense advance in Plato's political theory. Not that it contradicts anything that has gone before ; on the contrary it works out into a definite system the vague formula of the earlier dialogues. The first book restates the general position : politics is a science and it aims at the advantage, not of the ruler, but of the subject. Then, when we come to construct a city, we find that the fundamental principle upon which it is based is that men are not self-sufficient but need one another and that only by specializing each on one job can they secure efficiency. This principle is carried further and we find that the rule of knowledge now implies a ruling class who specialize in governing and in acquiring the necessary knowledge, backed by an auxiliary ruling class who specialize in protecting the state against attacks from within and without. Only a most carefully thought-out system of education can provide the right kind of man to be a guardian ; and the knowledge that we have always realized the ruler to need, is now seen to be the knowledge of eternal Ideas. Truly the philosopher, like Socrates in the *Gorgias*, is the only true practitioner of political science. Harmony and community of interest can only be attained among the guardians by destroying those two causes of self-interest, private property and the family. Finally a study of the close connexion between different forms of state and the different types of individual corresponding to them shows us why the statesman must truly make citizens better if he wishes to better the state.

The *Politicus* does not depart from Plato's fundamental belief that ethics and politics are ultimately one. But a real attempt is made to define politics as such, and the whole discussion is therefore far more restricted. Though even here the Eleatic stranger insists that the art of ruling is the same in a state and a household. King, householder and politician are practitioners of the same craft (259*c*). Starting from the general position that politics is a science, a form of knowledge, he attempts to define the statesman by the method of logical division in accordance with the Ideas—a method described at some length both here and in the *Sophist*. The first steps of the division are of considerable interest : knowledge is divided into the sciences which produce a physical object that did not exist before (πραϰτιϰή, 258*d. e*) and the cognitive (γνωστιϰή), like mathematics. Politics belongs to the latter class ; this may in turn be divided into those which are purely critical, like arithmetic, and those that direct the activities of others. Politics belongs to the directive [1] (ἐπιταϰτιϰή), not the purely critical class (ϰριτιϰή). And the directive sciences can be subdivided into those which give sovereign directions (i.e. out of their own knowledge, without reference to a higher authority) and those which merely carry out the directions of others. The rest of the process of dichotomy establishes the kind of living creature over which the king rules, and the various steps in the division of the animal kingdom are of less interest in this connexion. The king is, as it were, a shepherd of men, a manherd (267*b, c*). But many others besides the king will claim to belong to this last class. We must therefore investigate their claims.

At this point the argument is interrupted by the myth

---

[1] The names 'directive' and 'cognitive' are borrowed from Taylor, p. 394, as also the expression 'sovereign directions'.

(268d–274d),[1] the main point of which is as follows : The world, which is a body endowed with soul, is a created thing and it does not possess the power of eternally similar motions : its life is directed in two ways, one alternating with the other at great intervals of time. The first period is that in which the god himself takes command and subordinate gods have charge of the various races and parts in it. Everything runs smoothly and there is no war or discord of any kind. But a time comes when the god lets the world direct itself and the other gods also withdraw their guidance. The world soul is then responsible for itself and all other souls for their part of it. Everything goes into reverse, for, although the world tries to remember the directions of its creator, its partly bodily nature fails more and more and would lead it to complete destruction if it were not that the god, to avoid this, takes the helm again and another period of divine guidance sets in. There is no need to go into the details of the world's life under guidance. Men rise from the earth and gradually grow into babies, and everything else to match. There is humour here, but it is rather crabbed. The description of the golden age reads like a nightmare after an overdose of Empedocles. One point, however, is worth noting : the idyllic life of the age of Kronos with its vegetarian and clothesless simplicity made men happy only if we may suppose that they spent their leisure in the pursuit of philosophy (272c) ! This casts considerable doubt upon the desirability of the above picture, so similar to the first simple city of the *Republic*, and it would seem that Plato is ready

---

[1] This is by far the strangest myth in Plato. It is very awkwardly introduced as ' play ' because the younger Socrates is not yet too old for this (268e) and we get an unpleasant impression of the Eleatic talking down to his audience. Its relevance to the argument is emphasized (269e). In the body of the story we are reassured that it will soon be over (272d) and again that its relevance will soon be realized (274b). So also at the end (274e), and later we have a reference back to the huge bulk (θαυμαστὸν ὄγκον, 277b) of the myth. All this is very inartistic and quite unworthy of the author of the *Gorgias*, *Phaedo*, *Republic* and *Phaedrus* myths. There has been no myth since and Plato is not very happy in this return to his earlier manner. As for the substance, there seems to be a confusion, for while Plato speaks throughout of everything as reversed in the godless period, he also speaks of the world as slowly forgetting the directions of the god. We thus get two images, one of all life going into reverse, the other of a *gradual* departure from the ideal, a slowing down as it were with the danger of a complete stop. The two images are incompatible.

to see some merit after all in our godless age, and in the
' feverish city ' of the earlier work.[1]

There is no need to seek any deep meanings in the details of
the story. As in a Homeric simile, these details fill in the
picture but have no direct relevance to the chief point of
comparison. This main point is unequivocally clear from the
Eleatic's own words (274e) :

' When we were asked about the king and politician of our present
period of existence, we told of the shepherd of the human race that
lived in the opposite period. That is a god, not a man ; and in this
we made a serious mistake.'

To what does this refer ? Presumably to the earlier part of
the *Politicus* where we spoke of the king as possessed of knowledge, but enough has scarcely been said about him there to
justify the ' wondrous bulk ' of the myth unless the king be
understood to refer to the philosopher-king of the *Republic*,
endowed with perfect knowledge. That ruler is now relegated
to a mythical past and an equally mythical future. If we are
to define the statesman, we must find something less ideal.

Yet the philosopher-king is not given up without a struggle.
In a later passage (292b–302a) where he has been differentiating between kinds of government, e.g. according to the
number of rulers, or according as it is based on force or consent, the Eleatic suddenly declares these distinctions superficial. The kingly art was a form of knowledge. That is its
distinctive characteristic, and the fundamental difference is
between government based on knowledge and that based
only on law. It is only the man who does not possess knowledge who needs to be bound by law, or even by the consent
of his subjects. We do not require a doctor to persuade his
patients before he saves their lives or restores them to health,
nor do we worry whether he be rich or poor. In the same
way, so long as a ruler has the knowledge and aims at the
good, as long as he makes men better, we shall not submit
him to any restrictions whatever. The law is essentially a
second best only (294a). And there follows an excellent
description of its shortcomings.

[1] See Burnet, p. 291.

' The law cannot decree what is best with an exact realization of
the most just and good in every case. Men and actions change so
continually, that it is impossible for any science to make a single rule
that will fit every case once and for all.'

Notwithstanding that law is just such an imperfect general rule,
yet we need it in every department of life. In athletic con-
tests, for example, general instructions are issued by trainers
who cannot give sufficient individual attention to do otherwise (294*d*). A doctor will give instructions to be followed
during his absence, but he would not hesitate to change them
on his return. He would rely on his knowledge, not on the
general rules which that knowledge made.

So the state that is governed with full knowledge is the only
one governed rightly, whatever form the government may take.
But when knowledge is absent, then the golden rule is (297*d*)
' that no one dare to transgress the law on penalty of death'.
For if we could not trust our doctors not to aim at private profit
rather than health, even laymen would be justified in making
laws about medicine. It would not then be unreasonable even
to elect by lot representatives of the people to rule according
to law and to call them to account at the end of their term of
office. This, the Athenian system so bitterly criticized by
Socrates in the early dialogues because it did not obey the
expert, is now seen to be inevitable if we cannot trust our rulers
to possess that knowledge of right and wrong which cannot but
lead to good conduct.

But the bitterness of Plato's renunciation is very clear in
the next passage (299*b*) where the Eleatic goes on to say that it
will then also be necessary to prevent any one going beyond the
laws and discovering truth that may not be embodied in them.
Such a quest for wisdom will be called *corrupting the young* and
persuading others to lawlessness, ' for nothing must be wiser
than the law '. In this kind of state (299*e*) :

' Clearly all art and science (τέχναι) would be utterly lost to us,
and could never rise again because the law forbids investigation.
So that life, which is hard enough now, would not be worth living
at all.'

One is reminded of Socrates' words in the *Apology* (38*a*) that
the uncritical life is not worth living. Plato is in effect saying :

' You say that the philosopher-king is impossible. From what
I have seen of the world I'm inclined to agree with you. And
I further agree that an absolutely rigid system of laws is the
only alternative. But what an alternative ! ' (e.g. 301c–e).
This very clear exposition of the limitations of law and of
its essential inferiority to the direct application of knowledge
to particular cases must have read strangely to Greeks accustomed to look upon obedience to the law as the supreme
virtue of the citizen and the cause of all good in the state.
And the realization that no general rule can do full justice to
any particular case is something quite new in Plato. It is a
development that might have led him far if he had followed
it up in the rest of his philosophy.[1] It has been said that the
Politicus shows a more indulgent attitude to law than the
Republic.[2] I do not think that is the case. The true philosopher is really farther above the law in the later dialogue ; he
has risen so high as to join the gods. We are told in the
Republic that laws of detail are useless, but never that the best
laws, even those enacted by the philosopher-king himself,
are inevitably imperfect, and that he would find it essential
himself not to be bound by them. Whereas the *Politicus*
insists again and again that law is always a second best (δεύτερος
πλοῦς, 300c). The truth is that Plato, realizing more and
more the improbability of his ideal ever being realized, is
prepared to study more closely such kinds of government as
are necessarily imperfect and is in that sense more indulgent
to them.

In an examination of the different kinds of government, the
Eleatic adopts (291c ff.) the usual Greek classification into
monarchy, oligarchy and democracy.[3] He casts around for a
principle of further subdivision ; violence or consent, wealth
or poverty of the rulers, obedience to the law, are suggested.
The latter is finally adopted, but only after the discussion on
the relative merits of knowledge and law, with which we have
already dealt. Only when it has been made quite clear that

---

[1] Aristotle certainly took it to heart, and it is passages like this that make
the change from one philosopher to the other less of a sudden break than is
usually thought.
[2] Barker, p. 271.   [3] Cp. *Republic*, 338d.

the best government, that based on knowledge, is *hors concours* as it were, do we apply the criterion of obedience to the law and subdivide our three kinds of government in accordance with it. These can still be put in order of merit. Those that respect the law are better than those who do not : the best being constitutional monarchy, constitutional aristocracy next, democracy last. But, on the principle of *corruptio optimi pessima*, in the unconstitutional class tyranny is the worst, and democracy the least dangerous.

This is a poor defence of democracy, but it is very different from the violent denunciations in the *Republic* where it was inferior to all except tyranny. Rather despairingly Plato has now come round to the conclusion that if the scientific government of the philosopher-king is impossible, we can still hope for government in accordance with a constitution and right belief. Of these a constitutional monarchy is the most desirable. But if we cannot even be sure that the law will be respected and that men act on other than selfish motives, then democracy is the safest. And perhaps in this very imperfect world democracy needs no other defence ! Certainly dictatorship, government by the arbitrary will of one leader, is to be condemned beyond all others in practice, unless—Plato's gaze is still ruefully fixed upon the ideal state—he were a true lover of wisdom, which, he now agrees, is all but impossible.

Besides the classification of governments, the Eleatic concurrently pursues the purpose of the earlier dichotomy. At the close of the myth he points out that political science still needs to be differentiated from others (275*b*–276*b*). First of all he separates it from the shepherd ; the latter's charge includes the feeding of his flock, which the statesman does not.[1] Besides, only the mythical ruler deserves to be called shepherd of the human race.

The next step is to establish the difference between statecraft (βασιλικὴ τέχνη) and all other crafts in the state. The method to be used is illustrated by an example : the art of

---

[1] This rejection of ' feeding the flock ' as no part of the statesman's duty reflects incidentally Plato's tendency to ignore economic considerations. The statesman does not produce food, of course (nor does the shepherd), but we should certainly consider the regulation of the food supply as very much his business. See also 290*a*.

weaving, which is carefully differentiated from all allied crafts and from such as prepare the weaver's tools and materials (279*b*–283*a*). When this method is applied to statecraft, Plato elaborately distinguishes from it all the productive arts, the slaves' services, trade- and business-men, for are they not ever prepared to serve for money ? Heralds and civil servants are excluded by their very name ; and priests and soothsayers are rejected as mere messengers between men and gods, in spite of their prestige. Nor must we admit the tribe of orators and sophists who are met with in the lawless cities described above (cp. 291*b* and 303*d*).[1] But once these pretenders and rivals are disposed of, there remain the genuine contributors and helpers : the strategist, the judge, the orator who uses his powers to persuade men of what is good. These genuinely help the king, who directs their special capacities in the right way : to know how to speak is rhetoric, to know when to speak and when to be silent requires the direction of a higher art. The general should know how to win battles, but only the statesman can decide when to wage war at all. So the judge must impartially administer the law, but lawmaking is the king's business.[2] ' Statecraft does not itself act but rules over those arts whose function it is to act ' ; and so we come to the final definition (305*e*) :

' The name of statecraft then seems to belong to the art which controls all the particular arts, watches over the laws and all else in the state and weaves all together most successfully. And statecraft is the right name as it defines the extent of its function by the name of the community.'

In the concluding pages of the dialogue Plato develops the image of the statesman as a weaver, whose hard task it is to harmonize into one whole all the different elements in the state. Hardest of all is the task of weaving into one pattern those two

[1] Most of these classes of men have already been separated from the ' king ' by the dichotomies in the earlier part of the book.

[2] This seems to contradict what Plato said that law must be supreme. But now that he comes to define statesmanship he almost gets back to the ideal plane. On the other hand his satirical pen rather over-reached itself in the passages on law's inferiority to knowledge, unless indeed we take these as a *reductio ad absurdum* of the only alternative there is to government based on knowledge.

so different characters, the gentle and the spirited. This
description is very reminiscent of the requirements he desired
in his guardians, only whereas there the two qualities were to
be harmonized within the individual guardian's soul, here the
two different types of men are to be reconciled within one state.
Both moderation or gentleness (σωφροσύνη) and spiritedness or
courage (ἀνδρεία) are virtues, but their excess is vicious. Plato
looks upon the blending of those two qualities, which are here
analysed at some length, as the main problem for the management of men.

In this way does the *Politicus* explain and analyse the kingly
science of the *Euthydemus*. He seems to abandon the philosopher-king of the *Republic*, as a practical solution, and yet the
alternative is far from satisfactory and the final definition of
statecraft seems to imply the philosopher's knowledge all over
again. In spite of this, however, the *Politicus* is far more
realistic in its analysis of actual forms of government, and law
becomes both more definitely a second best, and at the same
time more of a necessity, than it was ever before.

So it is natural that an attempt should be made in the *Laws* [1]
to provide a code in accordance with which a city might be
governed in the world as it is. There is also a general restatement of general political principles, and the attitude adopted
throughout is not unlike that of the *Politicus*. The ideal ruler
is relegated to the age of Cronos in a passage that must be taken
as a reference back to the myth of that dialogue. Here too law
is admittedly but a second best, but necessary because no man
has the knowledge required to do without it (875*d*).

The first book begins with a discussion that continues the
contrast between moderation and courage, gentleness and

---

[1] A wrong idea of the nature of this, Plato's last, work is so widespread that
it should be said again that there is immensely more to be got out of it than
its unfortunate title would imply. Only four books, VIII, IX, XI, XII, are
concerned with a detailed legal code. Books I–III are a very general discussion of psychology, art, education, history and political theory ; IV–V
are a general preamble to the founding of the projected state, followed by a
discussion of its population, climate, &c. ; VI gives the offices of state,
methods of election and marriage laws ; VII is on education ; X discusses
religion. We have seen the important contributions made on several of
these subjects. In importance and general interest, the *Laws* yield first
place only to the *Republic*. It is, in fact, a final statement of Plato's philosophy without the metaphysics. See Taylor, pp. 462–497.

spiritedness found in the last pages of the *Politicus*. But in the *Laws* it is represented as a difference between the Athenian and the Dorian point of view. Cleinias the Cretan boasts that the laws of his country aim first and foremost at efficiency in war. This he justifies on the ground that war is the ' natural ' state between cities and individuals, and even, he adds at the Athenian's suggestion, between the conflicting desires of the same individual. Victory, therefore, is the supreme goal for all (625*e*–626*e*). The Athenian, on the contrary, says that we should aim at peace, not victory.

Just as a man should control his passions, rather than repress them, so the statesman should aim at harmony between classes, not at the victory of any one of them. There is nothing very new in this, we have seen that harmony was the aim to be attained in the earliest dialogues. But the presentation of the problem is new, and the discussion of it more thorough. The Cretan admits he is wrong and that he confused the means with the end (628*e*) ; the Athenian follows up his advantage and criticizes Spartan law because it develops one virtue only, courage, not justice or moderation or wisdom ; and only one form of courage : the capacity to endure pain. Hence the Spartan abroad is unable to resist pleasurable temptation (634*a*, cp. 661*e*).

The discussion between the militaristic Dorian who always relies on force and the Athenian who relies on persuasion is important because it prepares the ground for the principle introduced later that the law must not compel until it has attempted to persuade (719*e*–723*c*). This principle is followed throughout, and each law is introduced by a preamble which sets forth the reason for it and thus makes an appeal to the intelligence and the better feelings of the citizen. Then follows the law itself, which should be short and clear. After this the punishment for transgression. Plato thus gives practical examples of how the lawgiver should seek to obtain the consent, not the sullen obedience, of his fellow citizens. The law, he says, should be like a parent, not a tyrant.

The more practical outlook of the *Laws* is shown in the greater influence which circumstances are allowed to have upon both man and state. This is natural where the occasion is supposed to be the planning of an actual colony. At the very beginning (625*d*) Cleinias points out how topography affects a people's manner of fighting, which presumably means, on his excessively militaristic view, that it affects their whole life.[1] So the Athenian has much to say of that ' salty neighbour ' (705*e*) the sea, which brings commerce and the love of gain to cities, and also by making men rely on surprise attacks turns them into cowards. Later (747*d*) he speaks of the great influence which climatic conditions have upon the type of men a country produces. And there is one remarkable outburst (709*a*) :

> ' I was going to say that no law is made by man at all ; that misfortunes or disasters of all kinds that befall us make all the laws for us. The compulsion of war may overthrow the constitution and change the laws, or pestilence compels many changes, or the occurrence of a plague, or frequent unseasonable weather over a period of years. As he considers these things a man might rush to the conclusion, as I did just now, that mortal man never makes any laws, but that all human affairs are a matter of chance.'

He tempers this determinism by the thought of divine guidance and the important reflection that, even so, knowledge is still of the greatest use. For if a man is caught in a storm at sea, he cannot prevent the storm, but he will find the knowledge of navigation the more useful for that (709*c*). In spite of all Plato never gives up anywhere his belief that man's greatest need is knowledge.[2] To want things is not enough, we must know whether what we pray for is good for us (687*d*) ; only those who are wise should be entrusted with the care of the state ;[3] and the aim of the lawgiver is, as ever, to make the city wise, as well as harmonious and free (693*c*, 701*c*).

And so it is through lack of knowledge that past cities have failed. A great many cities and civilizations have, the Athenian tells us, been destroyed by pestilence or floods.[4] Our own civilization followed a flood. All knowledge and crafts were lost and only a few mountaineers survived. From them our civilization grew. First came a dynastic period of small clan chiefs. Hamlets soon grew at the foot of the mountain,

---

[1] Environment is fully given its due also in the picture of the development of nations in the third book.
[2] Any more than he gave up the theory of Ideas. See p. 48.
[3] 689*d*. See p. 254.   [4] 677*e* ff. ; cp. *Timaeus*, 22*c* ff.

these joined together and their original rulers became an aristocracy or maybe they chose a king. The flood is forgotten and a great city like Troy rises in the plain. After the Trojan war three great cities ruled in Greece : Argos, Messene and Sparta. Only Sparta remains, for they failed through lack of knowledge, and through their failure to co-operate (692*d*). The Athenian then gives a description of Persia, which, though successful under Cyrus became a typical despotism under Xerxes through his lack of education and self-control. A highly idealized picture of Athens of old and a very prejudiced account of the Persian war precede the statement that Athens degenerated through excess of freedom. This gives a convenient view of the two opposite excesses, too much repression on the one hand, licence on the other (699*e*).

Sparta is praised as a mixed constitution (692*a*, 712*d*) and when the Athenian comes to the colony he is concerned with, in order to avoid both excesses he adopts a constitution which is a mixture of monarchy and democracy (701*e*). The perfect form of state is avoided because it is liable to the worst abuses if not successful (711*b–d*). This idea of a mixed constitution as the best is something new in Plato and he is adopting it from Sparta though his colony is to be quite different.

A detailed examination of the colony founded in the *Laws* would show many points of contact with the *Republic*. The population is fixed and to be kept constant, in this case the number of citizen landowners is fixed at 5,040, a convenient number for further subdivisions (737*c*, 740*d*). The sexes are to have equal education and opportunities (805*a*). The principle of specialization is adopted (846*e* ff.) though it does not here lead to a guardian class or a professional army and rulers. The details of religious worship are left to Apollo and other oracles (738*c*). The danger of excessive wealth or poverty is frequently emphasized (e.g. 742*c*). There are four classes in the state with a property qualification, an arrangement very reminiscent of Solon's constitution.

As for property, complete communism is explicitly said to be the best (739*c*), but the citizens are to be allowed private property to the extent of four times the value of their allotment of land. This land, however, must be neither bought nor sold (741*b*). A strict census of property is to be enforced, and any false declaration severely punished (754*e*). Finally, external trade is to be under government control (847*c*). In all this the colony may truly be called an approximation to the ideal republic.

It is impossible to go into detail here either about the officers of state, their mode of election, and their duties, or to give any adequate account of the code of law that follows and which the various officials have to administer. At the head of affairs is a board of thirty-seven guardians of the law (νομοφύλακες), nominated by the citizen army and elected by a majority vote. They must be not less than fifty and not more than seventy years old. These guardians have general supervisory duties, and among the lesser matters entrusted to them are nominations for the board of generals, elected by the army as before. There is also a council of three hundred and sixty, one-twelfth of which is to direct affairs for one month. Further provisions are made for officials to look after the market, a board for matters in the country and another for the town. Here young men will have an opportunity to be co-opted and to familiarize themselves with administration. The most important official is the director of education. He is chosen in a special election in which only magistrates and officials (not members of the council) will participate. As for the other elections, the tendency is to put more responsibility on the wealthier classes by compelling their attendance while allowing the poor to remain absent.

The administration of justice is also carefully provided for. Throughout the *Laws*, as elsewhere in Plato, there is a very high conception of justice as ' corrective ', never merely punitive. This is, of course, a result of the Socratic belief that ' no one sins on purpose'.[1] There are two kinds of equality : that of giving the same to all and that of giving to each according to his deserts. It is the latter which justice should aim at (757*b*, *c*). An attempt should always be made to settle things between neighbours, but where that fails two kinds of courts are provided, for private and public suits, with appeal to courts of magistrates. In judging public wrongs the assembly must have a share, because he who has no share in the administration of justice is not truly a citizen (768*b*).

[1] See pp. 226 ff.

Change in the law is dangerous, but Plato allows for it, if somewhat grudgingly, as he also allows travel abroad for older men. They are to report to a special council of magistrates meeting at night through whom changes can be made.

As for Plato's code of law, it is hard and the punishment heavy. It is the moral rather than the physical damage that he always has in view. He warned us in the *Politicus* that the only alternative to knowledge is laws the transgression of which is punished by death. But in the last pages of the *Laws* he once more emphasizes the need of knowledge for his nocturnal council, who have charge of the laws.

APPENDIX I

BURNET AND THE *PHAEDO*

THE theories of Professors Burnet and Taylor are well known. According to them the picture which Plato gives of Socrates in the dialogues is historical and the theory of Ideas as we find it in the *Phaedo* and the *Republic* was held by the historical Socrates. They go even farther than this, and credit the theory in all essentials to the Pythagoreans. With this general point of view I do not propose to deal. It has not found general acceptance and is, to my mind, satisfactorily refuted, especially by W. D. Ross in the introduction to his edition of Aristotle's *Metaphysics* (pp. xxxii–xlv), and in a special paper of his (Proc. Class. Assoc., 1933), also by G. C. Field in his *Socrates and Plato*.

But Burnet bases his case to a large extent on an interpretation of the *Phaedo* which I believe mistaken.[1] He argues that the theory of Ideas is there introduced as something quite familiar to Socrates' audience, especially to Simmias and Kebes ; that Simmias and Kebes are Pythagoreans ; and that the theory is therefore in essence Pythagorean. This, he tells us farther, is what we are told by Aristotle. On this last point I will only refer the reader to Ross's discussions already mentioned, and to his notes on the passages of the *Metaphysics* quoted therein. For the rest of Burnet's argument, it is my immediate purpose to show that the first statement is not true, that the theory of Ideas is *not* introduced in the *Phaedo* as something familiar to Simmias and Kebes, and that there is little evidence that those two men were Pythagoreans in any real sense. My reason for doing so is that the statement about the familiarity of the theory has been accepted (mistakenly, as I believe) even by those who do not agree with Burnet's conclusions.[2]

The following considerations prove, it seems to me, that Simmias and Kebes are *not* represented as familiar with the theory of Ideas.

1. The analysis given in the text (pp. 15 ff.) of the five different occasions

---

[1] *E. G. Ph.*, 354 ff. ; *Phaedo*, xliii ff., and notes *passim* ; *From Thales to Plato*, pp. 154 ff. See also Taylor, pp. 174–208, and *Varia Socratica*, p. 56.
[2] e.g. Robin, *Phaedo* (Budé), p. xviii ; Ross, *Metaphysics* on 987*b* 10, Hackforth, p. 164. He discusses the evidence of the *Apology* against Burnet's general view on pp. 158–66.

on which the theory of Forms is discussed in the *Phaedo* shows that a different aspect of the theory is brought out on each occasion :

(a) in 65d–66a we are made to understand that there *are* realities which the mind or soul grasps without the help of the senses.

(b) in 72e–76c : these are the realities which the mind knew before birth, and of which we are reminded through sense-perception, in so far as the particulars ' imitate ' the Forms.

(c) 78c–80b : the absolute unchangeability of the Forms is emphasized, and their nature contrasted with the physical world.

(d) 100b–e : participation in the Forms is the cause of phenomena and of their qualities.

(e) 102d–105b : a further discussion of participation and a difficult distinction between properties and accidents derived therefrom.

This surely appears to be a gradual explanation of the theory of Ideas, the more difficult problems coming last. Of course each succeeding aspect of the theory is worked into the argument for immortality and made use of, for this is a well-constructed work of art and not (though its very success would make us forget it) an actual conversation. There is a good deal of explanation and discussion in each passage which seems to make it very unlikely that those to whom it is addressed are familiar with the Ideas ; they certainly are not familiar with its implications.

2. The impression of a carefully graded explanation of the theory is confirmed by the fact that the technical vocabulary seems to be graded in the same manner. It seems to have generally escaped notice that the words εἶδος and ἰδέα are not used to indicate the Forms until 103e and that after that they are used freely.[1] But apart from this the vocabulary seems to develop as follows : In 65d ff. we have : φαμέν τι εἶναι δίκαιον αὐτό . . . τῆς οὐσίας ὃ τυγχάνει ἕκαστον ὄν . . . αὐτὸ καθ' αὐτὸ εἰλικρινὲς ἕκαστον in 74a ff., such expressions as αὐτὸ τὸ ἴσον . . . αὐτὸ τὸ ὅ ἐστιν (ἴσον) (74d) ; ἐκείνου τοῦ ὅ ἐστιν ἴσον (75b) : αὐτὸ τὸ καλόν . . . ἅπαντα οἷς ἐπισφραγιζόμεθα τὸ αὐτὸ ὃ ἔστιν (75d).

In 78d ff. are added αὐτὴ ἡ οὐσία, αὐτὸ ἕκαστον ὅ ἐστι τὸ ὄν, μονοειδὲς ὂν αὐτὸ καθ' αὐτό, ὡσαύτως κατὰ ταὐτὰ ἔχει and at 80b we have the full contrast between the visible and the eternal worlds. The latter is called τὸ θεῖον, ἀθάνατον, νοητόν, μονοειδές, ἀδιάλυτον, ἀεὶ κατὰ ταὐτὰ ἔχον ἑαυτῷ.

In 100b : τὸ καλὸν αὐτὸ καθ' αὐτό, παρουσία at 100d, τῷ καλῷ τὰ καλὰ καλά, 100c.

In 103b : τὸ ἐν ἡμῖν, τὸ ἐν φύσει. Then at last εἶδος, ἰδέα and μορφή in 103e, as if from a feeling that now that everything has been explained the technical terms, which are used freely henceforth, will be understood.

3. This is all very different from the way the theory is introduced in the fifth book of the *Republic*, where Glaucon is definitely supposed to be familiar with it. Socrates has been asked to differentiate between the lovers

---

[1] At 78b, δύο εἴδη τῶν ὄντων is clearly irrelevant ; the word is used in its ordinary sense : ' two kinds of existence ', of which one is the physical world. Phaedo uses εἶδος for the Forms at 102b *in his own person* when he breaks off the story for a moment. This was evidently the natural way to refer to them and it makes it all the more remarkable that the word is not used by Socrates up to this point in the reported conversation, for certainly there has been plenty of opportunity.

of sights and sounds and the philosopher. This, he says, might be difficult
to explain to others, ' but you (Glaucon) will, I think, agree with what
follows '. He then goes on (475*e*) :

. . . *ἐπειδή ἐστιν ἐναντίον καλὸν αἰσχρῷ, δύο αὐτὼ εἶναι.*
πῶς δ' οὔ ;
οὐκοῦν ἐπειδὴ δύο, καὶ ἕν ἑκάτερον ;
καὶ τοῦτο.

καὶ περὶ δὴ δικαίου καὶ ἀδίκου καὶ ἀγαθοῦ καὶ κακοῦ καὶ πάντων τῶν εἰδῶν
πέρι ὁ αὐτὸς λόγος, αὐτὸ μὲν ἓν ἕκαστον εἶναι, τῇ δὲ τῶν πράξεων καὶ σωμάτων
καὶ ἀλλήλων κοινωνίᾳ πανταχοῦ φανταζόμενα πολλὰ φαίνεσθαι ἕκαστον.
And the argument proceeds from there. Not only is the word *εἶδος* used
in introducing the theory, but the whole feeling is different. The Ideas are
not something to be explained but something taken as known (*μανθάνω*,
477*c*) the theory is then used in argument, as in *Phaedo*, but the explanations
given are of a very different character.[1]

4. It should be noted also that Simmias brings forward the theory that the
soul is a harmony. This, as Socrates points out, is quite inconsistent with
the theory of Recollection and of knowledge as recollection of the Ideas.
Such a conception of the soul could not have been held by any one who was
acquainted with the epistemological implications of the theory of Forms.

5. We must now examine the particular phrases upon which Burnet
mainly bases his case to prove that Simmias and Kebes are ' enthusiastic
supporters ' of the theory of Ideas. That they are very much attracted by it
when it is explained to them I do not, of course, deny. It is true also that
Simmias abandons his definition of the soul as a harmony when it is shown
to clash with the theory, though this is by no means the only argument
brought against the view.

Much is made of Simmias' emphatic words : *φαμὲν μέντοι νὴ Δία* at 65*d*,
in answer to the question : *φαμέν τι εἶναι δίκαιον ἢ οὐδέν* ; and to
Socrates' next words : *καὶ αὖ καλόν γέ τι καὶ ἀγαθόν*; he replies : *πῶς δ'οὔ*.
Two points arise. First, that Simmias agrees without hesitation. But,
as Burnet himself says in his note, ' if we will only translate literally and
avoid loose philosophical terminology, there is nothing in the doctrine as
here set forth which should be unintelligible to any one who understands a
few propositions of Euclid and recognizes a standard of right conduct '.
This makes it clear that Socrates is proceeding step by step. Further,
Euthyphro agrees with almost as much enthusiasm (5*d πάντως δήπου*) though
the language there is far more technical and definite, e.g. *αὐτὸ δὲ ἑαυτῷ*
ὅμοιον καὶ ἔχον μίαν τινὰ ἰδέαν κ.τ.λ. Yet it is not suggested that Euthyphro was ' perfectly familiar ' with the theory of Ideas. The second point
of which Burnet makes much is the use of the first person plural. Taylor
(*V.S.*, 57 n.) goes so far as to suggest there are two distinct sets of ' we '
referring to two different groups. Burnet says ' the suggestion clearly is
that Socrates and Simmias are using the language of a school to which both
belong '. But is it ? Socrates frequently uses the first person plural, thus
associating others with himself in the search for truth. He does it in the
Laches (193*d* ff. and *passim*), in the *Lysis* (218 ff.), throughout the *Republic* and
elsewhere. I cannot feel that the first person plural used in this dialogue
throughout has any particular significance.

As for the *θρυλοῦμεν* of 76*d*, the *ἐπισφραγιζόμεθα* of 75*d* (which looks back

---

[1] I am not suggesting that the fact that the theory *is* familiar to Glaucon
need mean anything more than that it had been explained elsewhere.

to 74a) and the πολυθρύλητα of 100b, I see no reason why they should refer to anything but the frequent previous mention of the Forms in this very dialogue. No reader of the *Phaedo* will be surprised to find these ' eternal things ' referred to as πολυθρύλητα by this time. In fact he will find himself agreeing that they are ' the things we are always babbling about '. To see in any of this a reference to a ' school of philosophy ' is surely fanciful.

All these considerations have convinced me that Burnet was mistaken when he declared that the theory of Ideas is introduced in this dialogue as something familiar to Simmias and Kebes. There can be no doubt that Plato very carefully explains the theory step by step. It would surely be inartistic (though this is a purely subjective argument) to do this to an audience already fully familiar with it.

I cannot enter here into the vexed question of Pythagorean influence upon the development of the theory of Ideas. Clearly they had some. But there is no evidence in the *Phaedo* that will allow us to class Simmias and Kebes as Pythagoreans in any real sense. They have attended some lectures of Philolaus at Thebes (Φιλολάῳ συγγεγονότες, 61d). So did a good many Thebans, one imagines, just as Meno attended those of Gorgias. If they appear in Iamblichus' list of Pythagoreans, Xenophon (*Mem.*, I, 48) has them in a list of Socratics. Both may be based on little more than this dialogue. And what Socrates expects to find at 61d–e is that they have heard Philolaus on suicide, and that he has told them that a philosopher should be willing to face death. Kebes says he has heard ' nothing definite ' (οὐδὲν σαφές). What a disciple ! A moment later he says he has indeed heard from Philolaus that a man should not commit suicide. He heard this from others also but, he repeats, nothing definite. *And that is all about Philolaus.* The impression made upon the reader is that Kebes is a cultured person with a general interest in philosophy, not a philosopher. As for Simmias, he is, as we saw, the kind of person who can speak of the soul as a harmony without seeing, until it is pointed out to him, that this is incompatible with the theory of Recollection. I cannot but feel that we are to see in this the confused state of Simmias' mind rather than ' the inherent contradictions of fifth-century Pythagorean thought '.

Finally, if Burnet is right in suggesting that Phaedo tells the tale in the Pythagorean συνέδριον at Phlius (notes *ad init.*) I feel sure that Plato's purpose is to explain the theory of Ideas to those who know ' that the art of measurement is concerned with all things ' but who fail because ' they are not accustomed to study a subject by classifying it according to the Ideas ' (*Pol.*, 285a) rather than to indicate to his readers in any over-subtle manner that the Pythagoreans discovered the theory of Forms.

APPENDIX II

SOPHIST, 246a–249d

As explained in the text, I believe that Plato is here setting himself a problem, rather than solving it : that the Forms by themselves do not account for movement and life and that somehow (but he does not here say how) soul, as well as Ideas, must be included in reality in the full sense (in ' das im strengen Sinn Seiende ' as Ritter puts it, II, p. 130).

This passage of the *Sophist* has given rise to countless discussions, and to justify my view I must deal with the main points. For full reference I refer the reader to M. Diès' special monograph *La définition de l'être et la nature des Idées dans le Sophiste de Platon*, to his introduction to the Budé edition of dialogue, and his *Autour de Platon*, II, pp. 362 ff. The chief points in dispute are three :

1. The definition of the existent (τὸ ὄν) as that which has the power to act or to be acted upon (δύναμις εἴτ' εἰς τὸ ποιεῖν εἴτ' εἰς τὸ παθεῖν, 247e) has sometimes been taken to indicate a complete change in Platonic philosophy, especially by Zeller, who from this point on wants to regard the Ideas as active powers. He supports this view by a misunderstanding of 248d–249b, and of the passage from the *Philebus* discussed in App. IV below. As he puts it (II, 575, see also Apelt, p. 23 ff.) ' wir müssen den Begriff des Seins auf den der Kraft zurückführen '. This view is followed by Lutoslawski (433). Diès, however, has satisfactorily proved (*L'Etre*, 17 ff.) that the definition is introduced as provisional, remains so, and is discarded when it has done its work. In any case, as the only δύναμις attributed to the Ideas in this section is the power to be known, which is a δύναμις εἰς τὸ παθεῖν and so does not imply any ποιεῖν, Zeller's conclusion does not follow. Add to this that the Being which we are seeking to define includes that of the materialist as well as that of the friends of the Ideas, the definition must apply to σῶμα as well as to ἀσώματα εἴδη. It is not, therefore, a definition of Being as understood by Plato, hitherto at least.

2. In 248a–249d the stranger attacks the ' friends of the Ideas '. The difficulty is this : these philosophers speak of Becoming (γένεσις) and Being (οὐσία) and separate the two completely. The former we know by means of our bodily perceptions, the latter by means of the soul's reasoning (λογισμῷ). How can these two have any communication with one another (κοινωνία) ? The Idealists can in fact be convicted of contradiction : they admit that the Ideas are known, but they deny that the Ideas are acted upon in any way. Hence, to be consistent they should deny that to be known is a πάθος. But that is absurd. Now if they admit, as they must, that γιγνώσκεσθαι is a πάθος, then they must admit that the Ideas, being known,

295

are acted upon or, in other words, subject to κίνησις or activity. This is, however, impossible for those who hold, as the friends of the Ideas do, that the real is completely unmoved, not subject to κίνησις. This ends the argument directed explicitly against these Idealists who must now admit that their οὐσία is subject to at least ' the power of being acted upon '. The next paragraph is the most important. The stranger suddenly exclaims :

' By Heaven, shall we believe that there is no movement, life, soul or knowledge in what supremely is (ἐν τῷ παντελῶς ὄντι), that it neither loves nor knows, but stands motionless, in proud sanctity, without life or movement ? '

He then asserts that the παντελῶς ὄν must have mind and life, and therefore soul. Having soul, it will have motion. We must therefore agree that that which is in motion, and motion itself, must exist fully. And he proceeds to apply his findings.

The whole difficulty here lies in the words παντελῶς ὄν, and the problem seems to be this. The ' friends of the Ideas deny that anything is truly real which is subject to κίνησις of any kind. But to restrict the real in this way to what is absolutely immobile is unsatisfactory, first because such Ideas could not even be known, and further (since γιγνώσκεσθαι is a passivity) we must also include the knowing mind, which is a principle of active movement and causation, in true Reality, ἐν τῷ παντελῶς ὄντι. Now Plato, who was a believer in Ideas, could do this in two ways, either by endowing his Ideas themselves with mind (so Zeller), or by including in the world of true reality another kind of existent, namely soul, which contains the active principle of motion within itself. True reality, τὸ παντελῶς ὄν, will then include both Ideas and some kind of soul. I agree with Diès, and it is indeed the general opinion, that Plato did not do the former : the Ideas never became gods. But he did do the latter. And I must here refer the reader to my discussion of Plato's gods (pp. 161 ff.) to see how he did it, and how the inclusion of souls as existents in the full sense, was only the culmination of a long process of development in Plato's thought.

I do not believe that Diès is right (L'Etre, 48, 54) in the distinction he makes between οὐσία as endowed with passive, παντελῶς ὄν as endowed with active movement. The two words are, I believe, used synonymously. It is true that οὐσία is used of the Ideas, when quoting the Idealists in argument (or rather arguing against them and therefore using the word as they do). There is a difference of this kind between the Ideas and νοῦς, but that is not the point here. Nor can I agree that παντελῶς ὄν refers to the sensible world (ibid., 73 ff.). The references given by Diès do not convince me that these words could ever be applied to it. And surely it was not necessary to prove so emphatically that there was movement in the physical world ? Nor can the words refer to the whole universe, including the noetic with the sensible, as Diès now believes (II, 558 ff.). And even if it could, it would not mean that here. Plato had never denied that there was soul in the cosmos, either in the Phaedo or elsewhere. What the Phaedo does seem to deny is that anything which is subject to movement could be said to be in the full sense in which the Ideas are. The fact that the soul knows and claims kinship with the Ideas implies a contradiction (for to be known is a πάθος). Which is just the contradiction of which the passage before us accuses the ' friends of the Ideas '.

3. Who are the Friends of the Ideas ?

To any reader who had not been forewarned by scholarly discussions it would seem perfectly obvious that the author of the *Phaedo* and the *Republic* must at least be included among those here criticized. The language of the *Phaedo* can only be understood as creating just such a divorce between the phenomenal world and ' the real ' as is here indicated. Certainly the Ideas are there at perfect rest and not subject to $\varkappa \ell \nu \eta \sigma \iota \varsigma$. There is, of course, talk of participation, and the whole point of the *Sophist* is to point out to such Idealists that no such participation or imitation is possible unless they grant the Ideas at least passive $\delta \upsilon \nu \alpha \mu \iota \varsigma$, and unless they grant further that the mind is somehow part of the supreme reality. But, here as in the *Parmenides*, Plato may well have in mind also some of his disciples who carried this separation further than he did, or than he had intended, and had not profited by the efforts he had already made to bridge the gap. This is now the generally accepted view, it would appear, in Germany.

See Friedlander, II, 528 ; Ritter, II, 132 ; Wilamowitz, I, 564, includes also the Eleatics and other Idealists, and the argument certainly applies equally to them ; Gomperz, II, 596 ; Raeder, 328. All these at least include Plato himself. Natorp, 292 and Shorey, 594 take the reference to be to wrong-headed disciples. Diès does not commit himself, but thinks it improbable that Plato is criticizing himself. Brochard, 137, also remains in doubt.

Zeller thought the Megarian school were meant, but this is refuted by Gomperz, Diès and Wilamowitz.

Taylor, 385, and Burnet, 91 n. 1, and 280, find here also a reference to later Pythagoreans. This, of course, fits in with the rest of their point of view.

APPENDIX III

POLITICUS, 283b–285b

Too much importance has often been attached to certain unusual expressions in this passage and they have been taken to indicate some fundamental change in Plato's doctrine. Ritter even goes so far as to distinguish between two kinds of Ideas,[1] one to correspond to each of the two kinds of measurement here discussed. There is no trace of this in the text. As it is extremely dangerous in interpreting Plato to attach too much importance to single words and unusual phrases (indeed he delights in oxymoron at times as a way of challenging thought) I propose to give a summary of the whole passage first, adding the Greek words where necessary ; it will be the simplest way of making clear what I consider the correct interpretation of the debated words.

283c Let us consider the whole question of excess and defect (πᾶσαν τὴν ὑπερβολὴν καὶ ἔλλειψιν.) The science of measurement (μετρητική) is
d concerned with bigness and smallness, and the whole of excess and defect. And let us divide measurement in two parts : the first is concerned with the size of objects in relation to one another, the other with the necessary nature of the process of becoming (κατὰ τὴν τῆς γενέσεως ἀναγκαίαν οὐσίαν). You think that what is smaller is naturally so in relation to what is bigger and to nothing else, and vice
e versa. Yet what exceeds the mean (τὴν φύσιν μετρίου) or is exceeded by it we again speak of as really coming to be (ὄντως γιγνόμενον), and in this way (ἐν ᾧ) the good among us differ from the bad. Therefore (ἄρα) we must suppose these two ways in which the big and the small exist (οὐσίας) and they are thus judged, as we now see, in relation to each other and in relation to the mean.
284a Arts and crafts (τέχναι) and their products are thus divided. If they watch closely the more and the less than the mean, thinking not that this does not exist but that it is difficult (οὐχ ὡς οὐκ ὂν ἀλλ᾽ ὡς χαλεπόν),
b thus preserving the mean, their products are good.
c Our aim must be to see that more and less are measured not only in
d relation to one another but also to the realization of the mean (τὴν τοῦ μετρίου γένεσιν). The arts and sciences and the mean cannot
e exist without each other. Therefore there are two kinds of measurement ' one, those arts which measure number, size, depth, width, swiftness, in relation to their contraries, the other, those arts which measure in relation to the mean, the fitting, the opportune, the neces-

---

[1] II, 158 ff.
298

sary and all those things which are established by the middle between
the extremes '.
285a That is what many wise men (the Pythagoreans ?) say, that measurement is concerned with all that is. But because they are unaccustomed to classify things in accordance with the Forms, they class
b together whatever they think in some way alike, though it is different,
and also separate what should be together. One should examine all
the differences in the Forms, and include together in the nature of one
Form (γένους τινὸς οὐσίᾳ) all that properly belongs together within
one likeness (ἐντὸς μιᾶς ὁμοιότητος).

The meaning of this absolute mean I have tried to explain in the
text. It is not called an Idea because it is not, at least for the most
part, coextensive with it. Take the Idea Man. Clearly there are
within it many qualities, each made definite at a certain point.
For example, to revert to our illustration of human temperature :
the Form of man will contain heat in a certain mathematical ratio,
say 98 degrees Fahrenheit. That formula, 98 degrees, as applied
to heat, is part of the Idea Man. It is not the whole of it, nor is it
the Idea of heat. To speak of the ' mean ' as an Idea therefore
would only confuse us, as we are trying to establish the existence of
the absolute mean, or, in other words, to prove the existence of
objective reality in mathematical terms. What applies to my
example of temperature applies in the same way to all the other
qualities that go to make up the Idea of man. There is an ideal, ' a
mean ' for every virtue, for size, &c. And Plato dreamt of expressing the right point for every quality with as much precision as we
are able to do in the case of temperature. All these right points or
amounts together would presumably be found in the Idea of man,
and, all together at least, there only.
Once this point is established he goes on to criticize certain
philosophers (he is usually taken to refer to the Pythagoreans).
He says in effect that it is true, as they maintained, that measurement is the basis of all science. But that is not enough. You cannot reason and classify properly unless you do so in accordance with
the Forms. His meaning is surely obvious : you may know that
human temperature is a matter of calculation of heat (and let us
suppose you have the means of measuring it in degrees), but unless
you know the mean, the *right* temperature for man, you are not very
far advanced and you have no medical knowledge. That is to
calculate according to the mean, and also according to the Ideas.
But the latter implies even more. For unless you know and have
a proper understanding of the whole Idea of man, of man's function
and purpose as it were, unless you *see* the Idea as a whole with your
mind's eye, you will not know *why* 98 degrees is the proper temperature for man. If Plato is here criticizing the Pythagoreans, then
clearly he did not think that they had reached this point, if indeed
they had reached the second stage, which is doubtful. They know
that all art is measurement, but they fail to make the distinction

between purely relative calculation and calculation with the scientific mean in view.

The main points of the passage now being clear we may examine the startling expressions which are found in it, though I do not believe any of them too startling when left embedded in their context. Plato uses οὐσία, as he uses εἶδος, quite often very vaguely. So in 283e for διττὰς οὐσίας τοῦ μεγάλου we might as well have had δύο εἴδη τοῦ μεγάλου and the meaning is simply two kinds, two natures (= φύσεις) of bigness without, I believe, any reference to the degree of reality of either kind. And when the second kind of measurement is defined as κατὰ τὴν τῆς γενέσεως ἀναγκαίαν οὐσίαν the important word seems to be ἀναγκαίαν and we might as well have had τὴν τῆς γενέσεως ἀνάγκην. At any rate it must refer to that part of the process of becoming which is governed by the fixed and unalterable mean. It is the fixity that is important (it has nothing whatever to do with the very different use of ἀνάγκη in the Timaeus). The necessary and fixed condition of any becoming is the mean, the μέτριον, the exact, right ratio of any quality inherent in an Idea, and the whole phrase is equivalent to πρὸς τὸ μέτριον, e.g. in 283e 11. The Idea is indeed the necessary condition of the coming into existence of any particular. But it really makes little difference if we wish to press the phrase to mean ' the necessary reality of the process of becoming ' (though I think this emphasis on οὐσίαν is wrong) for the phenomena, in so far as they have any reality, have it just in so far as they express or imitate the Ideas, which they do in so far as they conform to the measure, mean or μέτριον inherent in them. That there was some degree of reality in the world of becoming is obvious even from the Line of the Republic, and was never denied by Plato.

And so that which stands in relation, be it excess or defect, to the mean and the Idea, is looked upon as trying to get as close to that mean as possible (just as the equal sticks imitate equality in the Phaedo). No phenomenon quite reaches this mean, but it is in so far as it is so related to the ' mean ' that it has any reality and can be said really to come to be. Which is the meaning of the phrase ὄντως γιγνόμενον.

All these expressions describe γένεσις, and only the scientific type of measurement can describe the process of coming to be. Purely relative measurement does not, and cannot, describe it. It can only say ' this is bigger than that '. It cannot say what this is, or to be more exact, what this becomes.

Once more : When I say that Socrates is hotter than Theaetetus I am not saying anything very essential about either of them. But when I say, ' Socrates' temperature is 100 degrees, he therefore has a fever,' I am relating Socrates to the absolute mean 98, thereby expressing a relationship between him and the Idea of man. I have knowledge of what he is, or becomes, I am relating him to that which is real in him, which is the extent to which he realizes the Idea of man as expressed by temperature. That is ' the being of his becoming ', and I am considering him as an ὄντως γιγνόμενον.

APPENDIX IV

PHILEBUS, 23c–27c

THE view adopted in the text is based mainly on two points : that the Ideas are to be classed under πέρας , and that the mixed class contains phenomena only ; in other words, that Plato is trying to account for the process of becoming. The first point, that the Ideas belong to the Definite or Limit, seems to me to follow from the following considerations.

1. The theory elaborated in this passage is quite obviously the same as that which is more briefly mentioned in 16c, and the two passages must be taken together. There can be no doubt that the henads or monads mentioned in 15a–b are the Ideas, for the difficulties put forward by Socrates in the next paragraph are obviously the old difficulties involved in participation in the Forms discussed in the *Parmenides*. Nor can any reader of the *Sophist* and the *Politicus* (not to mention the *Phaedrus*) doubt that in the process of διαίρεσις the search for a unit in division is the search for an εἶδος. That is explicitly stated in passages too numerous to mention. The process of division is again mentioned in 16d, in connexion with the πέρας—ἄπειρον theory (ἀεὶ μίαν ἰδέαν περὶ παντὸς ἑκάστοτε θεμένους ζητεῖν). There too we have ἕν—πολλά, πέρας—ἄπειρον as equivalent pairs. Division is a search for ἕν in each case, and we must proceed from the highest ἕν (the *summum genus*) through a definite number of subdivisions. Each of these is, of course, also a ἕν, a henad or Idea (μία ἰδέα).[1] It is also πέρας being impressed upon ἄπειρα. Clearly, here at least, the Idea is definitely classed with πέρας. And that holds for all the examples of classification given in the following pages.

2. I have said that the Ideas belong to πέρας. We meet them chiefly in this dialogue under their mathematical aspect. I have tried to show that the cosmic number of the *Republic* is the Idea of Good considered (mythically) as the supreme and all-inclusive mathematical formula of the world. Therefore the fact that only mathematical illustrations are used here will not disturb us. Some scholars have seen in the πέρας here the μαθηματικά which Aristotle says Plato placed between the Ideas and the particulars. In the Line of the *Republic* we should presumably find these in the lower section of the noetic world CE. There both CE and EB contain Ideas. So here, I suggest, in so far as Plato has these μαθηματικά in mind, they too are

---

[1] Bury, p. xlii, says εἴδη are the ἀριθμοί or πόσα which mediate between the One and the many. But in every division the εἶδος of any class is also a ἕν and must therefore be identified with πέρας.

to be found in πέρας but, at least in this dialogue, the two are not differentiated and would both be called Ideas, as in the *Republic*.

3. Zeller maintains that the Ideas come under αἰτία. This is directly due to his misinterpretation of the passages from the *Sophist* discussed above (App. II). If Plato was not there turning his Ideas into moving souls, but rather differentiating between the two we shall not be surprised to find φρόνησις, νοῦς and σοφία classed under αἰτία. The moving cause is, as it was already in the *Phaedrus*, soul, and wisdom and knowledge naturally belong to it. Far from being an argument in favour of including Ideas under αἰτία, this becomes a reason for excluding them. It is true that Ideas are called the cause of things in the *Phaedo* and the *Republic*. So they are in a sense, as it is the contemplation of them which leads the soul to act rightly, and the demiurge to create. They cause τῷ γιγνώσκεσθαι, not directly. Further, when the *Phaedo* and the *Republic* were written, the moving cause had not been satisfactorily distinguished or accounted for, which is the point that the passage in the *Sophist* (249c) brings to the fore.

The argument that if πέρας is mixed with ἄπειρον to form the mixed class this would make the Ideas immanent if they belong to πέρας is hardly worth refuting. For then any form of participation would make them immanent. Surely this is pressing the word ' mix ' too far.

That πέρας is not an active principle is true. Neither, if my interpretation of the passage in question from the *Sophist* is right, are the Ideas. If they were we should need no moving cause, and no demiurge.

4. As is well known, Jackson classed the Ideas under μικτόν. He distinguishes between the πόσον which is μέτριον and the many πόσα which only approximate to it. The former, together with the More-and-less (under the guidance of νοῦς) then makes a μικτόν which is an Idea ; the latter πόσα, impressed by νοῦς upon the More-and-less, make imperfect particulars. The objections to this are many, the chief one being that it does violence to the Platonic text with the sole purpose of evolving a Platonic doctrine which tallies with what Aristotle says about it. Also (i) πόσον and μέτριον are not 'plainly' different in 24c ; on the contrary, the words are synonymous.

(ii) Where do these imperfect πόσα come from ? Does the νοῦς that brings phenomena about work with imperfect formulae ? The particulars are then no longer imperfect approximations to perfect Ideas, but perfect copies of imperfect formulae. That is not Platonic.

(iii) Surely the reason why the particulars only approximate to the Ideas is to be found in the nature of the More-and-less, the Indeterminate of the *Philebus*, the ἐκμαγεῖον of the *Timaeus*, not, on any theory, in the model, the μέτριον or the αὐτοζῷον.

(iv) What is the relation of these faulty πόσα with the ἀριθμοί ? Jackson identifies them, but are they not *wrong* calculations ? To introduce them only adds to the confusion.

Rodier also places the Ideas under μικτά, as well as the particulars. We then have two processes of γένεσις. In the former the Ideas are μικτά, some higher Idea being πέρας. For the γένεσις of a particular a lower Idea is πέρας. This is ingenious, but there is nothing in Plato to make us suppose that he ever, and certainly not here, considered his Ideas as μικτά, even though there obviously is some interdependence between the Ideas.

This brings us to the second disputable point, that we are here concerned only with the coming to be of the physical world. If the Ideas are to be included only under πέρας, this cannot but be the case. It may be added, however, that, even if Plato realized the interdependence of Ideas, he would hardly have described the process as a γένεσις. But we need not hang our case on a word. The general sense of the passage makes the point clear : the metaphysical discussion arose from the fact that the mixed life, by which human life is obviously meant, has been found to include pleasure and pain as well as knowledge. From this we go on to discuss the meaning of ' mixed '. Hence the μικτόν from first to last naturally refers to the world of phenomena : there is not a shadow of a hint that it anywhere refers to anything else.[1] And while it is quite in Plato's manner to introduce as all but a digression an analysis that throws new light on his philosophy as a whole, it is hardly his way to revolutionize the very basis of that philosophy in a parenthesis. And I would again emphasize that when πέρας and ἄπειρον are first introduced it is in connexion with the method of διαίρεσις as applied to the physical world in accordance with the Ideas.

We are, in fact, once more dealing with the μετρητική which has the absolute μέτριον in view, described in the *Politicus*. As there, so here, it analyses the process of γένεσις. And here too I would hesitate to strain too far one or two curious expressions which do occur. We find, for example, γένεσις εἰς οὐσίαν, a coming to be. True, if we underline οὐσία, Being of a kind is granted to the physical world. But does this mean very much more than it ever did ? οὐσία is a pretty vague word at times, and the works of Aristotle were not yet written. And in Plato we must not argue from single words. At least he always tells us not to. The same is true of the word εἶδος where it is applied to the four factors of existence. We need not be disturbed by such phrases as τὰ δύο τῶν εἰδῶν and κατ' εἴδη in 23*d*, or τὸ δὲ τρίτον . . . τίνα ἰδέαν ἔχειν in 25*b*, or even by τὴν τοῦ ἀπείρου ἰδέαν in 16*d*. That is Plato's way, which is not infrequently irritating. But these expressions mean no more than the δύο εἴδη τῶν ὄντων applied to the physical and intelligible world in *Phaedo*, 79*a*. To argue from this that there are Ideas of all four factors, as Ritter seems to do (II, 183) is to confuse two distinct uses of the word.

My view is substantially in accord with that of Burnet (p. 332) and Friedländer (II, 573), as well as with Brochard in his excellent note (199). For full references see Rodier (pp. 79–93). Wilamowitz (I, p. 639) insists that the Ideas remain undisturbed, yet he identifies the Idea of Good with αἰτία, in a way I cannot understand. He takes the μικτόν to be the physical

---

[1] So τὸ καλούμενον ὅλον of 28*d*, and τό γε τοῦ πάντος σῶμα ἔμψυχον of 30*a* mean the physical world, as Bury takes them (p. xliv). Cp. τῶν ἀεὶ λεγομένων εἶναι in 16*c*.

world as does Bury (pp. lxiv–lxxxiv, and Appendix D and E), and Taylor (pp. 414 ff.) who, however, gives the Forms no place in the scheme. Natorp (pp. 336 ff.) equates all the Forms with πέρας, and rightly emphasizes that the problem here is quite different from that in the *Sophist*. Ritter (II, pp. 165–185) at first takes ἄπειρον as 'Stoff' and πέρας as Form, but then relapses into vagueness.

LIST OF BOOKS REFERRED TO IN THE NOTES

O. APELT : *Platonische Aufsätze*, Teubner, 1912.
J. ADAM : *The Republic of Plato*, Cambridge, 1920.
E. BARKER : *Plato and his Predecessors* (Greek Political Theory), Methuen, 1918.
H. BONITZ : *Platonische Studien*, Berlin (Vahlen), 1875.
BOVET : *Le Dieu de Platon d'après l'ordre chronologique des dialogues*, Paris (Alcan), 1902.
V. BROCHARD : *Etudes de philosophie ancienne et de philosophie moderne*, Paris (Vrin), 1926.
J. BURNET : *Greek Philosophy*, Part I (From Thales to Plato), Macmillan, 1920.
Early Greek Philosophy, London (Black), 1908.
Plato's Phaedo, Oxford, 1925.
Platonism, Univ. California, 1928.
Essays and Addresses, Chatto & Windus, 1929.
R. G. BURY : *The Philebus of Plato*, Cambridge, 1897.
The Symposium of Plato, Cambridge (Heffer) 1909.
L. CAMPBELL : *The Sophistes and Politicus of Plato*, Oxford, 1867.
H. DIELS : *Die Fragmente der Vorsokratiker*, Berlin, (Weidmann) 1922.
A. DIÈS : *Autour de Platon* (I and II), Paris (Beauchesne), 1927.
La définition de l'Etre et la nature des Idées dans le Sophiste de Platon, Paris (Vrin), 1932.
Le Sophiste (Budé, viii, 3), Paris, 1925.
E. B. ENGLAND : *The Laws of Plato*, Manchester U.P., 1921.
G. C. FIELD : *Plato and his Contemporaries*, Methuen, 1920.
Socrates and Plato, Parker, Oxford, 1913.
FINSLER : *Platon und die Aristotelische Poetik*, Leipzig, (Spirgatis).
P. FRIEDLÄNDER : *Platon : Eidos Paideia Dialogos* (I), Berlin (De Gruyter), 1928.
Die Platonische Schriften (II), Berlin, (De Gruyter) 1930.
Der Grosse Alkibiades, Bonn (Cohen), 1923.
P. FRUTIGER : *Les Mythes de Platon*, Paris (Alcan), 1930.
Th. GOMPERZ : *Greek Thinkers*, London (Murray), 1901–2.
R. HACKFORTH : *The Composition of Plato's Apology*, Cambridge, 1933.
E. HALEVY : *La Théorie platonicienne des Sciences*, Paris (Alcan), 1896.
J. HARWARD : *The Epinomis of Plato*, Oxford, 1928.
The Platonic Epistles, Cambridge, 1932.
J. HIRSCHBERGER : *Die Phronesis und die Philosophie Platons vor dem Staate*, Leipzig (Dietrich), 1932.
J. ITHURRIAGUE : *Les idées de Platon sur la condition de la femme au regard des traditions antiques*, 1931.

305

B. Jowett : *The Dialogues of Plato*, Macmillan, 1892.
A. P. Lafontaine : *Le Plaisir d'après Platon et Aristote*, Paris (Alcan), 1902.
R. Lagerborg : *Die Platonische Liebe*, Leipzig (Meiner), 1926.
W. Lutoslawski : *The Origin and Growth of Plato's Logic*, Longman Green, 1897.
S. Marck : *Die Platonische Ideenlehre in ihren Motiven*, Leipzig (Dietrich), 1932.
R. Mugnier : *Le Sens du mot θεῖος chez Platon*, Paris (Vrin), 1930.
G. Murray : *Five Stages of Greek Religion*, Oxford, 1925.
P. Natorp : *Platons Ideenlehre*, Leipzig (Meiner), 1921.
H. Raeder : *Platonische Entwickelung*, Leipzig (Teubner), 1905.
C. Ritter : *Platon* (I and II), München (Beck), 1910.
Neue Untersuchungen uber Platon, München (Beck), 1910.
Die Kerngedanken der Platonische Philosophie, München (Reinhardt), 1931.
The Essence of Plato's Philosophy, Allen and Unwin, 1933.
L. Robin : *La Théorie platonicienne des Idées et des Nombres d'après Aristote*, Paris (Alcan), 1908.
La Théorie platonicienne de l'Amour, Paris (Alcan), 1908.
Etudes sur la signification et la place de la Physique dans la philosophie de Platon, Paris (Alcan), 1919.
G. Rodier : *Etudes de Philosophie Grecque*, Paris (Vrin), 1926.
W. D. Ross : *Aristotle's Metaphysics*, Oxford, 1924.
P. Shorey : *What Plato Said*, Univ. Chicago Press, 1933.
The Unity of Plato's Thought, Univ. Chic. Decenn. Publ., 1st Ser. VI., 1904.
The Idea of Good in the Republic, Univ. Chic. Stud. Class. Phil. I, 1895.
The Republic (Loeb), Heineman, 1930.
R. Schaerer : *Ἐπιστήμη et Τέχνη*, Macon (Protat), 1930.
D. Tarrant : *The Hippias Major*, Cambridge, 1928.
A. E. Taylor : *Plato, The Man and his Work*, Methuen, 1927.
A Commentary on Plato's Timaeus, Oxford, 1928.
Varia Socratica, Parker (Oxford), 1911.
Plato and the Authorship of the Epinomis, Proc. Brit. Acad., XV.
U. Von Wilamowitz-Moellendorff : *Platon : sein Leben und seine Werken* (I), Berlin, 1909.
Platon : Beilagen und Textkritik (II), 1919.
E. Zeller : *Die Philosophie der Griechen*, Leipzig, 1875.

BIBLIOGRAPHICAL ESSAY

The purpose of this essay is twofold: (1) to highlight some of the literature considered most useful to students wishing to continue their study of Plato, and (2) to identify issues of scholarly importance which have been generated in the literature since the first appearance of *Plato's Thought*. Inevitably, the essay will read as something like a "Who's Who" or a "What's What" in Platonic scholarship. I shall not attempt to give a complete bibliographical account, and shall confine discussion and the bibliography, except in rare cases, to works in English. The items mentioned in the Essay are fully documented in the Bibliography which follows it, under the numerals by which they are tagged here.

A fuller bibliographical discussion is given by J. B. Skemp in *Greece and Rome, New Surveys in the Classics,* No. 10, Oxford, 1976. The volumes on Plato in Guthrie's *History* (7) contain an ample bibliography. A complete bibliography of studies of Plato from 1950 to 1957 has been compiled by H. Cherniss in *Lustrum* 1959 and 1969 (publ. in 1960 and 1961 resp.); and there are two bibliographies of subsequent literature: one by R. D. McKirahan, *Plato and Socrates, A Comprehensive Bibliography,* 1958–1973, New York and London, 1978, and one by L. Brisson in *Lustrum* 1977 (publ. 1979). A clearly written account of the history of Platonic scholarship is given by E. N. Tigerstedt, *Interpreting Plato,* Stockholm, 1977.

For comprehensive general treatments which analyse critically Plato's doctrines and arguments, see the volumes by I. M. Crombie (1) and the book by J. Gosling (6). Less analytical in approach are the volumes by Guthrie noted above. Platonic scholarship is being greatly enhanced by the new Clarendon Plato Series, of which five volumes have appeared to date: (8)–(12). These studies illustrate well the methods of contemporary analytical scholarship on Plato.

Fresh, accurate translations are followed by a generally high level of philosophical commentary. Among other commentaries on individual dialogues, especially to be recommended are R. E. Allen's study of the *Euthyphro* (13); E. R. Dodds' introduction and commentary to his edition of the *Gorgias* (20); and N. White's survey and essays on the *Republic* (27).

For the remainder of this essay it will be convenient to use the chapter titles of Grube's text as headings. A glance will show that the topics surveyed in the text have not enjoyed equal prominence in subsequent scholarship. The theory of Forms and its associated metaphysical and epistemological doctrines have by far had the lion's share of attention. There is a good reason for this: although the theory receives little space in the dialogues, it is nevertheless at the center of Plato's philosophy. Furthermore, its historical influence and its contemporary interest are greater than any other aspect of Plato's philosophy. No need, then, to apologize for this imbalance.

Preface

Both the question of the chronology of the Platonic dialogues and the "Socratic question" have received further attention. An important unsettled matter is the date of the *Cratylus,* though see J. V. Luce (114). By far the most controversial chronological issue, with far-reaching implications for our assessment of the development and the interpretation of much of Plato's philosophy, is the determination of the relative place of the *Timaeus* in the Platonic corpus. Challenging the traditional view of this dialogue as one of Plato's very latest, G. E. L. Owen (128) adduced philological, philosophical and historical consideration to argue powerfully for placing the dialogue prior to the *Parmenides* and the *Theaetetus,* dialogues which usher in Plato's "critical" phase. H. F. Cherniss countered the challenge four years later (81) and seems to have persuaded many of the correctness of the traditional dating. Others have not been convinced by the rejoinder, and the issue is by no means settled.

The Socratic question is a complex of two questions: (1) do we have any materials from which to construct an account of Socrates that is historically reliable, and are the Platonic dialogues among such materials; and (2) if so, which dialogues can be distinguished from others as furnishing these materials? The answer to the first question that is most generally accepted is an affirmative one: some of Plato's dialogues are historically more reliable than other sources such as Xenophon [see Vlastos (153) and Lacey (111)]. On the second question, most scholars agree that the dialogues which precede the *Phaedo* (with the *Meno* being transitional) depict the doctrines, arguments, methods and indeed the personality of the historical Socrates.

A sort of "Platonic question", somewhat similar to the Socratic question, has also been raised in the literature of the last decades. Do Plato's dialogues (and letters, if they are genuine) provide us with the record of Plato's philosophical thinking, or are his most fully developed views not to be found there? Several German scholars, notably Kraemer (53) and Gaiser (46) revived and defended the view that Plato did not commit his philosophical doctrines to writing, but developed a set of "esoteric", "unwritten doctrines", of which we find hints in Aristotle and elsewhere. On this view, Plato's "real" philosophy is inaccessible to us. The view has been undermined by Vlastos in a careful review of Kraemer's book (157), though it reappears, surprisingly, in the books by Findlay (3) and (4), who appears to have taken no account of Vlastos' criticism.

The Theory of Ideas

The book by Sir David Ross (63) is still standard, though parts of its account have been challenged. A readable introduction to Plato's metaphysics and epistemology with a fairly traditional interpretation is the book by Raven (60). A recent work which is more sophisticated philosophically and in the extent of its scholarship is that by White (74). The second volume of Crombie (referred to above) is also valuable.

After the demise of the Burnet–Taylor thesis, which claimed that the Platonic theory of Forms is already present in the earliest dialogues (see Grube, above, pp. 7-10; cf. pp. 291-294), the alternative view, that "form talk" in the Socratic dialogues is of no metaphysical consequence, held sway until it was powerfully challenged by Allen (13). Though agreeing with this view that the Platonic theory of the *Phaedo* and the *Republic* could not be read back into these dialogues, he maintained that nevertheless *a* theory of Forms is implicit in

Socrates' procedure in searching for definitions. Allen's view
has been favorably received by many, though it has been
criticized by, e.g., J. Rist (135).

It is generally agreed that the theory of separated Forms
makes its first appearance in the *Phaedo* (see Grube, Appendix
I above), and motivates the Platonic "vision" that is so
characteristic of the middle dialogues. The logical under-
pinnings of the theory have been investigated in several recent
studies. The major questions are these: does Plato require a
Form to correspond to every predicate (or "name", as he puts it
in a passage which seems to lay down this requirement, *Rep.*
596a), or do his arguments restrict the class of predicates for
which Forms are required? If so, is the restriction deliberate?
On one influential account, proposed by Owen (125), Plato's
actual arguments restrict him to requiring Forms only for "incomplete predicates", predicates which need to be completed
in some way if they are to apply without ambiguity to things (in
the sensible world). So if a thing may be called "equal", it is
because it is equal *to* something; if it may be called
"beautiful", it is because it is beautiful in a certain respect,
relation or context, and so forth. For Plato claims, anything in
this world which is equal or beautiful is also unequal or ugly. It
is this infection by the "compresence of opposites" which dis-
qualifies sensible things from exhibiting beauty and equality,
and so forth, "purely" or "perfectly". There are, however, pure
and perfect exemplifications of these characteristics, namely
the Forms. The Equal is indeed equal, but not equal relatively
to anything; the Beautiful is indeed beautiful, but not relatively to anything. Owen went on to suggest that after the *Phaedo*
and the *Republic,* and specifically in the *Timaeus,* Plato's
preoccupation with universal flux required an expansion of the
set of incomplete predicates to include all predicates, for they
all apply to their subjects only at certain times and not at
others.

The notion that there are pure or perfect exemplifications of
these characteristics which in the sensible world always turn up
with their opposites, and hence "impurely", and that the
Forms are such exemplifications, has led some scholars to question the logical integrity of the theory. For embedded in this
notion is the idea of "self-predication" referred to in the In-

troduction. If the Form the Beautiful is purely beautiful, by contrast to which the beautiful things of this world are deficiently beautiful, imperfect copies of a perfect original, then, in order to sustain the comparison, the Form must be beautiful in the same sense as its copy. But if this is so, the theory is vulnerable to the "Third Man" argument (on which see the Introduction, and the following).

Plato frequently says in the *Republic* and elsewhere that Forms are "more real" than sensible things. What does he mean? It has been usual to interpret such statements as specifying a difference in the degree of existence enjoyed by Forms and sensibles: Forms exist fully, but sensible things only partially. Questioning the sense of this interpretation and its basis in the Platonic texts, Vlastos (150) argued for interpreting the statements as specifying a difference in the degree in which Forms and their participant sensibles are characterized by the relevant predicate; to say that the Beautiful is "more real" than beautiful sensibles is to say that it is more beautiful. This interpretation is supported independently by important recent work by Charles Kahn (52) on the Greek verb "to be", a study of far-reaching implications for our understanding of Greek ontology. Vlastos' interpretation has been challenged, however, by Guthrie (7) and Brentlinger (79).

Just what are the "many sensibles" to which Plato contrasts the Forms? The usual view is that they are spatio-temporal particulars. An alternative view has been proposed by Gosling (95): he takes them to be sensible quality-types, such as "being brightly colored" (as an example of one of the many beautifuls). Gosling's view has had a mixed reception. There are indeed contexts in which Plato's statements are best read that way, but on the whole one cannot say that Plato restricts the range of expressions like "the many beautifuls" either to sensible quality-types or to sensible particulars.

The issues around the "Third Man" argument have been discussed in the Introduction. The literature is vast and still growing, and only the most influential can be mentioned. Recent discussion begins with the paper by Vlastos (147) in 1954. He argued (1) that two assumptions, not explicit in the text of the *Parmenides* which gives the argument, are needed as premises for the validity of the argument; (2) that with the addition of these premises the argument is only vacuously valid, for the two premises jointly entail a self-contradiction; (3) that the theory of Forms of the middle dialogues does indeed require both premises, and is thus "logically moribund"; and (4) that Plato, failing to identify the premises and their logical incompatibility, was in a state of "honest perplexity" about the import of the argument for his theory of Forms. The various components of this interpretation did not go unchallenged. Geach (93) objected to the claim that the Form possesses its character *univocally* with the sensible thing, suggesting instead an *analogical* relation. Sellars (141) criticized Vlastos' reconstruction of the argument and his diagnosis of Plato's state of mind, focussing particularly on the interpretation of "self-predication". Vlastos has responded to both critics, (149) and (148), and Sellars has argued further in (142). Some years later C. Strang (144), offering a new analysis and interpretation of the argument, argued that Plato was well aware of the troubles of self-predication, exposed them by the regress of the *Parmenides* and thereafter abandoned it along with paradeigmatism (the thesis that each Form is itself the perfect exemplification of the character it represents) and the attendant "Copy Theory" (the thesis that sensible things are imitations or copies, however imperfect, of Forms), components of the middle dialogues' theory of Forms. More recently, Vlastos has published a reconsideration of the argument in the light of his critics (151), and has propounded a new view of the earlier self-predicative expressions, which he, following Peterson (133) calls "Pauline predications" (155).

What becomes of the theory of Forms after the critique of the *Parmenides?* Much depends on where one places the *Timaeus.* It is obvious that in that dialogue Forms do appear as paradigms and the Copy Theory is present in full force. This has encouraged proponents of an early *Timaeus,* but has not daunted their critics who, either with Cherniss (81) deny that the "Third Man" argument has any force against paradeigmatism or the Copy Theory properly understood; or with Lee (112) propose that these are given a new construction in the *Timaeus* which is not vulnerable to the critique of that argument. Barring the *Timaeus,* however, can any text supporting paradeigmatism be found in the later dialogues?

Cherniss cites a passage in the *Statesman* as such a text, but the citation is disqualified by Owen (129).

What is abundantly clear is the fact that Plato's enthusiastic faith in the metaphysical, epistemological and ethical resources of the theory of Forms is absent from the later dialogues (exempting the *Timaeus*). The ethical and aesthetic Forms all but disappear from the later works, and one finds instead a disciplined, dispassionate logical investigation into what we would call formal or logical concepts like unity, being, sameness, difference and the like, and the implication of the relations among these for thought and language. These highly abstract entities (one need not doubt that they continued for Plato to have a mind-independent existence) are the successors to the paradeigmatic Forms of the middle dialogues, and they testify to a radical shift in Plato's philosophical interests and temper. The new interests and temper are more congenial to modern analytical scholarship, and much recent work on Plato has concentrated on the metaphysics, epistemology, logic and the philosophy of language of his later dialogues. A brief survey of the scholarship on these topics concludes the present section.

In 1939 Gilbert Ryle published an influential study on the *Parmenides* (137), less important for its interpretation than for the way in which it associated problems which Plato raises in the later dialogues with problems to which contemporary twentieth-century philosophers and logicians such as Russell were addressing themselves. Through the work of Ryle and others Plato was drawn into contemporary discussions. Such interest in Plato encouraged a reexamination of arguments in the *Cratylus*, the *Theaetetus*, the *Sophist* and the *Philebus*. Thus N. Kretzmann (110) and C. Kahn (105) have given important accounts of the philosophy of language in the *Cratylus*. Much attention has been devoted, with great profit, to Plato's account of "being" in the *Sophist* and its implications for logic and language. Plato appears to mark off one use of "to be" from another, but what is the distinction? Is it between an existential and other uses of the verb? This traditional view, endorsed by Ackrill (77), is disputed by Owen (127) who argued that Plato is distinguishing between two incomplete uses of the verb "to be": that in which it functions as an identity sign from that in which it introduces a predicate. A detailed study of the question has been offered by M. Frede (45). Plato's metaphysical argument in the *Sophist* for the "interweaving of Forms", and the service this theory renders as the foundation of language has been discussed in papers by Ackrill (76) and Moravcsik (117), and problems of logic and language in the *Sophist* are dealt with by Wiggins (159). The metaphysics of the *Philebus,* with its fundamental distinction between *peras* and *to apeiron* (limit and the unlimited), is discussed by Crombie (1), vol. II, pp. 423–440, by Gosling (9) *ad loc.* and in the book by G. Striker (71).

Much recent work has been done on the various arguments in the *Theaetetus.* Ever since Robinson effectively challenged the traditional view [propounded explicitly by Cornford (16)] that the arguments of that dialogue are meant to show that no satisfactory account of knowledge can be given which dispenses with the theory of Forms (136), scholars have been disinclined to associate Plato's examination of various accounts of knowledge with that theory. The arguments are viewed as inquiries into the concept of knowledge, quite apart from what the objects of knowledge might be. McDowell's commentary is excellent (11), and among the more important papers are those by Cooper (82), Burnyeat (80) and Fine (89).

Pleasure

Plato's ethical theory has been discussed in two important books. The first, by J. Gould (47), focusses primarily on the early and late dialogues, noting a change in Plato's ethical outlook and accounting for the change by attending to the middle dialogues. The other, by T. Irwin (51), is a rigorously argued study of the ethics of the early and middle dialogues. Irwin distinguishes sharply the Platonic from the Socratic ethical theory. Both books are controversial.

Plato's ethics encompasses more than his treatment of pleasure. In this section I restrict mention to studies on pleasure; for other elements in Plato's ethical theory see under *Education* and *Statecraft.*

Did Socrates himself accept the hedonistic premises of the argument against "the many" in the *Protagoras?* That question is by no means settled. It is answered affirmatively in recent studies by Taylor (12) and Irwin (51), negatively by Gulley (50), Sullivan (143), Vlastos (152) and Santas (140). For the treatment of pleasure in the *Gorgias* see the commentaries by Dodds (20) and Irwin (10). Plato's treatment of pleasure in the middle dialogues has not received independent attention. Limited discussion of it will be found in the general studies and the relevant commentaries.

The systematic examination of pleasure in the *Philebus* and its claim to be "the good" is analysed by Gosling in his commentary (9). Cooper (84) gives an account of the claims of various kinds of knowledge and pleasure to be goods. Plato's discussion of false pleasures has generated some controversy in the literature; see the papers by Gosling (94) and (96), Kenny (106), Dybikowski (88) and Penner (130).

Eros

Recent writers on this topic have tended to compare Platonic *eros* favorably or unfavorably with other conceptions of love. Thus A. Nygren, a Swedish theologian, published an influential study (57) whose main subject is the Christian concept of *agape,* contrasted with various Greek conceptions of *eros,* particularly the Platonic. Nygren has characterized Platonic love as acquisitive and egocentric, as opposed to Christian love, which is spontaneous, unmotivated and indifferent to the value of the beloved. A more sympathetic treatment is given by T. Gould (48) who contrasts Platonic love not merely with the Christian, but also with Freudian and romantic conceptions of love.

An important recent essay by Vlastos (156) examines Platonic *eros* sensitively, yet finds it wanting in a crucial respect: it fails to accommodate love of persons for their own sake, and as individuals. Persons are loved as mere instantiations of abstract qualities such as beauty, which are the proper objects of Platonic love. In an essay which is in part a rejoinder to Vlastos' estimate, Kosman (108) argues that Platonic love is love of one's true self, one's true nature which one no longer possesses, and that, more generally, love for the Beautiful is a desire for the realization of things as they truly are.

The climax of Plato's thoughts on *eros,* the ascent to the Beautiful in the *Symposium,* has been studied by Cornford

(85), Markus (116) and Moravcsik (118).

The Soul

A careful, scholarly account of the course of Plato's views about the soul is provided by T. Robinson (62). A valuable historical sketch which provides a useful background to Plato's psychology is an account by D. Furley (92) of earlier Greek concepts of the soul. The essays by Dodds (87), Guthrie (99) and Hall (102) are also useful.

Of philosophical interest are the arguments in the *Phaedo* for the immortality of the soul; see the commentaries by Hackforth (23), Bluck (14) and Gallop (8). Plato's final argument, which he thought was conclusive, has been analysed in the studies by Keyt (107), O'Brien (124), Hartman (103) and D. Frede (91).

The Socratic idea of "caring for one's soul" and the moral psychology of the *Republic* will be discussed below under *Education* and *Statecraft*.

The Gods

Plato's religious beliefs and attitudes have not received much attention in the literature. No comprehensive account has been published since that of Solmsen (68), who discusses Plato's religious ideas against the background of his social and political views. There is a brief account of Plato's theism by Hackforth (100) based on the later dialogues.

To what extent is the "creation account" of the *Timaeus* to be taken literally, i.e., as implying that the present world order had a temporal beginning? This question, debated since antiquity, is answered in favor of a temporal beginning by Vlastos (146). This view, though not the "majority view", is endorsed by Hackforth (101). Vlastos has given a fuller account of the Platonic *cosmos* in (73).

An instructive comparative study of Plato and Christianity which resists the tendency to Christianize Plato (or to Platonize Christianity) is provided by Verdenius (145).

Art

Surprisingly little of value has been published on Plato's

aesthetic views. Highly recommended is a monograph by Verdenius (72), the first chapter of which has been reprinted in Vlastos (39). Of interest also are the short accounts by Oates (58) and Murdoch (56), and an article by Grey (98).

Education

The Socratic "paradox" that virtue is knowledge has inspired a large volume of discussion. The major studies are those by Santas (139) and (140) and Vlastos (152), and the discussions in the books by Taylor (12) and Irwin (51). Further bibliographical data are available in these studies. Irwin argues that Socrates holds virtue to be only instrumentally valuable to the attainment of happiness, and not (also) constitutive of it. Such an interpretation construes the Socratic injunction to "care for the soul" as equally instrumental toward, rather than constitutive of, happiness, and so Irwin takes it. A perceptive analysis of the Socratic soul and of the analogy between psychic health and physical health is given by Santas (66) ch. VIII, sec. 6.

In the *Protagoras* Socrates argues for the identity of virtue and knowledge by first arguing for the unity of the virtues. What is the "unity" in question? In an influential article Penner (132) has argued that it is identity (so also Irwin and Taylor). Vlastos (155) has argued, on the other hand, that the virtues remain ontologically distinct; their unity is their inseparability.

Socrates' educational method is the *elenchus,* the systematic examination of definitions and other propositions elicited from his interlocutors. Analysis of this method is now a standard component of any major study of the early dialogues: see the books by Robinson (61), Gulley (50), Irwin (51) and Santas (66). The philosophical method announced and employed in the middle dialogues is the method of hypothesis which is put to its highest use in the science of dialectic, as that science is described in the *Republic.* Interpretations of this method are given by Robinson (61), Sayre (67) and Bluck (14). The method of dialectic that is adumbrated in the *Phaedrus* and is described and practiced in the later dialogues seems to be altogether different: it is the method of (collection and) division, and it has been studied by Lloyd (113), Ackrill (78) and

Moravcsik (119).

Plato's proposals for the education of the guardians in the *Republic* have come under fire, but since the criticism is part of a larger attack on Plato's political program, it will be discussed in the section immediately following.

Statecraft

Although Socrates (according to the early dialogues) was profoundly disturbed by the political disintegration of his day, it was left to Plato, whose despair at the moral corruption of contemporary politics was no less, to respond by proposing a well defined political theory whose implementation, he profoundly believed, would be the salvation of society. This is the theory of the *Republic*. But what, ultimately, is the character of that theory? Is it totalitarian, akin to twentieth-century manifestations of totalitarianism, or does it provide the foundation for modern democracy? In the 1930s R. H. S. Crossman (43) saw alarming parallels between Plato's political proposal and the rise of totalitarianism on the European continent. But the attack against Plato on behalf of the "open society" was most vigorously levelled by Sir Karl Popper (59). Others, however, were quick to exonerate Plato [see Levinson (54) and Wild (75)]. A series of papers on the issue has been collected by R. Bambrough (31). Recently Vlastos (158) has published a critique of Popper which, though it does not exonerate Plato from the charge of totalitarianism, does vindicate his integrity, and shows how Popper's charge of inegalitarianism needs to be drastically qualified.

The question about the nature and the rewards of justice runs the length of the *Republic,* and Plato's argument to the effect that the just and only the just are happy has raised important questions. First, is the connection between justice and happiness a *utilitarian* connection? That is, is justice recommended as merely a means to happiness? An affirmative answer to this question was first proposed by H. A. Prichard in his famous Inaugural Lecture in 1928 (134); more recently it was revived by M. B. Foster (90), but it is rejected by J. D. Mabbott (115) in a criticism of Foster's view. Second, is Plato's argument valid? D. Sachs claimed to have identified a fallacy in the argument (138), but R. Demos (86) has countered with an exoneration of Plato from the charge. The argument that "justice pays" when justice is understood as an internal ordering of a person's soul has been discussed in important studies of the moral psychology of the *Republic* by Vlastos (154), Kraut (109) and Cooper (83). A general study of the theoretical background to Plato's idea of the philosopher-king has been offered by Rosamund Kent Sprague (69).

The political program of the *Laws* has not received nearly the amount of attention as that accorded to the *Republic*. We have, however, a valuable full-length study by G. Morrow (55), as well as a shorter essay (120).

BIBLIOGRAPHY

General

(1) I.M. Crombie, *An Examination of Plato's Doctrines,* vol. I, *Plato on Man and Society,* London, 1962, and vol. II, *Plato on Knowledge and Reality,* London, 1963.

(2) G.C. Field, *The Philosophy of Plato,* 2nd ed., Oxford, 1969.

(3) J.N. Findlay, *Plato: the Written and Unwritten Doctrines,* London, 1974.

(4) _____, *Plato and Platonism: An Introduction,* New York, 1978.

(5) P. Friedlander, *Plato,* tr. H. Meyerhoff, vols. I–III, London, 1958, 1964 and 1969.

(6) J. Gosling, *Plato,* London, 1973.

(7) W.K.C. Guthrie, *A History of Greek Philosophy,* vol. IV, *Plato, the Man and his Dialogues: Earlier Period,* Cambridge, 1975, and vol. V, *The Later Plato and the Academy,* Cambridge, 1978.

Commentaries and Studies of Individual Dialogues

The Clarendon Plato Series:

(8) D. Gallop, *Plato: Phaedo,* Oxford, 1975.

(9) J. Gosling, *Plato: Philebus,* Oxford, 1975.

(10)   T. Irwin, *Plato: Gorgias,* Oxford, 1980.

(11)   J. McDowell, *Plato: Theaetetus,* Oxford, 1973.

(12)   C.C.W. Taylor, *Plato: Protagoras,* Oxford, 1976.

Others:

(13)   R.E. Allen, *Plato's 'Euthyphro' and the Earlier Theory of Forms,* London and New York, 1970.

(14)   R.S. Bluck, *Plato's Phaedo,* London, 1955.

(15)   _____, *Plato's Meno,* Cambridge, 1964.

(16)   F.M. Cornford, *Plato's Theory of Knowledge,* London, 1935.

(17)   _____, *Plato's Cosmology,* London, 1937.

(18)   _____, *Plato and Parmenides,* London, 1939.

(19)   R.C. Cross and A.D. Woozley, *Plato's Republic: A Philosophical Commentary,* London, 1964.

(20)   E.R. Dodds, *Plato, Gorgias,* Oxford, 1959.

(21)   R. Hackforth, *Plato's Examination of Pleasure,* Cambridge, 1945, reprinted as *Plato's Philebus,* Cambridge, 1972.

(22)   _____, *Plato's Phaedrus,* Cambridge, 1952.

(23)   _____, *Plato's Phaedo,* Cambridge, 1955.

(24)   N.R. Murphy, *The Interpretation of Plato's Republic,* Oxford, 1951.

(25)   A.E. Taylor, *A Commentary on Plato's Timaeus,* Oxford, 1928.

(26)   R. Weingartner, *The Unity of the Platonic Dialogue: the Cratylus, the Protagoras, the Parmenides,* Indianapolis and New York, 1973.

(27)   N. White, *A Companion to Plato's Republic,* Indianapolis and Cambridge, 1979.

Collections of Articles

(28) R.E. Allen, ed., *Studies in Plato's Metaphysics*, London and New York, 1965.

(29) J.P. Anton and G.L. Kustas, eds., *Essays in Ancient Greek Philosophy*, Albany, 1971.

(30) R. Bambrough, ed., *New Essays in Plato and Aristotle*, London and New York, 1965.

(31) _____, ed., *Plato, Popper and Politics*, Cambridge and New York, 1967.

(32) H.F. Cherniss, *Selected Papers*, ed. by L. Taran, Leiden, 1977.

(33) A. Grande, ed., *Paideia: Special Plato Issue*, Buffalo, 1976.

(34) E.N. Lee, A.D.P. Mourelatos, R.M. Rorty, eds., *Exegesis and Argument: Studies in Greek Philosophy Presented to Gregory Vlastos*, Assen, 1973.

(35) J.M.E. Moravcsik, ed., *Patterns in Plato's Thought*, Dordrecht, 1973.

(36) H.F. North, ed., *Interpretations of Plato, Mnemosyne* suppl. vol. 50, Leiden, 1977.

(37) G. Vlastos, ed., *The Philiosophy of Socrates*, New York, 1971.

(38) _____, ed., *Plato I: Metaphysics and Epistemology*, New York, 1971.

(39) _____, ed., *Plato II: Ethics, Politics and Philosophy of Art and Religion*, New York, 1971.

(40) _____, *Platonic Studies*, Princeton, 1973.

(41) W.H. Werkmeister, ed., *Facets of Plato's Philosophy*, *Phronesis* suppl. vol. 2, Assen, 1976.

Books

(42) I.M. Crombie, *Plato: the Midwife's Apprentice*,

London, 1964.

(43) R.H.S. Crossman, *Plato Today*, London, 1937.

(44) G.C. Field, *Plato and his Contemporaries*, London, 1930.

(45) M. Frede, *Praedikation und Existenzaussage, Hypomnemata*, vol. 18, Goettingen, 1967.

(46) K. Gaiser, *Platon's Ungeschriebene Lehre*, Stuttgart, 1963.

(47) J. Gould, *The Development of Plato's Ethics*, Cambridge, 1955.

(48) T. Gould, *Platonic Love*, London, 1963.

(49) N. Gulley, *Plato's Theory of Knowledge*, London, 1962.

(50) _____, *The Philosophy of Socrates*, London, 1968.

(51) T. Irwin, *Plato's Moral Theory: the Early and Middle Dialogues*, Oxford, 1977.

(52) C.H. Kahn, *The Verb 'Be' in Ancient Greek*, Dordrecht, 1973.

(53) H.J. Kraemer, *Arete bei Platon und Aristoteles: Zum Wesen und zur Geschichte der platonischen Ontologie*, Heidelberg, 1959.

(54) R.B. Levinson, *In Defense of Plato*, Cambridge, Mass., 1953.

(55) G.R. Morrow, *Plato's Cretan City*, Princeton, 1960.

(56) I. Murdoch, *The Fire and the Sun*, Oxford, 1977.

(57) A. Nygren, *Agape and Eros*, tr. P.S. Watson, Harper Torchbook, New York, 1969.

(58) W. Oates, *Plato's View of Art*, New York, 1972.

(59) Sir Karl Popper, *The Open Society and its Enemies*, vol. I, *The Spell of Plato*, 5th ed., London, 1966.

(60) J.E. Raven, *Plato's Thought in the Making*, Cambridge, 1965.

(61) R. Robinson, *Plato's Earlier Dialectic,* 2nd ed., Oxford, 1953.

(62) T.M. Robinson, *Plato's Psychology,* Toronto, 1970.

(63) Sir David Ross, *Plato's Theory of Ideas,* Oxford, 1951.

(64) W.G. Runciman, *Plato's Later Epistemology,* Cambridge, 1962.

(65) G. Ryle, *Plato's Progress,* Cambridge, 1966.

(66) G. Santas, *Socrates,* London, Boston and Henley, 1979.

(67) K. Sayre, *Plato's Analytic Method,* Chicago, 1969.

(68) F. Solmsen, *Plato's Theology,* Ithaca, 1942.

(69) R.K. Sprague, *Plato's Philosopher King,* Columbia, 1976.

(70) J. Stenzel, *Plato's Method of Dialectic,* tr. D.J. Allan, Oxford, 1940.

(71) G. Striker, *Peras und Apeiron, Hypomnemata,* vol. 30, Goettingen, 1970.

(72) W.J. Verdenius, *Mimesis: Plato's Doctrine of Artistic Imitation and its Meaning for Us,* Leiden, 1949.

(73) G. Vlastos, *Plato's Universe,* Seattle, 1975 and Oxford, 1975.

(74) N. White, *Plato on Knowledge and Reality,* Indianapolis, 1976.

(75) J. Wild, *Plato's Modern Enemies and the Theory of Natural Law,* Chicago, 1953.

Articles:

(76) J.L. Ackrill, *"SYMPLOKE EIDON",* in (28), 199–206, and (38), 201–209.

(77) _____, "Plato and the Copula: Sophist 251–259", in (28), 207–218, and (38), 210–222.

(78) _____, "In Defense of Platonic Division", in *Ryle,*

O.P. Wood and G. Pitcher, eds., New York, 1970, 373-392.

(79) J.A. Brentlinger, "Particulars in Plato's Middle Dialogues", *Archiv für Geschichte der Philosophie*, vol. 54, 1972, 116-52.

(80) M.F. Burnyeat, "The Material and Sources of Plato's Dream", *Phronesis*, vol. 15, 1970, 101-122.

(81) H.F. Cherniss, "The Relation of the *Timaeus* to Plato's Later Dialogues", in (28), 339-378, and (32), 298-339.

(82) J. Cooper, "Plato on Sense Perception and Knowledge: *Theaetetus* 184 to 186", *Phronesis*, vol. 15, 1970, 123-146.

(83) _____, "The Psychology of Justice in Plato", *American Philosophical Quarterly*, vol. 14, 1977, 151-157.

(84) _____, "Plato's Theory of Human Good in the *Philebus*", *Journal of Philosophy*, vol. 74, 1977, 714-730.

(85) F.M. Cornford, "The Doctrine of Eros in Plato's *Symposium*", in (39), 119-131.

(86) R. Demos, "A Fallacy in Plato's *Republic?*" in (39), 52-56.

(87) E.R. Dodds, "Plato and the Irrational Soul", in (39), 206-229.

(88) J.C. Dybikowski, "False Pleasures and the *Philebus*", *Phronesis*, vol. 15, 1970, 147-165.

(89) G. Fine, "Knowledge and *Logos* in the *Theaetetus*", *Philosophical Review*, vol. 88, 1979.

(90) M.B. Foster, "A Mistake in Plato's *Republic*", *Mind*, N.S. vol. 46, 1937, 386ff.

(91) D. Frede, "The Final Proof of Immortality of the Soul in Plato's *Phaedo*, 102a-107a", *Phronesis*, vol. 23, 1978, 27-41.

(92) D. Furley, "The Early History of the Concept of Soul", *Bulletin of the Institute of Classical Studies of the University of London,* vol. 3, 1956, 1–18.

(93) P. Geach, "The Third Man Again", in (28), 265–278.

(94) J. Gosling, "False Pleasures: *Philebus* 35c–41b", *Phronesis,* vol. 4, 1959, 44–53.

(95) _____, "*Republic* V: *ta polla kala,* etc." *Phronesis,* vol. 5, 1960, 116–128.

(96) _____, "Father Kenny on False Pleasures", *Phronesis,* vol. 6, 1961, 41–45.

(97) _____, "*Doxa* and *Dunamis* in Plato's *Republic*", *Phronesis,* vol. 13, 1968, 119–130.

(98) D.R. Grey, "Art in the *Republic*", *Philosophy,* vol. 27, 1952, 291–310.

(99) W.K.C. Guthrie, "Plato's Views on the Nature of the Soul", in (39), 230–243.

(100) R. Hackforth, "Plato's Theism", in (28), 439–447.

(101) _____, "Plato's Cosmogony", *Classical Quarterly,* N.S. vol. 9, 1959, 17–22.

(102) R.W. Hall, "*Psyche* as Differentiated Unity in the Philosophy of Plato", *Phronesis,* vol. 8, 1963, 63–82.

(103) E. Hartman, "Predication and Immortality in Plato's *Phaedo*", *Archiv für Geschichte der Philosophie,* vol. 54, 1972, 215–228.

(104) T. Irwin, "Plato's Heracliteanism", *Philosophical Quarterly,* vol. 27, 1977, 1–13.

(105) C.H. Kahn, "Language and Ontology in the *Cratylus*", in (34), 152–176.

(106) A. Kenny, "False Pleasures in the *Philebus:* A Reply to Mr. Gosling", *Phronesis,* vol. 5, 1960, 45–52.

(107) D. Keyt, "The Fallacies in *Phaedo* 102a–107b", *Phronesis,* vol. 8, 1963, 167–172.

(108) L.A. Kosman, "Platonic Love", in (41), 53–69.

(109) R. Kraut, "Reason and Justice in Plato's *Republic*", in (34), 207-224.

(110) N. Kretzmann, "Plato on the Correctness of Names", *American Philosophical Quarterly*, vol. 8, 1971, 126-138.

(111) A.R. Lacey, "Our Knowledge of Socrates", in (37), 22-49.

(112) E.N. Lee, "On the Metaphysics of the Image in Plato's *Timaeus*", *The Monist*, vol. 50, 1966, 341-368.

(113) A.C. Lloyd, "Plato's Description of Division", in (28), 219-230.

(114) J.V. Luce, "The Date of the *Cratylus*", *American Journal of Philology*, vol. 85, 1964, 136-152.

(115) J.D. Mabbott, "Is Plato's *Republic* Utilitarian?", in (39), 57-65.

(116) R.A. Markus, "The Dialectic of Eros in Plato's *Symposium*", in (39), 132-143.

(117) J.M.E. Moravcsik, "Being and Meaning in the *Sophist*", *Acta Philosophica Fennica*, vol. 14, 1962, 23-78.

(118) _____, "Reason and Eros in the 'Ascent'-passage of the *Symposium*", in (29), 285-302.

(119) _____, "The Anatomy of Plato's Divisions", in (34), 324-348.

(120) G.R. Morrow, "Plato and the Rule of Law", in (39), 144-165.

(121) A. Nehamas, "Predication and Forms of Opposites in the *Phaedo*", *Review of Metaphysics*, vol. 26, 1973, 461-491.

(122) _____, "Plato on the Imperfection of the Sensible World", *American Philosophical Quarterly*, vol. 12, 1975, 105-117.

(123) _____, "Self-Predication and Plato's Theory of

Forms", *American Philosophical Quarterly,* vol. 16, 1979, 93–103.

(124) D. O'Brien, "The Last Argument of Plato's *Phaedo",* *Classical Quarterly,* vol. 17, 1967, 189–231, and vol. 18, 1968, 95–106.

(125) G.E.L. Owen, "A Proof in the *PERI IDEON",* in (28), 293–312.

(126) _____, "Notes on Ryle's Plato", in *Ryle,* O.P. Wood and G. Pitcher, eds., New York, 1970, 341–372.

(127) _____, "Plato on Not-Being", in (38), 223–267.

(128) _____, "The Place of the *Timaeus* in Plato's Dialogues", in (28), 313–338.

(129) _____, "Plato on the Undepictable", in (34), 349–361.

(130) T. Penner, "False Anticipatory Pleasures: *Philebus* 36a3–41a6", *Phronesis,* vol. 15, 1970, 166–178.

(131) _____, "Thought and Desire in Plato", in (39), 96–118.

(132) _____, "The Unity of Virtue", *Philosophical Review,* vol. 82, 1973, 35–68.

(133) S. Peterson, "A Reasonable Self-Predication Premise for the Third Man Argument", *Philosophical Review,* vol. 82, 1973, 451–470.

(134) H.A. Prichard, "Duty and Interest", in *Moral Obligation, and Duty and Interest,* Oxford, 1968, 203–238.

(135) J.M. Rist, "Plato's 'Earlier Theory of Forms'", *Phoenix,* vol. 29, 1975, 336–357.

(136) R. Robinson, "Forms and Error in Plato's *Theaetetus",* *Philosophical Review,* vol. 59, 1950, 3–30.

(137) G. Ryle, "Plato's *Parmenides",* in (28), 97–148.

(138) D. Sachs, "A Fallacy in Plato's *Republic",* in (39), 35–51.

(139) G. Santas, "The Socratic Paradoxes", *Philosophical*

Review, vol. 73, 1964, 147-164. [Reprinted as ch. VI in (66).]

(140) _____, "Plato's *Protagoras* and Explanations of Weakness", in (37), 264-298. [Reprinted as ch. VII in (66).]

(141) W. Sellars, "Vlastos and the 'Third Man'", *Philosophical Review,* vol. 64, 1955, 405-437.

(142) _____, "Vlastos and the 'Third Man': A rejoinder", in *Philosophical Perspectives,* Springfield, 1967, 55-72.

(143) J.P. Sullivan, "The Hedonism in Plato's *Protagoras"*, *Phronesis,* vol. 6, 1961, 10-28.

(144) C. Strang, "Plato and the Third Man", in (38), 184-200.

(145) W.J. Verdenius, "Plato and Christianity", *Ratio,* vol. 5, 1963, 15-32.

(146) G. Vlastos, "The Disorderly Motion in the *Timaeus"*, and "Creation in the *Timaeus:* Is it a Fiction?" in (28), 379-420.

(147) _____, "The Third Man Argument in the *Parmenides"*, in (28), 231-264.

(148) _____, "Addenda to the TMA: A Reply to Professor Sellars", *Philosophical Review,* vol. 64, 1955, 438-448.

(149) _____, "Postscript to the Third Man: A Reply to Mr. Geach", in (28), 279-292.

(150) _____, "Degrees of Reality in Plato", in (30), 1-19, and (40), 58-75.

(151) _____, "Plato's 'Third Man' Argument (*Parm.* 132A1-B2): Text and Logic", and appendices, in (40), 342-365.

(152) _____, "Socrates on *Acrasia"*, *Phoenix,* vol. 23, 1969, 71-88.

(153) _____, "The Paradox of Socrates", in (37), 1-21.

(154) _____, "Justice and Happiness in the *Republic*", in (39), 66-95.

(155) _____, "The Unity of the Virtues in the *Protagoras*", and appendix in (40), 221-269.

(156) _____, "The Individual as Object of Love in Plato", and appendices, in (40), 3-42.

(157) _____, "On Plato's Oral Doctrine", in (40), 379-403.

(158) _____, "The Theory of Social Justice in the *Polis* in Plato's *Republic*", in (36), 1-40.

(159) D. Wiggins, "Sentence Meaning, Negation and Plato's Problem of Not-Being", in (38), 268-303.

INDEX OF REFERENCES TO PLATO'S WORKS

INDEX OF GREEK WORDS

INDEX OF PROPER NAMES

GENERAL INDEX

Activity (Movement) :
  in Ideal world : 40, 296 ;
  pleasure as — : 69 ;
  in early education : 246
Allegory :
  does not redeem mythology,
    155
Anthropomorphism : 151, 153-4
Art :—in *Apology* : 180 ; *Ion* : 180-2 ;
    Republic : 182-92 ; *Phaedrus* :
    192-4 : 210-14 ; *Sophist* :
    194-5 ; *Philebus* : 195-6 ;
    Laws : 196-202 ; *Gorgias* :
    208-10 ;
  relies on inspiration : 180-1, 190-
    194 ;
  emotional appeal : 181, 185,
    203 ;
  educational value : 182-5, 194,
    196-7, 203, 205, 235, 245,
    248 ;
  as imitation : 184-5, 187-9, 190-
    195, 202-7 ;
  banished from *Republic* : 186, 189-
    190, 192 ;
  criteria : 198-200, 212 ;
  and pleasure : 80, 182, 186, 195-
    199, 200, 209-10, 245 ;
  censorship : 192, 197, 200, 205-6 ;
  and psychology : 214-15 ;
  requires knowledge : 190, 199,
    210-12 ;
  painting : 187, 188, 190, 194
  see also μουσική
Astronomy :
  in education : 238, 250 ;
  and mathematics : 176
Atheism : of three kinds attached :
    145, 171-6

Be : meanings of the verb ' to be ' :
    36, 38-9, 42
Beauty : 20, 47, 53, 62, 65, 109
Being :
  as object of knowledge : 23, 38 ;
  nature of— : 38-9, 47
  see also Ideas

Belief (opinion) :
  contrasted with knowledge : 23,
    37 ;
  true and false : 77, 208 ;
  and virtue : *see* Virtue

Causes :
  The Ideas as — : 19 ;
  The four — : 46, 301-2
Cave : Parable of the — : 28
Chance :—and design in the uni-
    verse : 172
Christianity :
  contrasted with Platonism : 121,
    150-1, 153, 155-6, 169-70
Cinema :
  as parallel to tragedy : 206
Communism :
  in *Republic* : 65-6, 269-71 ; in
    Laws : 287
Concept :
  Ideas not concepts : 33, 49, 168
Convention :
  opposed to the ' natural ' : 51, 54,
    172
Courage :
  in *Republic* : 272
  as knowledge, 217-18, 221 ;
  and ' moderation,' 236, 284

Death :
  Philosophy as practice for — :
    125-6
  Is there a Form of — ? : 167
Definition :
  Socratic — : 4, 11 ;
  of courage : 218 ;
  of Eros : 100, 106, 109, 212;
  of sophrosyne : 218-19 ;
  of the self : 219-20 ;
  of virtue : 11-12
Demiurge :
  162-4, 169-70, 177
Diairesis :
  as logical method : 31-2, 41-2,
    44-5, 73, 277

341